TREASON & BETRAYAL

THE RISE AND FALL OF INDIVIDUAL #1

ALSO BY KENNETH FOARD McCALLION

The Essential Guide to Donald Trump

Shoreham and the Rise and Fall of the Nuclear Power Industry

TREASON & BETRAYAL

THE RISE AND FALL OF INDIVIDUAL #1

Kenneth Foard McCallion

Bryant Park Press
An imprint of HHI Media

Bryant Park Press
An imprint of HHI Media

Book Design by Danielle Allyssa

Jacket Design by Danielle Allyssa

Jacket Photography by Sharon Dominick/iStock

Manufactured in the United States of America

ISBN: 978-0-9979292-7-0

To Susan, Brendan, Meghan and Foard,
for their patience and support

And to Ian and other members of the U.S. Armed Forces, past and
present, who have dedicated their lives to the defense of our country
and its democratic institutions,

and

Special Thanks to Damara Carousis and my other students at
Fairfield University whose encouragement, excellent suggestions and
research made this possible.

TABLE OF CONTENTS

CAST OF CHARACTERS

ROMAN ABRAMOVICH

Russian billionaire worth $11.4 B owns stakes in steel giant Evraz, Norilsk Nickel and the U.K.'s Chelsea soccer team. He has close ties to Putin and suspected ties to Russian organized crime. He and his now ex-wife Dasha Zhukova were close friends with Jared and Ivanka Kushner, and Dasha attended the Trump Inauguration with Ivanka. He also controls the world's second largest aluminum company which, through a Canadian steel subsidiary, supplied much of the piping for the controversial Keystone XL pipeline that Obama halted but Trump has green-lighted. Trump signed an executive order in March 2017 basically exempting Abramovich's companies from the requirement that U.S. pipelines be built with U.S. steel.

ARAS AGALAROV

Russian billionaire and co-host with Trump of 2013 Miss Universe pageant with Trump in Moscow. Rob Goldstone, the publicist for Aras and his son Emin arranged for the infamous June 9, 2016 meeting at Trump Tower where Donald Trump Jr., Paul Manafort and Jared Kushner met with a group of Russians for the purpose of transferring Russian-obtained "dirt" on Hillary Clinton to the Trump Campaign. Based on a statement drafted by his father, Donald J. Trump, Don Jr. initially told the press that the meeting was held to discuss adoptions of Russian children by Americans, but on July 8, 2017, he admitted in a tweet that he had agreed to the meeting with the understanding that he would receive information damaging to Hillary Clinton.

EMIN AGALAROV — Aras Agalarov's son and Russian pop star.

RINAT AKHMETSHIN — The Russian lobbyist who attended the June 9, 2016 Trump Tower meeting with Don Jr., Manafort and Kushner.

JAMES A. BAKER — Former FBI General Counsel who discussed with Deputy Attorney General Rod Rosenstein the possibility of secretly recording the conversations between Rosenstein and Trump. Baker testified in a private session before Congress: "The FBI's investigation must be viewed in the context of the bureau's decades-long effort to detect, disrupt and defeat the intelligence activities of the governments of the Soviet Union and later the Russian Federation that are contrary to the fundamental and long-term interests of the United States. The FBI's counter- intelligence investigation regarding the 2016 campaign fundamentally was not about Donald Trump but was about Russia. Full stop. It was always about Russia. It was about what Russia was, and is, doing and planning. Of course, if that investigation revealed that anyone—Russian or American—committed crimes in connection with Russian intelligence activities or unlawfully interfered with the investigation, the FBI has an obligation under the law to investigate such crimes and to seek to bring those responsible to justice. The FBI's enduring counterintelligence mission is the reason the Russia investigation will, and should, continue—no matter who is fired, pardoned or impeached."

STEVE BANNON

This former executive chairman of Breitbart News, sometimes referred to as "Trump's Rasputin," served as White House Chief Strategist in the Trump Administration during the first seven months of Trump's term. He is quoted in Michael Wolff 's book, Fire and Fury, as having described the June 9, 2016 Trump Tower meeting between members of the Trump Team and the Russians as "treasonous."

MARIA BUTINA

This Russian citizen and covert Russian agent pleaded guilty on December 13, 2018 to conspiracy against the United States and acting illegally as an unregistered Russian agent in the United States. Posing as a U.S. student and the founder of "Right to Bear Arms," a Russian front organization for Russian intelligence operations, she attempted to infiltrate Republican political circles, the National Rifle Association (NRA) and the National Prayer Breakfast in order to influence U.S. relations with Russia before and after the 2016 presidential election.

MICHAEL CAPUTO

This former senior Trump campaign advisor with ties to the Kremlin testified before the House Intelligence Committee in a closed session for more than three hours (CNN). Rep. Jackie Speier described Caputo during Congressional hearing as part of a "tarantula" web of links to Russia and Putin's "image consultant." Caputo, who lived for many years in Russia, also did extensive PR work for Gazprom, Russia's giant state-owned energy company.

STEPHANIE CLIFFORD

Adult film star known as "Stormy Daniels," who received $130,000 in hush money from Trump attorney and fixer Michael Cohen shortly before the November 8, 2016 presidential election so that she would not publicly disclose her affair with Trump. Cohen admitted at the time of his guilty plea and sentencing in federal court that he made the payments with the full knowledge and consent of then-candidate Trump, who is described in the federal filings as "Individual-1."

SAM CLOVIS

Trump Campaign's national co-chair and chief policy advisor is the unnamed "campaign supervisor" in court documents filed by the Special Counsel's office who exchanged emails with George Papadopoulos about the offers from the Russian agents to give the Trump Campaign "dirt" on Hillary Clinton and set up a meeting between Trump and Putin. Clovis, who responded to the emails by telling Papadopoulos, "Great work," has reportedly been interviewed by Special Counsel Mueller's office and testified in the grand jury handling the Russia investigation.

MICHAEL D. COHEN

Trump's former longtime personal lawyer and "fixer," who pleaded guilty to tax evasion, bank fraud, campaign finance violations and lying to Congress. He was sentenced to three years in jail and over $1 million in fines. Cohen has testified that, at Trump's direction, he continued negotiations on the Trump Tower Moscow project well into the summer of

2016, and that he lied to Congress about those negotiations with the Russians having ceased in January 2016. A December 2018 filing by the Special
Counsel's offices described how Cohen had lied to
Congress about the length of the negotiations over
the Moscow Tower and about Trump's involvement with this project. Cohen is cooperating with
federal prosecutors. On January 17, 2019 Buzz-
Feed News reported that Trump directed Cohen to
lie to Congress about the Moscow Project,[1] but the
following day, the Special Counsel's office disputed the BuzzFeed News story, at least as to certain
descriptions and "characterizations" as to Cohen's
false testimony to Congress about Trump's role in
the Moscow Tower negotiations.[2]

JAMES B. COMEY   Former F.B.I. Director, who was fired by Trump
on May 9, 2017 for failing to comply with Trump's
requests that he go easy on the FBI's investigation
of Michael Flynn and the entire investigation of
collusion between the Trump Campaign and the
Russians. Comey's firing and Trump's subsequent
admission to NBC's Lester Holt that the firing was
related to the Russia investigation triggered an FBI
counterintelligence investigation of Trump to determine whether he was a national security risk.

1   Leopold, Jason and Cormier, Anthony, *"President Trump directed His Attorney Michael Cohen To Lie to congress about the Moscow Tower Project,"* BuzzFeed News, January 17, 2019, https://
www.buzzfeednews.com/article/jasonleopold/trump-russia-cohen-moscow-tower.mueller-investiga-
tion?ref=bfnsplash
2   Mazzetti, Mark and LaFraniere, Sharon, *"Mueller Statement Disputes Report That Trump Directed Cohen to Lie,"* The New York Times. January 18. 2019 https://www.nytimes.com/2019/01/18/us/
politics/buzzfeed-cohen-russia-tower.

KELLYANNE CONWAY

American pollster, political consultant, and pundit who was a senior staffer on the Trump Campaign and is currently serving as Counselor to the President in the Trump Administration. She is reported to have coined the phrase "alternative facts" in describing White House press secretary Sean Spicer's description of the Trump Inauguration crowd as "the largest audience ever to witness an Inauguration, period."

RANDY CREDICO

Former associate of Roger Stone, who Stone has referred to as his "principal source" regarding communications with WikiLeaks.

KRISTIN DAVIS

Known as the "Manhattan Madam" for formerly running a high-end escort service, she is also a longstanding friend of Roger Stone. Davis was subpoenaed to testify before the federal grand jury hearing evidence of Special Counsel Mueller's Russia probe, presumably about her dealings with Stone.

RICK DEARBORN

President Donald Trump's former deputy chief of staff. His name first surfaced in connection to the Russia investigation on August 23, 2017 when CNN reported Congressional inves- tigators were looking at an email Dearborn sent in June 2016 referencing someone looking to arrange a meeting between Trump campaign officials and Russian president Vladimir Putin. CNN also reported that Dearborn helped arrange Trump's April 2016 address at the Mayflower Hotel where Russian Ambassador Sergey Kislyak was in attendance. Congressional investigators reportedly are looking into whether Dearborn had any role in arranging Senator Sessions' previously undisclosed meetings with Kislyak in July and September 2016.

OLEG V. DERIPASKA

He paid Paul Manafort millions of dollars to reburnish his image in Washington and to get the U.S. sanctions against him lifted. Manafort also owed him millions of dollars that were supposed to be used for an investment venture, but the debt seems to have been forgiven after Manafort was named Trump's Campaign Chairman. The go-between for Deripaska and Manafort was Konstantin Kilimnik, a Russian GRU intelligence agent working for Manafort in Kiev, Ukraine. Manafort offered Deripaska "private briefings" on the campaign during the 2016 election campaign. On December 19, 2018, the Trump Administration announced its intention to lift sanctions on some of Deripaska's Russian aluminum companies. On January 21, 2019, it was reported by the New York Times that the lifting of sanctions benefitted Deripaska to the tune of millions of dollars.

KIRILL DMITRIEV

A Russian banker who met with Eric Prince in the Seychelles in January 2017, possibly to establish a "back channel" communications link between the Trump team and the Kremlin.

BORIS EPSHTEYN

A Russian-born attorney and Trump campaign and administration advisor on Russian and Ukrainian matters. Epshteyn previously arranged trade shows for Russia and the City of Moscow in the U.S., and frequently appeared on TV as a surrogate for Trump whenever a pro-Russian apologist was needed to explain away Russia's annexation of Crimea or other sanctionable violations of international law.

ANTHONY "TONY" FABRIZIO — Fabrizio's company, Fabrizio, Lee & Associates, which claims on its website to be "one of the leading survey research and campaign strategists in the nation," was the chief pollster firm for the Trump Campaign. Fabrizio was copied in on emails between Paul Manafort and Russian intelligence agent Konstantin Kilimnik, who received internal proprietary polling data sent by Manafort. Fabrizio is reported to have been interviewed by the Special Counsel in February of 2018.

MICHAEL T. FLYNN — Trump's first national security adviser, who pleaded guilty to lying to the F.B.I. about conversations with Russian ambassador Kislyak regarding U.S. sanctions and the Russian response to them in December 2016, during the Transition. Flynn was paid over $65,000 by various Russian companies with links to the Kremlin, and was paid to attend a dinner celebrating the anniversary of RT, a Russian propaganda outlet, where Flynn sat at the same table as Russian President Vladimir Putin.

RICK GATES — 2016 deputy chairman of Trump Campaign who pleaded guilty to financial fraud and lying to the F.B.I. He continues to cooperate with the Mueller probe and has not yet been sentenced.

DAVID GEOVANIS — A Moscow-based American businessman with longstanding ties to Trump. Geovanis helped organize the 1996 trip to Moscow by Trump, who was pursuing what became one of his life-long obsessions, which was to build a Trump Tower in Moscow. Also on the 1996 trip were real estate moguls Bennett LeBow and Howard Lorber, who later became substantial contributors to Trump's 2016 campaign, and who were personally acknowledged by Trump from the podium after Trump won the 2016 New York Republican primary. Lober is reported by the New York Times as being one of the Trump family associates who spoke with Donald Trump Jr. from blocked numbers around the time of the infamous June 9, 2016 Trump Tower meeting with Russian operatives peddling "dirt" on Hillary Clinton to Manafort, Kushner and Don Jr. of the Trump campaign.

ROB GOLDSTONE

British-born publicist who repeatedly served as an intermediary between the Trumps and the Agalarovs. He also set up and attended the June 9, 2016 meeting at Trump Tower between Trump team members Don Jr., Paul Manafort and Jared Kushner. They met with a gaggle of Russians offering "dirt" on Hillary Clinton, but who were really angling for Trump's help in getting U.S. sanctions on Russia lifted.

J.D. GORDON

Trump campaign national security advisor who helped soften the plank in the Republican platform relating to U.S. assistance to Ukraine so as to be less anti-Russian. He is also reported as having a social relationship with Russian agent Maria Butina in 2016.

SEBASTIAN GORKA

A Trump advisor and media surrogate during the

2016 presidential campaign and with the Trump Administration until August 25, 2017.

SERGEY N. GORKOV Head of Russian state-run bank under American sanctions, who Russian ambassador Kislyak said had a direct line to Putin. He met with Jared Kushner at Trump Tower in December 2016 after Kislyak suggested the meeting. Jared says it was a social meeting, while Gorkov says it was all about Kushner's real estate business.

GUCCIFER 2.0 Online persona created by Russian intelligence officers and used to share hacked files from Democratic sources; Roger Stone has mutually complimentary exchanges with Guccifer about all the progress being made by the Russians to hack into U.S. databases and disseminate derogatory information about the Clinton Campaign.

HOPE HICKS Former longtime Trump aide and former communications director, who suggested aboard Air Force One with Trump present that Don Jr.'s emails about the June 9, 2016 Trump Tower meeting with the Russians should never be publicly released.

INTERNET RESEARCH AGENCY Russian organization and troll factory that directed Russia's social media disinformation campaign during the 2016 election.

KONSTANTIN V. KILIMNIK Longtime Manafort associate and Russian GRU intelligence agent who is currently under indictment with Manafort for witness tampering, and is believed to be hiding in Russia.

SERGEY I. KISLYAK

Former Russian ambassador to the United States and suspected Russian FSB intelligence agent, who seems to have met virtually every Trump Campaign member worth meeting, including Jeff Sessions, Jared Kushner, George Papadopoulos, Carter Page, etc. Michael Flynn phoned Kislyak in December 2016 to discuss U.S. sanctions policy towards Russia, which Flynn later lied about to the FBI, was indicted, and then pleaded guilty. On May 10, 2017, the day after Trump fired FBI Director James Comey, Trump met in the Oval Office with Kislyak and Russian Foreign Minister Sergei Lavrov with no other Americans present. Trump gleefully reported to the Russians: "I just fired the head of the F.B.I. He was crazy, a real nut job." Mr. Trump added, "I faced great pressure because of Russia. That's taken off." Trump also disclosed highly classified information to the Russians during this Oval Office meeting regarding an Islamic State plot, thus compromising a key source of a U.S. ally, believed to be Israel.

IKE KAVELADZE

Business associate of Aras Agalarov and suspected money launderer who attended June 9, 2016 Trump Tower meeting.

JARED KUSHNER

Trump's son-in-law, senior adviser and "Secretary of Everything." On January 24, 2019, NBC News Reported that Kushner was rejected for a security clearance by two White House security specialists after his FBI background check raised red flags regarding potential foreign contacts, foreign travel and meetings with Russian officials where he asked for a "back channel" link to the Kremlin. He was eventually given clearance over these objections, but denied CIA higher level security clearance.

SERGEY LAVROV

Russian Foreign Minister who is prominently mentioned in the Steele Dossier. Lavrov and Russian Ambassador Kislyak attended the May 10, 2017 Oval Office meeting with Trump, where Trump bragged about firing Comey and disclosed highly confidential information to the Russians.

BENNETT LEBOW

A New York-based real estate developer and chairman of the Vector Group who accompanied Trump on his 1996 trip to Moscow to scope out the proposed site of a Moscow Trump Tower, which Trump pursued for the next two decades.

COREY LEWANDOWSKI

Trump's first campaign manager from January 2015 to June 2016. He signed off on Carter Page's trip to Moscow in July 2016.

HOWARD LOBER

A New York-based real estate developer and chairman of Prudential Douglas Elliman, a residential brokerage in New York. He was a major Trump 2016 campaign contributor who accompanied Trump and fellow real-estate mogul Bennett LeBow on a 1996 trip to Moscow organized by Moscow-based American businessman David Geovanis. The Moscow trip was one of many efforts by Trump over the years to make his dream of a Moscow Trump Tower a reality.

PAUL MANAFORT

A lawyer and political consultant who joined Trump's presidential campaign team in March 2016, and was campaign chairman from June to

August 2016; he was convicted on financial fraud charges, pled guilty to other charges, and then secretly passed information on to the White House after agreeing to cooperate with the Special Counsel's investigation. He was indicted for witness tampering, along with Konstantin Kilimnik, a Russian GRU intelligence agent who served as Manafort's right-hand man in Ukraine and Russia. Manafort is reported to have passed Trump Campaign research and polling data onto the Russians and Ukrainians via Kilimnik and others, thus establishing a direct "collusion" link between the Trump Campaign and the Russians. Manafort received millions of dollars from Oleg Deripaska, Russian billionaire and Putin ally, and offered through Kilimnik to give Deripaska "private briefings" while Manafort was serving as Trump Campaign Chairman.

JAMES MATTIS

This Secretary of Defense and retired four-star Marine Corp General resigned on December 20, 2018 following Trump's twitter announcement that he planned to pull U.S. troops out of Syria and Afghanistan. In his resignation letter, Mattis implicitly criticized Trump for undermining America's alliances, including NATO, and for not defending core democratic principles: "One core belief I have always held is that our strength as a nation is inextricably linked to the strength of our unique and comprehensive system of alliances and partnerships. While the US remains the indispensable nation in the free world, we cannot protect our interests or serve that role effectively without maintaining strong alliances and showing respect to those allies."

K.T. MCFARLAND — Former deputy national security adviser who was with Trump at Mar-A-Largo in Florida during December 2016 when Flynn made multiple calls to Russian ambassador Kislyak to discuss U.S. sanctions against Russia and Russia's response.

DONALD F. MCGAHN II — Former White House counsel through October 17, 2018. McGahn was extensively interviewed by Special Counsel Mueller's team. He talked Trump out of firing Mueller at least once.

JOSEPH MIFSUD — London-based academic from Malta with ties to Russian intelligence. He told former Trump campaign adviser George Papadopoulos that the Russians had access to "thousands of emails" relating to Hillary Clinton. He is named as "Foreign Contact 1" in FBI affidavit relating to Papadopoulos.

STEPHEN MILLER — Trump's senior advisor for policy has been interviewed by Special Counsel investigators regarding his role in the drafting of a letter relating to the firing of FBI Director James Comey. He was also one of the attendees at a March 2016 meeting where George Papadopoulos spoke about getting Trump and Putin together for a meeting.

SERGEI MILLIAN — Born in Belarus, he has been the president of the Russian-American Chamber of Commerce in the USA since 2006. He claims to have significant business ties to Trump going back to 2007, when Trump attended a "Millionaire Fair" in Moscow. Millian claims he was the "exclusive broker" to promote one of Trump's real estate projects in Russia and other former Soviet states.

ROBERT S. MUELLER III

Appointed as Special Counsel by Deputy Attorney General Rod Rosenstein on May 17, 2017 to head up investigation of Russian interference in the 2016 Presidential election and related matters. He previously served as the sixth Director of the Federal Bureau of Investigation from 2001 to 2013.

GEORGE NADER

A Lebanese-American businessman and adviser to UAE Crown Prince Mohammed bin Zayed Al-Nahyan ("MBZ"). He has also worked for Blackwater. He appeared before the grand jury investigating Russian interference in the 2016 elections and related matters in March 2018. It is believed that he has testified that the January 2017 meeting between Erik Prince and Russian banker Kirill Dmitriev was set up in advance in order to establish a "back channel" means of communication between the Trump team and Moscow. If so, then his testimony may contradict Prince's testimony before the House Intelligence Committee to the effect that it was a chance business meeting in the Seychelles.

JERROLD "JERRY" NADLER

New York Congressman since 1992, became the Chairman of the powerful House Judiciary Committee in January 2019 when the Democrats seized control of the majority of the House of Representatives.

ALEXANDER NIX

Suspended Cambridge Analytica CEO has admitted that he tried to make contact with WikiLeaks about missing Hillary Clinton emails. It has been reported that Nix answered some of the House Intelligence Committee's questions by video teleconference.

CARTER PAGE

A petroleum industry consultant and former foreign-policy adviser to Trump during the 2016 Presidential election campaign. Before joining the Trump campaign, where he was a vocal advocate both in the U.S. and in Russia for the U.S. to relax its sanctions policy against Russia, Page was targeted in 2013 by a group of Russian spies as a possible recruit who could obtain U.S. documents and information helpful to the Russians. A FISA surveillance application filed by the FBI in October 2016, a month before the election, said: "The FBI believes that Page has been collaborating and conspiring with the Russian government."

LISA PAGE

Former FBI attorney who has told House Judiciary and Oversight Committee investigators in private testimony: "In the Russian Federation and in President Putin himself, you have an individual whose aim is to disrupt the Western alliance and whose aim is to make Western democracy more fractious in order to weaken our ability, America's ability and the West's ability to spread our democratic ideals." She added: "That's the goal, to make us less of a moral authority to spread democratic values," and that "with respect to Western ideals and who it is and what it is we stand for as Americans, Russia poses the most dangerous threat to that way of life."

GEORGE PAPADOPOULOS

2016 Trump campaign foreign policy adviser who tried to set up a meeting between Trump and Putin and dealt with Russian agents about getting "dirt" on Hillary Clinton. On October 5, 2017, Papadopoulos pleaded guilty to making false statements to FBI agents about the timing and the possible significance of his contacts in 2016 relating to U.S.-Russia relations and the Trump campaign. He served time in federal prison and is currently undergoing a 12-month supervised release.

BRAD PARSCALE   The digital director of the Trump Campaign.

DMITRY PESKOV   Kremlin spokesperson who spoke to Trump's attorney Michael Cohen in January 2016 regarding the potential Trump Moscow real estate project.

RICHARD PINEDO   A California man who sold bank accounts online and pleaded guilty to identity fraud charges brought by the special counsel. He was sentenced to six months in prison and six months of home detention.

JOHN D. PODESTA   Hillary Clinton's campaign chairman whose emails were stolen by Russian hackers.

REINCE PRIEBUS   Former White House chief of staff.

YEVGENY PRIGOZHIN   Often referred to as "Putin's chef," he is suspected of having spearheaded Putin's campaign to interfere with the 2016 U.S. elections. He and 12 other Russians are defendants in one of the Mueller indictments.

ERIK PRINCE   This founder of Blackwater has told the House Intelligence Committee that in January 2017 he met with Al Nahyan Mo- hammed bin Zayed, the Crown prince of Abu Dhabi in the Seychelles, and then met with Kirill Dmitriev, a Russian banker who was also at the island resort at the time. It is suspected that Prince and Dmitriev discussed the setting up of a "back channel" communications link between the Trump team and the Kremlin.

VLADAMIR V. PUTIN   Former KGB agent and President of Russia who authorized the cyberattack on the U.S. by Russian operatives during the 2016 U.S. presidential election, and expertly orchestrated -- through a combination of flattery, economic and financial in- ducements and kompromat -- the manipulation and possible recruitment of Trump as a witting or un- witting Russian asset or agent.

ROD ROSENSTEIN   Deputy Attorney General overseeing the Special Counsel's investigation following Attorney General Sessions' recusal.

DMITRY RYBOLOVIEV   Russian billionaire who overpaid Trump for the purchase of a mansion for $95 million (Trump says $100 million) in Palm Beach, Florida in 2008. Ryboloviev never moved into the mansion, which was described as "unlivable," and it was eventually torn down. His plane has been spotted close to where Trump was located, but no direct meetings have been confirmed.

FELIX SATER   Russian émigré, convicted felon, organized crime associate and longtime Trump business associate. He escorted the Trump children in Moscow and has worked on several proposed projects for Trump in Russia.

IGOR SECHIN   Executive chairman of Russian state oil company

Rosneft who, according to the Steele Dossier, met with Carter Page in July 2016 in Moscow.

JEFF SESSIONS Former Attorney general, former senator and former Trump campaign adviser, who recused himself from oversight of the Russia investigation and the Special Counsel's investigation.

GLEN SIMPSON Co-founder of Fusion GPS, the research firm that hired British ex-spy Christopher Steele to investigate Trump's possible ties to Russia. He testified before the Senate Judiciary Committee in private session.

SEAN SPICER Trump's first White House press secretary and dissembler-in-chief.

CHRISTOPHER STEELE Former British MI-6 intelligence agent who spent an extensive amount of time in Russia and developed many contacts there. Based upon these contacts and his firm's investigation, he produced the Dossier that essentially concludes that Trump had been compromised by the Russians.

ROGER J. STONE JR. Longtime Trump adviser and political consultant, noted for his use of opposition research and "dirty tricks." He is the subject of a portion of the Special Counsel's investigation, relating to contacts between the Trump Campaign and Julian Assange of WikiLeaks, which was used by the Russians to disseminate much of the illegally hacked data and documents obtained from the Hillary Clinton campaign and other Democratic sources. Stone was arrested on January 25, 2019 on charges of obstruction of justice, making false statements and witness tampering. According to Stone's indictment, he told "senior Trump Campaign officials" about stolen emails in WikiLeaks possession in June or July 2016, prior to WikiLeaks releasing its first batch of Democratic emails on July 22, 2016. A senior Trump Campaign Official then "was directed" to contact Stone to find out what other damaging information WikiLeaks had that could be helpful to the Trump Campaign. On October 4, 2016, Stone told Steve Bannon that WikiLeaks would be releasing "a load every week" and, sure enough, on October 7, 2016 WikiLeaks released, 6,000 of John Podesta's emails.

JASON SULLIVAN

Social media expert and associate of Roger Stone. He was subpoenaed to appear before the federal grand jury hearing evidence gathered as part of the Special Counsel's investigation. He prepared a strategy document prepared for Stone entitled, "Welcome To The Age of Weaponized Social Media."

ALEXANDER TORSHIN

A key Putin political ally in Russia and deputy governor of the Central Bank of Russia, at least until he recently announced his retirement. Torshin's assistant, Maria Butina, recently pled guilty in the U.S. to charges of spying for Russia and attempting to infiltrate various U.S. groups, including the NRA.

DONALD J. TRUMP

Current occupant of the White House, despite having lost the 2016 general election by 2.7 million votes and having been substantially aided by

a massive disinformation campaign and cyber- attack on our electoral and other democratic systems
that appears to have been coordinated with Trump
Campaign operatives with the knowledge and consent of Trump himself. Trump is reported to be
the current subject of an FBI counterintelligence
investigation to determine whether he has been
compromised and is acting as a Russian agent, and
whether as a result, the U.S. national security was
placed (and still is) at risk.

DONALD TRUMP JR.   Trump's eldest son was active in Trump's presidential campaign and was instrumental in organizing
the June 9, 2016 meeting at Trump Tower, where
he and others associated with the Trump Campaign met with a group of Russians in the hopes
of getting illegal "dirt" that the Russians had on
Hillary Clinton through Russian cybercrimes. Instead, they apparently got a lecture on the evils of
U.S. sanctions against Russia, which the Russians
expected the Trump Administration to lift if and
when he was elected.

YULIA TYMOSHENKO   The former Prime Minister of Ukraine and
pro-Western opposition leader who was impris-
oned and prosecuted by the pro-Russian Ukrainian
Yanukovich regime on trumped-up and politically
motivate charges. Paul Manfort engineered much
of the "whitewash" investigation and report prepared by the Skadden law firm, including Alex van
der Zwaan, of the circumstances surrounding Tymoshenko's jailing and prosecution.

VIKTOR Г. VEKSELBERG   A powerful Russian oligarch who is worth roughly $13 billion, making him one of the richest men in both Russia and the world. He wired $500,000 to an LLC controlled by Michael Cohen, Trump's personal lawyer and "fixer." The Special Counsel's office is investigating the relationship, if any, between these contacts and payments and the Trump campaign/administration.

NATALIA VESELNITSKAYA   A Russian lawyer and government operative who attended the June 9, 2016 Trump Tower meeting with Don Jr., Manafort and Kushner. On January 8, 2019, this key figure in the Special Counsel's investigation, was charged by federal prosecutors in Manhattan of seeking to improperly interfere with an earlier Department of Justice investigation of money laundering by the Russian company Prevezon and a powerful Russian businessman believed to have close ties to Putin. Apparently, she pretended in federal court in Manhattan that she was purely a private defense lawyer when she was, in fact, working for the Russian government.

WIKILEAKS/JULIAN ASSANGE   A self-described "anti-secrecy organization" that is a de facto arm of Russian intelligence, releasing tens of thousands of hacked emails from Hillary Clinton's campaign and the Democratic National Committee that it obtained from the Russians. Its founder, Julian Assange, also maintained various contacts with Trump Campaign operatives that are the subject of the Special Counsel's investigation.

SALLY Q. YATES   Former acting attorney general who warned the Trump White House that Michael Flynn had lied to Vice President Mike Pence and others about the substance of his conversations with Russian ambassador Kislyak in December 2016. She was fired by Trump for refusing to enforce the Muslim travel ban, which she considered to be illegal.

VIKTOR YANUKOVICH

Former pro-Russian President of Ukraine who was ousted in February-March 2014 and fled to Russia for protection by Putin. He and his political party, the Party of Regions, paid Paul Manafort millions of dollars "off the books" for consulting work.

AL NAHYAN MOHAMMED BIN ZAYED

Crown prince of Abu Dhabi who attended a January 2017 meeting in the Seychelles with Trump supporter and Blackwater founder Erik Prince. Prince has told the House Intelligence Committee that he met with Al-Nahyan, who then suggested that he meet with Kirill Dmitriev, a Russian banker who was also at the island resort at the time. It is suspected that Prince and Dmitriev discussed the setting up of a "backchannel" communications link between the Trump team and the Kremlin.

DASHA ZHUKOVA

Ex-wife of Russian billionaire Roman Abramovich and close friend of Ivanka Trump.

ALEX VAN DER ZWAAN

Dutch lawyer who worked out of London office of mega-law firm Skadden Arps on an investigation and report relating to the Ukrainian government's incarceration and prosecution of Ukrainian pro-Western opposition political leader and former Prime Minister Yulia Tymoshenko. Van der Zwaan and perhaps other attorneys coordinated with Paul Manafort, Rick Gates and possibly Russian-Ukrainian operative Konstantin Kilimnik. Van der Zwaan pleaded guilty to lying to FBI agents who interviewed him in London about conversations with Gates and Kilimnik.

PROLOGUE

"This American carnage stops right here and stops right now."

Donald J. Trump, January 20, 2017

It was a grey overcast day in Washington on January 20, 2017, the day that Donald J. Trump was sworn in as the 45th President of the United States. The weather matched the mood of the majority of Americans who had voted for Hillary Clinton, but whose candidate was denied the election as a result of an anachronistic Electoral College system, a lackluster Clinton Campaign that had ignored key battleground states such as Michigan and Wisconsin, and of course substantial help from the Russians.

But the most significant assault on American democracy did not result from the illegal hacking and cyber attacks by Russian agents on our electoral system and social media. Rather, it came from Donald Trump's full-scale assault on American ideals and values, which had long been this country's most powerful weapons in its arsenal of democracy.

In his grim inauguration speech, Trump basically announced the end of American Exceptionalism -- the hallowed concept and conviction that the United States has a special mission and place in history. Instead of extolling the virtues of our democracy and calling upon its citizens to raise the torch of liberty in every corner of this country and around the world, Trump took the cynical view that the United States was no better or worse than Russia or any other authoritarian country, and that all our government should be doing is to "put America first" by concentrating

1

on building our country's economic wealth over all other considerations, and by not worrying about other concerns such as human rights or even democratic rights and freedoms around the world.

Trump's denouncement of America's commitment to liberty and justice for all was a frontal attack on the guiding principles forming the bedrock of our democracy and America's faith in itself and its transcendent mission. The Declaration of Independence had been a clarion call that resonated not only on this continent but around the world, declaring that the pursuit of life, liberty and the pursuit of happiness was the cherished goal of all Americans and freedom-loving people the world over. Now Trump was seeking to extinguish that fire by declaring that America was no longer the beacon of liberty, and that every country – especially Russia – should be permitted to do whatever it wanted in its own country and in its sphere of influence (i.e. Ukraine), and that if they dismembered neighboring countries or slaughtered its own people who were fighting for greater civil and human rights, that this was of no importance to the U.S. In other words, Trump was articulating precisely what Putin and others in the Kremlin wanted to hear, which is that Trump would give them the green light to rebuild the Russian Empire without fear of opposition or retaliation by the U.S. In doing so, Trump was demonstrating that he was a traitor to the traditional American democratic ideals.

The enduring concept of American Exceptionalism dates back to French writer Alexis de Tocqueville's reflections on America in his 1835/1840 work, Democracy in America, where he concluded: "The position of the Americans is therefore quite exceptional, and it may be believed that no democratic people will ever be placed in a similar one."

Abraham Lincoln echoed this theme of American uniqueness when he noted in his Gettysburg address in 1863 that one of the things that set us apart from all other countries in history was the sacred duty of the United States to ensure that "government of the people, by the people, for the people, shall not perish from the earth."

Since the end of the Civil War, and up until January 20, 2017, the idea of American Exceptionalism has infused the rhetoric of virtually every modern President and political leader. In April 1917, near the end of the First World War, President Woodrow Wilson exhorted Americans to fulfill the country's destiny to make the world "Safe for Democracy."

In his State of the Union address in January 1941, when the future of liberal democracies in their world war against fascism hung in the balance, President Franklin Delano Roosevelt sent a message to its besieged democratic allies around the globe, reassuring them that "We Americans are vitally concerned in your defense of freedom. We are putting forth our energies, our resources, and our organizing powers to give you the strength to regain and maintain a free world … This is our purpose and our pledge."

Fifty-eight years ago, in his Inaugural speech in January 1961, President John F. Kennedy's reminded Americans that it was our country's fundamental duty to protect human rights "at home and around the world." He pledged that America would "bear any burden, meet any hardship, support any friend, oppose any foe to assure the survival and the success of liberty."

Ronald Reagan inspired us with his soaring rhetoric about America being a "Shining City on the Hill," a beacon of freedom, hope, and liberty that was – and always be -- the model and example for all the world.

President Obama, in April 2009, publicly acknowledged Americas "extraordinary role in leading the world towards peace and prosperity," while cautioning that such a lofty goal could only be achieved through effective partnerships with other countries. He also often reminded us that America is, at its core, a good and caring nation that must work tirelessly in the cause of democracy and human rights around the world.

With Trump, this powerful concept of American Exceptionalism, which has been enshrined in our nation's psyche for almost two hundred years, was declared to be dead and buried. Or so Donald Trump and his enablers would like us to believe.

In the immortal words of Stephen Colbert, Trump, in his easily forgettable Inaugural speech, basically compared America to a "dumpster fire." America's longstanding mission to preserve and protect the causes of democracy, freedom and human rights around the world had, according to the Trump gospel, virtually devastated the country. In Trump's view, American internationalism and free trade policies, fueled in large measure by a belief in America's special place in the world, had reduced America to a virtual wasteland. Trump painted a dark "Mad Max" picture of a country with "rusted-out factories scattered like tombstones across the landscape of our nation." and rampant "American Carnage" in our inner cities.

Of course, Trump's vision of America was a totally false one, or at least grossly misleading, and he most probably knew it. But this kind of dark rhetoric that he honed on the campaign trail seemed to work, so now that he was sworn in as President, he seemed incapable of letting his distorted vision of America evolve into something that more closely resembled reality.

In the dark parallel universe painted by Trump in his inauguration speech, there was not even one acknowledgment that any of the former Presidents sitting behind him had done anything other than to let America go to hell in a handbasket. Since, according to the Trump Doctrine, only he and he alone can save the country from catastrophe, he could not possibly bring himself to thank the outgoing President – Barrack Obama -- for literally saving the country's economy from the virtual freefall that it was in when he took office in January 2009. He could not acknowledge that, under President Obama's stewardship, the unemployment has dropped from a high of 10% in January 2009 down to under 5%, that poverty and welfare dependency fell sharply fallen throughout the country, and that 20 million more Americans enjoy health insurance coverage, or at least until the Republican leadership guts the Affordable Care Act.

Questioning the value of America's international alliances such as NATO, which have kept the peace in Europe for at least the past five decades, Trump had latched onto the slogan of "American First," which was used by fascist sympathizers and isolationists such as Charles Lindberg during the late 1930s to try to keep America from coming to the aid of the Western European democracies that were being threatened, reasoning that Hitler's plan to exterminate all European Jews and minority groups was none of America's business.

In his Inaugural Address, Trump did make a passing reference to seeking "friendship and goodwill with the nations of the world," but, instead, announced that our interaction with other nations would be solely motivated by a new commitment to serve America's interests first, which presumably no longer included an interest in promoting freedom and human rights in other parts of the world, or combatting Climate Change, unless – in the unlikely event – that there was some economic or strategic advantage to the United States in promoting such causes.

In short, Trump tried his best to drive a stake through the heart of American Exceptionalism, and the concept that America is the last best hope for freedom and democracy. Hopefully, the flame of liberty will not and cannot be extinguished by Trump or anyone else seeking to denounce and deride fundamental American principles, but such a dark and self-obsessed view of the world and Americas place in it will inevitably cause damage to the essence of what this country stands as long as the proponent of such foreign and treasonous views continues to occupy the White House.

Although Trump still occupies the White House, continuing to serve the interests of a foreign hostile power and promoting hostile ideas that are fundamentally inconsistent with American democratic ideals, there are strong indications that America will not only survive the Trump phenomenon but may rebound even more strongly once he is removed.

Starting on January 21, 2017, hundreds of thousands of Americans participated in the Women's March on Washington, putting Trump and his cronies on notice that their dedication to eliminating the scourge of Trumpism was more powerful than ever, and that they would not rest until this fundamental threat to our democracy was driven from power. After all, America has been a beacon of liberty and protector of human rights throughout the world for generations now, and this shining torch can never be extinguished, either by Trump or by any other petty despot who dared to attack America's core values and restrict our basic liberties.

As Woodrow Wilson proclaimed over one hundred years ago, "The history of liberty is a history of resistance." Tens and hundreds of thousands of Americans have answered the call, either by marching in the streets, attending rallies, picketing, petitioning, writing letters and the thousands of other ways that an aroused citizenry can speak truth to power.

America has also begun to realize that Trump is either unwilling or unqualified to carry out the basic constitutional duties of the President, including the duty to preserve and protect this great country when it is threatened and under siege, and that he has irrevocably sided with America's arch-enemy by now consistently acting in a manner that is antithetical to the best interests of the United States. In other words, America has begun to wake up to the grim reality that we have a traitor in our midst, and that he is willing to do virtually anything – including the firing of an FBI Director who refuses to deviate from the Rule of Law -- to hold onto the levers of power and to obstruct, side-track and suppress the Justice Department's investigation into his Campaign's active coordination and complicity with Russia's efforts to damage our democracy and to elevate one of its own compliant assets to the White House.

Ironically, there probably would have never been a Special Counsel's investigation of Russian interference in the 2016 presidential election and the numerous contacts between the Russians and Trump Campaign operatives if Trump had not fired FBI Director James Comey on May 9, 2017. About one week later, on May 17, 2017, Deputy Attorney General Rod J. Rosenstein announced to the appointment of former FBI Director Robert S. Mueller III to serve as Special Counsel. The Comey firing also triggered the launch of a counterintelligence investigation by federal law enforcement officials as to whether Trump was working on behalf of Russia against American interests.

Now that the Special Counsel's investigation has been concluded, and it has been announced that no more indictments will be forthcoming from the Mueller team, it can be fairly said that the Special Counsel has left an impressive prosecutorial record. The raw statistics alone are impressive: 34 individuals and three companies were indicted, convicted or plead guilty to felony charges, including Trump's Campaign Chairman (Paul Manafort), Trump's Deputy Campaign Manager (Rick Gates), Trump's first National Security Advisor (Michael Flynn), Trump's personal lawyer and "fixer"

(Michael Cohen), Trump Campaign national security advisor (George Papadopoulos), Trump advisor (Roger Stone), and a rogue's gallery of Russian spies and hackers with direct ties to Kremlin.

Reviews of the Mueller Report may be an entirely different matter. Twenty-two months into the investigation, on Friday, March 22, 2019, Special Counsel Mueller sent his final report to Attorney General William Barr. While the Mueller Report itself is not publicly available as of this book's publication, and certain confidential portions of the Report are unlikely to be released for the foreseeable future, Attorney General Barr released a summary letter to Congress on Sunday, March 24, 2019, stating that "the Special Counsel's investigation did not find that the Trump campaign or anyone associated with it conspired or coordinated with Russia in its efforts to influence the 2016 U.S. presidential election."

On the issue of whether Trump obstructed justice, the Barr letter reports that Mueller "ultimately determined not to make a traditional prosecutorial judgment" on this important issue, and that "while [the Mueller Report] does not conclude that the President committed a crime, it also does not exonerate him." Barr also reported, however, that in his view and apparently in that of Deputy Attorney General Rod Rosenstein, "the evidence developed during the Special Counsel's investigation is not sufficient to establish that the President committed an obstruction-of-justice offense."

The puzzling "no collusion" finding by Mueller is particularly troubling since this conclusion was apparently reached without any actual interview or sworn testimony by Trump as to, for example, what was going through his mind when he invited the Russians to hack into the Clinton Campaign's database to find her "missing" emails or when he appeared to have advance knowledge of one or more of the WikiLeaks data dumps.

Donald Trump Jr. apparently also got a free pass from Mueller without requiring him to answer questions under oath as to what he was thinking when he set up the Trump Tower meeting with the Russians in the hope and expectation that they would turn over hacked emails and other Clinton "dirt." Since "intent" is always a necessary element in a criminal conspiracy, and the silent operation of the mind can only be divined by either the words or actions of an individual, or by asking him or her what they were thinking at the time, it is difficult to reconcile the decision not to interview these seemingly important witnesses and Mueller's sterling reputation as a thorough prosecutor. Could Trump have been given a "pass" on an interview merely because he was a sitting President, and could Don Jr. have been given a pass because they were "First Family?" Or is there a more reasonable explanation, which is that Don Jr. is the "target" of an ongoing criminal investigation, and Mueller did not want to jeopardize that ongoing investigation by interrogating him now while he is still technically a "target?"

Since the U.S. does not officially believe in "royalty," and our system of laws is premised on the concept that "No man is above the law," how then can a conclusion be reached that neither Trump nor any of his inner circle conspired with the Russians when neither Trump nor at least one other key player (Don Jr.) were even asked to explain what they were doing when they met with Russian, talked about getting access to Clinton "dirt," and discussed the lifting of U.S. sanctions on Russia.

Mueller's conclusion of "no collusion" must also be carefully scrutinized, since it appears to be based on a very narrow reading of what constituted Russian interference in the 2016 election. As summarized in Barr's March 24th letter to Congress, the Special Counsel's investigation focused on two major aspects of Russian interference. The first involved attempts by a Russian organization, the Internet Research Agency (IRA) to conduct disinformation and social media operations in the U.S., with the aim of interfering in the election, and the second involved Russian government efforts "to conduct computer hacking operations designed to gather and disseminate information to influence the elections."

Just as with polling data, where answers to a question are likely to vary widely depending on how the poll question is phrased, the narrow definition of "Russian interference" as posed in Barr's March 24th letter (and presumably the Mueller Report) almost dictates a negative answer to the question of whether the Trump campaign "conspired or coordinated with Russia." With regard to the first prong identified in the Barr letter, no one to my knowledge has even suggested that anyone in the Trump campaign directly conspired with Russia's Internet Research Agency ("IRA"). Nor are there any allegations to my knowledge that anyone connected with the Trump campaign directly conspired with Russia's "hacking operations" that, as summarized in the Barr letter, gathered emails from "the Clinton campaign and other Democratic Organizations." So if the question is framed as: "Did the Trump campaign or anyone associated with it conspire with the IRA's disinformation and social media campaign in the U.S. or with the Russian government's hacking operations?", the answer inevitably is a resounding "No."

The question naturally arises from the Barr letter's (and Mueller's) conclusion of "no conspiracy" between the Trump campaign and the Russians is why did so many Trump campaign officials lie about their contacts with Russian officials during the campaign and transition period? Jeff Sessions, Jared Kushner, Don Jr., Michael Flynn, Carter Page, George Papadopoulos, and others either lied about their meetings with Russian Ambassador Kislyak and other Russian officials, or they intentionally failed to disclose those meetings on government disclosure forms they were required to file with U.S. law enforcement agencies. The obvious reason for why they lied about these meetings and phone conversations with the Russians was not that was that they were discussing how the Russians could best go about hacking into Clinton Campaign and DNC databases to get "dirt" on Clinton, or how the Trump Campaign could assist Russia with its disinformation and social media campaign in the U.S. Rather, these contacts were more broadly focused on how the Trump campaign, transition team and administration would adopt a pro-Russian policy agenda, such as reducing or eliminating the crippling U.S. financial and economic sanctions on Russia and accepting Russia's de facto annexation of Crimea, in return for Russia's independent efforts to damage the Clinton campaign and to get Trump elected.

To put it another way, this broader conspiracy between the Trump campaign and the Russians had little or nothing to do with the nuts and bolts of Russian hacking operations and disinformation campaign on U.S. social media, and a lot to do with the Trump campaign's and transition team's secret alliance with the Russians to undercut -- and then reverse -- the Obama Administration's strong policy of punishing Russia financially for its military intervention in Ukraine and other provocations in violation of international law, as well as the watering down of the Republican Platform regarding U.S. support for the Ukrainian government in its efforts to defend itself against Russian aggression. This broader conspiracy to tilt U.S. policy in favor of Russia, while knowing that doing so was contrary to the U.S.'s best interests, is precisely why Trump campaign operatives consistently lied about their contacts with the Russians, since they knew --either consciously or at some basic visceral level -- that these contacts with the Russians were contrary to U.S. interests or, at the very least, contrary to existing U.S. policy towards Russia as formulated by the Obama Administration. This broad conspiracy against the United States, which is a violation of Title 18 of the United States Code, Section 371, among other criminal provisions, is precisely the statute that Special Prosecutor Mueller used in numerous indictments for tax fraud, violations of the Foreign Agents Registration Act (FARA) and other fraudulent acts against U.S. agencies, but which he apparently declined to pursue with regard to the broader conspiracy between Russian and Trump campaign operatives to sell out U.S. interests in favor of Russia's interests, and to give aid and comfort to a foreign hostile power at the expense of one's own country, which is the textbook definition of Treason, and most certainly amounts to Betrayal.

Of particular concern regarding the Barr letter's summary of the Mueller Report is that, while it acknowledges that the illegally hacked material used against Clinton during the 2016 presidential campaign was "publicly disseminated ...through various intermediaries, including WikiLeaks," the Special Counsel (as explained by Barr) apparently did not consider WikiLeaks to have fallen within the definition of "Russian government" for purposes of assessing collusion, even though it is almost universally accepted – and certainly by the U.S. intelligence community – that WikiLeaks was, for all intents and purposes, an arm or agency of the Russian government. If the Special Counsel and Barr had considered WikiLeaks to just be another Russian agency (which it functionally was and still is), then the question of whether Trump campaign operatives conspired with the Russian government to disseminate hacked information damaging to Clinton and the Democrats may well have been "Yes." After all, Roger Stone was indicted, at least in part, for lying about his contacts with both WikiLeaks and a Russian intelligence front known as "Guccifer 2.0." Through Roger Stone and other Trump campaign operatives, the Trump campaign and Trump himself appear to have had advanced knowledge as to when WikiLeaks would be making additional "data dumps," and that Trump and his team both agreed with and ascribed to the criminal conspiratorial goals of the Russian/WikiLeaks plan to interfere with the U.S. election through the dissemination of these stolen materials.

It is also difficult to square what we know of the Mueller Report's "no collusion" finding with reliable press reports from generally well-reputed press and media outlets about the contacts between high-level Trump campaign officials and Russian agents. For example, it has been reliably reported that Trump Campaign Chairman Paul Manafort and Deputy Chairman Rick Gates met at the Grand Havana Room at 666 Fifth Avenue in Manhattan (Jared Kushner's building) with Konstantin Kilimnik (a known Russian operative closely connected to GRU Russian intelligence operations who was one of the people indicted by the Special Counsel's office), and that Manafort passed on to Kilimnik U.S. polling data. For what purpose you may ask would Manafort give a Russian government-connected operative U.S. polling data during the 2016 presidential campaign other than to help Russia with its disinformation campaign targeting swing U.S. voters? I can't think of any other purpose, and I doubt that the experienced prosecutors on the Mueller team would conclude otherwise. However, if Mueller or Barr narrowly restricted their analysis to evidence relating to contacts between Trump team members and full-time Russian government employees or officials, they may well have excluded contacts with Kilimnik and others who are closely connected to the Kremlin but may not technically be in the full-time employ of the Russian government.

Another example of a "smoking gun" meeting that Mueller and Barr may have excluded from their analysis of whether Trump campaign operatives conspired with "the Russian government" to influence the election is the June 9, 2016 Trump Tower meeting between Don Jr., Jared Kushner and Paul Manafort with a group of Russians, including Natalia Veselnitskaya, a Russian attorney closely connected with the Russian government but who may not have literally been a Russian government employee or official as of the date of the meeting. In my view, and I believe in the view of many legal analysts closely following the Russia/Trump investigation, such a narrow definition of the term "Russian government" would be unwarranted and unfortunate, since there should be no serious dispute that Veselnitskaya was an "agent" and authorized representative of the Russian government for purposes of a conspiracy or "collusion" analysis. Indeed, when the meeting was set up with Don Jr., it was represented by the Rob Goldstone, the British publicist who was acting as the liaison between the Russian and Trump camps, that Veselnitskaya would be speaking on behalf of the "Crown prosecutor of Russia," a reference to Yury Yakovlevich Chaika, the Prosecutor General of Russia, with whom Veselnitskaya has had a close and longstanding relationship. Goldstone specifically advised Don Jr. by email that "the Crown prosecutor of Russia" had "offered to provide the Trump campaign with some official documents and information that would incriminate Hillary ... and would be very useful to your father." The email went on to say that the offer was "part of Russia and its government's support for Mr. Trump." Don Jr. wrote back: "If it's what you say I love it." Since all that is needed for a criminal conspiracy is an express or tacit understanding or agreement in furtherance of an unlawful goal, sometimes referred to as a "meeting of the minds," and some act in furtherance of that conspiracy, it is difficult to understand how Mueller and Barr could have concluded that there was no conspiracy here without defining the underlying crime so narrowly, i.e., the

Russian hacking and disinformation campaign, that the subject matter of the Trump Tower meeting could be construed as falling outside the scope of the Special Counsel's investigation. In other words, by the standards asserted in the Barr letter as to what constituted "election interference," Barr (and perhaps Mueller) were able to reach the strained conclusion that this meeting did not "count" for purposes of determining whether there was a "tacit agreement ... on election interference." Thus, the Barr letter itself (and perhaps the Mueller Report when we see it) required a lot of legal "spin" and contortions to reach a "no collusion" conclusion.

One thing is sure, though, which is that Trump is getting exactly what he hoped for when he appointed Barr as his Attorney General. Not only did Trump get a "no collusion" letter that is filled with partial sentence quotes from the Mueller Report, but he also got a "no obstruction-of-justice" finding by Barr after a weekend review, when Mueller had taken 22-months to investigate the matter and could not draw any definitive conclusions on that issue.

Although the Barr letter's summary of Mueller's "no collusion" conclusion is extremely cursory, and the full Mueller Report itself undoubtedly contains much more detail, there is already a vast reservoir of information that can be gleaned from the Mueller indictments themselves, as well as from the publicly available sentencing memoranda and court filing by the Special Counsel's office. When these materials are combined with mountain of information publicly disclosed over the past several years as a result of reliable investigative reporting, there is already ample evidence to reach a conclusion that is the direct opposite of what Mueller apparently concluded, and that the Trump Team coordinated on numerous levels with Russian agents and operatives (including WikiLeaks) in their efforts not only to broadly assist Russia with achieving goals that were contrary to existing U.S. foreign policy and antithetical to U.S. interests, as well as to more narrowly influence the 2016 presidential election and to swing it in Trump's favor.

There is also substantial public evidence that Trump himself welcomed and approved of the efforts by his operatives to obtain information from the Russians that would be helpful to his campaign and harmful to that of Hillary Clinton. Given Trump's "hands-on" and "command and control" management style, even former Trump advisor Steve Bannon has publicly agreed with the general consensus that there was "zero" chance that Trump did not know about the critical June 9, 2017 meeting that Don Jr. arranged at Trump Tower with a group of high-level Russian operatives.

Similarly, there is – at least in the judgment of this writer and most other "Trump watchers" – virtually "zero" chance that Trump did not authorize and know about the many other significant points of contact between his campaign and Russian operatives that were either specifically designed to give his campaign a boost and to sink that of Hillary Clinton, or were designed to undercut the then-current hardline U.S. policy towards Russia. A few examples should more than suffice to make this point:

- During a 2016 news conference, Trump invited Russia to assist his campaign and harm Clinton's by hacking into U.S. databases to find the "missing" Clinton emails. "Russia, if you're listening, I hope you're able to find the 30,000 emails that are missing," Trump stated. "I think you will probably be rewarded mightily by our press." According to documents filed by the Special Counsel's office in July 2018, in connection with Mueller's indictment of 12 Russian GRU intelligence officers, the Russian agents complied with Trump's request by intensifying their hacking operations. According to the indictments, the Russians continued through the green light publicly given to them to expand their operations into the hacking of state election boards.

- Michael Cohen, Trump's personal lawyer and "fixer," suggested in his testimony before Congress on February 27, 2019 that Trump knew about the infamous June 9, 2016 meeting at Trump Tower between Don Jr. and other senior officials in the Trump Campaign with Russians claiming that they could provide "dirt" on Hillary Clinton.

- There is substantial evidence that Trump and his Campaign had prior knowledge and a "heads up" that a treasure trove of damaging information about Hillary Clinton was about to be unleashed by WikiLeaks in the summer of 2016. For example, Michael Cohen testified before Congress that he was in Trump's office in July 2016 during the 2016 campaign when Roger Stone told Trump over a speakerphone that he had just spoken to Julian Assange of WikiLeaks and that additional stolen emails and other "dirt" on Hillary Clinton would be released in the next few days. Cohen testified that Stone told Trump that Assange had told him that there would be a "massive dump of emails that would damage Hillary Clinton's campaign."

- The Special Counsel's indictment released on January 25, 2019 charged Trump's "dirty trickster" Roger Stone with having followed the directions of a top Trump campaign official during the 2016 presidential campaign, and that this high-level Trump Campaign official had dispatched Stone to get information from WikiLeaks about the thousands of hacked Democratic emails. There is a high probability that either (1) Trump was the only one senior enough in the campaign to have "directed" Stone to take this action, or (2) that no other senior campaign official would have sent Stone on his WikiLeaks mission without Trump's blessing.

• On December 29, 2016, Trump's National Security Advisor Michael Flynn had conversations with Russian ambassador Sergey Kislyak during the transition period as part of a coordinated effort by the Trump team to influence foreign policy before the inauguration, undercut the Obama Administration's sanctions against Russia for meddling in the 2016 election, and to signal to the Russians that U.S. sanctions would likely be eased or lifted once Trump was sworn in. The next day (Dec. 30, 2016), President Vladimir Putin announced that Russia would not retaliate against the U.S. for the sanctions.

• Flynn was directed by a "very senior member" of Trump's transition team (presumably Jared Kushner) to call Russian Ambassador Kislyak on December 22, 2016, and to ask him to have Russia delay or defeat a UN Security Council resolution condemning Israel for its settlement policy. The Obama Administration abstained, and the resolution passed. Given the major foreign policy implications of this call to this Russian official, it is extremely unlikely that Kushner would have directed Flynn to do this without Trump's knowledge and consent.

• Trump hired Paul Manafort as his Campaign Chairman when it was public knowledge at the time that Manafort had long-standing relationships with Russian and Ukrainian oligarchs and political leaders with close ties to the Kremlin, and that Manafort could help him solidify his own relationship and that of his campaign with high-level Russian operatives and Kremlin insiders.

Manafort lived up to and even exceeded Trump's expectations by, among other things, attending the June 9, 2017 Trump Tower meeting with the Russians, offering "private briefings" on the presidential campaign to Oleg Deripaska, a Kremlin insider and Putin crony, providing an ongoing liaison between Trump Campaign officials and Russian intelligence operatives via Konstantin Kilimnik, a Russian GRU intelligence agent who had been working with and "handling" Manafort for many years on behalf of the Kremlin, and, at the Grand Havana Room at 666 Fifth Avenue in Manhattan (a building owned by Jared Kushner), providing Kilimnik and Russian intelligence critical U.S. polling data that could be used to target key precincts in key states as part of Russia's disinformation campaign and interference with the 2016 election.

- Jared Kushner, Trump's son-in-law and chief advisor, had numerous off-the-record meetings with Russian officials and bankers, both with Michael Flynn and by himself, where Kushner repeatedly tried to open a "back door" communication channel with the Kremlin on behalf of the Trump Team, so that he and other Trump operatives could communicate with the Russians without the prying eyes of U.S. law enforcement and intelligence agencies knowing what was being discussed. It is inconceivable that Kushner would have made such direct overtures to the Russians on numerous sensitive subjects without Trump's knowledge and consent.

- Trump Campaign advisor George Papadopoulos was urged by senior Trump Campaign officials to meet with Russians and to forge closer ties between the Trump Team and the Russian government. Papadopoulos complied with these requests and had at least several meetings with Russian operatives believed to have close ties with the Kremlin and Russian intelligence operations. In August 2016, for example, a top campaign official (believed to be national campaign co-chairman Sam Clovis) urged Papadopoulos to travel to Europe and to Russia if necessary, to meet with various Russian operatives who were offering "dirt" on Hillary Clinton, access to Putin or other forms of Russian assistance to the Trump Campaign.

- Trump Campaign advisor Carter Page also had numerous points of contact with Russian operatives during the 2016 Campaign and was even given permission by a senior campaign official (presumably with Trump's O.K.) to fly to Moscow during the campaign for a "conference" where he met with various Russian officials and operatives. At the time Trump publicly announced the fact that Page was joining his campaign as a foreign policy advisor, Trump must have known of Page's longstanding and extremely outspoken pro-Russian stance on the Russian sanction issues, and that he had been caught up in and described as "Male-1" in a major U.S. counterintelligence investigation in 2015 that had led to the arrest and federal conviction of at least two of these Russian intelligence operatives.

There is thus substantial evidence already in the public record that the numerous points of contact between Trump campaign/transition operatives and the Russians were intended largely to assure Russia that Trump was "on board" with its major foreign policy objectives, even though those objectives just happened to be contrary to U.S. national and strategic interests, and to encourage, aid and abet Russia in its own illegal hacking efforts and its disinformation campaign, even though the Trump Team stopped short of any "hands-on" participation in Russia's hacking and disinformation campaign.

When Michael Isikoff and David Corn wrote *Russian Roulette* last year, they must have been prescient as to what the Mueller Report would finally say about the Special Counsel's investigation. In the final page of the book, they wrote:

> During the campaign, Trump had encouraged Russia's hacking and dumping – of which he was the chief beneficiary. He had praised the WikiLeaks releases, promoting them, and calling for more – even after he had received a secret U.S. government briefing stating that the cyber break-ins and the dissemination of Democratic files were part of a Russian covert operation to undermine the election. He had spoken positively about Putin and suggested he was eager to undo sanctions and cut deals with the Kremlin – even as the Russia information war fare campaign was underway. Whether or not the investigations would ever turn up hard evidence of direct collusion, Trump's actions – his adamant and consistent denial of any Russian role – had provided Putin cover. In that sense, he had aided and abetted Moscow's attack on American democracy.[1]

In other words, the Mueller investigation was never intended to address the larger question posed by Trump's pro-Russian words and actions, which were fully supported by the pro-Russian team members with which he surrounded himself. This larger question is whether Trump and his campaign aided, abetted and provided "comfort" to a hostile foreign power, i.e. Russia, such that the conduct of Trump and members of his team can be properly considered to be treasonous and a betrayal of their own country's interests. I believe that the answer to that question, as explained in this book, is a resounding "Yes."

There is also ample evidence that Trump attempted to obstruct the investigation by U.S. law enforcement and intelligence agencies into the ties between his campaign and the Russians, and none of the conclusory statements by a Trump appointed Attorney General who is already on record as basically stating that a sitting president cannot obstruct justice can obscure that fact. For example:

- On February 14, 2017, Trump privately met with FBI Director James Comey in the Oval Office, asking Director Comey to, in words or substance, make sure that the FBI drops the investigation of former National Security Advisor Michael Flynn.

- On the same day (Feb. 14, 2017), Trump spoke privately with Daniel Coats, the Director of National Intelligence, and Mike Pompeo, the CIA Director, asking them to persuade Comey to "back off" the investigation of Michael Flynn.

- During March and April 2017, Trump told Comey in multiple phone calls that he wanted Comey to "lift the cloud" of the Russia investigation.

- In March 2017, Trump made separate appeals to the Director of National Intelligence, Daniel Coats, and to Adm. Michael S. Rogers, the Director of the National Security Agency, urging them to publicly deny the existence of any evidence of collusion during the 2016 election.

- On March 30, 2017, Trump asked Comey again in another phone call what could be done to "lift the cloud" of the Russia investigation from his administration, stressing that "the cloud" was interfering with his ability to make deals for the country and that "he hoped [Comey] could find a way to get out that he wasn't being investigated."

- On April 11, 2017, Trump again called Comey, asking him to release a statement that he (Trump) was not personally under investigation. Trump states, according to Comey: "Because I have been very loyal to you, very loyal; we had that thing you know."

- Frustrated at the fact that Comey had not followed his veiled directives to quash the Flynn investigation and the entire Russian/Trump probe, and given the fact that Comey had not complied with his "request" to make a statement exonerating him, Trump fires Comey as FBI Director on May 9, 2017, in a last-ditch effort to kill the investigation that by then had reached deeply into the White House.

- On May 10, 2017, while Trump was alone in the Oval Office with Russian Ambassador Kislyak and Russian Foreign Minister Sergei Lavrov, Trump confided in these Russian officials that firing of FBI Director James Comey the day before had taken "great pressure" off him. He described Comey as a "nut job," had "taken off" the "great pressure" of the Russia investigation. Trump explains to the Russians: "I just fired the head of the FBI. He was crazy, a real nut job." He also states: "I faced great pressure because of Russia. That's taken off."

- On May 11, 2017, Trump confirmed to NBC's Lester Holt during an interview on national TV that he had decided to fire

Comey because of "the Russia thing."

• During June 2017, Trump ordered White House counsel Don McGahn to fire Special Counsel Robert Mueller, backing off only when McGahn threatens to quit.

• On July 8, 2017, while aboard Air Force One, Trump attempted to obstruct and divert prosecutorial and public attention away from the clear "collusion" inference to be drawn from the June 9, 2016 Trump Tower meeting with the Russian by drafting a false public statement for his son, Don Jr., absurdly claiming that the meeting was about "adoption policy." A statement released by Don Jr., based upon his father's false narrative, stated that this now infamous meeting was about "the adoption [program] of Russian children that was active and popular with American families years ago and was since ended by the Russian government." Within a matter of days, however, Don Jr. was forced to retract his "adoption" story concocted by his father, and in the emails he released, it was clear that Don Jr. and other members of Team Trump were looking for "dirt" on Hillary Clinton, and then when Don Jr. was told that the Russians could deliver the goods on Clinton, he responded: "I love it!"

• Michael Cohen publicly testified before Congress on February 27, 2019, that Trump had previously told him "in code" to lie to Congress in August 2017 about the fact that Trump and Cohen had been actively working on a Trump Moscow Tower project well into the presidential primary campaign period in 2016.

It can also be concluded at this point with a high degree of confidence that, while the winding up of the Special Counsel's operation is unquestionably an important inflection point in the Russia/Trump investigation, it does not mark the end of the legal troubles faced by Trump, his family, and his inner circle. At most, it only marks the end of the beginning.

Although there will be no more indictments from Mueller' office now that he has concluded his investigation, but this is because he has passed the investigative and prosecutorial baton to various units within the Justice Department, particularly the U.S. Attorney's for the Southern District of New York, the District of Columbia and in other federal districts. Don Jr., Jared Kushner, and others may be breathing collective sighs of relief now that Mueller is closing up shop without indicting them, but it is likely that this is just a temporary reprieve and that there are numerous federal and state prosecutors who have their sights on these two and several others within the Trump orbit, and these continuing investigations will now be forging full steam ahead now that they no longer have to give deference to the Mueller probe.

In short, for the first time in its long history, America is not only faced with the challenge of having an agent of a foreign hostile power holding the Office of the Presidency, but having a sitting president in the White House who is willing to use the awesome powers of that otherwise great office to hold onto his position and its perquisites by any means necessary, regardless of whether they are lawful or not. Trump has demonstrated time and time again that he is fully capable of obstructing and impeding any and all investigations and prosecutions that threaten him or his family. However, as the Mueller indictments and a vibrant free press have shown time and time again, America's core democratic institutions may have been severely shaken, but they are not broken, and we will eventually emerge from this stress test of Trumpism stronger than ever. We are not there yet, but we have started to turn the corner. The investigations and prosecutions by the Special Counsel and the U.S. Attorney's Office for the Southern District of New York have already demonstrated that the federal justice system is still functioning reasonably well, and if Congress can continue to reassert its constitutional duties of oversight and investigation, the Republic will not only survive but may well thrive. We can right our democratic ship of state, but only if we continue to have the collective resolve to do so.

CHAPTER 1

THE SIBERIAN CANDIDATE

TO BETRAY

1. To give aid or information to an enemy of; commit treason against; betray one's country.

2. To inform upon or deliver into the hands of an enemy in violation of a trust or allegiance.[1]

One of the best – and most terrifying – movies I saw when I was growing up in the New York City suburbs was *The Manchurian Candidate*. In this 1962 thriller, a Korean War soldier named Raymond Shaw is brainwashed by his Communist captors and then allowed to "escape" back to U.N. lines. Shaw is given a hero's welcome back in the United States and is awarded the Congressional Medal of Honor. Russian and Chinese agents, however, secretly planned to use Shaw to subvert and destroy American democracy, and almost succeeded in achieving that goal.

The other soldiers in Shaw's platoon were also programmed to say nice things about him, including the oft-repeated classic line: "Raymond Shaw is the kindest, warmest, bravest, most wonderful human being I've ever known in my life." This kind of over-the-top hyperbole and robotic language is one of the "tells" that the director of *The Manchurian Candidate* gives to the audience to show that the characters in the film have been brainwashed and have no real control of themselves.

Trump's first televised Cabinet meeting on June 12, 2017 had much the same feel and tone. After reviewing the alleged successes of his first 143 days in office, Trump made the following remarkable claim: "Never has there been a president....with few exceptions...who's passed more legislation, who's done more things…than I have."[2] Really? What about Abraham Lincoln, who led the country through a bloody Civil War, or Franklin D. Roosevelt, whose New Deal led us out of the Great Depression and through World War II? Given the fact that the Trump Administration's "signature" executive order during its first months was the so-called "travel ban", which was blocked by several federal judges, Trump's pompous statement was especially startling. Since Trump has entered office, barely any significant legislation had been passed in Congress.

Once Trump had finished praising himself, he invited his new Cabinet members to honor him. They dutifully complied, with one after the other lavishly extolling his virtues and his accomplishments, without a hint of reservation or irony. For example, White House Chief of Staff Reince Priebus said: "We thank you for the opportunity and blessing to serve your agenda."[3] Each Cabinet member tried to outdo the last in flattering their boss as if they were competitors in the boardroom of "The Apprentice" or some other reality TV show. Trump ate it up. While a more secure or humble man would have been embarrassed by this unrestrained outpouring of adulation, Trump seemed to be loving it.

As I watched this Cabinet meeting on TV, I could not help but think that Trump and a majority of his Cabinet members were acting as if they were brainwashed members of some former lost platoon that had only recently been returned to this country as "sleeper agents." Of course, this could not possibly be literally true. But it is difficult to come up with a rational explanation as to why Trump's senior advisors were so solicitous and accommodating. Trump and his advisors were also oddly reticent to criticize Russia, the U.S.'s long-standing enemy, especially since Russia had engaged in several aggressive actions towards its neighboring countries, such as Ukraine, a policy that is clearly contrary to the strategic interests of the United States and its Western European allies. We also now know that Russia engaged in a carefully planned and coordinated attack on our core American democratic institutions during the 2016 Presidential campaign, and that this threat is continuing.

Why do Trump and other senior Administration officials have such great difficulty accepting the universal judgment of U.S. intelligence agencies that Russia successfully mounted a vast disinformation campaign on multiple social media platforms? Why does Trump and other senior Administration officials have such great difficulty accepting the fact that Russians hacked into U.S. databases to collect sensitive and confidential information to sow confusion and dissension in our political processes? Throughout our nation's long history, Americans have rallied around the flag to defend our country whenever it has sustained a massive hostile attack or been threatened, as shown, for example, after the Pearl Harbor and September 11th attacks.

So, why did the White House and Republican leadership in Congress during the first two years of Trump's term fail to acknowledge the seriousness of the Russian threat and ask all Americans to unite to face this threat? To find the answer to this crucial question, it is necessary to take a close look at the man at the top. What is it about Donald J. Trump that leads him to have become Russia's #1 booster, to the point where he is acting more in the interests of Russia than that of his own country, the nation he has sworn to preserve and protect?

If there had been any doubt that Trump fully intended to turn the White House over to the Russians, such doubts were dispelled on May 10, 2017, when Trump hosted a chummy "victory" meeting with Russian Foreign Minister Sergey Lavrov and Russian Ambassador Kislyak in the

Oval Office. The meeting, which was covered only by the Russian press (since the U.S. press had been excluded) came only hours after Trump had fired FBI Director James Comey for failing to tamp down or terminate the FBI's investigation of whether the Trump Campaign had colluded with the Russians to interfere in the 2016 U.S. elections. Looking ecstatic, Trump referred to Comey during the meeting with the Russians as a "nut job" and confided to his high-level Russian friends that the firing of Comey had relieved "great pressure" on him.

Such an invitation to the leaders of a hostile foreign power to enter the Oval Office — generally considered to be the inner sanctum of American democracy — was unprecedented, but Trump broke with precedent because, as a White House spokesperson stated, Putin had explicitly asked for it. Apparently, when Putin asks Trump for something, he gets it. What was particularly unnerving about the meeting was that Trump excluded all other Americans from the room but permitted the assembly to be covered by Russian reporters — in the Oval Office! The images of Trump smiling and putting his arm genially on Lavrov's back were nauseating. Lavrov and Putin had been working together since 2004 with the goal of making Russia great again, and now they were announcing to the world that Russia was finally back on top, that the West's attempts to isolate and sanction Russia had failed, and that they had a lapdog in the White House to prove it. It seemed that every time Putin told Trump to jump, the only thing that Trump would ask was "how high"?

What exactly did Trump and Putin talk about during their November 2018 meeting in Buenos Aires at the G20 meeting? We will probably never know, since no American other than Melania Trump was present, so there are no U.S.- generated notes or recordings that can inform our government officials or the American public as to what the two of them discussed. But the Russians know what was discussed because they had their own translator present and undoubtedly recorded the conversation as well. On other other occasions where Trump has met with Putin where he did have an American notetaker or translator present, he had sworn the notetaker to secrecy and, for good measure, confiscated the notes. So what is it that Trump is hiding, and why is he being so secretive and acting so strangely?

On December 19, 2018, Trump again shocked many, if not most, Americans by announcing that he was pulling U.S. troops out of Syria within the next few weeks.[4] One of Russia's longstanding goals had been to get the U.S. out of Syria, which they considered Russia's proxy and puppet in the Middle East. Trump was now complying with this request from Putin. This move was directly contrary to the advice of Secretary of Defense James Mattis and most of the U.S. military and civilian leadership. Trump had been advised for months that such a precipitous move would be disastrous, not only jeopardizing the U.S.'s strategic interests in the region, but leaving our Kurdish allies exposed to the impending onslaught by the Turkish military. The Turks had been preparing for a concerted drive against the Kurdish forces in Syria and seemed poised to unleash it. The following day, Trump announced that he was moving up the timetable for a major withdrawal of U.S. troops from Afghanistan, another primary goal of the Russians.

These unilateral decisions by Trump proved to be the last straw for Secretary Mattis, who submitted a resignation letter that was highly critical of Trump's worldview and foreign policy. In a thinly veiled swipe at Trump's seemingly inexplicable affinity for Putin and all things Russian, Mattis noted, "I believe we must be resolute and unambiguous to those countries whose strategic interests are increasingly at odds with our own."

Mattis further wrote:

> It is clear that China and Russia, for example, want to shape a world consistent with their authoritarian model — gaining veto authority over other nations' economic, diplomatic and security decisions — to promote their own interests at the expense of their neighbors, America, and our allies.[5]

Mattis essentially accused Trump of trying to tear down the global political order that has successfully served the U.S. in the post-World War II era, which has been primarily based on the building of NATO and other alliances with like-minded liberal democracies that share a common sense of values and worldviews. "Treating allies with respect" was a common thread in Mattis's remarks, serving as a rebuke to Trump's "America First" doctrine suggesting that the U.S. can "go it alone" in a dangerous and unpredictable world.

On January 2, 2019, during another Cabinet meeting, Trump also set off alarm bells by bizarrely misstating the former Soviet Union's involvement in Afghanistan, using words and phrases that appear to have been directly borrowed from a recent Russian-Putinist propaganda campaign to justify the Soviet Union's invasion of Afghanistan in 1979.[6] "The reason Russia was in Afghanistan was because terrorists were going into Russia," Trump explained, spouting a gross misstatement of history that has gained absolutely no traction outside the Kremlin. He added: "They were right to be there."[7]

So why did Trump see fit to use a nationally televised Cabinet meeting to promulgate Russian talking points and revisionist history on Afghanistan when there were clearly far more pressing matters to attend to, such as the recent government shutdown?[8] And perhaps more importantly, is Trump's wholesale adoption of Russian propaganda an indication that he has been seriously compromised and is now acting as a *de facto* Russian agent? In addition, since we know that Trump rarely reads anything, and this disinformation would certainly not be contained in any briefing materials he is receiving from U.S. intelligence agencies, who is feeding him this nonsense? Who is he talking to who would stovepipe these Russian talking points into his head? As the *Washington Post*'s Glenn Kessler has asked, "Is it possible that Trump's remarks on Afghanistan ... reflect a conversation he had with Putin?"[9] Rachel Maddow of MSNBC also theorized on her show, "Somebody has apparently given President Trump the old Soviet Union talking points on why that invasion was an awesome idea."[10] The question is: how is Trump getting this information? Is he secretly getting this from a Russian "handler," and is this "handler" Putin himself?

So, how did this come to pass, that a sitting U.S. president is acting as if he were a Russian agent? Why is it that Trump seems incapable of criticizing Putin or the Kremlin, and feels compelled to only say nice things about them regardless of what they are doing?

Many of these questions remain unanswered, even though we are more than half-way into Trump's term. For example, when, where, and how did Trump and Putin first meet? This may seem like a simple question, but over the years, Trump has made various conflicting claims that he has met with Putin and that they "got along great," or, alternatively, that he never met him before moving into the White House.

In 2013, Trump told David Letterman during an appearance on his show: "He's a tough guy. I met him once."[11] Well, almost correct, but not quite. During Trump's Miss Universe pageant in Moscow, Trump received word that Putin was going to stop by to meet him at the event. However, some unexpected diplomatic obligation arose requiring a change of plans for Putin. He did send Trump a gift as a small token of his appreciation, which Trump undoubtedly continues to treasure to this day.

In 2015, during a talk show with host Michael Savage, Trump was asked whether he had ever met with Putin. Trump answered: "One time, yes. Long time ago." He added: "Got along with him great, by the way."[12] In November 2015, Trump said that he got to know Putin "very well" during a joint television appearance on *60 Minutes*.[13] However, this was impossible since Trump's segment was taped in New York, while Putin's segment was taped in Russia.

As the 2016 Presidential Campaign heated up and journalists increasingly began asking Trump why he was so warm and uncritical of Russia, he changed his story. In June 2016, Trump flatly told reporters: "I never met Putin, I don't know who Putin is."[14] However, the following month, in July 2016, when pressed by George Stephanopoulos in an interview on ABC, Trump stated: "I don't think I've ever met him. I mean if he's in the same room or something. But I don't think so."[15]

Putin, at least, was consistent on the issue. Putin denied meeting Trump before Trump assumed the Presidency, telling Megyn Kelly on NBC in June 2017: "There was a time when he used to come to Moscow. But you know, I never met with him."[16]

Even if Trump did not actually meet with Putin, there could be no question that Trump felt an affinity and affection for the Russian President, to the point that Trump imagined his feeling was being reciprocated with the same intensity. Trump publicly bragged about his close relationship to Putin, claiming that Putin had referred to him as "a genius," although there is no record of Putin ever making such comment. Very odd indeed. Where did this "bromance" come from and why does Trump feel such an affinity for this brutal autocrat who was intent on destroying – or at least severely weakening – NATO and the entire Western democratic alliance?

Trump had first to somehow manage to become the President of the United States before achieving his real ambition: to personally meet with Putin and ultimately win the respect of leaders of Russia, a country he had always dreamed of doing business with. The first confirmed face-to-face meeting between Trump and Putin came in early July 2017, when they met during a sideline meeting at the G20 summit in Hamburg, Germany. "It is an honor to be with you," Trump told Putin, barely able to contain himself.[17]

The two leaders again met one year later, in July 2018, in Helsinki. America and most of the rest of the free world were shocked by Trump's disgraceful performance. Shocked, but not surprised. The President of the United States acted as if he were some Russian lapdog, or perhaps the ultimate Siberian Candidate. Trump stood onstage alongside Russian President Vladimir Putin and accepted the former KGB officer's denials regarding his country's interference with the U.S. 2016 Presidential elections. Trump's head nodded up and down as Putin denied any involvement, and even continued to respond affirmatively when Putin admitted to wanting Trump to win the 2016 election "because he [Trump] talked about bringing the U.S. Russia relationship back to normal."[18]

Trump was repeatedly asked by reporters which one he believed: Putin or his own intelligence community. Trump's answer was, in substance: Putin. Trump's later attempt to "walk back" his answer was decidedly unpersuasive, especially when he said that he did not think that Russia had any motive to try to damage the U.S. electoral system. "My people came to me. Dan Coats [the National Intelligence Director] came to me, and some others," Trump said. "They said they think it's Russia. I have President Putin. He just said it's not Russia. I will say this: I don't see any reason why it would be."[19] Meanwhile, Trump's own Director of National Intelligence was ringing the alarm bells, publicly stating that "the warning lights are blinking red again" as to the threat level facing the U.S., just as they were blinking before 9/11.

Sen. John McCain undoubtedly spoke for most Americans, when he called it "one of the most disgraceful performances by an American president in memory."[20] Sen. Bob Casey of Pennsylvania said Trump had "shamed the office of the presidency" with his "dangerous and reckless" reaction to Putin — "a new low and profound embarrassment for America."[21] Former CIA Director John Brennan, calling it "nothing short of treasonous."[22]

Trump's comments proved to be even too much for the Republican Congressional leadership. House Speaker Paul Ryan rejected the idea of "moral equivalence" between the U.S. and the Russian Federation.[23] Senate Majority Leader Mitch McConnell stated that "the Russians are not our friends and I entirely agree with the assessment of our intelligence community,"[24] which was that Russia had interfered with our election process.

The putrid smell of treason and betrayal is most assuredly in the air. The question is: what are we going to do about it?

CHAPTER 2

TRAITORS IN THE WHITE HOUSE

"There's a smell of treason in the air."

Douglas Brinkley, March 20, 2017

On March 20, 2017, FBI Director James Comey publicly confirmed for the first time that the FBI was investigating possible collusion between Trump campaign officials and associates with Russia as part of an effort by a hostile foreign power to influence the outcome of the 2016 U.S. election in Trump's favor. Testifying before the House Permanent Select Committee on Intelligence, Comey also confirmed what many Americans had already suspected: Trump had lied by falsely accusing his predecessor, President Barack Obama, of wiretapping Trump's headquarters during the 2016 presidential campaign.

This was an extraordinary moment. For perhaps the first time in American history, an FBI Director publicly stated that a sitting president had been lying to the American people, and that this same president and his minions were under investigation for having betrayed their own country and their fellow citizens by giving aid and comfort to a foreign hostile power. "There's a smell of treason in the air," presidential historian Douglas Brinkley said, after hearing Comey's Congressional testimony on March 20, 2017.[1] "Imagine if J. Edgar Hoover or any other FBI director would have testified against a sitting president? It would have been a mind-boggling event."

Now, after more than two years, a critical mass of evidence has publicly emerged indicating that Trump and at least some of his key campaign advisors and Administration officials have actively encouraged, conspired with, and colluded with the Russians to disseminate illegally hacked documents critical of Trump's Democratic opponent and to otherwise improperly influence the election. On January 8, 2019, for example, we learned what many of us had strongly suspected, which is that Trump Campaign operatives had shared proprietary polling data and other information with the Russians, presumably in order to facilitate their efforts to specifically target their disinformation and election disruption efforts in the 2016 presidential campaign. Specifically, a court document filed by senior Trump Campaign official Paul Manafort's legal team inadvertently revealed that he had shared polling data with a business associate tied to Russian intelligence, who is believed to be Konstantin Kilimnik.[2]

Perhaps even more significantly, on January 11, 2019, *The New York Times* reported that, immediately after Trump fired FBI Director Comey on May 9, 2017, senior U.S. Department of Justice officials authorized the FBI to open up a Counterintelligence investigation into whether "the president's own actions constituted a possible threat to national security" and whether he was "working on behalf of Russia against American interests."[3] One of the goals of the investigation was to determine "whether Mr. Trump was knowingly working for Russia or had unwittingly fallen under Moscow's influence." The FBI investigation of Trump apparently also had a criminal aspect to it, which was above and beyond the counterintelligence aspect, which was whether the firing of Comey constituted an obstruction of justice.

Although we do not have any official or final results of the FBI investigation of Trump, there is already enough information publicly available to conclude with a high degree of reliability that, yes indeed, Trump is the first President of the United States who has betrayed his country and his fellow citizens by putting his own personal financial and political interests, as well as those of a hostile foreign power, over the interests of his own country. In other words, the evidence already strongly indicates that Trump has sold us out, that he is working primarily for Russia and himself, not the United States, and that his actions and continued occupancy of the White House constitute a monumental national security crisis every single day that he remains there.

This is as remarkable as it is alarming. Before Trump, the U.S. had an uninterrupted string of 44 Presidents – some of whom were outstanding, some just okay, and a few clunkers – with nary a hint of severe treasonous behavior or betrayal by any one of them.[4] None of them betrayed their oath "to preserve, protect and defend the Constitution of the United States."[5] None of them even arguably committed an act that met the narrow Constitutional definition of treason,[6] requiring evidence of the taking up of arms against the United States or giving "aid and comfort" to its enemies. None of them even qualified for the looser and more general definition of "traitor,"[7] which involves the betrayal of one's country in favor of the interests of another. Most certainly, none of them sold out to a hostile foreign power, placing their own personal interests or those of another nation over the interests of the U.S.

And then, there is the curious case of Donald J. Trump.

President Andrew Johnson – who assumed the presidency upon the assassination of Abraham Lincoln at the conclusion of the Civil War – was impeached by the House of Representatives in part based upon criticism that he was too lenient to the southern leaders who had led their states to secede from the Union. However, Johnson's efforts to reconcile with the former rebel states and their leaders were never seriously considered to be an act of treason. The war had already come to its conclusion, and the Confederacy could no longer be regarded as an "enemy" of the U.S. Johnson's efforts to "reconstruct" those rebel states to the Union with a minimum amount of rancor and resentment could never be seriously considered to be an act of treason.

Indeed, the charge of treason or betrayal of one's country has rarely been invoked in U.S. history, in part because it is a grave offense that few Americans have ever contemplated, no less acted upon. Treason and betrayal require the subordination of the interests and ideals of one's country to one's selfish interests and those of a hostile foreign power. To commit a treasonous act, the wrongdoer must ignore his or her obligations as a citizen of the United States to never act in a manner that will harm the interests of the country and its democratic institutions. In the case of a President, an act of treason or betrayal also violates the solemn oath of office that must be taken by every President.[8] Neither Andrew Johnson nor any other president has – until now – engaged in the course of conduct that could reasonably be construed as constituting treason or betrayal of the country.

Without limiting the scope of the inquiry to just Presidents, there have been few traitors in all of American history, which is remarkable for a country that has been in existence for 243 years. Leaving aside the particular case of Robert E. Lee and the countless southern soldiers who took up arms against the United States in the Civil War, one has to go back to the American Revolution to find a clear example of an American leader who decided to sell out his country. Benedict Arnold was a Major General in the Continental Army under the leadership of George Washington when he decided to switch sides and aid the British forces. Arnold was never held to account for his treachery, and peacefully lived out his days in England after the British troops surrendered at Yorktown in 1781; his name, however, lives on in infamy in U.S. history as a synonym for traitor.

Aaron Burr is a close second in the annals of American traitors since this former Vice President of the United States under Thomas Jefferson schemed with English and Spanish agents to annex a large portion of the southwestern U.S. to form a new country, where Burr, of course, intended to rule as its leader. Burr was tried for treason in 1807 but was acquitted, despite the substantial evidence introduced against him.

Also early on in United States history, two of the leaders of the 1794 uprising of farmers and distillers in western Pennsylvania known as the Whiskey Rebellion were convicted of treason and sentenced to be hung, although they were pardoned by then-President George Washington before the sentence was carried out. Much later, at the height of the Cold War, Julius and Ethel Rosenberg were convicted and executed in 1953 under the Espionage Act for having passed on top-secret documents relating to America's atomic bomb program to Russian agents, but they were never actually charged with treason.[9]

The Founding Fathers were very careful to narrowly limit the definition of "treason" to only the most serious of offenses involving the betrayal of one's country. Since the term "treason" had been used to cover may real, and perceived offenses under English common law, the Framers of the U.S. Constitution specifically limited the definition of "treason" in Article III, Section 3, Clause 1 of the Constitution. The article provides as follows: "Treason against the United States shall consist only in levying War against them, or in adhering to their enemies, giving them Aid and Comfort."[10] The U.S. Constitution also defines "treason" as one of the three grounds – Treason, Bribery, and "High Crimes and Misdemeanors" – for the impeachment of a President.[11]

The charge of "treason," therefore, cannot be leveled lightly, either against a sitting President or any citizen. Benedict Arnold's treachery could have stopped the fledgling republic in its tracks if George Washington had not been quickly alerted to Arnold's substantial assistance to the British forces. Burr's aborted attempt to carve off a piece of the U.S. for himself and his co-conspirators could have also caused significant damage to the U.S. if his plot had succeeded. And yet, there remains no American – at least in recent history – who has arguably come close to the damage already caused to this country and its democratic institutions by Donald J. Trump. As President of the United States, Trump is unquestionably the most powerful person on the planet, with his hand on the levers of awesome powers that can drastically affect the course of American history and that of the world, either for good or for evil. To say that the fate of the world is in the hands of the President of the U.S. is not a mere hyperbole, given the destructive consequences of a nuclear exchange that can be triggered by an unstable or cornered narcissistic President.

History teaches us that it was not merely fate or good fortune that accounts for the American success story for so many decades and now centuries, any more than it was mere happenstance that the Roman Empire dominated the world stage well into the Sixth Century. In 1787, spurred on by the growing economic troubles of the fledgling independent country and the trauma of violence that came to be known as the Shay's Rebellion, the Founding Fathers of our country carefully crafted the U.S. Constitution in Philadelphia. The U.S. Constitution is perhaps the most dramatic example of political genius the world has ever known. The founders conceived of a government with three separate yet interrelated branches –

legislative, executive and judicial – that contained checks and balances to avoid the potential despotic pitfalls of a monarchy or other unitary form of government. They also guaranteed, through the First Amendment, freedom of speech, religion, and of the press, all of which are so vital to a thriving democracy. They struck a critical balance between a pure democracy and a representative republic through the establishment of two houses of Congress, with one – the House of Representatives – being the "People's House," whose members of Congress are elected directly by the popular vote, and a Senate, where each state is allocated two Senators, no matter how large or small the state.

Although an act of pure genius, the Constitution our founders drafted was far from perfect. It did not give women the right to vote, and it did not prohibit slavery. It has sometimes been said that "the perfect is the enemy of the good," and the issues relating to racial and gender equality were not dealt with in the U.S. Constitution drafted in 1787, or were handled poorly in the interests of political expediency in order to win the necessary ratification by all the states. Some of these critical issues were later dealt with through additional amendments to the Constitution, and a good argument can be made that the country has not yet completed the process of correcting fundamental errors in the Constitution.

That the Constitution is still a "work in progress" is perhaps most graphically demonstrated by the fact that two Presidents – George W. Bush and Donald J. Trump – have been elected in recent history with less than a majority of the popular vote. This anomaly is because we have an Electoral College process, which is little more than a troublesome vestigial organ that should have been removed from the body politic long ago. The Electoral College no longer serves its original purpose, which was to prevent an unqualified person with authoritarian tendencies or unscrupulous principles, or who was the puppet of a foreign power, from assuming the high office of the Presidency.[12] The election of Donald J. Trump to the U.S. Presidency demonstrated once again that the Electoral College has utterly failed to serve as a final tripwire designed to protect the American people from having an unqualified or unprincipled person occupying the White House.

The founders did, however, brilliantly address a wide range of issues and scenarios that might face the nation in the future. These issues included the procedure for impeaching and removing a President during the four-year term between elections. Most of what we now accept as Constitutional norms were never explicitly outlined in the Constitution, but, instead, were developed over time and have become embedded within established Constitutional law principles. For example, there is nothing in the Constitution stating that the Supreme Court has the final say as to what the Constitution or U.S. statutes really mean, even though we now accept the federal judiciary's primacy as to such matters almost without question. We have to remind ourselves that it was not until the Supreme Court decided *Marbury v. Madison*[13] that the Court first articulated the view that it was the final arbiter on constitutional and statutory issues, and perhaps more importantly, Congress and the President accepted that view without protest.

Other portions of our democratic fabric of government are also more a matter of tradition, such as the generally accepted norm that the U.S. Justice Department and its important investigative arm, the FBI, should pursue their investigations and criminal prosecutions without regard to political considerations and without political interference from the President or anyone else. Every federal prosecutor takes a solemn oath to pursue the goals of justice "without fear or favor," and know that they have an obligation not to let political considerations or even pressure from the White House influence their professional judgment. The U.S. Department of Justice is an agency of the Executive Branch and nominally falls within the responsibility of the President. So, is a President just doing his duty when he orders the Justice Department to investigate one of his political rivals while going easy on one of his political allies, or is he obstructing the proper administration of justice and perverting the justice system for political ends? The truth, then, is in the details, and is often hidden deep within the facts and circumstances of a particular case. The general principle that "No man is above the law" and that the Justice Department should be primarily staffed by career prosecutors who carry out their duties free of political bias or favor, has become embedded in our democratic system of government. Or so we thought. Any deviation from those established norms should set off alarm bells ringing across the land.

Some other potentially important questions about our democratic system have never been resolved, mainly because the country has never been forced to squarely face them. For example, while Article I, Section 3 of the Constitution explicitly provides that a President can be indicted and tried for criminal offenses *after* he leaves office,[14] it is silent on the question of whether a sitting President can be charged and tried for crimes while still holding office.[15] Many Americans may think that a sitting President is immune from criminal prosecution since that is apparently the position outlined in current Department of Justice guidelines. But guidelines are just that —guidelines; they are not the U.S. Constitution or even federal law. As we see on an almost daily basis, there can always be exceptions to guidelines, as demonstrated by some U.S. judges who constantly grapple with the U.S. Sentencing Guidelines to determine whether a particular criminal defendant's sentence should follow the Guidelines or deviate from them.[16] Criminal penalties, in the end, depend on the particular facts and circumstances of a case, possible mitigating factors relating to the defendant himself, or whether his or her remorse or acceptance of responsibility for the offense – or his/her cooperation with law enforcement and the prosecutors – warrants the imposition of a lesser sentence.[17]

President Richard Nixon was actually named as an unindicted co-conspirator by the Watergate Grand Jury.[18] We will never know how the Supreme Court would have ruled on the issue of presidential immunity from prosecution if the government prosecutors had pressed the issue and actually asked the grand jury to return an indictment against Nixon while he was still in office, since Nixon resigned and, on September 8, 1974, was immediately pardoned by his successor, President Gerald Ford.

Similarly, the charging documents and plea agreement entered into between government prosecutors and Trump attorney Michael Cohen essentially named President Trump as an unindicted co-conspirator.[19] Cohen told the federal judge under oath on August 21, 2018 that it was Trump who had directed him to make the hush money payments to the two women, Stormy Daniels and Karen McDougal, that Trump wanted to silence, at least until after the November 2016 presidential election.[20] The government referred to Trump in its filing relating to the Cohen pleas agreement as "Individual-1."[21]

It should also be remembered that in 1973, Vice President Spiro Agnew was convicted of tax evasion relating to bribery charges stemming from his tenure as Governor of Maryland. Under his plea agreement, Agnew pleaded *nolo contendere* (no contest) to one count of tax evasion and simultaneously resigned as Vice President.[22] While some commentators have cited the Agnew case as legal precedent for the proposition that a sitting Vice President can be indicted,[23] the issue was never actually decided in federal court in light of Agnew's guilty plea and resignation.

However, in response to submissions by Agnew's lawyers in federal court, the Justice Department, in 1973, did take the position that sitting Vice Presidents are not immune from indictment and prosecution.[24] The Justice Department maintains this position to this day,[25] which is arguably at odds with the current policy of the Justice Department regarding a sitting President. Given the number of days that Trump has spent at one or more of his golf resorts during his first two years in office, it is increasingly difficult to rationalize an immunity defense for the president – but not the vice-president – because the president is far too busy to be distracted by criminal indictments. The argument that he needs to devote his precious executive time helping his lawyers prepare his criminal defense is dubious, at best.

So, we find ourselves with a system of democratic government that has survived for an extraordinarily long period but is comprised of a fairly intricate set of written constitutional principles, with an overlay of unwritten, but critically important, democratic norms and traditions. These elements have withstood the test of time because of American citizens, no matter what their political affiliations or policy differences, have accepted those democratic norms for the good of the country, even if adherence to those norms proves to be personally disastrous.

When the Supreme Court decided in *United States v. Nixon*[26] that the White House had to turn over the tapes to the Special Prosecutor's office containing damning evidence, President Nixon did not hesitate to turn over copies of those tapes, even though he knew or should have known that the contents of those tapes would sink his presidency. He did this, presumably, because it is an accepted norm that the Supreme Court has the final word on issues of law. The Judiciary does not have its own police force or enforcement mechanism capable of enforcing its decisions by, for example, occupying the White House and forcibly taking tapes from a President who refuses to give them up. Nevertheless, Nixon turned over the Watergate tapes, and the rest is history.

But what if we had a President who did not accept democratic norms that have served this country so well throughout its history? What if we had a President who, as the founders feared, would owe a secret allegiance to a hostile foreign power, such as Russia, rather than to his own country? What if we had a President who realized that his own personal and financial interests had grown more closely intertwined with those of Russia than of his own country? What if he wanted an "offshore" safe haven for his business and personal interests that were beyond the reach of U.S. government prosecutors and the federal justice system? Would it be more important to keep on the good side of Putin and the Kremlin than to carry out his official duties to protect and defend the United States?

Which brings us inevitably to the current incumbent of the White House: Donald J. Trump. There is a growing mountain of evidence that Mr. Trump has betrayed the interests of the United States to such an extent that he is the first U.S. president to be guilty of treason. He may well have sold out his country by giving aid and comfort to an enemy engaged in an ongoing assault on our country and its core institutions.

Mr. Trump embraced Vladimir Putin and all things Russian, even when Russia has acted in matters directly contrary to the interests of the United States. He has begun to mimic the most authoritarian impulses of Putin and other autocratic despots around the world who have either compromised or entirely dispensed with the democratic processes of their own countries. In Russia, despite early signs of hope for democracy following the collapse of the Soviet Union, the trappings of democracy, such as "free elections" and a "free press," have become little more than thinly disguised window dressing. Virtually all political and economic power is now concentrated in the hands of Putin and his inner circle of oligarchs. A similar disturbing pattern has emerged in Turkey, Poland, Hungary, and other countries, where democratic institutions and an independent judiciary have been neutralized, and their governments are now either totally autocratically controlled or "illiberal democracies," at best.

Trump has repeatedly demonstrated that he is, by instinct and temperament, much more comfortable in an autocratic setting, such as the one in Russia. He is naturally drawn to countries where an uncritical press is little more than the propaganda arm of the state, or in the most extreme example, with the Crown Prince of Saudi Arabia, whose response to press criticism is to have the offending journalist brutally murdered and dismembered at a Saudi government consulate in Turkey. Trump's reaction to this and other outrages has been studied indifference, sending a loud and clear message across the U.S. and around the globe that the U.S. is no longer a beacon of democracy, protector of the powerless and the oppressed, and the champion of justice. Instead, Trump's clear message is that the U.S. is just another enormous economic power and consumer market and that it will just look the other way if faced with substantial human rights or humanitarian issues as long as the offending country – in this case, Saudi Arabia – continues to buy billions of dollars of our military hardware and other products. In other words, the U.S. is "open for business as usual," but closed to any serious or principled efforts to preserve and protect struggling democratic institutions around the world if there is no economic profit in it. "America First," as used by Trump, refers to this country's financial and economic power, not its political, electoral or democratic institutions. Members of the press who insist on haranguing the President with implicitly critical and pointed questions are declared to be "the Enemy of the People." Members of the federal judiciary who strike down Administration policies are ridiculed and denigrated, suggesting that an independent judiciary and the Rule of Law should become casualties of a slow-motion autocratic coup, just as has happened in several other countries over the past decade, and which could also happen here as well.

A strong case can be made that Russia is indeed an "enemy" of the United States for purposes of determining whether Trump has violated the constitutional and statutory provisions defining "treason" even if there has been no formal declaration of war between the U.S. and Russia.[27] An equally strong case can be made that the current White House incumbent is a "traitor" in the more popularly accepted sense of that term. There is overwhelming evidence that Trump has put his own financial and political interests ahead of those of his country, in that he actively sought and received material assistance from the Russians during the 2015 and 2016 Presidential election season, and such election interference substantially impaired and damaged our country's electoral and democratic processes. Trump also secretly pursued a lucrative real-estate project in Moscow requiring the personal approval of President Putin while in the midst of the Presidential primary and general election campaign. As a candidate, he consistently softened his official stance on Russian aggression in Crimea and elsewhere and signaled that he would "reconsider" the U.S.'s sanctions policy against Russia in return for Putin's approval of the Moscow Tower project, which was expected to bring hundreds of millions in revenue to Trump and his organization. Russian money had already bailed out the Trump Organization on more than one occasion, especially after six successive bankruptcies by Trump organization casinos[28] and the withdrawal by major banking lenders of any additional financing for the Trump organization. Without Russian money, which had become plentiful during Russia's rapid privatization process, with billions of rubles landing in the pockets of the Russian leadership and oligarchs virtually overnight, Trump and his entire operation would have been likely to have come crashing down around his head.

To say that Trump is indebted to the Russians financially would be a gross understatement, and when Russia dangled the keys to the White House before him during his presidential campaign, the deal was doubly sealed, since he was now both politically and financially wedded to the Russians. The inescapable truth is that Trump is now emotionally and financially more attached to Russia than the U.S. After all, hadn't they invested hundreds of millions in his projects, when U.S. banks were cutting him off? Hadn't they invited him to Moscow and said nice things about him? Wasn't their press corps courteous and respectful, as opposed to those pushy U.S. correspondents like CNN's Mike Acosta, who insisted on asking him embarrassing questions and refused to give up the mic?[29]

This *quid pro quo* arrangement between Trump's Team and the Russians, whether explicit or implicit, substantially undercut the U.S. policy as set by the Obama White House. The Obama policy was to be tough on Russia and to increase sanctions against Putin and his oligarchs for their repeated violations of international norms of behavior, including the illegal annexation of Crimea and invasion of other portions of Ukraine, the killing of dissident journalists, and other human rights violations.

Trump dramatically escalated his willingness to sell out the U.S.'s strong interest in maintaining the integrity of its political institutions and electoral processes by publicly inviting Wikileaks – a recognized *de facto* arm of Russian intelligence – to unlawfully disseminate hacked Hillary Clinton emails.[30] By the summer of 2016, it was widely known that the Clinton emails had been collected by Russian intelligence operatives and distributed through various Russian-related outlets, including "DC Leaks" and Wikileaks. Donald Trump, Jr., Paul Manafort, Jared Kushner and others associated with the Trump campaign welcomed a Russian delegation to Trump Tower on June 9, 2016, to discuss how the Trump campaign could gain access to stolen Hillary Clinton emails.[31]

After Trump's surprise electoral college victory, Trump and his transition team continued to engage in a treasonous course of conduct designed to further both Trump's and Russia's financial, political and strategic interests, all at the expense of U.S. national interests. On December 29, 2016, Obama announced that the U.S. was imposing additional economic sanctions on Russia in retaliation of a U.S. intelligence report that Russia had interfered in the U.S. elections through a series of cyber attacks on our electoral systems as well as though a concerted disinformation campaign through social media.[32] Trump, through his national security advisor Michael Flynn and others, sent a clear message to Moscow via Russian Ambassador Kislyak that Russia should not retaliate in kind but, rather, should wait until Trump was sworn in as President.[33] Trump and Flynn were either explicitly or implicitly promising that the severe sanctions on Russia would be "revisited" and lifted and that Trump was also willing to continue to do Russia's bidding on other fronts.

Trump was already ratcheting up his criticism of NATO, the most successful military alliance in world history, which had repeatedly frustrated Russian expansionist intentions in Eastern Europe and the Baltic States and was – along with the U.S. and Western European imposed sanctions – the most troublesome thorn in the side of Mother Russia.[34] Trump's suggestion that maybe the U.S. would not honor Article 5 of the NATO treaty, which required all NATO members to come to the defense of any one member that was attacked, was met with collective shock by our European allies and delight by Putin and his Kremlin cronies.[35]

Although the drama and chaos in the White House continue unabated, and the outcome still unknown, one thing is sure, which is that the U.S. democratic political system has been undergoing a severe stress test. While nothing is certain these days, it is more likely than not that our system of government will survive relatively intact, but severely damaged. Just like a surviving victim of a heart attack may never recover 100%, there is no guarantee that the U.S. system of governance will be as open and robust as it was in the pre-Trump era. What is certain, however, is that the current White House incumbent has repeatedly sold out U.S. interests in favor of his own interests and that of his state sponsor, Russia, and that he is the first American President who can genuinely be described as a traitor.

This country has several options open to it in dealing with this national emergency: indictment, impeachment, and the possibility of resignation are always open to him. The country could cross its collective fingers and hope that nothing catastrophic will happen in the next two years, just as the in the past few years we have avoided involvement in any additional or devastating wars or global conflagrations. Why not just wait until, in all likelihood, he will be voted out of office in November 2020? Why put the country through the agony of impeachment proceedings or a public indictment and prosecution?

The problem with this thinking is that it must be remembered that no serious commentator thought that Trump would actually win the election in November 2016. We know FBI James Comey did not think so, which emboldened him to publicly castigate Hillary Clinton for her "reckless" behavior concerning the handling of her emails. Comey reasonably believed that Clinton would be elected as the next President of the U.S. no matter what he said, so why not placate the Republicans in Congress by taking a few pot shots at Clinton? At the same time, Comey failed to disclose to Congress and the American public that the FBI and the Justice Department had a major ongoing investigation into the Trump Campaign for collusion and coordination with the Russians to interfere with the 2016 election.

So, if you are being lulled into a sense of complacency, thinking that there is no way that Trump can continue to occupy the White House more than another two years, just remember what happened in 2016. Will we be able to prevent another successful cyber attack on our electoral system and social media by Russia during the 2020 campaign? Will Trump continue to play by the rules that he has not yet broken over the next two years, by restraining himself from declaring war on Iran or some other country to distract public attention from the Russia investigation and other crises of his own making? Will he comply with orders of the Supreme Court as Nixon did during Watergate, or will he feel so cornered and persecuted in the White House that he starts refusing to comply with lawful court orders? Is a declaration of martial law under some "trumped-up" pretext really out of the question? Will he precipitate a constitutional crisis by firing Mueller, and then insisting that his Attorney General bring the Russia investigation to a quick close, just as the House Republicans quietly closed the books on the Russia investigation and prematurely declared that there was no evidence of collusion between the Trump Campaign and Russia? There are thus numerous permutations of plausible fact patterns that could spell disaster for the U.S. over the next two years.

The country really cannot afford to just wait and hope for the best. Immediate action is required. Now.

CHAPTER 3

POOR LITTLE RICH KID:
THE EARLY YEARS

It was Aristotle who said, "Give me the child until he's seven and I will show you the man." This maxim certainly applies to Donald J. Trump, since it can be persuasively argued that he is much the same person now as he was when he was a young man.

Trump was born in June 1946, the fourth of five children. His father, Fred Trump, was a successful builder and real estate developer in Queens, New York, and his Scottish-born wife, Mary, was an immigrant to the U.S. who had come here to get away from the poverty and despair on the Isle of Lewis.[1] The Trump family lived in a 23-room, red-brick, faux Georgian mansion in the wealthy Jamaica Estates neighborhood of Queens.[2] The Trumps had a chauffeur, a cook, a color TV, and two Cadillacs with consecutive personalized numbered plates, which was unusual for a New York family back in the 1950s.[3]

According to *Trump Revealed*, a biography compiled in 2016 by Washington Post journalists who spoke to dozens of former neighbors and other people familiar with the Trumps, the psychological profile of the young Donald Trump is nearly identical to that of the man occupying the White House.[4] For example, when Dennis Burnham was a toddler, his family lived next door to the Trumps. When his mother briefly put Dennis in a playpen in their garden, the young Donald, then aged five or six, stood at the fence throwing rocks at the little boy.[5] After that, Dennis' horrified mother warned him to "stay away from the Trumps" as they didn't want him "beaten up by the family bully." Another local child, Steven Nachtigall, now a 66-year-old doctor, said he never forgot Trump since he was "a loudmouth bully" who was fond of beating up younger and smaller kids in the neighborhood. Nachtigall vividly remembered Trump because "it was so unusual and terrifying at that age." Young Donald also is reported to have picked mercilessly on his own little brother, Robert, a quiet and sensitive child. Donald apparently later boasted that he once stole Robert's building blocks, gluing them together so that his brother could never use them again.[6]

Trump admitted to being a troublemaker in primary school. "I liked to stir things up and liked to test people," he said years later. "It wasn't malicious so much as it was aggressive." Trump bragged that when he was only eight, he almost got expelled from school for giving his music teacher a black eye 'because I didn't think he knew anything about music.'"[7] Unsurprisingly, Trump's story was exaggerated. The teacher, Charles Walker, remembered Trump as an attention-seeker, recalling "Donny" as a "little s**t."[8] Trump was athletic, particular when it came to baseball, but he had a bad temper. A teammate recalled lending Trump his baseball bat, which Trump furiously smashed on the concrete pavement, cracking it and rendering it useless. Trump never apologized. Fred Trump toughened up his children by banning them from having pets and urging them to be "killers" in everything they did.

In 1959, when the young Trump was caught sneaking off into Manhattan on Saturdays, the 13-year-old Donald was sent off to the New York Military Academy about 70 miles north of New York City, where he had to conform to a harsh military-style regime. Trump thrived in the

hyper-competitive atmosphere there. He had a confidence and ostenta-
tiousness that matched his privileged background and his father's business
success.

"When I look at myself in first grade [age six], and I look at myself
now, I'm basically the same," Trump told a biographer.[9] If "character is
destiny," as the Greek philosopher Heraclitus is quoted as saying, then
Trump's character was well-formed at a young age, and his destiny had
thoroughly reflected that character. Little did we know, however, until November 8, 2016, that our own common destiny and that of our country
would be so closely linked to his child-like and petulant character.

Over the years, and especially when he seriously entered the political
arena, Trump carefully modified his personal narrative to make it more
appealing to the every day American voter. He never claimed that he had
grown up poor, or that he had a total rags-to-riches personal history. But
he did take some liberties with his own narrative, especially the part dealing with the degree to which his father Fred Trump had helped him build
his real estate fortune.

During the Republican presidential primaries in 2015 and 2016, Trump
depicted himself as essentially a self-made billionaire who started with
only $1 million from his real estate mogul father, Fred Trump, and that
he was able to parlay this relatively small stake into a real estate empire.
Americans like to think of themselves as Horatio Alger types, who can
pull themselves up by their bootstraps in a country where — according to
the American Dream — everyone has an equal opportunity to succeed.
Conversely, we do not like to think of America as a land where the vast
majority of our wealth is concentrated in a relatively small but entrenched
upper class, where inherited wealth that is passed down from generation

to generation by an economic aristocracy is a much more significant factor in determining one's success than intelligence, education, or hard-work.[10]

The "American dream" is – in reality – mostly a myth, given the growing economic disparities between the very wealthiest Americans and the rest of us. But like any myth, it is hard to dispel and perhaps should not be dispelled, since some day in the future the myth of America as the land of limitless opportunity for all may become a reality. It all depends on whether we really are willing to try to make it so.[11]

At least for now, we want our Presidents and other high elected officials to have led a life of accomplishment and success before we are willing to give them our vote. These accomplishments can be either in the public or the private sector, in the military or in business. It really does not make much difference, as long as a candidate can prove that he succeeded mostly under his or her own steam and that nothing (or almost nothing) was just handed to them on a silver platter.

So, Candidate Trump's personal narrative about having built his real estate empire through dint of hard work and smarts was essential to his success and a key ingredient in his attractiveness to millions of Americans. According to Trump's persuasive narrative, if Donald J. Trump could achieve great success in business, then he might also be able to "drain the swamp" in Washington, D.C. and make the government work as efficiently and successfully as the Trump Organization supposedly did.

It was not until almost two years into Trump's presidency that reporters from *The New York Times* were able to conclude a painstaking investigation of Trump's finances. The *Times* found that, instead of the $1million that he said he had received from his father, Trump actually had received at least $413 million in today's dollars, "much of it through tax dodges in the 1990s."[12]

In other words, Trump's carefully crafted narrative, which was that "I built what I built by myself," was false. According to the investigation by the *Times*, "the president's parents, Fred and Mary Trump, transferred well over $1 billion in wealth to their children. This could have produced a tax bill of at least $550 million under the 55 percent tax rate then imposed on gifts and inheritances."[13] Instead, the Trumps only paid a total of $52.2 million in taxes or about 5 percent of what they had passed on to Donald Trump and their other children.[14] In short, Donald Trump was a knowing participant in the dubious tax schemes and outright fraud that helped his parents avoid the payment of most of the tax bill that should have been due.[15]

Even before the completion of the *Times'* investigation of Trump's finances, other journalists and biographers – including Wayne Barrett, Gwenda Blair, David Cay Johnston, and Timothy L. O'Brien – had challenged Trump's self-flattering narrative, especially the claim of being worth $10 billion. When *Times* reporter Tim O'Brien suggested, in *Trump Nation*, that Trump was not worth the $10 billion he claimed to have amassed, and was worth a mere $1 billion or less, Trump sued him for defamation and lost.[16] It was also reported that Fred Trump had once helped his son make a bond payment on an Atlantic City casino by buying $3.5 million in casino chips. Added together, the amounts that Fred gave him were closer to $14 million than the $1 million that Trump acknowledged receiving.[17] But none of the prior research on Trump's finances came anywhere near to the $413 million that the Times documented as having come from his parents.

The publication of the *Times'* October 2018 investigation into the Trump's finances was devastating to Trump's carefully nurtured self-image as a self-made billionaire. As the *Times* reported:

By age 3, Mr. Trump was earning $200,000 a year in today's dollars from his father's empire. He was a millionaire by age 8. By the time he was 17, his father had given him part ownership of a 52-unit apartment building. Soon after Mr. Trump graduated from college, he was receiving the equivalent of $1 million a year from his father. The money increased with the years, to more than $5 million annually in his 40s and 50s.[18]

According to the *Times'* documentation, there were over 295 separate revenue streams that Fred Trump ingeniously created to funnel money to his son Donald, who despite his father's largesse, always seemed to be on the brink of one disaster or another. As the *Times'* report explained it:

Fred Trump was relentless and creative in finding ways to channel this wealth to his children. He made Donald not just his salaried employee but also his property manager, landlord, banker and consultant. He gave him loan after loan, many never repaid. He provided money for his car, money for his employees, money to buy stocks, money for his first Manhattan offices and money to renovate those offices. He gave him three trust funds. He gave him shares in multiple partnerships. He gave him $10,000 Christmas checks. He gave him laundry revenue from his buildings.[19]

The *Times* also revealed how Fred Trump gradually transferred ownership of eight buildings with 1,032 apartments to his children, with the first transfer to Donald occurring just before his 16th birthday on June 1, 1962 when he transferred a plot of land in Queens to a newly created corporation, making his children the owners of record, and then constructing a 52-unit rental building. By the time that young Donald was in high school, his share of the profits was about $17,000 in today's dollars, and his share grew to over $300,000 a year soon after he graduated from college.

At the age of 29, Trump did succeed in acquiring the former Commodore Hotel on 42nd Street, which was then converted into the Grand Hyatt Hotel, but as Wayne Barrett and others have reported, Trump could not possibly have succeeded with the Grand Hyatt project if his father had not co-signed the many contracts that the deal required.[20] Fred also lent Trump seven and a half million dollars to get started as a casino owner in Atlantic City.[21] The $7.5 million was in addition to the previously mentioned casino chips Fred purchased to help Donald make the bond payments.

Although Trump had limited success as a traditional real estate developer, which involves the actual development, construction and marketing of real estate projects, he was a truly accomplished self-promoter. Trump put his name on residential towers financed and built by others, making millions on just his brand name alone, just as sports stars and other celebrities make their money by giving companies the right to use their name and image on sportswear and other products. Trump built his brand name up to the point that it was generating hundreds of millions of dollars. Donald Trump's capacity for shameless self-promotion was epic and probably gave him an edge over his less egomaniacal competitors to win the Presidency.

Back in May of 1984, Trump wanted in the worst way to get on the *Forbes Magazine* 400 list of the wealthiest people in the world. He decided to take matters into his own hands and placed a phone call to Jonathan Greenberg, a journalist who then worked for *Forbes*.[22] Trump used a fake name, "John Barron," falsely claiming to be a publicist for Donald Trump and eventually succeeding in conning his way onto the Forbes 400 list. In an opinion piece that he later wrote for *The Washington Post*, Greenberg describes not only what happened back then, but the significance of Trump's con games had for his later success as a presidential candidate:

> His confident deceptions were so big that they had an unexpected effect: Instead of believing that they were outright fabrications, my Forbes colleagues and I saw them simply as vain embellishments on the

truth. We were so wrong.

> This was a model Trump would use for the rest of his career, telling a lie so cosmic that people believed that *some* kernel of it had to be real. The tactic landed him a place he hadn't earned on the Forbes list — and led to future accolades, press coverage and deals. It eventually paved a path toward the presidency.

Trump's later "Make America Great Again" campaign has much the same ring to it. When did America stop being great? Trump never really says, but the message is clear: Vote for me. I am successful, I am brash, and as your leader, I will make this devastated country Number One again!

During the 2016 presidential campaign, *The Washington Post* published a recording of a 1991 interview that "Miller" — another pseudonym that Trump used – gave to *People* magazine. On the tape, "Miller" asserted that Trump is "starting to do tremendously well financially," and that "actresses just call to see if they can go out with him and things."

Also during the campaign, a former editor of the *New York Post*'s Page Six gossip section penned a confession in *Politico Magazine*: "I helped make the myth of Donald Trump," Susan Mulcahy wrote. "And for that, I am very, very sorry."[23] She explained: "If you worked for a newspaper in New York in the 1980s, you had to write about Trump," continuing, "As editor of the *New York Post's* Page Six, and later as a columnist for *New York Newsday*, I needed to fill a lot of space, ideally with juicy stories of the rich and powerful, and Trump more than obliged."[24]

Although Trump had a keen knack for self-promotion, he could not have achieved an undeserved reputation as a charming, brash entrepreneur with an unfailing ability for business without the help of some key people.[25] Perhaps the most important of these critical enablers of the Trump image is Tony Schwartz, the real writer of *The Art of the Deal*, the

1987 best-seller that created the myth that Trump was a genuine American real estate and business genius.

Schwartz spent countless hours with Trump, following him around for days on end, taking notes and listening in on Trump's phone conversations. It soon dawned on Schwartz that he was dealing with a man who had deep-seated personality and character flaws and that he was "pathologically impulsive and self-centered."[26]

Schwartz remained silent during the entire Republican primary season stretching from 2015 to mid-2016, but when Trump won the Republican presidential nomination, he felt that he could no longer remain silent:

> "I put lipstick on a pig," he said. "I feel a deep sense of remorse that I contributed to presenting Trump in a way that brought him wider attention and made him more appealing than he is." He went on, "I genuinely believe that if Trump wins and gets the nuclear codes there is an excellent possibility it will lead to the end of civilization."[27]

And that was just the restrained version of Schwartz's evaluation of Trump. He added that if he wrote the book about the real Donald J. Trump, it would be called "The Sociopath."[28]

Schwartz has also explained how Trump raised the art of lying to an entirely new level. "He lied strategically. He had a complete lack of conscience about it." According to Schwartz, since most people are "constrained by the truth," Trump's indifference to it "gave him a strange advantage."[29]

By 1987, when *The Art of the Deal* was first published, Trump's life and his world was starting to unravel. Trump and Ivana were getting divorced, which cost him $25 million. Meanwhile, Trump was going through what O'Brien refers to as "a crazy shopping spree that resulted in unmanageable debt." His purchase of the Plaza Hotel in Manhattan was heavily leveraged with debt, and he was also paying carrying costs of about $20 million on the development rights to the Hudson rail yard on the West Side of Manhattan, where he bragged that he was going to build "the tallest building in the world." However, in 1987, the City denied him permission to construct such a tall skyscraper, a major setback that he minimized in *The Art of the Deal*, saying "I can afford to wait." But when O'Brien closely examined Trump's finances, he concluded: "The reality is that he *couldn't* afford to wait. He was telling the media that the carrying costs were three million dollars, when in fact they were more like twenty million."

At the same time, Trump was also building a third casino in Atlantic City, the Taj Mahal, which he promised would be "the biggest casino in history." The reality, however, was that Trump was losing millions of dollars a day on his casinos, with no bottom in sight. He bought the Eastern Air Lines shuttle that operated out of New York, Boston, and Washington, renaming it the Trump Shuttle, and acquired a giant yacht, the Trump Princess.

In 1992, journalist David Cay Johnston published *Temples of Chance*, which showed in detail that Trump's net worth statement from 1990 showed that Trump owed $300 million more to his creditors than all of his assets were worth. In other words, Trump was effectively bankrupt. In 1993, Trump's company was forced into bankruptcy by the banks, and over the next span of years, Trump filed for bankruptcy protection six times for his various companies.

But just when Trump appeared to be in a free-fall, he was "discovered" by Mark Burnett, the reality TV producer, who read *The Art of the Deal* and decided to base a new reality TV show on the concept. The show was "The Apprentice," featuring Trump as an enormously successful real estate developer and entrepreneur, not the failing businessman who was hanging on by his fingernails.

A star was born. The rest is history.

CHAPTER 4

A USEFUL IDIOT

There were some early warning signs that the young Donald Trump might later be particularly susceptible to the snares and entreaties of a hostile foreign power that was seeking his assistance to undermine the American political system, sow dissension and confusion, and to advance its own interests to the detriment of the United States. While a full psychological evaluation of Mr. Trump is beyond the scope of this book,[1] and certainly beyond the competence of the author, law enforcement and intelligence agents in the U.S., Russia, and virtually every other country regularly engage in psychological profiling in order to identify the most likely targets for "turning," "flipping" or "compromising."[2]

Some targets of criminal investigations or intelligence operations will never turn on their own organized criminal gang or their country no matter how much pressure is put on them. They would never switch sides and spy or gather evidence on their own people, no matter what the penalty or the inducement. And then there are those who, either through chronic insecurity, overinflated egos or other factors are susceptible to being induced or seduced by flattery, gifts and money into cooperating with agents and operatives for the other side. Sometimes the target that is "turned" does not even realize until it is too late that they are damaging their own team, which usually makes little or no difference to them as long as the results are favorable to themselves personally. If they get a little richer, or if their egos are receiving constant gratification, it is of little importance what happens to their other gang members or their fellow countrymen. In addition to large doses of flattery to the chronically insecure target that you wish to compromise, it also helps immensely if that person is of average or low intelligence, but thinks that he (or she) is a genius. Like, really smart.

The Russians have a name for a person who can be turned or compromised without even knowing it: useful idiot. This is, unfortunately, what Individual-1 has become. A useful idiot who just so happens (as luck would have it for the Russians) to be occupying the White House. Although the origins of the phrase are obscure, and its attribution to Vladimir Lenin is probably incorrect,[3] it is generally intended to refer to persons in the U.S. or other countries in the West who are either knowingly or unwittingly helping Russia by espousing certain views or causes, or taking such actions, that have the end result of benefitting Russia. In 1959, Congressman Ed Derwinski of Illinois wrote an editorial from a Chicago paper into the Congressional Record, referring to Americans who traveled to the Soviet Union to promote peace as "what Lenin calls useful idiots in the Communist game."[4] The editorial board of the New York Times applied the term to Trump, writing on December 15, 2016: "There could be no more "useful idiot," to use Lenin's term of art, than an American president who doesn't know he's being played by a wily foreign power."[5] The editorial noted that, despite Trump's continuing denials that there were no direct contacts between the Trump Campaign and the Russians, two days after the election, on November 10, 2016, Sergei Ryabkov, Russia's deputy foreign minister, admitted that "there were contacts" between Moscow and Mr. Trump's campaign.

Earlier that same year, in August 2016, Michael J. Morell, the acting director and deputy director of the Central Intelligence Agency from 2010 to 2013, also came to the same conclusion. He discribed Trump's relationship with Russia this way: "In the intelligence business, we would say that Mr. Putin had recruited Mr. Trump as an unwitting agent of the Russian Federation."[6] Mr. Morell referred to the traits that made Trump an easy target for the Russians to turn. The list included:

> his obvious need for self-aggrandizement, his overreaction to perceived slights, his tendency to make decisions based on intuition, his refusal to change his views based on new information, his routine carelessness with the facts, his unwillingness to listen to others and his lack of respect for the rule of law.[7]

Trump was apparently an easy mark for the Russians. To state the now obvious: "President Vladimir V. Putin of Russia was a career intelligence officer, trained to identify vulnerabilities in an individual and to exploit them. That is exactly what he did early in the primaries. Mr. Putin played upon Mr. Trump's vulnerabilities by complimenting him. He responded just as Mr. Putin had calculated."[8]

In other words, the reasons for Trump's apparent willingness to take policy positions consistent with those of Russia and inconsistent with American interests may not necessarily be linked to a carefully thought-out and rational analysis of the personal economic gains he might reap by siding with Russia. Instead, Trump's irresistable attraction to all things Russian may be just a product of his extreme psychological insecurity and susceptibility to flattery. Whatever the underlying reason, though, the results are the same. Trump has endorsed Russian espionage against the United States to influence the electoral process and swing the election his way. He has refused to denounce Russia's annexation of Crimea; and by questioning the U.S. commitment to NATO, he is giving a green light "to a possible Russian invasion of the Baltic States."[9]

Of course, during the 2016 presidential election campaign, Trump thought that he was the one who was in control and "playing" the Russians, rather than being the one being played by them. His plan was apparently a simple one. He could say nice things about Vladimir Putin and Russia all he wanted without any adverse consequence since he was just a private citizen who had no governmental or foreign policy obligations, right? And he would never have any such responsibilities since he was never going to be elected as President. Everyone knew that, right? Once the campaign was over, he would then be free to monetize his enhanced reputation and brand name by finally completing that lucrative Trump Moscow Tower. The Kremlin could not possibly refuse him now since he had so dutifully assisted Russia's efforts to delegitimize the entire American political process and diminish America's reputation in the eyes of the whole world.

That was the plan and a good one at that. But then something horrible and unexpected happened. On November 8, 2016, Trump was elected President of the United States, and there was no way he could back down now. He had to go ahead with it and make the best of a bad situation. Once he was elected, things went from bad to worse. The "Russia thing" would not go away, and there was nothing he could do – even firing the FBI Director – that could stop the nightmare.

On January 3, 2018, New York Magazine's publication of an excerpt of Michael Wolff's new book, *Fire and Fury: Inside the Trump White House*, ignited a political firestorm.[10] The excerpt, which was entitled "Donald Trump Didn't Want to Become President" explained that the Trump Campaign planned to lose the election so that Trump and his team could get back to doing what they loved best: making money. Trump was described on election night as follows: "It looked as if he had seen a ghost."[11] The article also painted a picture of an out-of-control White House, a rudderless ship with a captain who was, at his best, mentally unstable and of low intelligence.

Given his chronic insecurity about his intelligence and mental state, Trump could not resist immediately responding on twitter to the Wolff book's allegations, stating that his "two greatest assets" were his "mental stability" and "being, like, really smart."[12] Trump also described himself as "a very stable genius," having been elected as President of the United States "on [his] first try."[13] His early-morning tweet storm also slammed the "fake news mainstream media" for questioning his "mental stability and intelligence."

Trump's twitter storm, however, only added fuel to the fire. How many "stable geniuses" have to publicly defend their stability and their genius on twitter? Very odd indeed.

Trump's insecurity regarding his intellectual and mental prowess not only made him an easy target for the Russians, Saudis and other autocratic governments to compromise through effusive and ego-massaging flattery, but it also has predictably led him to spend much of his waking hours trying to convince others that he is "really smart" and well educated. Conversely, due to his chronic insecurity, Trump has felt compelled to publicly berate his critics for their lack of intelligence or education. Whenever his intellectual capacity is questioned or mocked, Trump has always been quick to remind people that he graduated from an Ivy League college. At a speech in Phoenix, Arizona on July 11, 2015, Trump repeated multiple times: "I went to the Wharton School of Finance," adding, "I'm, like, a really smart person."[14]

Although Wharton is primarily known for its graduate M.B.A. program, Trump did not receive any graduate degree from the University of Pennsylvania's Wharton Business School. Instead, Trump transferred into Wharton's undergraduate program after spending two years at Fordham University in New York, and after an undistinguished academic career there, graduated two years later in 1968 with a Bachelor in Science degree.[15]

In a television interview on NBC's "Meet the Press" on August 16, 2015, he described Wharton as "probably the hardest there is to get into." He added, "Some of the great business minds in the world have gone to Wharton."[16] Moderator Chuck Todd responded: "Why do you have to tell us all the time that you went to Wharton?" Todd added, "People know you're successful."

During Trump's rise to the top of the real estate development world, various news publications exaggerated his academic achievements at Wharton. The *New York Times* reported in 1973 and 1976 that he graduated first in his class.[17] However, in a 1985 biography of Trump, Jerome Tuccille accurately wrote that he was not an honor student and "spent a lot of time on outside business activities."[18] Another biographer, Gwenda Blair, wrote in 2001 that Trump was admitted to Wharton as a special favor by a "friendly" admissions officer who had known Trump's older brother, Freddy.[19]

Despite Trump's repeated mention of Wharton, his own classmates hardly remember him.[20] "He was not in any kind of leadership. I certainly doubt he was the smartest guy in the class," said Steve Perelman, a 1968 Wharton classmate and a former *Daily Pennsylvanian* news editor.[21] Trump was barely seen around campus on weekends, remained uninvolved in most campus activities and his picture was even absent from the yearbook.[22] Although Trump has never been known to be shy or self-effacing, and there is no lack of Trump hotels, casinos and golf courses emblazoned with his name, no building on Penn's campus bears his name, despite his virtually constant name-dropping about having graduated from Wharton.

The Wharton School and the University of Pennsylvania, of which it is a part, have been noticeably reticent in response to the election of one of their own to the Presidency. Penn's last presidential affiliation was with William Henry Harrison, who spent only one semester there.[23] You would think that Penn and its Wharton School would want to celebrate the rise of one of its alumni to the highest office in the land. Indeed, my own fellow classmate, President George W. Bush was warmly welcomed as a commencement speaker in 2001 at Yale University,[24] where he had graduated with the Class of 1968, and in 2012, President Obama spoke at the graduation ceremonies for Columbia University's sister school, Barnard, although the ceremony was actually held on the Columbia campus.[25] Even Hillary Clinton, who lost the election to Trump (although winning the popular vote) has been besieged with an avalanche of requests to speak at various universities since the 2016 election.

However, Trump has, as far as I can tell, never been asked to speak at the University of Pennsylvania since ascending to the presidency. One clue to this mystery can be found by perusing *The Daily Pennsylvanian* for comments from students and alumni. One typical comment is as follows: "Trump deserves NOTHING in the way of gratitude after what he's done to the USA and the planet since becoming POTUS."[26] Penn has declined comment to multiple news sources on the topic of Trump's presidency and attendance at the University.[27]

Whether due to chronic insecurity or braggadocio or some other motivating factor, Trump not only seems obsessed with convincing people that he is well educated, but also that he has a higher IQ than anyone else.[28] "Sorry losers and haters, but my IQ is one of the highest -and you all know it!" he tweeted in May 2013. "Please don't feel so stupid or insecure, it's not your fault."[29]

In 2016, then-presidential candidate Trump challenged Mayor Sadiq Khan of London: "Let's do an IQ test," thus displaying a woeful ignorance of what intelligence testing really involves.[30] Whatever it is, it is definitely not a sporting contest.

More recently, Trump has accused numerous critics, such as Robert De Niro ("very low-IQ") and Mika Brzezinski ("dumb as a rock"), of falling within the lower end of the intelligence spectrum. According to Trump, former Vice President Joe Biden is "not very bright;" former rival Hillary Clinton is "very dumb;" Ohio Gov. John Kasich is a "dummy;" former Massachusetts Gov. Mitt Romney is "one of the dumbest and worst candidates in the history of Republican politics." Republican political strategist Rick Wilson is "dumb as a rock;" U.S. Sen. Rand Paul, R-Ky., is "without a properly functioning brain;" and as to Supreme Court Justice Ruth Bader Ginsburg, Trump tweeted, "her mind is shot."[31]

Some commentators have pointed out that a disproportionate share of Trump's targets for his "low IQ" tweets have been African-Americans, and may be evidence of Trump's racial bias.[32] "Lebron James was just interviewed by the dumbest man on television, Don Lemon," wrote Trump of the NBA superstar interview with the CNN talk show host.[33] Trump added: "He made Lebron look smart, which isn't easy to do." Trump made these comments one day after speaking at a rally in Pennsylvania and ripping into Rep. Maxine Waters, D-Calif., who is black, as having a "very low IQ."[34] However, Trump has also insulted the intelligence of so many non-African Americans that it must tentatively be concluded that he is indeed an equal opportunity insulter in chief.

Although ignorance of specific well-known facts of American history may well be a sign of just plain ignorance rather than of low intelligence, Trump's display of his woeful ignorance of basic facts occurs so frequently that it would appear there is, in fact, a correlation between the two in his case. For example, Trump has spoken as though he thought famed abolitionist orator Frederick Douglass (1818-1895) were still alive.[35] Many times he's told audiences that the F-35 stealth fighter is *literally* invisible in combat.[36] He's exhibited confusion about the difference between HIV and HPV, between climate and weather, and between England, Great Britain and the United Kingdom.[37]

Trump boasts about how little he reads, and his Twitter rants are filled with misspellings and punctuation errors.[38] Former Secretary of State Rex Tillerson did not deny reports that he called Trump "an (expletive) moron," and in the recent behind-the-scenes book *Fire and Fury*, author Michael Wolff quotes top White House officials referring to Trump a "dope" or an "idiot."[39] One of his former professors at the University of Pennsylvania reportedly said, "Donald Trump was the dumbest g------ student I ever had."[40]

Although it is unlikely that he has a low IQ, and it is difficult to fathom how such a large number (but less than a majority) of American voters could have voted for him if he were truly mentally challenged, Trump has displayed a tendency towards laziness and is notorious for never (or barely ever) reading anything. He gets more of his information ("or disinformation") from Fox News than he does from his briefing books, which he rarely reads. But perhaps this reading-phobia is because he suffers from ADHD (Attention Deficit Hyperactivity Disorder), or dyslexia and not from a low IQ. Some experts have suggested that the Trump phenomenon may force us to rethink the meaning of "smart" and "dumb," as well as the importance of a person's IQ.[41] Perhaps we are underestimating the importance of another factor – *forcefulness* – sometimes referred to as the "Eisner factor."[42]

Michael Eisner, the former Disney Chairman/CEO and American business icon a few decades ago, was quoted as saying: "Around here, a strong POV [point of view] is worth about 80 IQ points." Eisner meant that a person with a forceful personality can be persuasive and more successful than a person who may be smarter and has given an issue greater thought, but who speaks less forcefully and with a lesser degree of "certainty."[43]

When Hillary Clinton's suggested during one of the 2016 presidential debates that a President Trump would be a "puppet" for the Russian regime, Trump instinctively blurted back, "No, no puppet, no puppet. You're the puppet."[44] While not thoughtful or artful, and sounding more like a childlike response to a schoolyard taunt than anything else, it was at least a short, *forceful* and succinct response to a remark that Trump basically had no real answer to, because almost everyone knew it was true.

Gideon Rachman has suggested in the *Financial Times* that Trump isn't a genius in the conventional, intellectual sense, but that "Mr. Trump has a legitimate claim to three other kinds of 'genius': political genius, instinctive genius, and evil genius."[45] So Mr. Trump should probably start talking less about his IQ and his "very, very large brain" (there is no evidence that the mere size of one's brain is an indicator of intelligence), and more about his innate political genius. "Evil genius" works too.

One thing is for sure, the Russians definitely have Trump's "number" and that – either through flattery, economic inducements, compromising material (kompromat) or other factors – they now have the President of the United States in their pocket and can manipulate him whenever they please, to the benefit of Russia and the detriment of the U.S.

CHAPTER 5

THE DONALD AND THE DRAFT

An ordinary candidate with no record of military service might have been deterred by common sense or good judgment from publicly attacking an iconic war hero and former prisoner of war in Vietnam on his military record and reputation for bravery. But Donald J. Trump was no ordinary candidate. He had already demonstrated a puzzling tendency to raise subject matters and to go to places that perhaps a wiser man might fear to tread.

So, on July 19, 2015, while campaigning for the Republican presidential nomination in Iowa, Donald Trump interjected an additional degree of excitement into the race by questioning the credentials of Arizona Senator John McCain and former prisoner of war in Vietnam as a war hero: "He's not a war hero," said Trump. "He's a war hero because he was captured. I like people who weren't captured." As a naval aviator, McCain had been shot down during the Vietnam War and held prisoner for more than five years at the prisoner of war camp known as "the Hanoi Hilton," refusing early release even after being repeatedly beaten.

Trump's comments drew cries of outrage and condemnation from his rivals and senior Republican officials on a scale far more significant than even Trump's repeated portrayals of Mexican immigrants as rapists and murderers. Republican candidates who have been honorably discharged from military service, and especially veterans such as recently-deceased Senator McCain who had been injured and permanently disabled, are universally held in near-reverence by virtually all Republicans – and indeed most Americans. McCain, in particular, held a special place in Republican hagiography, after having survived repeated torture during his five-years of detention by his North Vietnamese captors, leaving him partially disabled and not able to raise one arm above his head. He was also the recipient of the Purple Heart, a Silver Star and the Distinguished Flying Cross.

Trump, however, refused to back down from his comments about McCain. After all, McCain had been pestering Trump throughout the Republican primary season, criticizing him for jeopardizing bipartisan efforts in Congress to pass legislation reforming the immigration laws. McCain was incensed, publicly accusing Trump of "fir[ing] up the crazies."

Trump was not to be intimidated by McCain's war record. After all, Trump himself had faced his own challenges and exhibited his own kind of heroism when he struggled with the risks posed by sexually transmitted diseases, an occupational hazard during the young Trump's club-hopping and philandering days. In a 1997 interview with shock jock Howard Stern, Trump talked about how he had been "lucky" not to have contracted diseases when he was sleeping around; it was his own "personal Vietnam." Trump elaborated: "I've been so lucky regarding that whole world. It is a dangerous world out there. It's scary, like Vietnam. Sort of like the Vietnam-era," Trump said in a video. "It is my personal Vietnam. I feel like a great and courageous soldier."

Trump also likened his military-themed boarding school experience at the New York Military Academy as essentially equivalent to having been trained in the military. Of course, he never had to run the risk of anyone shooting at him, but wearing a military-type uniform and playing soldier can – I suppose – feel just like the real thing. Almost as real as the "Call of Duty" video game!

Inevitably, Trump's near-contemptuous disdain for McCain and his military service in Vietnam led to questions as to how Trump had been able to avoid the military draft that was drawing in tens, if not hundreds of thousands, of young men into the war. At various times, Trump had said that he was not drafted because he got a high lottery number, but an examination of Trump's draft board file shows that, for most of the years when eligible for the draft, he avoided it on medical grounds. "If I would have gotten a low number, I would have been drafted. I would have proudly served," he told ABC News in 2015. "But I got a number, I think it was 356. That's right at the very end. And they didn't get – I don't believe – past even 300, so I was – I was not chosen because of the fact that I had a very high lottery number." According to records at the National Archives, Trump did receive a draft number of 356 out of 365, but by the time that the draft went into effect in December 1969, he was already shielded from the draft by a "1-Y" medical deferment.

Shortly after his 18th birthday, Trump registered with the Selective Service on June 24, 1964. His Selective Service card noted that Trump was 6-foot-2 and 180 pounds, and under a section on the card titled "physical characteristics," it stated that Trump has a birthmark on both heels. There is no mention of any disability on his Selective Service card. Registering made Trump a candidate for a military draft, which was about to ramp up as U.S. involvement in Vietnam grew.

The first U.S. troops arrived in Vietnam on March 8, 1965, with 3,500 United States Marines coming ashore at Da Nang as the first wave of U.S. combat troops into South Vietnam, adding to the 25,000 U.S. military advisers already in place. U.S. troop numbers peaked in 1968 when President Lyndon Johnson approved an increase in the number of forces in Vietnam to 549,500. One out of every ten Americans who served in Vietnam was a casualty; out of 2.7 million who served, 58,220 were killed and 304,000 wounded. The war ended with the fall of Saigon on April 30, 1975.

After graduating from the New York Military Academy, Trump decided to stay in New York, enrolling at Fordham University in the fall of 1964. He would remain there for two years, before transferring to the Wharton School at the University of Pennsylvania, where he would study business.

Trump received four education deferments while in college. The first education deferment came on July 28, 1964, several weeks before he began his freshman year at Fordham. Trump received similar deferments his sophomore, junior and senior years. The deferments ended once he graduated from the University of Pennsylvania in 1968, making the then-22-year-old Trump eligible to be drafted. On October 15, 1968, several months after graduating from Penn and returning to New York, Trump was granted a 1-Y medical deferment. In an interview with *The New York Times*, Trump said he received the medical deferment because of bone spurs in his heels. The National Archives and Records Administration confirmed that Trump's medical deferment from the draft resulted from a September 1968 physical exam that "disqualified" him from service. "I had a doctor that gave me a letter — a very strong letter on the heels," Trump told *The New York Times*.

Over the years, Trump has been vague as to whether the bone spur problem was related to one or two of his feet, and if one foot, which foot that was. Donald Trump biographer, Michael D'Antonio, recalls that when Trump took off his shoes and tried to show him his bone spurs when they met years ago, he couldn't see anything. Trump also said during the presidential campaign in 2016 that he could not recall who had signed off on the medical documentation relating to his bone spur(s). "You are talking a lot of years," Trump said. He said that he still had some paperwork relating to the exemption that he would provide, but never did.

In late December 2018, questions about Trump's medical exemption from the Vietnam War draft arose again after *The New York Times* reported that a podiatrist might have diagnosed him with bone spurs as a favor to his father, Fred Trump. The daughters of the podiatrist, Dr. Larry Braunstein, who died in 2007, told reporters that their father often told the story of coming to the aid of the young Donald Trump during the Vietnam War as a favor to his father. Dr. Braunstein's ground floor office was located below Edgerton Apartments in Jamaica, Queens, one of the dozens of the buildings owned by the Trumps in the 1960s. "What he got was access to Fred Trump," Elysa Braunstein said. "If there was anything wrong in the building, my dad would call, and Trump would take care of it immediately. That was the small favor he got." There is also some indication that a second podiatrist, Dr. Manny Weinstein, who died in 1995, also had some involvement in Trump's medical deferment. Perhaps not coincidentally, Dr. Weinstein moved into an apartment owned by Fred Trump the same year that Donald Trump got his exemption.

Trump's portrayal of McCain as a loser because he had gotten shot down and imprisoned in 1967 during the Vietnam War raised questions as to whether Trump had been a "draft dodger." His draft deferment history during the Vietnam draft years was clearly inconsistent with his secondary school record, where, according to his former coach at the New York Military Academy, he was "quite the athlete." Trump was on the varsity baseball, soccer, and football teams, and seemed like a perfect candidate for military service. He won the "Proficient Cadet" award for two years running and "Honor Cadet" for all of the four years he was there. In 2005,

Trump was inducted into the school's Hall of Fame because his sports achievements were considered so impressive. While at the New York Military Academy, Trump was scouted by the Boston Red Sox and the Philadelphia Phillies, as well as by the U.S. Military Academy at West Point.

The inescapable conclusion is that, as biographer Gwenda Blair noted in "Donald Trump: Master Apprentice," Trump dodged the draft "despite his athletic prowess," that the "bone spur" medical deferment was an excuse concocted by Trump's father and at least one podiatrist beholding to Trump Sr., and that the Donald willingly went along with this charade.

While there may be a danger in reading too much into the young Trump's successful efforts to dodge the draft, it did reinforce one basic lesson that served him well over the years. When confronted with a problem – such as the risk of being drafted like tens of thousands of other poor shmucks and shipped off to some Southeast Asian jungle where there was a good chance that you could end up being shipped back in a box – you should call upon well connected friends and family to "fix" the problem and make it go away. All it took was a doctor's note to the draft board and – presto, magic – the problem disappears.

This lesson, that patriotism and military service are for suckers, and that any problem can be fixed as long as you know the right people, was later reinforced by Trump's first fixer, the legendary Roy Cohn. Cohn helped Trump learn how to grease the political and governmental wheels, manipulate the press, pay off the corrupt unions and organized crime to gain a competitive advantage in the real estate development field. Trump's second major "fixer" – attorney Michael Cohen – dutifully arranged to clean up Trump's messes with porn stars and Playboy models who were threatening to go to the press. Finally, and most importantly, in collaboration with Michael Cohen, it was also Felix Sater and other well-connected individuals to the Russian mob and Kremlin insiders who gave Trump access to the hundreds of millions of dollars of cash that he needed to keep his real estate empire afloat after a string of casino losses and bankruptcies brought him to the edge of the financial abyss. When the Russians dangled the keys to a lucrative Trump Moscow Tower project under his nose, and as a bonus, threw their considerable weight behind an effort to throw the election Trump's way, or at least help him avoid an embarrassing total wipeout in the presidential election, Trump never hesitated for a second.

Remember the golden rule, Trump said to himself. "He who has the gold, rules." Patriotism and "service to country" are for suckers, he had learned. Antiquated terms like "treason" and "betrayal" meant nothing. It was just good business to throw in your lot with the Russians. Putin was a winner. Trump was a winner. Nothing else matters.

CHAPTER 6

BOUGHT AND PAID FOR

It is difficult as an American to accept the remarkable fact that we have a president occupying the White House who is bought and paid for by the Russians. How could this happen? Well, it did not happen overnight. It happened gradually over time.

This is how it happened.

Other than his father, Donald J. Trump's primary mentor and role model during his formidable years was the infamous mob lawyer, Roy Cohn. Cohn had risen to fame as Chief Counsel to Senator Joseph McCarthy during the McCarthy hearings in the late 1950s. Senator McCarthy capitalized on the "Red Scare" gripping the nation by calling before his Senate Hearing Committee dozens of government officials, labor leaders and Hollywood scriptwriters and producers who were suspected of being "card-carrying Communists" or Communist sympathizers ("fellow travelers"). Trump's crusade to build a $70 billion wall on our southern border,[1] to supposedly prevent hoards of brown-skinned illegal immigrants from entering the country and then raping and pillaging their way across America's heartland, has a decided similar ring to it as the McCarthy witchhunt of the 1950s. Senator Joe McCarthy convinced many Americans that Communists had embedded themselves within our government, our military and even in Hollywood as part of a conspiracy to destroy our democracy and to take away our liberties.

Senator McCarthy's downfall finally came when he started accusing members of the U.S. military of communist leanings. The generals pushed back, with the famous public reprimand of U.S. Army attorney Joseph Nye Welch: "Until this moment, little did I dream that you could be so reckless and so cruel... Have you left no sense of decency!"[2]

After the McCarthy Hearings, Roy Cohn went into the private practice of law in New York and quickly earned a reputation as one of the top mob lawyers in the City, if not the country. As a young federal prosecutor in the Brooklyn Organized Crime Strike Force, I actually had the opportunity to try my first federal criminal trial against Cohn. Later, I had to deal with Cohn once again when he represented Donald Trump in a mob shakedown and extortion investigation relating to real estate construction projects throughout the City.

Cohn operated out of a townhouse on East 68th Street in Manhattan, where clients Anthony "Fat Tony" Salerno and Paul "Big Paul" Castellano were regular visitors. Besides getting advice on their legal problems, as a former secretary later recalled to Wayne Barrett in his 1992 book, *Trump: The Deals and the Downfall*,[3] the visits by the mob bosses to their lawyer's office allowed them to talk shop without having to worry about FBI wiretaps.

In order to break into the Manhattan real estate market, Donald Trump needed three things: (1) loan guarantees from his father, Fred Trump; (2) "sweetheart" deals with the Mafia, which at that time controlled the construction trades and the construction unions; and (3) "dirty" Russian money that needed to be "laundered" through the purchase of Trump real estate and condominiums. While Fred Trump provided the first of these three requirements, Trump had to rely on Roy Cohn to make the necessary introductions for the other two vital elements.

To help build his first two Manhattan projects – the former Commodore Hotel site (now Grand Hyatt New York) on East 42nd Street, and the Trump Tower on Fifth Avenue – Trump had to cut a deal with several major Mafia figures and their companies. The foundations for Trump's Manhattan projects were made with redi-mix cement, and the only redi-mix cement company at the time that could be totally counted on to get the job done without union strikes or other disruptions was S&A Concrete Co., a concern partly owned by Anthony "Fat Tony" Salerno, the boss of the Genovese Crime Family. Fortuitously, Trump and Salerno were both represented by attorney Roy Cohn. The deal that was struck was simple, yet extremely effective. During a "sit down" at Cohn's East Side townhouse, Trump and Salerno struck a deal whereby Trump would guarantee that all his Manhattan construction contracts for cement would go to S&A Concrete, which would be inflated by about 5 to 10%. The excess cash in the deals was split between the bosses of the Genovese and Gambino organized crime families operating in New York City.[4] In return, Trump was assured that there would be no union strikes or walk-outs on any of Trump's Manhattan projects.

Since the powerful organized crime families operating in New York City at the time controlled the labor unions, they were in a position to guarantee "labor peace" to Trump even if the unions went out on strike at other job sites. This gave Trump a significant competitive advantage over other Manhattan developers who did not enjoy the advantages of having Roy Cohn as their "godfather," or "rabbi" as he was sometimes called, with a close, cozy relationship with both the Mafia and the labor unions. As reported by Pulitzer Prize-winning journalist Tom Robbins, Cohn told a reporter that Trump called him "fifteen to twenty times a day, asking what's the status of this, what's the status of that."[5]

S&A Concrete's redi-mix trucks were driven by union drivers from Teamster Local 282, whose President, John Cody, answered in turn to the Genovese and Gambino organized crime bosses. Trump entered into a contract with Local 282 that required Trump to pay at least two "working teamster foremen" on each of his construction projects. In actuality, Trump was paying for two no-show "non-working teamster foremen," whose salaries were funneled to the Mafia family bosses who guaranteed the "labor peace" that Trump was paying for.

As a young federal prosecutor at the time with the U.S. Dept. of Justice's Brooklyn Organized Crime Strike Force, I was one of the federal prosecutors who, along with a team of FBI and U.S. Labor Department agents, investigated and successfully prosecuted Cody on various criminal labor law violations known as the Hobbs Act. The Act prohibits union leaders from shaking down and extorting legitimate businesses. We got much of our assistance in this investigation from Sigmund Sommers, another New York developer who was building the North Shore Towers on the Queens-Nassau County line, and who had also entered into an extortionate "sweetheart" deal with Cody and his mob-controlled Local 282.

However, when FBI agents and federal prosecutors approached Trump and Roy Cohn for assistance in the investigation of Local 282 and its mob-ties, we were completely stonewalled. Trump alternatively said, through Cohn, that he didn't know anything and refused to acknowledge that he was paying for no-show teamsters on the Trump Tower project, or he just refused to answer our questions and "took the Fifth." Some of the more junior federal prosecutors – such as myself – recommended that Trump be indicted for lying to federal agents and obstructing the federal investigation, but we were overruled by our higher-ups in Washington. Our bosses wanted us to only concentrate on prosecutions of organized crime controlled labor union leaders, who at that time had a virtual stranglehold on construction projects in New York City and who could indefinitely close down any developer who refused to play ball with them.

Trump and Cohn also entered into several corrupt relationships with organized crime figures to rebuild the Grand Hyatt Hotel on East 42nd Street in Manhattan. According to Tom Robbins, Trump had chosen a notorious demolition company secretly owned in part, according to the FBI, by a top Philadelphia mobster who doubled as crime lord of Atlantic City. To pour concrete for the new hotel, Trump picked a company that – like S&A Concrete – was controlled by organized crime. The ostensible President of the company was a man named Biff Halloran, but he answered to the Mafia bosses, just as did every other cement company that wanted to do business in New York City. Halloran was convicted a few years later for his role in what prosecutors dubbed a mob-run cartel that jacked up construction prices throughout the city.[6] For the carpentry contract, according to Tom Robbins, "Trump settled on a Genovese family-controlled enterprise that was central to another mob price-fixing racket, as found by a subsequent federal probe."[7]

Based upon his cozy relationship with organized crime-controlled unions and contractors, Trump was able to slash his labor costs by using undocumented Polish workers to demolish the Bonwit Teller building, which led to the construction of the Trump Tower. On paper, the demolition contractor was a union company, as were all of Trump's vendors at the time. But according to *The Marshall Project*, "Local 95 of the demolition workers was essentially a subsidiary of the Genovese crime family, and few union rules were enforced. Most of the workers were undocumented immigrants from Poland, and they were paid so little and so sporadically that many were forced to sleep on the job site."[8] A rank and file union dissident later sued Trump for failing to pay pension and medical benefits required under the union contract. Trump denied knowing about conditions at the work site."[9] Despite his denials, Trump and his associates were found guilty in 1991 of conspiring to avoid paying pension and welfare fund contributions to the union.[10]

In addition to traditional Mafia-style organized crime, Trump – primarily through Roy Cohn – also developed strong ties to Russian organized crime figures, who had a lock on some areas of Brooklyn, such as Brighton Beach, where Russian emigres tended to congregate, but who were gradually moving their criminal operations into Manhattan and the other regions of New York City. When Trump Tower opened in 1983, some of the first condominium buyers were Russian mobsters. No doubt they saw an excellent opportunity to park some of their illegally-obtained cash in the U.S. Trump welcomed these mobsters with open arms, no questions asked, even though any quick background check would have disclosed that they were closely connected to Semion Mogilevich, the head of the most powerful and dangerous of the Russian mob organizations.[11] Vadim Trincher,[12] a professional poker player and Russian organized crime associate, purchased a $5 million condo on the 63rd floor of Trump Tower, from which he and Anatoly Golubchik ran an illegal sports betting ring in Trump Tower that catered primarily to Russian oligarchs. Hillel (Helly) Nahmad, a co-defendant of Golubchik and Trincher's in an organized crime prosecution stemming from their illegal gambling operations in Trump Tower, paid more than $21 million for the entire 51st floor of Trump Tower, where he ran a high stakes poker game that catered to millionaire and billionaire clients.

According to an 84-page indictment, Trincher, and Golubchik's sports betting operation operated under the protection of "Vor" Alimzhan Tokhtakhounov, a Ukrainian-born Mafia Don who was a VIP guest at the 2013 Miss Universe pageant Trump hosted in Moscow. Tokhtakhounov, who lives in Russia, was also implicated for bribing Olympic officials in 2002 in Salt Lake City. Another top Russian boss who owned an apartment in Trump Tower was Vyacheslav Kirillovich Ivankov, who came to the U.S. and rose to become one of the most potent Russian mobsters in America. Ivankov was arrested in 1995 and sent to prison for conspiring to extort $3.5 million from two Russian emigres who ran an investment advisory company in lower Manhattan.

David Bogatin, another Russian-born mobster, ran a gasoline-bootlegging scheme in the early 1980s that was so lucrative that he spent nearly $6 million to buy five separate condos in Trump Tower. According to an investigation by journalist James S. Henry, Trump was personally involved in the sale of the condos. Bogatin pleaded guilty to tax evasion relating to the gasoline that he was illegally selling but jumped bail before he could be sentenced to prison. Before he fled, he turned over the mortgages on his Trump Tower condos to a Genovese crime family associate, who liquidated the mortgages through a Mafia-controlled bank in New York.

Perhaps Trump's closest Russian organized crime relationship was with Felix Sater, who was born in Russia and whose father was reputed to be a Russian organized crime lieutenant. Sater had pleaded guilty in 1998 to racketeering in a stock manipulation scheme involving the Genovese and Bonanno crime families and had done some jail time for stabbing another broker in the face with a margarita glass during an altercation in a bar. Sater, who had to wear a court-ordered ankle bracelet much of the time, played a role in some high-profile Trump projects and carried a

Trump Organization business card with the title "Senior Advisor to Donald Trump." He worked out of an office on the 24th floor of Trump Tower, two levels below Donald Trump.

Sater and his business partners in Bayrock hatched a plan to build Trump towers in U.S. cities and across the former Soviet bloc. Trump liked the idea and gave Sater's company the rights to explore projects in Moscow as well as in Florida and New York. As Sater boasted to potential investors, and according to testimony in a 2008 court case: "I can build a Trump Tower, because of my relationship with Trump."

Despite Trump's frequent boast about his high IQ and excellent memory, he struggled to remember Sater in a deposition taken on November 5, 2013. Trump testified under oath that he would not recognize Sater if they were sitting in the same room. Similarly, in a 2015 interview with the Associated Press, he said, "Felix Sater, boy, I have to even think about it."

Sater's sworn testimony painted a much different and more accurate picture in a 2008 libel case that Trump brought against journalist Tim O'Brien, arguing that O'Brien's book, *Trump Nation: The Art of Being the Donald,* damaged his reputation and cost him projects that Bayrock and others had been pursuing. Sater testified that he visited Trump's office frequently over a six-year period to talk business with Trump. Sater recalled flying to Colorado with Trump and said that Trump once asked him to escort his children Donald Jr. and Ivanka around Moscow.[13]

Trump and his lawyers have stated that he was not aware of Sater's criminal past when he first signed on to do business with Sater's firm, Bayrock Group. However, even after Sater's background was disclosed in a 2007 *New York Times* article, Sater continued to use Trump Organization office space and business cards. When Trump's children Donald Jr. and

Ivanka went to Moscow in 2006, Sater squired them around the city. It is also reported that Sater arranged for Ivanka to actually sit in Putin's chair, where she got a kick out of twirling around a couple of times.

Sater's criminal background became a serious problem for Trump when one of the company's most significant projects, the Trump International Hotel and Tower in Fort Lauderdale, Florida became engulfed in legal disputes after construction was stalled in 2009. Outraged condominium buyers filed a lawsuit, claiming, among other things, that Trump and others had failed to tell them about the criminal past of a critical member of the development team. Trump walked away from the failing project, saying he held no responsibility since he had merely licensed his name to the effort.[14]

Despite the lawsuits and occasional setbacks, Russian money sustained Trump throughout the 1980s, 1990s and after that. According to a *Bloomberg* investigation into the Trump World Tower, which started construction in 1998, "a third of the units sold on floors 76 through 83 by 2004 involved people or limited liability companies connected to Russia and neighboring states," according to sales agent Debra Stotts.[15] They had "big buyers from Russia and Ukraine and Kazakhstan," she added. Additionally, Broker Dolly Lenz sold "about 65 units in Trump World Tower" to Russian buyers looking for real estate.[16] Lenz explained that she had contacts in Moscow looking to invest in the United States and that they "all wanted to meet Donald. They became very friendly."[17] In 2002, "the push to sell units in Trump World to Russians expanded," when Sotheby's International Realty reportedly teamed up with Kirsanova Realty, a Russian company.[18]

Trump SoHo, also located in Manhattan, began construction in 2007 and was substantially funded with money obtained from sources in Russia and the former Soviet Union. Much of the funding for Trump SoHo came from the Bayrock Group, all of whose principals -- including Tevfik Arif, Tamir Sapir, and Alexander Mashkevich – came from the former Soviet Union and had close ties to both the Kremlin and Russian organized crime.[19] The owners of Bayrock were a virtual rogues gallery of career criminals who were involved in criminal activities ranging from money laundering and smuggling to running a prostitution ring.[20] For example, Mashkevich has been repeatedly accused of bribery and money laundering involving projects in Kazakhstan,[21] and had settled a case in 1996 without admitting guilt.[22] The same can be said for some of the Trump Soho's clientele. For example, Viktor Khrapunov, who is the former mayor of Almaty, Kazakhstan, went to trial July 2018 for allegedly purchasing condominiums in the building with stolen public monies, which were allegedly laundered through a network of offshore shell companies while serving as the country's energy minister.[23]

So, why did Trump affiliate himself with such a sketchy crew? The answer is simple. The Russians largely dealt in cash – lots of cash, and Trump needed boatloads of cash to make up for the fact that most legitimate banks refused to fund any Trump projects after successive failures and bankruptcies involving his casinos and related businesses. During the development of Trump SoHo, Eric Trump, in a moment of candor, told a reporter that "the best property buyers now are Russians," who "can go around without a mortgage loan from American banks, that require income checks and they can buy apartments with cash."[24]

Trump also took advantage of the Russian money pouring into Miami real estate by cultivating a relationship with Elena Baronoff, a Russian-American socialite, whose real estate company targeted Russian and other Eastern European buyers from an office in the lobby of the Trump International Beach Resort in Miami.[25] The Trump organization was so successful in attracting Russian buyers to an area immediately north of Miami called Sunny Isles, that the area soon became known as "Little Moscow." [26] At least 20 units in Trump Towers I, II, and III at Sunny Isles were purchased by individuals with Russian passports or addresses.[27] Individuals with Russian passports or addresses also were reported to have bought 16 units in Trump Palace, twenty-seven units in Trump Royale, and 13 in Trump Hollywood. Russian money bailed Trump out of a Palm Beach mansion that he had purchased,[28] but was generally considered to be a "white elephant" for which he had overpaid. In 2008, Russian fertilizer magnate Dmitry Rybolovlev took this mansion off Trump's hands for $53 million more than Trump had paid for it four years earlier.[29] Some of these Russian buyers brought more than just money to the Trump Organization; they also brought valuable links to Russian organized crime which, by this time, had virtually merged with the Russian government power structure under Putin.

Until he began running for president, Trump frequently boasted in numerous interviews about the amount of Russian money that flowed through his projects.[30] Similarly, in 2008, Donald Jr. told investors in Moscow that "Russians make up a pretty disproportionate cross-section of a lot of our assets."[31] Eric Trump also told a golf reporter in 2014 that the Trump Organization was able to expand during the financial crisis because "We don't rely on American banks. We have all the funding we need out of Russia."[32] In short, Russian money was keeping the Trump Empire afloat, and if Putin and others in the Kremlin pulled the plug on this cash outflow of hundreds of millions of dollars from Russia into Trump properties, the entire Trump Organization would have come to a screeching halt virtually overnight. Small wonder then that Trump felt compelled to say nice things about Putin and Russia, and was willing to sacrifice important U.S. interests to do Russia's bidding.

CHAPTER 7

A BRIEF HISTORY OF TREASON

Treason is the most serious crime that a citizen can commit against his own country.[1] It is a crime of betrayal. Traitors are universally depicted in literature and in the arts as among the most despicable human beings on the planet. In Dante Alighieri's Inferno, for example, the ninth and lowest circle of Hell was reserved for traitors. The names of Judas Iscariot, who betrayed Jesus,[2] and Benedict Arnold, a General in the Continental Army who betrayed the American revolutionary cause by secretly working for the British forces, have become synonymous with the term "traitor." Marcus Junius Brutus, who betrayed Rome and, with Cassius, murdered Julius Caesar in the Roman Senate, is also high up on the infamous list of most notorious traitors.

Under English law, treason against the King was known as "high treason." Any person who committed treason was commonly labeled as a "traitor." Perhaps the most infamous of English traitors was Guy Fawkes, who tried to assassinate King James I.[3] Having failed in his objective, Fawkes was convicted of treason and was sentenced to be hanged, drawn and quartered.

Given the gravity of the offense, it is no coincidence that the Framers of the Constitution listed "treason" as the first of the three grounds for impeachment under Article II, Section 4 of the U.S. Constitution.[4]

Treason may mean different things to different people, and the term is often misused. For example, shortly before Election Day in November 2016, the Republican chairman of the House Homeland Security Committee, Rep. Mike McCaul, claimed that Hillary Clinton had committed "treason" by mishandling classified State Department emails.[5] Similarly, on October 27, 2017, Sebastian Gorka, the controversial former deputy assistant to President Trump,[6] charged during an interview on Fox News with Sean Hannity that recent allegations against Hillary Clinton relating to a uranium deal were comparable to espionage committed by Julius and Ethel Rosenberg, who "got the [electric] chair."[7]

Similarly, after his first State of the Union Address to Congress on January 30, 2018, President Trump referred to the fact that the Democratic legislators refused to stand up and applaud any of the proposals as "treasonous."[8] More recently, Trump has re-tweeted a meme depicting Hillary Clinton, Rod Rosenstein (the Deputy Attorney General), James Comey (the former FBI Director) and other critics and opponents of his Administration to be jailed traitors behind bars.[9]

However, the most famous of U.S. politicians who used charges of "treason" to attract notoriety was Republican Senator Joseph McCarthy of Wisconsin.[10] As chair of the Senate Permanent Investigations Subcommittee, from April to June 1954 McCarthy conducted a series of televised "red-baiting" hearings, commonly referred to as the Army-McCarthy Hearings, accusing the Army and various governmental departments of being infested with "treasonous" Communists, as well as Communist sympathizers and their "fellow travelers." He even went so far as to accuse Democrats of being guilty of "twenty years of treason" for failing to stop the spread of Communism.

To counter McCarthy's attack on its integrity, the Army hired Boston lawyer Joseph Welch to represent it and to make its case. At a session on June 9, 1954, McCarthy charged that one of Welch's attorneys had ties to a Communist organization.[11] Welch responded with the now famous rebuke: "Until this moment, Senator, I think I never really gauged your cruelty or your recklessness." When McCarthy continued his attack, Welch interrupted, calling McCarthy's bluff once and for all: "Let us not assassinate this lad further, Senator. You have done enough. Have you no sense of decency?"[12] McCarthy quickly deflated like a punctured balloon. Literally overnight, the American press and people turned on him in revulsion, as if finally realizing that the Emperor had no clothes.

McCarthy's charges of treason and harboring Communist sympathizers against the Army are eerily similar to Trump's repeated accusations that the leadership of the FBI and the Justice Department has not been sufficiently "loyal" to him. He has repeatedly charged that there is a dark conspiracy against him and his Administration, a conspiracy involving "deep state" Democratic-sympathizers embedded in the FBI, Justice Department, CIA, State Department and other key government agencies. According to Trump, these "deep staters" are determined to thwart his efforts to forge a closer relationship with Russia and, instead, persist in pursuing a "fake" investigation into collusion between Team Trump and the Russians.

The close similarities between McCarthy's "red-baiting" demagoguery and Trump's dark mutterings about "treason," lack of "loyalty", and deep-state conspiracies against him are not entirely coincidental. Trump, like McCarthy before him, craves publicity and the limelight at any cost, including the truth, and has risen to the top of the political ladder by astutely dividing the American people to the maximum extent possible, spreading fear, distrust, and paranoia for his own personal political advantage.

Both McCarthy and Trump also relied heavily on Roy Cohn, the evil genius who served as chief counsel to McCarthy's congressional sub-committee and then, after returning to the private practice of law in New York (until eventually disbarred) represented a series of organized crime bosses and their associates in various high-profile criminal trials. At the same time, Cohn took the young Donald J. Trump under his wing, mentoring him on how to manipulate the press for maximum exposure. Cohn taught him the black arts of how to successfully use corrupt "sweetheart" labor contracts with organized crime-controlled construction trade unions to gain an unfair competitive advantage in the real estate development field.

Donald Trump's reckless charges of "treason" against the Democratic caucus in Congress for sitting on their hands during his State of the Union Address was as baseless as Senator Joe McCarthy's unsupported charges that the Democrats were guilty of "twenty years of treason."

Perhaps because the word "treason" is such a supercharged term that tends to be grossly misused and often misunderstood, the Framers decided to specifically define "treason" in Article III, Section 3, Clause 1 of the Constitution. The Article III provides: "Treason against the United States shall consist only in levying War against them, or in adhering to their Enemies, giving them Aid and Comfort."[13]

Since President Trump cannot fairly be accused of having literally taken up arms and "levying" war against the U.S., it is the second part of the definition of treason, i.e., giving aid and comfort to our country's enemies, that is the one applicable to him and those around him. Thus, the threshold questions that must be answered are as follows: (1) Is Russia an enemy of the United States,[14] and if so, (2) did Trump give Russian "aid and comfort" justifying criminal prosecution or impeachment?

Before we get to those questions, however, we should briefly review the history of treason. There have been relatively few cases where Americans have been charged with treason or the related offense of "espionage." These cases give us some insight as to whether the term "treason" applies to the swirling allegations of "collusion" between members of the Trump Team (or Trump himself) with the successful Russian efforts to interfere with the 2016 election and the country's democratic processes.

Given the severe and irreversible nature of the penalty normally meted out when an official was found guilty of treason, i.e., death, and the absence of any clear-cut definition under English law for "treason," the Framers decided to both narrow the definition by restricting it to "levying war" against the United States and, secondly, giving "aid and comfort" to its enemies.

In No. 43 of the *Federalist Papers*, James Madison wrote:

As treason may be committed against the United States the authority of the United States ought to be enabled to punish it: but as new tangled and artificial treasons have been the great engines by which violent factions, the natural offspring of free governments, have usually wreaked their alternate malignity on each other, the Convention has with great judgment opposed a barrier to this peculiar danger by inserting a Constitutional definition of the crime.[15]

Thus, the Founders were deeply concerned that accusations and prosecutions for Treason did not include ordinary political dissent or political disagreements, and in a more contemporary application, it cannot be said to apply to the negligent handling of arguably classified emails or other material.

Shortly after the U.S. Constitution was enacted and adopted by the states, the first Congress passed the Crimes Act of 1790 (sometimes referred to as the Federal Criminal Code of 1790),[16] which included a definition of the crimes of "treason"[17] and "misprision of treason," which makes it a crime to fail to disclose knowledge that another person or persons are planning to commit – or already are committing – treason.[18]

Since the Constitution came into effect, there have been fewer than 40 federal prosecutions for treason and even fewer convictions.[19] Several men were convicted of treason in connection with the 1794 Whiskey Rebellion but were pardoned by President George Washington.[20]

The Aaron Burr Treason Case

The most famous treason trial was that of Aaron Burr, who is one of the most fascinating characters in American history. After losing the 1800 presidential election to Thomas Jefferson, Burr served as the nation's third vice president from 1801-1805.[21] He planned to run again for the presidency in 1804, but his political career abruptly ended on July 11, 1804, when he took the day off from his duties as Vice President of the United States to shoot and kill former Treasury Secretary Alexander Hamilton in a duel at Weehawken Heights, New Jersey. It was the culmination of a longstanding rivalry between the two. The duel was precipitated in part by the fact that Burr had defeated Hamilton's father-in-law, Philip Schuyler, for one of the two New York Senate seats in 1791. As Secretary of the Treasury, Hamilton desperately needed all of the support he could get for his Federalist Party policies, which favored a strong central bank and one national currency, so the loss of the Senate seat to Burr was upsetting.

On April 24, 1804, a letter was published in the Albany Register written by Dr. Charles D. Cooper to Hamilton's father-in-law, former U.S. Sen. Philip Schuyler, suggesting that Hamilton had made previous statements critical of Burr.[22] When Burr confronted Hamilton and asked him to repudiate Dr. Cooper's letter, Hamilton basically shrugged it off, stating that, in essence, he had no control over what Dr. Cooper thought or wrote. Burr then challenged Hamilton to a duel, which Hamilton accepted.[23]

Burr succeeded in mortally wounding Hamilton during the fight, who died the following day. Burr was subsequently indicted for murder in both New York and New Jersey, and he wisely avoided those two states while serving out the remainder of his vice-presidential term. Having his political ambitions crushed by the fact he was a better shot than Hamilton, Burr – with his ambitions still burning – came up with another plan to rise to the top. Burr can be accused of many faults, but "thinking too small" was not one of them. He planned to form a new country – to be led by him, of course – in a portion of the western territories of the U.S. and he plotted to raise a rebellion in New Orleans, and elsewhere, in order to build his new nation. He even toyed with the idea of invading and conquering Mexico.

Burr's conspiracy to commit treason started one month after killing Hamilton when he met with Britain's minister to the U.S., Anthony Merry, who reported that Burr was planning to separate a portion of the western part of the U.S. with military force. He also met with the Spanish minister to the U.S., Marques de Casa Yrujo, and broached the subject, but neither Britain nor Spain decided to help Burr with his ambitious plans. In early 1805, while still supposedly acting as Vice President of the United States, Burr went west to raise an army that would either invade Mexico or carve off a portion of the U.S. to form an independent country under his leadership.

Burr met with one of his co-conspirators, Herman Blennerhassett, on an island located in the Ohio River, then part of Virginia. Later, Burr joined forces with General James Wilkinson, where they assembled an army of about 7,000 men to carry out the plan. Burr, however, left the island before any actions were taken to actually implement the program. After Burr had gone, Wilkinson got cold feet and informed President Jefferson of the plans to mount a rebellion and to take a significant portion of U.S. territory to form a new country.

Burr was arrested in March 1807 while he was trying to flee to Florida, which was then under Spanish control. He was then taken to Virginia to stand trial before Chief Justice John Marshall. At that time, Supreme Court judges also acted as appellate (or circuit) judges. His bail was set at $5,000.

On June 24, 1807, the grand jury for the Virginia federal circuit indicted Burr, charging him with one count of treason and one count of a high misdemeanor for "unlawfully, falsely, maliciously, and traitorously ... intending to raise and levy war" against the U.S.

The trial began on August 10, 1807, and lasted about one month. On September 1, 1807, President Jefferson, still incensed at what he considered to be Burr's clear-cut act of treason and disloyalty to the United States, sent a special message to Congress, declaring, in essence, that Burr's guilt was "placed beyond question." Jefferson also gave incriminating evidence against Burr to George Hay, the U.S. attorney in charge of the prosecution, and also offered pardons to Burr's co-conspirators if they agreed to turn state's evidence and testify against Burr.

The evidence against Burr seemed to be overwhelming on its face since numerous witnesses for the prosecution painted a vivid picture of Burr and other conspirators plotting to annex a portion of the U.S. by force of arms and to mount a war against Mexico. However, the prosecution ran into trouble. The essence of the treason charge was that Burr committed an overt act on December 10, 1806 by assembling a military force on Blennerhassett Island for purposes of waging war against the United States. The problem was that the evidence showed that Burr was not on the island on that particular date, but rather hundreds of miles away from there.

The second problem was that Chief Justice Marshall instructed the jurors that they could convict Burr of treason as a co-conspirator if they found that at least two witnesses provided testimony that some overt act was committed in furtherance of the conspiracy. However, General Wilkinson was the only witness who testified as to Burr's direct involvement in the alleged plot to commit treason.

In a 30-page written opinion,[24] Chief Justice Marshall wrote that the charge of treason may be established by either evidence that the defendant did so by "levying war, or by giving aid and comfort to those who were levying war...."[25] In other words, treason may be committed by those who do not themselves bear arms, but aid and abet acts of war against the United States. He referred to such culpable parties as "accessories to treason" or those who are "leagued in the conspiracy," all of who could be "declared to be traitors." However, to be found to have been a party to a conspiracy to commit treason, the party must "perform a part" by committing an "overt act" in furtherance of the conspiracy.[26] In the end, after only 25 minutes of deliberation, the jury found Burr to be "not guilty."

Undeterred by Burr's acquittal on the treason charges, Jefferson and U.S. Attorney Hay prosecuted Burr on the "high misdemeanor" charges, and over 50 witnesses were called to testify at the five-week trial presided over by Chief Justice Marshall and another judge, Cyrus Griffin. Much to President Jefferson's frustration, the jury acquitted Burr once again.[27]

Hay then filed a motion to prosecute Burr for treason in Ohio, alleging that Burr conspired to levy war against the U.S. government in Ohio, as well as Virginia. Marshall ultimately ruled, however, that Burr could only be tried for misdemeanor charges in Ohio. Jefferson and Hay finally gave up at this point and ceased all further prosecution efforts against Burr.

Treason and the Civil War

During the Civil War, treason trials were held in Indianapolis against the so-called "Copperheads" for conspiring with the Confederacy against the United States.[28] After the war, the issue arose as to whether the leaders of the Confederate States of America should be indicted for treason as part of a "harsh" peace, or whether these leaders should be given amnesty to facilitate the more rapid re-integration of the seceding states back into the Union.

When General Robert E. Lee surrendered at Appomattox Courthouse in April 1865 on behalf of the Army of Northern Virginia, Gen. Ulysses S. Grant assured all Confederate soldiers and officers full amnesty. The only condition that Grant required was that the soldiers return to their homes and refrain from any further acts of hostility. Other Union generals issued similar terms of amnesty when accepting Confederate surrenders.[29]

In the end, Jefferson Davis, the Confederate president, was the only Confederate leader who was indicted for treason, and he was held in prison for two years. However, this indictment was dropped in 1869 when it was feared that he would be acquitted by a jury in Virginia.[30] President

Andrew Johnson granted immunity to all Confederate officials as one of his final acts before he left office in 1869.

Treason After World War II

After World War II, Iva Toguri D'Aquino was convicted of treason in 1949 for wartime radio broadcasts under the name of "Tokyo Rose." She was sentenced to a ten-year prison term.

There were no prosecutions explicitly for treason during the period of the Cold War with the Soviet Union; however, Julius and Ethel Rosenberg were notably tried, convicted and executed on June 19, 1953, for handing over nuclear secrets to the Russians as part of a conspiracy to commit espionage.[31] One likely reason why the federal prosecutors charged the Rosenbergs with espionage rather than treason was that both the 1798 Alien and Sedition Acts and the Espionage Act of 1917 have much broader definitions of what constitutes such an offense against the United States than the Constitution's Article III definition of treason.

Jonathan Jay Pollard was a former intelligence analyst for the United States government when he was arrested on November 21, 1985 and charged with spying for Israel. In 1987, as part of a plea agreement, Pollard pleaded guilty to spying for and providing top-secret classified information to Israel. He was sentenced to life in prison for violations of the Espionage Act, but on November 20, 2015, he was released on parole.[32] For years, the Israelis disavowed Mr. Pollard, but eventually granted him citizenship, acknowledging his work for them.[33] Some Americans, and certainly Israel, felt that Pollard's sentence was too harsh, in view of the fact that he was spying for an American ally, not one of America's adversaries or enemies. However, the prevalent view among Americans and the U.S.

government was that the betrayal of one's country is the most serious offense that an American can commit, no matter whether the treasonous conduct is for a friend or foe. "He wasn't an Israeli," said Joseph E. di Genova, the U.S. attorney who prosecuted Pollard. "He was an American citizen who betrayed his country for money."[34]

So, what can we infer from the absence of actual criminal treason prosecutions or, in the case of presidents and other public officers, impeachment proceedings based upon treason in recent American history? Is it because there has been an absence of traitors in our midst or in high office, or is the charge of "treason" under constitutional or criminal statutory standards simply inapplicable because, it is argued, that without a formal declaration of war, another country – no matter how hostile or adversarial – cannot be considered to be our nation's "enemy."

As discussed in the next chapter, a strong argument can be made that conspiracy and collusion with a hostile foreign power such as Russia can, in fact, constitute the crime of treason or the predicate for impeachment of a sitting president.

CHAPTER 8

IS RUSSIA AN ENEMY OF THE U.S.?

This brings us back to a fundamental question: Is Russia an enemy of the United States, and if so, are President Trump and members of his team guilty of treason for having given "aid and comfort" to Russia either during the 2016 election, the transition period, or during the Trump Administration? And, finally, even if they are not technically liable for having committed treason, can they still correctly be considered as "traitors" for having betrayed their country?

The President's Broad Constitutional Powers to Defend the Country In Response to an Enemy Attack, Even In the Absence of a Congressional Declaration of War

Under the English legal system at the time of the Constitutional Convention, the King had both the power to wage war and the power to declare war. The Founders decided to divide those two responsibilities between the Executive (*i.e.,* the President) and Congress. Congress was given the power to declare war under Article I, Section 8 of the Constitution, which provides: "Congress shall have power to ... declare War."[1] As of the time of the Convention, a declaration of war had already come to be considered as little more than a formality. As Alexander Hamilton observed, "the ceremony of a formal denunciation of war has of late fallen into disuse." *The Federalist* No. 25, at 165 (Alexander Hamilton) (Clinton Rossiter ed., 1961).

At the same time, however, Congress gave the President the power to make war and defend the country. Article II, Section 2 states that the "President shall be Commander in Chief of the Army and Navy of the United States, and of the Militia of the several States when called into the actual Service of the United States." U.S. Const. Art. II, § 2, cl. 1. He is further vested with all of "the executive Power" and the duty to execute the laws. U.S. Const. Art. II, § 1. These powers, therefore, give the President broad constitutional authority to use military force in response to threats to the national security of the United States.

It is inconceivable that the Founders thought that the President did not have the power – and indeed the duty – to take all necessary measures to repel a surprise attack by the enemy or hostile forces even without a formal declaration of war by Congress.[2] The Founders may well have, to some extent, been dreamers, since they conceived of and established a democratic form of government that the world had never seen before. However, they were also practical men. They understood that the President's constitutional power to defend the United States and its people should be interpreted in light of their express intention to create a federal government that was, in the words of Alexander Hamilton, "clothed with all the powers requisite to [the] complete execution of its trust."[3]

The security of the nation has always unquestionably been a central component of the government's ability to execute that sacred public trust. As Hamilton explained, because "the circumstances which may affect the public safety are [not] reducible within certain determinate limits, . . . it must be admitted, as a necessary consequence that there can be no limitation of that authority which is to provide for the defense and protection of the community in any matter essential to its efficiency."[4]

The Supreme Court has consistently held that the conduct of foreign affairs and protection of the national security from, among other things, enemy attacks, are "'central' Presidential domains."[5] The President's constitutional powers in these areas flow from the specific grants of authority in Article II that make the President both the Chief Executive of the Nation and the Commander in Chief.[6] Based upon these explicit constitutional grants of authority, the Supreme Court has "recognized 'the generally accepted view that foreign policy [is] the province and responsibility of the Executive.'"[7]

Conducting military hostilities is a central tool for the exercise of the President's plenary control over the conduct of foreign policy. There can be no doubt that the use of force protects the Nation's security and helps it achieve its foreign policy goals. Construing the Constitution to grant such power to another branch could prevent the President from exercising his core constitutional responsibilities in foreign affairs. Even in the cases in which the Supreme Court has limited executive authority, it has also emphasized that we should not construe legislative prerogatives to prevent the Executive Branch "from accomplishing its constitutionally assigned functions."[8]

Thus, the scope of a President's powers to protect national security must be construed to authorize the most effective defense of the country and its interests in accordance "with the realistic purposes of the entire instrument."[9] This includes the authority and, indeed, duty for the President to defend the country by all means possible in the event of an attack by an enemy, hostile power, terrorist group or person. Conversely, the President is to refrain from giving "aid and comfort" to an enemy or belligerent that has attacked America under the penalty of being impeached as a traitor.

America's Forceful Response to Its Many Enemies Throughout History, Without a Formal Declaration of War

The longstanding undeclared hostilities between the U.S. and another country is not unusual in American history. Throughout its history, the U.S. has been engaged in numerous conflicts with other belligerent nations and non-state actors, without any declarations of war.[10] On at least 125 occasions, Presidents have acted without prior express military authorization from Congress.[11] These include the Philippine–American War from 1898–1903, the military actions by U.S. troops in Nicaragua in 1927, the NATO bombing campaign of Yugoslavia in 1999, the U.S. military actions and drone strikes in response to the September 11, 2001 terrorist attack on the U.S. and, more recently, the 2017 missile strikes on Syria ordered by President Trump.[12]

America's "Enemies" Since World War II

There have been no formal declarations of war by Congress since World War II, following Japan's attack on Pearl Harbor on December 7, 1941.[13] Nevertheless, it must be conceded that the United States has struggled with foreign enemies throughout its post-war period, and the giving of "aid and comfort" to such enemies by an American citizen would correctly be considered as an act of treason.

The Korean War was perhaps the most notable of these undeclared conflicts. Technically, it was never really a "war;" rather, it was considered a "police action" authorized by U.N. Resolutions, not by an act of Congress.[14] Nevertheless, this did not prevent the loss of tens of thousands of American casualties on the Korean peninsula, and 28,500 U.S. troops continue to man the Demilitarized Zone dividing North and South Korea.

In other words, there is still no "peace" in Korea,[15] but technically there was never a "war."

Similarly, the Vietnam War, which cost at least 58,000 American lives, was fought without any declaration of war, even though the Gulf of Tonkin Resolution that Congress passed on August 7, 1964 authorized President Johnson to take any measures he believed were necessary to retaliate and to promote the maintenance of international peace and security in southeast Asia.[16]

Although the U.S. and the Soviet Union were not technically at war during the post World War II period known as the Cold War, there is no question that the two countries were declared enemies throughout that period. The hostile relations between them nearly ended up in a "hot war" with the Cuban missile crisis in 1963, as well as at other points in time. Although there was some thaw in relations between Russia and the U.S. after the collapse of the Soviet Union, the hostile relations between the two countries resumed after Vladimir Putin assumed the reins of power in Russia on December 31, 1999, following the resignation of President Boris Yelsin. Since then, Russia's expansionist policies have made it a significant competitor and hostile adversary of both the U.S. and its NATO allies, especially after its annexation of Crimea and active military intervention in eastern Ukraine on behalf of the pro-Russian separatists.

Finally, Russia's decision to engage in asymmetrical warfare with the U.S. by launching a cyber attack designed to disrupt and interfere with the 2016 elections removed any remaining doubts that Russia is an enemy of the United States. In addition, the fact that, according to U.S. intelligence reports, Russia continued its cyber attacks on the U.S. electoral system during the 2018 mid-term elections,[17] and has also conducted cyber attacks on U.S. power plants and other critical infrastructure,[18] conclusively indicates that Russia remains undeterred in its resolve to continue to take active hostile measures against the U.S.

The War Powers Act

Following the withdrawal of most American troops from the Vietnam War in 1973, the issue of whether and to what extent the President could deploy forces without a declaration of war was extensively debated in Congress. This debate led to the War Powers Resolution,[19] which clearly defined how many soldiers could be deployed by the President and for how long. It also required formal reports by the President to Congress regarding the status of such deployments and limited the total amount of time that American forces could be deployed without a formal declaration of war.

Although the constitutionality of the War Powers Act has never been tested, it was followed during the invasions and incursions into Grenada, Panama, and Somalia. One major exception was when President Clinton's ordered the deployment of U.S. troops in the 78-day NATO air campaign against Yugoslavia during the Kosovo War.

In a September 25, 2001, Memo discussing the President's inherent power to order military action as Commander-in-Chief, it was concluded that the President did, in fact, have such broad powers and had often exercised them in the past:

> You have asked for our opinion as to the scope of the President's authority to take military action in response to the terrorist attacks on the United States on September 11, 2001. We conclude that the President has the broad constitutional power to use military force. Congress has acknowledged this inherent executive power in both the War Powers Resolution, Pub. L. No. 93-148, 87 Stat. 555 (1973), codified at

50 U.S.C. §§ 1541-1548 (the "WPR"), and in the Joint The resolution passed by Congress on September 14, 2001, Pub. L. No. 107-40, 115 Stat. 224 (2001).

Further, the President has the constitutional power not only to retaliate against any person, organization, or state suspected of involvement in terrorist attacks on the United States, but also against foreign states suspected of harboring or supporting such organizations. Finally, the President may deploy military force preemptively against terrorist organizations or the states that harbor or support them, whether or not they can be linked to the specific terrorist incidents of September 11.[20]

Since September 11th, both Presidents George W. Bush and Barack Obama used this "broad constitutional power to use military force" referred to in this Memo and other documents to attack al-Qaeda and other terrorist organizations, and to charge any American citizen who actively participated or gave "aid and comfort" to al-Qaeda with treason. For example, on October 11, 2006, the United States government filed charges against Adam Yahiye Gadahn for his appearance on widely-circulated videos as a spokesman for al-Qaeda, threatening attacks on American soil.[21] At the direction of President Obama, who apparently authorized Gadahn's "termination with extreme prejudice," he was later killed on January 19, 2015, in an unmanned drone strike in Waziristan, Pakistan.[22]

During the Obama Administration, some members of Congress expressed concern during March of 2011 that the decision of President Barack Obama to order the U.S. military to participate in air attacks in Libyan exceeded his constitutional authority.[23] In response, President Obama set forth his defense and explanation for ordering the attack in a two-page letter, stating that as commander in chief, he had the constitutional authority to authorize the strikes, which were limited in scope and duration, and necessary to prevent a humanitarian disaster in Libya.[24] U.S. participation in the Libyan attack was also justified because Libya, as a longstanding state sponsor of terrorism, was an undeclared "enemy" of the U.S. and its allies. Libya's leader, Moammar Gaddafi, had directed numerous terrorist attacks against U.S. nationals and others, bombing a Berlin disco in 1986 and a passenger aircraft over Lockerbie, Scotland, in 1988. Indeed, after the Berlin attack, President Ronald Reagan had ordered -- without specific congressional authority -- U.S. airstrikes against Libya.

Some commentators who defended President Obama's 2011 decision to impose a "no-fly zone" in Libya pointed out that during the Constitutional Convention, "the power to 'declare war' was substituted for the power to 'make war.'" The change was meant to define congressional authority specifically to clarify that the president could use military force without first seeking Congress's permission."[25] The President's use of military force without prior Congressional authorization could, therefore, be considered as consistent with the particular concern expressed by James Madison at the Constitutional Convention that the president should be able to "repel a sudden attack."[26]

Russia's Cyberattacks on the U.S. And Interference With the U.S. Electoral and Democratic Systems Confirm That It Is An "Enemy" of the U.S. Just As Much (Or More) As Al-Qaeda and Other Terrorist Groups

Just as terrorist organizations and hostile states who sponsor terrorism are considered to be "enemies" of the U.S. even in the absence of a formal declaration of war, it can reasonably be argued that Russia's ongoing cyber attacks on the U.S. are hostile acts by an enemy state. It follows, therefore, that any U.S. citizen who provides "aid and comfort" to them is guilty of treason.

Although Russia's cyber warfare on the U.S. has not produced the same graphic scenes of physical destruction and loss of life that accompanied the Pearl Harbor or 9/11 attacks, it may be argued that the results have been equally devastating. In April 2015, CNN reported that Russian hackers had penetrated sensitive parts of the White House computers, and the FBI, Secret Service, and other U.S. intelligence agencies categorized the attacks as "among the most sophisticated attacks ever launched against U.S. government systems."[27] Also in 2015, CNN reported that Russian hackers had breached the U.S. State Department email system in what was described as the "worst ever" cyber attack intrusion against a federal agency.[28]

In February 2016, senior Kremlin advisor and top Russian cyber official Andrey Krutskikh told the Russian national security conference in Moscow that Russian was working on new strategies for the "information arena" that was equivalent to testing a nuclear bomb and would "allow us to talk to the Americans as equals."[29]

In 2016, the release of hacked emails belonging to the Democratic National Committee, John Podesta and Colin Powell, among others, were identified by U.S. intelligence services and private sector analysts to have been hacked by the Russians and then released through DC Leaks and WikiLeaks, both of whom by that time had basically become arms of the Russian intelligence.

Since at least March 2016, Russian government cyber actors -- also referred to as "threat actors" -- targeted government entities and multiple U.S. critical infrastructure sectors, including the energy, nuclear, commercial facilities, water, aviation, and critical manufacturing sectors. On March 15, 2018, the U.S. Computer Emergency Response Team released an alert warning that the Russian government was executing "a multi-stage intrusion campaign by Russian government cyber actors who targeted small commercial facilities' networks where they staged malware, conducted spear phishing, and gained remote access into energy sector networks."[30] The Russian hackers targeted at least a dozen U.S. power plants, in addition to water processing, aviation, and government facilities.[31] According to this "Alert," after obtaining access, the Russian government cyber actors conducted network reconnaissance and collected information about Industrial Control Systems (ICS). In other words, by penetrating these critical U.S. infrastructures, the Russians have the capability of disrupting or completely shutting down these essential U.S. operations. It is possible that they can literally turn out the lights in a wide range of towns and cities throughout the U.S., at least for a while. So Russia's cyber attacks on the U.S. have not been limited to bots and trolls penetrating social media platforms and hacking into information databases; Russia has also targeted virtually all of the U.S. critical infrastructure.

On July 13, 2018, three days before Trump's disastrous meeting with Putin in Helsinki, Finland, the U.S. Department of Justice announced the indictment of 12 Russian intelligence officers on charges relating to the hacking of the Democratic National Committee and the Clinton presidential campaign.[32] The 29-page indictment contains a highly detailed description of how the Russian government systematically planned and executed a broad-ranging cyberattack that was intended to sabotage the Clinton campaign, aid Trump, and generally spread chaos throughout the American political scene in the months leading up to the November 2016 presidential election. There were "phishing" attacks designed to deceive Democratic operatives into giving up passwords and other critical information, to money laundering, to attempts to break into state election boards. In several respects, the Russian agents were brazen in their approach, as if they didn't really care if American officials and law enforcement knew that they were meddling in the U.S. election, and even paying for their social media accounts in rubles, rather than dollars. They must have known that the U.S. was relatively powerless to stop them, so why not taunt them in the process.

In announcing the indictment, Rod Rosenstein, the Deputy Attorney General, reminded us that "there will always be adversaries who work to exacerbate domestic differences and try to confuse, divide and conquer us."[33] He added, "So long as we are united in our commitment to the shared values enshrined in the Constitution, they will not succeed." What Rosenstein didn't say, however, was that the Russia agents may well have had an ally in the White House who was assisting them in compromising and weakening our country's democratic infrastructure, and that there was a real possibility that they were achieving that objective.[34] Indeed, on the day that the indictment was handed down, Trump commented that he believed that the focus on Russia's election meddling made it more difficult for him to establish closer ties with Russia.[35] Unsurprisingly, the Kremlin agreed. The Russian Foreign Ministry said that the indictment was meant to 'spoil the atmosphere before the Russian-American summit."[36]

Thus, Russia is a hostile power and enemy of the U.S., just as much as any terrorist organization. It logically follows, then, that any U.S. citizen – including the president -- who knowingly gives aid and comfort to Russia's attacks on the U.S. may be indicted and prosecuted for treason, as well as any related crimes, such as conspiracy against the United States and obstruction of justice. The only open question, then, is whether a sitting president may be indicted and prosecuted for treason while he is still in office, as opposed to having to wait until he voluntarily or involuntarily leaves office, and whether impeachment is the only constitutional option open to while the president still holds office.[37]

CHAPTER 9

ALL THE PRESIDENT'S (PRO-RUSSIAN) MEN

Although the men surrounding Trump during the Campaign and in the White House were undoubtedly handpicked by Trump himself, the result would have been the same if some Moscow handler had selected them for him. Many, if not most, of Trump's key advisors were known to be pro-Russian, even when U.S. interests diverged from those of Russia. These were precisely the people that Trump wanted around him so that they could help him implement his pro-Russian strategy if he managed to assume the Presidency.

Michael T. Flynn

During the 2016 Presidential campaign, Trump selected retired Lieutenant General Michael T. Flynn as one of his major foreign policy advisors, even though (or perhaps because) it was widely known that, after resigning as Director of the Defense Intelligence Agency (DIA) in 2014, Flynn became a regular contributor to RT, the Kremlin's wholly-owned English-language TV station.[1] In December 2015, Flynn further embellished his pro-Kremlin credentials by showing up in Moscow at RT's 10th Anniversary Gala, where he was photographed sitting at a table next to Vladimir Putin himself.[2] Apparently overwhelmed with enthusiasm, Flynn led a standing ovation for the Russian leader.[3]

Flynn was well paid by the Russians for his services,[4] which was used by the Russian propaganda machine to show that Russia had friends at the highest levels of the U.S. military establishment, and relations between the two countries were bound to improve considerably if Trump emerged as the Republican presidential candidate and won the race for the White House.

Flynn had attracted Putin's attention by being outspoken in favor of closer ties between the U.S. and Russia, notwithstanding its aggressive action in Ukraine and elsewhere. In an interview with Michael Isikoff of *Yahoo News* at the Republican National Convention on July 18, 2016, Flynn acknowledged that he had been paid to attend RT's lavish anniversary party, where he was unabashedly complimentary about Russian President Vladimir Putin.[5] When asked why he would want to be so closely associated with a Kremlin propaganda platform, Flynn said he sees no distinction between RT and other news outlets. 'What's CNN? What's MSNBC? Come on!' said Flynn."[6] In other words, Flynn was making the outlandish suggestion that CNN and MSNBC are propaganda outlets for the U.S. government, like the Voice of America, and were not independent news networks.

However, by working in Russia's interests and getting paid for it, Flynn walked himself into a massive problem with the U.S. military justice and criminal laws. Flynn was required to – but did not – get clearance from the Pentagon for either his Moscow trip or for the payment by Russia for his services, thus exposing himself to possible disciplinary and criminal sanctions.[7] Compounding his problems was the fact that the U.S. Constitution's emoluments clause prohibits both active and retired military officers from accepting foreign government payments without the permission of Congress.[8] Flynn's chummy relationship with Putin raised many eyebrows in the intelligence community, and his outspoken criticism of U.S. policy towards Russia also dismayed his former military colleagues, including retired Gen. Stanley A. McChrystal and retired Admiral Michael Mullen, a former chairman of the Joint Chiefs of Staff. According to *The Washington Post*, they contacted Flynn and asked him to show greater restraint in his public comments.[9]

During their tense transitional meeting at the White House after the election, outgoing President Obama warned Trump not to give Flynn any significant position in the new administration, signaling to Trump the growing consensus in the U.S. intelligence community that Flynn's ties to Russia posed a national security risk.[10] Trump ignored Obama's warnings about Flynn, since he seemed intent on putting together a pro-Russian Campaign, Transition Team and Administration that would be pleasing to Putin and the Kremlin. Trump's apparent motive was to advance his intense interest in building a Trump Tower in Moscow and to keep the Russian money flowing into his luxury condominium developments in the U.S. and around the world. In other words, the fact that Flynn had developed close ties with Russia was – in Trump's view – a virtue, not a liability.

During the 2016 Presidential campaign, Flynn became one of Trump's most vocal and outspoken advocates at numerous campaign rallies. At the July 2016 Republican National Convention in Cleveland, Ohio, an intense and almost rabid-looking Flynn led the delegates in the now infamous "Lock Her Up" chant, calling for the prosecution, conviction and incarceration of Trump's political rival, Hillary Clinton, for the capital offense of having failed to properly secure her emails. He assured the adoring delegates that he knew the national security business far better than Hillary Clinton, and that "if I did a tenth, a tenth of what she did, I would be in jail today."[11]

Flynn's knowledge and experience regarding matters of national security was put to the test in late December 2016 during the transition when, with the knowledge and consent of Trump and K.T. McFarland, one of Trump's other senior advisors, Flynn placed several phone calls to Sergey Kislyak, the then Russian Ambassador to the United States.[12] Flynn and Kislyak talked on the phone about the additional sanctions that the Obama Administration had just imposed on Russia in the wake of a U.S. intelligence report concluding that Russia had interfered in the 2016 Presidential election. The U.S. Embassy in Moscow was bracing itself for a substantial Russian-ordered exodus to take place immediately following the Obama Administration's announcements of the new sanctions and the expulsion of Russian diplomats and known intelligence operatives from the U.S.

Worried that the Obama "get tough with Russia" policy would tie Trump's hands once he took over the reins of power, McFarland and Flynn immediately conferred by phone and came up with a plan for Team Trump to send a "back-door" signal to the Russians. Flynn would ask Russia to hold off with any retaliation plans until after Trump had moved into the White House. Given some time, the clear implication was that Trump would then lift the crippling Russian sanctions.

Flynn was directed to call Ambassador Kislyak and to clearly convey to him the Trump Team's urgent request, which he did on December 29, 2016. In fact, Flynn had multiple phone calls and text messages with Kislyak during this same time frame, all of which were intercepted by U.S. intelligence and law enforcement agents.[13] Flynn then reported back to McFarland at Trump's Mar-A-Lago resort in West Palm Beach, Florida, who presumably was briefing Trump on these critical developments.[14]

By speaking with Kislyak by phone and then later lying about the substance of those phone calls to the FBI,[15] Flynn displayed not only a colossal lapse of integrity and judgment, but also violated rule #1 that any knowledgeable person must know: when speaking by phone to a high-level Russian official, there is a 99.9% probability that your conversation is being recorded by the FBI, the CIA, or some other U.S. intelligence organization. Yet, Flynn brazenly lied repeatedly about these phone calls to FBI agents, which he must have known at the time was a federal crime punishable by up to 5 years in federal prison, pursuant to Title 18 of the United States Code, Section 1001, which does not require that the lie be made under oath.

Since Flynn had an extensive background in national security and U.S. foreign policy, he also knew he was breaking rule #2: when dealing with a foreign official when you are not an official U.S. governmental representative, you must not engage in any back-door meddling with U.S. foreign policy. If you do meddle it is a violation of the Logan Act, a longstanding U.S. law prohibiting private citizens from interfering with U.S. foreign policy.[16] As it is often described, the U.S. can only have one foreign policy at a time, so Flynn and the rest of the Trump Team were apparently attempting to undercut official U.S. policy as of December 29, 2016 by engaging in its own back-door diplomacy that was directly contrary to the official Obama Administration's position regarding Russia.

To the surprise of virtually everyone – but certainly not to Trump, Flynn, and McFarland – Vladimir Putin announced the following day, on December 30, 2016, that Russia had decided to hold off responding to the Obama sanctions until after Trump was sworn in as the next U.S. President.[17] The hastily concocted Trump Team plan to influence U.S./Russian relations had magically worked, in no small measure based upon Flynn's signal to the Russians that if they were patient for another few weeks, their goal of having the harsh U.S. sanctions lifted would be realized.

When news reports began circulating to the effect that Flynn – like Jeff Sessions and a host of other Trump advisors – had spoken with the Russian Ambassador, Flynn lied about the substance of the conversation to Vice President-elect Mike Pence.[18] Pence dutifully repeated on the Sunday morning talk shows Flynn's categorical denials about having discussed anything remotely having to do with sanctions with Kislyak. From that moment on, the Russians knew that Flynn was compromised and that they had him figuratively in their pocket. They knew that Flynn was lying about the phone conversations. They had achieved with Flynn what every Russian intelligence officer hopes for, "Kompromat," the compromise of a valuable U.S. asset with information with which they can be blackmailed.

The U.S. Justice Department also knew that Flynn had been compromised, so Acting Attorney General Sally Yates rushed over to the White House immediately after the January 20, 2017 Inauguration to warn White House officials that Flynn had been compromised.[19] Trump's response was to wait several weeks before taking action on this information, which should have sent alarm bells ringing throughout the White House leading to the immediate sacking of Flynn from his position as National Security Advisor. Instead, Flynn continued to have top security clearance and access to the most sensitive information and was only fired when *The Washington Post* published a story on February 13, 2017 about the Flynn/Kislyak connection.[20]

Trump also fired the messenger, Sally Yates, on January 30, 2017, after she instructed Justice Department attorneys to not make any legal argument defending Executive Order 13769, which temporarily banned the admission of refugees and barred travel from certain Muslim-majority countries.[21] Yates took the legal position that the order was not defensible in court or consistent with the Constitution.

Flynn pleaded guilty to having lied to the FBI in early December 2017 and began cooperating with the FBI and Special Counsel Mueller's team. One of the first things that he must have told them was that Trump was fully informed of all his interactions with the Russians during the transition period and that he had indeed authorized these contacts. According to a Sentencing Memo that the federal prosecutors later released, Flynn had 19 interview sessions with the Special Counsel's office and other federal investigators, and they represented to the Court that his cooperation had been so successful, that he should not be sentenced to any jail time by the federal judge.

In other words, Flynn provided federal prosecutors with one of the critical pieces of the puzzle, which was whether Trump himself had authorized these significant contacts with Russian officials either during the Campaign or the Transition period. The answer that Flynn provided was an emphatic "Yes."[22]

Michael D. Cohen

Michael D. Cohen, Trump's personal lawyer and self-described "fixer," came from a family with longstanding connections to Russian organized crime figures in Brooklyn.[23] Cohen's uncle, Morton Levine, owned the El Caribe Country Club, a Brooklyn catering hall that was a well-known hangout for Russian gangsters. Cohen and his siblings all had an ownership interest in the club, which was rented for many years to Evsei Agron, the top Russian mafia boss of Brooklyn's Brighton Beach, as well as to his successors, Marat Balagula and Boris Nayfeld.[24]

Cohen's father-in-law, Fima Shusterman, was a naturalized U.S. citizen from Ukraine who was in the garment business and owned a fleet of taxicabs with his partners, Shalva Botier and Edward Zubok. All three of them were convicted of a money-laundering related offense in 1993. Shusterman was also suspected by federal law enforcement of being a silent business partner with Trump, as well as a conduit for wealthy Russian oligarchs and investors to launder their money by buying up condominiums in various Trump real estate projects.[25] Shusterman, who owned at least four New York taxi companies, also set Cohen up in the yellow cab business. Cohen eventually held 260 yellow cab medallions with his Ukrainian-born partner, the "taxi king" Simon V. Garber, until the two had a falling out in 2012.[26]

Glenn Simpson of Fusion GPS, who had hired former British MI-6 agent Michael Steele to investigate Trump's Russian connections during the 2016 presidential election campaign, testified before the House Intelligence Committee that Cohen "had a lot of connections to the former Soviet Union, and that he seemed to have associations with Russian organized crime figures in New York and Florida."[27]

Cohen also drew the attention of federal law enforcement who received a tip from an informant that Cohen and several other attorneys were helping various Russian money launderers purchase apartment in Sunny Isles Beach, Florida, just north of Miami. The area became known as "Little Moscow" due to the vast amounts of Russian money and Russian-speaking residents it attracted.[28] The street signs were even in Russian. Trump's brand name was on several of these Sunny Isles towers, and as Donald Trump Jr. bragged, Russian money kept "pouring in."[29] An investigation by Reuters found that at least 63 individuals with Russian passports or addresses bought at least $98.4 million worth of property in the seven Trump-branded luxury towers.[30] About one-third of the 2044 units at Sunny Isles were owned by limited liability companies, which were generally designed to hide the identity of the condominium unit's real owner.[31] Executives from Gazprom and other Russian natural resource giants also owned units in Trump's Sunny Isles towers. Trump and Cohen's genius – or evil genius – was that, instead of Russian criminal money being passive, incidental income, it became a central part of their business plan.[32] While many real estate developers had benefited from the purchase of their units by Russians who wanted to either hide or launder their money, Trump – with Michael Cohen's help – specifically marketed the Sunny Isle apartments to Russian criminals who needed a place to park their millions of ill-gotten cash for a couple of years.

Trump rewarded Cohen for his stellar performance in attracting Russian money into the Sunny Isle Towers projects by bringing Cohen into the Trump Organization in 2006. Eventually, Cohen became Trump's personal lawyer and fixer, just as the notorious Roy Cohn had been for Trump decades earlier. When payoffs were required to buy the silence of a former adult film star (Stormy Daniels) and a former Playboy model (Karen McDougal) in the closing weeks of the 2016 Presidential campaign so that their affairs with Trump would not become public knowledge, Cohen was the obvious "go to" man to arrange for these secret payments through various shell corporations.[33]

During most of the 2016 Presidential campaign, Cohen was Trump's intermediary with the Russians to move his cherished Trump Moscow Tower project along, which would have brought hundreds of millions of dollars to Trump and his organization once it was completed. Cohen arranged for Trump to sign a letter of intent for the project, which provided for tens of millions in financing from a Russian bank that was subject to

U.S. sanctions.[34] Although Cohen later falsely testified to a Congressional Committee that Trump had dropped the project before the February 1, 2016 Iowa Caucuses, Trump continued to pursue this Moscow project through at least June of 2016.[35] For this project to be successful, Trump needed the approval of Putin himself and the rest of the Kremlin leadership, which explains why Trump could only bring himself to say nice things about Putin and Russia during the Presidential primary and general election seasons. As was later disclosed, Trump and Cohen even went so far as to offer Putin a $50 million penthouse apartment in the Moscow Tower as a gift, once it was completed.[36]

Following Trump's surprise election victory in November 2016, Cohen also dabbled in U.S. foreign policy by involving himself in the formulation of a "peace plan" with pro-Russian operatives in Ukraine.[37] The essences of this plan was that the U.S. would totally capitulate to Russia's demands by withdrawing all of its objections to Russia's annexation of Crimea and lift all U.S. economic sanctions against Russia.

On April 9, 2018, Cohen's world (and to some extent Trump's) came crashing down when the FBI executed a search warrant of Cohen's home, office, and hotel room, carting off box-loads of sensitive documents and tape recordings.[38] These documents and records proved to contain a treasure trove of information and leads about Trump's personal and business dealings.

On November 29, 2018, Special Counsel Mueller's office dropped a bombshell on the White House when Michael Cohen pleaded guilty to lying to Congress about Trump's Moscow Tower project.[39] Cohen, Trump's former lawyer and fixer, clearly signaled in federal court in lower Manhattan that he was now fully cooperating with the special counsel's probe into the extent to which Russia interfered in the 2016 Presidential election and whether it had the active participation of the Trump team in those efforts.[40]

Previously, Cohen had told Congress, the press, and anyone else who asked that Trump had stopped pursuing a Trump Tower deal in Moscow well before the Iowa Caucuses in January 2016.[41] If that was the case, then the Moscow Tower project could not have been a factor in explaining Trump's "bromance" with Vladimir Putin and apparent inability to say anything critical of Russia, even when it invaded Ukraine and forcibly seized Crimea.[42]

With Cohen's November 29, 2018 plea agreement, the public learned for the first time from Cohen that Trump was still actively seeking the Kremlin's approval for the Trump Moscow project well into the 2016 Presidential primaries, and that Cohen discussed the status of the project with Trump on at least three occasions. He also briefed Trump's family members about it.[43] Cohen also admitted to agreeing to travel to Russia for meetings on the project and confirmed that the "Individual-1" described in the court documents filed in connection with Cohen's plea agreement was, in fact, Trump.[44]

The Cohen revelations in open court confirmed the growing mountain of evidence that the Mueller team has already gathered from numerous sources, including documents seized during the federal raid on Cohen's office and hotel suite.[45] This evidence strongly indicated that both Trump's business and political interests were closely tied to Russia during the entire 2015-2016 period, during which he was simultaneously seeking the approval of Putin and the Kremlin leadership of the Moscow hotel project, as well as assistance from Russia and its intelligence organizations in the 2016 Presidential election.[46]

To accomplish these two closely intertwined goals, it seems increasingly clear Trump acted through a growing circle of close personal associates (such as Michael Cohen and Roger Stone), family members (such as Don Jr. and Jared Kushner) and campaign operatives (such as Paul Manafort, Rick Gates, George Papadopoulos and Carter Page). These players were actively involved in advancing Trump's business interests with the Russian leadership while at to the same time securing Russia's support for his presidential bid.[47]

On December 12, 2018, Cohen was sentenced by a federal judge to a three-year prison term and over $1 million in fines, for a long list of crimes including having violated federal Campaign Finance laws and for having lied to a Congressional Committee about Trump's Moscow project.[48] Trump was described in the government's sentencing memo as the "Individual-1", who had conspired with Cohen to violate federal law.[49] The only reason Trump himself was not indicted was that the Justice Department guidelines barred the indictment of a sitting president.[50]

At his sentencing, Cohen made it absolutely clear that, while he accepted personal responsibility for violating the federal campaign laws and lying to Congress, he was acting on the directions of the man in the White House who is currently serving as President of the United States. Cohen's allocution in open court left no room for doubt that it was Trump who ordered the under-the-table payments. Trump's motivation was to violate the campaign laws by preventing knowledge of his extra-marital affairs from becoming publicly known, at least before Election Day. At the sentencing hearing on December 12, 2018, presiding Judge William Pauley summed up the importance of Cohen's — and by implication Trump's — violations of the campaign finance laws by stating that "our democratic institutions depend on the honesty of our citizenry in dealing with the government."[51]

On the same day that Cohen was sentenced, federal prosecutors also disclosed that they had entered into a "non-prosecution" agreement with AMI, the parent company to the National Enquirer.[52] AMI admitted that it made a $150,000 payment to Karen McDougal "in concert with" the Trump presidential campaign, in order to ensure that McDougal did not make public her damaging allegations about Trump before the 2016 presidential election.[53] This meant that federal prosecutors had a second reliable source – in addition to Cohen – that was prepared to testify that Trump personally knew of and directed these secret payments be made to avoid damaging disclosures before the November 2016 election and that Trump was personally in the room during discussions about these payments.[54] In other words, federal prosecutors had collected all of the ingredients necessary for Article I of an impeachment proceeding against Trump, or an indictment of the President.

On February 27, 2019, Michael Cohen publicly testifies before the House Committee on Oversight and Reform, portraying Trump as a con man, a cheat and a racist.[55] Cohen provided the Committee with documentary evidence supporting his testimony that Trump reimbursed him for the $130,000 he had laid out from a personal line of credit to pay $130,000 in hush money to Stormy Daniels, the porn star with whom Trump had an affair, and for which Cohen was indicted and plead guilty to federal Campaign Finance Law violations. Cohen produced a check for $35,000 dated August 1, 2017 drawn on Trump's personal bank account that bore Trump's distinctive signature. He also produced another $35,000 from Trump's trust account signed by his son, Don Jr. and Allen Weisselberg, the Trump Organizations longstanding chief financial officer. Cohen testified that he discussed these reimbursement payments from Trump, that he says involved 11 installments, with Trump during his first visit to the Oval Office after Trump had been sworn in as president. Importantly, Cohen testified that Trump directed him to lie about Trump's knowledge of the payments to Daniels.

Cohen also suggested in his testimony that Trump knew about the infamous June 9, 2016 meeting at Trump Tower between Don Jr. and other senior officials in the Trump Campaign with Russians claiming that they could provide "dirt" on Hillary Clinton. Cohen also testified that Trump told him in "code" in a way to suggest that Cohen lie to Congress about the time period during the 2016 election campaign that Trump and Cohen were still negotiating on a possible Trump Tower project in Moscow. Cohen also testified that he was in Trump's office in July 2016 during the 2016 campaign when Roger Cohen told Trump over a speakerphone that he had just spoken to Julian Assange of WikiLeaks and that additional stolen emails and other "dirt" on Hillary Clinton would be released in the next few days. Cohen testified that Stone told Trump that Assange had told him that there would be a "massive dump of emails that would damage Hillary Clinton's campaign." This testimony strongly inferred that Trump had advance knowledge of the coordination between his campaign operatives and the Russian/WikiLeaks conspirators who were hacking/stealing information and then publicly disclosing it with the dual purpose of damaging the Clinton Campaign and helping Trump get elected. [56]

Paul Manafort, Rick Gates, Konstantin Kilimnik, and Alex van der Zwaan

When Trump selected Paul Manafort to become a senior advisor and then Chairman of his Campaign, it seemed to many knowledgeable observers to be an odd choice. Although Manafort had been involved in the McCain Presidential campaign, he had spent most of his time over the past decade or two working overseas for various dictators, autocrats, and human rights violators. Manafort's dubious client list included President Marcos, who was eventually forced to flee the Philippines, and the despotic leaders of the Dominican Republic, Nigeria, Kenya, Equatorial Guinea, and Somalia. These men held onto the levers of power in their respective countries through violence, terror, the conscription of child soldiers, the sale of blood diamonds and the torture and murder of political opponents. A 1992 report from the Center for Public Integrity listed the consulting firm of "Black, Manafort, Stone, and Kelly" as one of the charter members of "The Torturers' Lobby," which included the firms that profited the most by doing business with foreign governments that violated their people's human rights.[57]

Just as he had done for numerous other despots, Manafort used all of his considerable skills in his makeover of Viktor Yanukovich, the pro-Russian President of Ukraine. Manafort molded this rough-hewn apparatchik into a cosmopolitan contemporary-looking statesman. Under Manafort's tutelage, the Yanukovich regime also ratcheted up its anti-Western European rhetoric as part of a campaign to prevent Ukraine from pursuing membership in the European Union. Yanukovich started pandering to the worst fears of the Russian-speaking minority in industrialized Eastern Ukraine, spreading totally fabricated rumors that any alliance with the EU would lead to the persecution of the Russian-speaking minorities. Also, when NATO held some naval exercises in the Mediterranean near Crimea, Yanukovich followed Manafort's advice and denounced these exercises as an infringement on Ukrainian sovereignty and as part of a European plot to force Ukraine to join the EU.

Alarmed that a U.S. citizen had become so involved in driving Ukrainian foreign policy into the arms of the Russians, American Ambassador William Taylor warned Manafort at a meeting in the U.S. Embassy in Kiev in 2006 that his work for Yanukovich and his anti-NATO rhetoric was counter to U.S. interests, and Ambassador Taylor further expressed his concerns in a State Department cable that later became public that one of Yanukovich's and Manafort's closest Ukrainian oligarchs – Dimitri Firtash – was closely associated with Russian organized crime leader Semion Mogalevich.[58] Manafort just ignored him and continued to advise the Ukrainian pro-Russian political forces to do everything in their power to keep Ukraine out of the EU and NATO. All other appeals to Manafort's patriotism by U.S. officials were equally rebuffed, and Manafort continued to be the primary Western spokesperson and apologist for Yanukovich and his pro-Russian allies in Ukraine.

In August 2016, *The New York Times* reported that a secret handwritten ledger maintained by the Yanukovich Administration, in Kiev, Ukraine, listed Manafort as the intended recipient of $12.7 million in "off the books" and undisclosed cash payments from 2007 to 2012.[59] The money was from Yanukovich's pro-Russian political party, the Party of Regions, for his work on behalf of this pro-Russian autocrat, who was deposed during a popular uprising in February 2014.[60] Government investigators in Ukraine describe the ledger as evidence of a corrupt network to loot Ukrainian assets and to influence elections during the period when Manafort was a chief adviser to Viktor Yanukovich. These secret Ukrainian ledgers also apparently contained information regarding an $18 million deal to sell Ukrainian cable TV assets to a partnership organized by Manafort and Oleg Deripaska, a Russian oligarch and a close ally of President Putin.[61]

Two days later, on August 17, 2016, *The Associated Press* reported that in 2012 Manafort and Rick Gates, Manafort's then-deputy in the Trump campaign organization, helped Yanukovich's pro-Russian governing party in Ukraine secretly route at least $2.2 million in payments to two prominent Washington lobbying firms for the purpose of influencing U.S. policy towards the Yanukovich regime.[62] Manafort and Gates apparently had helped steer money from a pro-Yanukovych nonprofit, the European Centre for a Modern Ukraine, to these two Washington lobbying firms: Podesta Group Inc. and Mercury LLC.[63]

By moving the Yanukovich party's money through this ostensibly nonprofit organization to the U.S. lobbying firms, Manafort and Gates concocted a scheme to disguise the real source of the funds, which all originated with the pro-Russian Ukraine government. Manafort and Gates wanted to structure the transaction in such a way that it would appear that a foreign government was trying to influence U.S. policy, especially since the U.S. policy and American interests at the time favored a Ukraine government that was more closely aligned with Western interests rather than those of Russia. The European Centre assisted this illegal scheme in making it seem as if the lobbying effort was not being conducted by a foreign power.[64]

After being introduced by Manafort and Gates to the lobbying firms, the European nonprofit paid the Podesta Group $1.13 million between June 2012 and April 2014 to lobby Congress, the White House National Security Council, the State Department, and other federal agencies, according to U.S. lobbying records. The nonprofit also paid $1.07 million over roughly the same period to Mercury to lobby Congress. Among other things, these lobbyists used their considerable political influence in Washington to defeat an effort to have the U.S. Congress pass a resolution condemning the pro-Russian Yanukovich government for its imprisonment of former Prime Minister Tymoshenko and other human rights violations.

Both the direct $12.7 million in cash payments to Manafort by Yanukovich's pro-Russian political party and the scheme to route $2.2 million in lobbying money from Ukraine to the Washington lobbyists violated the U.S. Foreign Agents Registration Act (FARA). FARA is a U.S. law requiring all U.S. lobbyists representing foreign leaders or their political parties to provide the U.S. Department of Justice with detailed reports regarding their actions.

In addition to his lucrative political consulting work for Yanukovich, Manafort also profited handsomely from the money laundering services that he provided to Russian and pro-Russian Ukrainian oligarchs who wanted to move some of their ill-gotten gains through U.S. and offshore bank accounts to disguise the questionable origin of the money. With a commitment of an initial $25 million from pro-Russian Ukrainian oligarch, Dimitri Firtash, Manafort formed CMZ Ventures in New York with an office located on the 20th floor of 1501 Broadway in Manhattan. In addition to Manafort (the "M" in CMZ), the two other name partners in the Company were Brad Zackson, a real estate broker with the Donald Trump organization, and Arthur Cohen, a longstanding real estate developer in the New York area. Firtash was the "silent partner" in the Company and the source of the funding. Manafort also knew (or should have known) that by teaming up with Firtash, he was also doing business with Firtash's primary backer, Seymeon Mogalevich, the godfather of Russian organized crime.

Manafort also had succeeded in establishing a close relationship with Oleg Deripaska —a Russian oligarch who was part of Putin's inner circle. Starting in about 2006, Manafort received millions of dollars from Deripaska. Manafort worked on his behalf in Washington, trying to get U.S. sanctions lifted so that Deripaska could visit the U.S. and invest some of his fortune in the U.S. Additionally, Deripaska invested millions of dollars in a Manafort-controlled company, Pericles LLC, that was supposed to invest in various real estate projects in the U.S. and the Caribbean but never did so. The money just "disappeared" according to court papers later filed by Deripaska's lawyers, and for a while, Manafort also went "missing."

In late March 2016, Manafort surfaced in a leadership role with the Trump Campaign, posing as a wealthy international political consultant with close ties to Russian money sources who was offering his services to Trump without charge.[65] Unknown at the time was that Manafort, who had a near-insatiable appetite for money, had blown through virtually all of the millions of dollars he had been collecting from the Russians and the pro-Russian Ukrainians. Manafort needed a high-profile job with Trump in the worst way so that he could show his powerful Russian friends that he could provide them access to a pro-Russian presidential candidate who would be in a position to help them if only they could pull off the political upset of the century – which surprisingly they did.

Trump hired Manafort for his close Russian connections and promise that he could hook Trump up with real power sources in Russia. Trump wanted contacts who could clear away any of the "red tape" delaying Trump's Moscow Tower project. Manafort almost immediately contacted his longtime associate in Kiev who was a known GRU (Russian military intelligence) officer – Konstantin Kilimnik [66]– to let Oleg Deripaska know that Manafort was now back on top and that he could arrange for "private briefings" on Trump to Deripaska, with no questions asked.[67] After that, Deripaska and his lawyers apparently stopped pursuing Manafort for return of the missing $17 million from the Pericles deal.

Paul Manafort was also at least one of the intermediaries between the Trump Campaign and WikiLeaks, which was closely linked to the GRU and the FSB (formerly known as the KGB). According to a report by *The Guardian* on November 27, 2018, Manafort met with Julian Assange inside the Ecuadorian embassy in London in 2013, 2015, and then again in March of 2016.[68] If accurate, this information is stunning, since it provides further proof of the links – through WikiLeaks – between the Trump Campaign and the Russian intelligence operatives who were collecting illegally hacked documents used to severely damage the Hillary Clinton Campaign.[69]

By March of 2016, Russian intelligence operatives already had established close ties with Wikileaks and Assange. With the acquisition of a treasure trove of documents from the hacked emails from the Clinton Campaign and the Democratic Congressional Campaign Committee in late March and early April 2016, U.S. intelligence agencies were able to confirm that Wikileaks had essentially become an arm of Russian intelligence.[70] Assange himself publicly confirmed on June 12, 2016, during a BBC interview that he had damning emails relating to Clinton.[71]

Manafort successfully navigated the Trump Campaign through the Republican National Convention into the general election, but then a series of news articles started appearing in mid-August 2016, disclosing further details regarding the extent of Manafort's ties with the pro-Russian Yanukovich Administration and the millions that he had allegedly received in "off-the-books" cash payment. Manafort's role in the Trump campaign was quickly downgraded, and then he was finally cut loose entirely from the campaign on August 9, 2016.[72] His faithful deputy, Rick Gates, stayed on, who continued to maintain the close working relationship between the Trump campaign and the pro-Putin forces in Russia and Ukraine, primarily through Kilimnik, their GRU-affiliated associate.

Even though Manafort did not continue to hold any official position in the Trump Campaign, he continued to stay in touch with Trump directly, as well as indirectly through his longtime deputy, Rick Gates, who continued to work on the Trump Campaign and the Transition Team. After all, Trump and Manafort had much in common. They were both enamored with money and with all things Russian, especially since Russian money had provided both of them with the lifestyle to which they had become accustomed, and which they could never really give up.[73]

As soon as the Special Counsel's office was established in May 2017, it took over the ongoing federal investigation of Manafort and Gates, which had been going on for several years and was being handled primarily by the FBI and the U.S. Attorney's Office for the Southern District of New York (SDNY). A part of the federal investigation of Manafort and Gates was based on the money-laundering activities of Manafort and Gates that was contained in a civil RICO suit that was pending in the U.S. District Court for the Southern District of New York (SDNY) that had been brought on behalf of Yulia Tymoshenko and others by my law firm, McCallion & Associates LLP.[74] SDNY prosecutors – and later the Special Counsel's office – followed up on leads provided by the civil RICO case by issuing subpoenas for the records of CMZ Ventures as part of their investigation of Manafort's Russian and Ukrainian ties and his money laundering efforts involving the U.S.[75]

Of particular interest to SDNY prosecutors and FBI agents working with them were documents that my office filed on April 4, 2014 in connection with the civil RICO case showing the depth of Manafort's relationship with Putin and his entire inner circle, particularly Oleg Deripaska, the Russian oligarch who is perhaps the closest of the Kremlin inner-circle to Putin. It was later disclosed that Manafort received millions of dollars each year, and court documents relating to Manafort's indictment revealed that Manafort had a $10 million loan from Deripaska in 2010.[76]

One of the documents left behind in Kiev when Yankovich and his cronies fled in late February 2014 was a Russian translation of an email/ memo dated August 24, 2012, from Gregory B. Craig to Paul Manafort. Craig was a partner at the Skadden Arps law firm, which was working at that time on an allegedly "independent" investigation and report regarding the Tymoshenko criminal prosecutions.[77] The clear inference of the document that was recovered, as well as that of the continuing investigation, was that Manafort orchestrated and "coordinated" the Skadden law firm's "independent" investigation with the Ukrainian government. The intention was that Yanukovich and his racketeering co-conspirators could be kept fully informed of what the Skadden "team" members were looking at, what they were looking for, and where their "investigation" was headed.

For example, an early draft of Skadden's report that had been annotated by Ukrainian government officials, who appeared to be pushing the Americans for a more sympathetic interpretation of the case.[78] Unsurprisingly, the final draft of the Skadden Report that was released to the press, after apparently beening heavily edited by Manafort and his pro-Russian clients in Kiev, concluded that the Tymoshenko prosecution by the Ukraine government – although slightly flawed – was not politically motivated.[79]

One of the principal attorneys at the Skadden law firm that worked on this effort to basically exculpate the Ukraine government for its prosecution and political "show trial" of Tymoshenko was Alex van der Zwaan, a Dutch attorney who was fluent in Russian and whose father-in-law was reported to have considerable influence in the Russian government.

Of particular interest to federal investigators was that the Skadden "investigation" and report was that the Ukraine government, with the complicity of van der Zwaan, Manafort and Gates, were grossly understating the amount of money that they were receiving from the Ukraine government for their work. The Ukraine Ministry of Justice was representing that the entire contract price relating to the hiring of the Skadden Firm was less than $12,000 USD, which meant that the law firm contract did not have to be let out for public bid. This contract amount was absurdly low, since our own estimates were that the Skadden firm's legal bills would have easily run into the millions of dollars. We shared our suspicions and all of the information that we had with the FBI and federal prosecutors, including information regarding Manafort's questionable activities in Russia and Ukraine, and offshore money laundering activities. Then we waited to see what the federal investigation would turn up.

As we later learned through the criminal information and plea agreement of van der Zwaan on February 20, 2018, the FBI interviewed him in London on November 3, 2017 about these matters, and his response was to basically "stonewall" them. He falsely told the agents that his last communication with Rick Gates had been in mid-August 2016, that it consisted of only an innocuous text message, and that his last communication with "Person A" – who is described as a Russian individual who had been affiliated with the Russian military intelligence agency known as the GRU – was in 2014. This "Person A" is reliably believed to be Konstantin V. Kilimnik, the longtime associate of Manafort and Gates who was also a Russian intelligence agent with the GRU.[80]

In truth and in fact, however, van der Zwaan well knew, according to the criminal information, that he had spoken to both Gates and Kilimnik in September 2016, when Gates first contacted him and told van der

Zwaan to call Kilimnik to discuss a criminal indictment that they believed the Ukrainian government was about to file against Manafort and others.[81]

As the Special Counsel's sentencing memo later disclosed, van der Zwaan had recorded his conversation with Kilimnik but did not think that the FBI had a copy of the recording at the time he was interviewed by the FBI.[82] Just as Michael Flynn had broken the cardinal rule #1 when speaking with the FBI about conversations you may have had with a Russian official or agent, van der Zwaan should have also assumed that his conversations with Kilimnik, a suspected Russian agent, were intercepted by the FBI or one of the U.S. intelligence agencies tasked with keeping tabs on the Russians.

The government memo states:

> In van der Zwaan's recorded conversation with Person A [Kilimnik], in Russian, Person A suggested that 'there were additional payments,' that '[t]he official contract was only a part of the iceberg,' and that the story may become a blow for 'you and me personally.'[83]

When government prosecutors served van der Zwaan with a grand jury subpoena seeking this tape recording and any other physical evidence and documents pertaining to the investigation, van der Zwaan failed to do so. The government, of course, had a copy of the recorded conversation obtained "by other means." Van der Zwaan was also charged in the criminal information with having knowingly withheld and destroyed other salient documents, including an email from "Person A" on September 12, 2016, in which van der Zwaan was asked to "exchange a few words via WhatsApp or Telegram." The government's sentencing memo further noted that "van der Zwaan is a person of ample financial means—both personally and through his father-in-law, a prominent Russian oligarch, who has paid substantial sums to the defendant and his wife."[84]

The government's description of van der Zwaan as "a person of ample financial means" does not do justice to the privileged background and incredible wealth that this young man had. He graduated with a law degree from the prestigious King's College London; he spoke four languages fluently – Russian, Dutch, English, and French. Van der Zwaan's wedding at a lavish English countryside estate was featured in the Russian edition of Tatler magazine.[85]

One particularly intriguing fact set forth in the Special Counsel's March 27, 2018 sentencing memo relating to van der Zwaan is that it goes out of its way to make mention of van der Zwaan's father-in-law, German Khan, a billionaire businessman born in Ukraine who owns Alfa Group, one of Russia's largest financial and industrial investment companies.[86] The Alfa Group is prominently featured in the Steele Dossier as one of the companies that facilitated the communications between the Russians and the Trump Team.[87] Steele's memo, which is sometimes referred to as "Company Intelligence Report" or CIR 112, is entitled: 'RUSSIA/ US PRESIDENTIAL ELECTION: KREMIN-ALPHA [sic] GROUP CO-OPERATION.' This memo strongly suggests that Alfa and its executives – which would include German Khan – 'cooperated' in an alleged Kremlin-orchestrated campaign to interfere in the 2016 U.S. Presidential election." It further alleges a close relationship between Alpha Group and Putin, including that '[s]ignificant favors, continue to be done in both directions' and that [Khan's two partners in Alfa] 'FRIDMAN and AVEN [are] still giving informal advice to PUTIN, especially on the US.'"[88] On April 3, 2018, Alex van der Zwaan was sentence to a prison term of 30 days a $20,000 fine.[89]

In the early morning hours of July 25, 2017, FBI and other federal agents executed a search warrant at Manafort's private residence in Northern Virginia.[90] They carted off Manafort's personal computer, various documents believed to be tax records and foreign banking records, and took photographs of his vast wardrobe, which were later used to support the government claims that Manafort had used the millions in illegally laundered funds he obtained from Russian oligarchs and the Ukraine government to lead a lavish lifestyle here in the U.S. If this was Mueller's way of getting Manafort's attention and to impress upon him the seriousness of the federal investigation and potential charges against him, this search should have done the trick.

On October 29-30 2017, government prosecutors filed a 12-count grand jury indictment in the District of Columbia (Washington, D.C.) against Paul Manafort and Trump's ex-Deputy Campaign Chairman, Richard W. (Rick) Gates III, charging them with a wide variety of federal crimes, including conspiracy to launder money, conspiracy against the United States, acting as unregistered agents of a foreign principal, false and misleading FARA statements and other charges.[91] Specifically, the indictment charged them with having hidden tens of millions of dollars that they received from former Ukrainian President Viktor Yanukovich and his pro-Russian Party of Regions and Opposition Bloc during the period from 2006 to 2015, which included the time period starting in March 2014 when Yanukovich fled Ukraine after a popular uprising, landing in Moscow under Putin's protection. The indictment further charged them with having funneled millions of dollars into the U.S. through various offshore bank accounts, without payment of U.S. taxes, and that they used those monies to maintain lavish lifestyles in the United States. They also used this money to conduct lobbying efforts in Washington for Yanukovich, his political party and the Government of Ukraine without registering and providing disclosures as foreign agents under the Foreign Agent Registration Act (FARA).

The indictment also alleged that Manafort and Gates "lobbied multiple members of Congress and their staffs about Ukraine sanctions, the validity of Ukraine elections, and the propriety of Yanukovych's imprisoning his presidential rival, Yulia Tymoshenko (who had served as Ukraine president before Yanukovych)." Although substantially accurate, this portion of the indictment triggered a Russian-orchestrated campaign to discredit the indictment and the entire Mueller investigation, based on the relatively minor factual error that Tymoshenko, who had served twice as Ukraine's prime minister, had never served as that country's president before being jailed in 2011 on trumped-up and politically-motivated embezzlement charges.[92] On October 31, 2017, shortly after the Manafort and Gates indictment was publicly released, Russia's foreign ministry cited this factual error in the indictment as proof the allegations are "cooked up" and not part of a "serious investigation."[93]

On February 22, 2018, a federal grand jury in Alexandria, Virginia filed a new set of charges against Manafort and Gates, charging them with 32 counts of tax, financial, and bank fraud charges.[94] Buried among the many other charges was the allegation that the chief executive of a Chicago bank. CEO Steve Calk of Federal Savings Bank, "expedited" approval of $16 million in loans for Paul Manafort. The allegation was that the loan was approved after Manafort discussed with Calk a possible role for the executive in the Trump Campaign and administration.[95]

This second indictment of Manafort and Gates proved to be too much for Gates to bear. The heat being placed on him by the Special Counsel's office had become far too intense, and the financial strain placed on him as a result of the legal fees he was forced to incur was rapidly depleting his family's resources. On February 23, 2018, Rick Gates pleaded guilty to one count of conspiracy against the United States and one count of making false statements to the FBI.[96] In exchange for an agreement to plead guilty and to cooperate with federal prosecutors, the government dropped the other charges relating to money laundering, acting as an unregistered foreign agent, and making other false statements.[97] On November 14, 2018, Special Counsel Mueller's office pushed back the sentencing of Gates, representing in federal court that Gates was still cooperating on "several ongoing investigations."[98]

On June 8, 2018, the grand jury returned a superseding indictment charging Manafort and his longtime associate and Russian GRU intelligence agent Konstantin Kilimnik with obstruction of justice and conspiracy to obstruct justice for their alleged efforts to contact and influence potential witnesses.[99]

On August 21, 2018, a federal jury in Alexandria, Virginia found Manafort guilty of 8 of 18 counts of financial fraud.[100] He continued to face the additional charges pending in federal court in Washington, D.C., as well as the counts in the Virginia federal case where the jury was unable to reach a verdict.

A few weeks later, on September 14, 2018, Manafort entered into a plea agreement whereby he agreed to plead guilty to two of the many counts in the indictment charging him with having engaged in a conspiracy involving money laundering, tax fraud, failing to report foreign bank accounts, violating rules requiring registration of foreign agents, lying and witness tampering.[101] Manafort also agreed to forfeit to the government his $7.3 million mansion in the Hamptons and his $3 million Trump Tower condo[102] and to fully cooperate with the Special Counsel's ongoing investigation.

In connection with Manafort's guilty plea, the government released substantial new evidence of a 2012 dirty-tricks campaign that Manafort had orchestrated to smear the former Ukrainian prime minister Yulia Tymoshenko and to label her as an anti-Semite.[103] At that time, Tymoshenko was still in a Ukrainian prison, and then Secretary of State Clinton was one of the leading international voices calling for her release.[104] Manafort and Gates were actively working for then-Ukraine President Yanukovich, whose Party of Regions was facing off against the opposition party led by Tymoshenko in the 2012 Ukrainian elections.

According to the documents released by the Special Counsel's office, Manafort bragged that he could "plant some stink" on her.[105] Manafort "orchestrated a scheme to have, as he wrote in a contemporaneous communication, '[O]bama jews' put pressure on the Administration to disavow Tymoshenko and support Yanukovych," prosecutors wrote. Specifically, the government memo explained that Manafort "sought to undermine United States support for Tymoshenko by spreading stories in the United States that a senior Cabinet official …[Hillary Clinton] was supporting anti-Semitism because the official supported Tymoshenko, who in turn had formed a political alliance with a Ukraine party that espoused anti-Semitic views." His 2012 plan was an effort to "tarnish Tymoshenko in the United States" and pressure the Obama administration to distance itself from her. However, the plan did not work, since Tymoshenko's party did well in the 2012 elections, and there are reports that she is planning a presidential run next year. Also, the Obama administration continued to criticize Yanukovych and to call Tymoshenko's prosecution unfair.

On Monday, November 26, 2018, the Special Counsel's office filed a report with the U.S. District Court in Washington, D.C., stating that Manafort had lied to federal investigators and violated his plea agreement.[106] The prosecutors concluded in this report that, based upon Manafort's breach of the plea agreement, the Special Counsel's office was no longer bound to recommend a reduced sentence for him based upon his cooperation and "acceptance of responsibility." Shortly after, it was reported that Manafort had been secretly communicating with the White House during the period that he was supposedly cooperating with the government investigation, and was thereby passing on valuable information about the nature and direction of the investigation into collusion between the Trump Team and the Russians.[107]

This was not the first time that Manafort had been accused of breaching his plea agreement and committing additional crimes. In June 2018, Manafort was charged by the prosecutors of witness tampering, which led to the decision by U.S. District Court Judge Amy Berman Jackson to revoke Manafort's 10 million bond and send him back to jail.[108]

On March 7, 2019, Judge T.S. Ellis of the federal district court in Alexandria, Virginia stunned most observers in the courtroom by imposing a mere 47- month sentence on Manafort. This amounted to little more than a slap on the wrist, considering the fact that Manafort was clearly the highest profile and unrepentant white-collar criminals to be sentenced in federal court in recent history.

Manafort had been facing up to 25 years in prison for the banking fraud charges for which he had been convicted by a jury in the summer of 2018. Federal prosecutors had argued that Manafort deserved a prison sentence of between 19 and 25 years, plus millions of dollars in fines and restitution for the crimes.

Judge Ellis's light sentence was particularly disturbing, given the fact that Manafort showed little or no remorse, and even lied under oath following a plea deal after the trial, which deal the federal prosecutors were permitted to cancel. Also surprising was Judge Ellis' comments that he thought the government's sentencing recommendation was "excessive," even though it was well within established federal sentencing guidelines that are applied uniformly throughout the country. Judge Ellis also added that he believed Manafort "lived an otherwise blameless life," which reflected a complete lack of understanding of Manafort's longstanding caree as a political consultant and operative for the most autocratic and brutal dictators throughout the globe over the past couple of decades.

Judge Ellis's sentencing remarks regarding Manafort also failed to show any appreciation for the fact that the Special Counsel's intense interest in Manafort was triggered for the same reasons that President Trump chose him to be his Campaign Chairman during the 2016 presidential campaign, which was that Manafort had a direct pipeline to the Kremlin and was able to deliver substantial Russian help in an a surprising electoral coup that landed Trump in the White House.

Although it is painfully clear Manafort never came completely clean with the Special Counsel's office as to his deep and longstanding ties with Russian intelligence, Manafort was also able, during 2016, to deliver to the Trump Campaign a direct liaison to Russian intelligence. Konstantin Kilimnik, a Russian GRU intelligence, was Manafort's right-hand man in Moscow and in Kyiv, Ukraine, where they both worked for a number of years under the auspices of the pro-Russian President, Viktor Yanukovich. In retrospect, it now appears clear that Kilimnik was actually Manafort's Russian "handler," who was assigned by Moscow to maximize Manafort's potential as a Russian asset both in Ukraine and in the U.S. Until Yanukovich was ousted as Ukraine President in February 2014 in a popular uprising and fled to Moscow, Manafort, Rick Gates and Kilimnik had helped Yanukovich chart a pro-Russian and anti-U.S. policy for Ukraine, for which Manafort was paid tens of millions of dollars, including the 12.7 million that was paid "off-the-books" and reflected on the "black ledger" found among the documents left behind when Yanokovich and his cronies fled Ukraine and sought sanctuary in Russia.

Trump also must have known when he hired Manafort that Manafort had a very cozy relationship with Oleg Deripaska, a prominent Russian oligarch and member of Putin's inner circle. Manafort had received millions from Deripaska over the years for trying to get U.S. sanctions lifted against Deripaska, and when Manafort rose to the head of the Trump Campaign, one of Manafort's first emails was to his Russian operative, Kilimnik, discussing how then could be "made whole" by monetizing Manafort's new-won access to Candidate Trump and offering "private briefings" to Deripaska on the Trump Campaign's efforts to implement a pro-Russian agenda, which they accomplished by watering down the Ukraine plank at the Republican National Convention by eliminating any promise to provide Ukraine with the defensive missile systems that beleaguered Ukraine needed to prevent further Russian encroachments and annexation of territory, as Russia had already done in Crimea.

Manafort also attended the now infamous June 9, 2016 Trump Tower meeting arranged between Don Jr. and Russian operatives who had promised to give the Trump Campaign incriminating political "dirt" on Hillary Clinton that could then be Trump operatives to bludgeon the Democratic candidate for the remainder of the presidential election cycle. Indeed, as Trump's primary liaison with his Russian allies, Manafort's presence at such a high-level meeting with the Russians was a virtual requirement by both Team Trump and Team Russia since Manafort and Kilimnik were in charge of all liaison and coordination between these two working partners who were working towards the same ultimate goal, which was to manage through all means necessary to pull off the intelligence and political coup of the century, which was to have Trump — essentially a Russian asset and operative -- capture and occupy the White House. This would be an achievement beyond anything ever before imagined by Putin, even in his most vodka-induced fantasies, and Manafort and Kilimnik were the linchpins in this successful campaign. We now even know that Manafort, Gates and Kilimnik met at the Grand Havana Room at the top of Jared Kushner's building on Fifth Avenue in Manhattan on August 2, 2016 to cinch the Trump/Russian alliance by passing on U.S. polling data to Kilimnik, which could only have been used by the Russians to facilitate the targeting of their disinformation campaign in U.S. social media, so that key precincts in key battleground states were targeted for the dissemination of anti-Clinton and pro-Trump messaging. As Andrew Weissmann, one of the Special Counsel prosecutors told Judge Amy Berman Jackson in a recent hearing, this Grand Havana Room meeting went "very much to the heart of what the Special Counsel's Office is investigating," namely the relationship between Russian intelligence and the Trump Campaign.

On March 13, 2019, Manafort was sentenced to 43 additional months in prison by Judge Jackson in a Washington, D.C. federal courthouse, which brought Manafort's total sentence on both sets of federal charges up to 7.5 years.

Judge Jackson made it perfectly clear today at Manafort's sentencing hearing that she was disgusted with Manafort's deceptive behavior and his failure to accept genuine responsibility for his crimes. She noted that it is "hard to overstate the number of lies, the amount of fraud and the extraordinary amount of money involved." She also suggested that he was undermining American values and interests, by acting as an unregistered foreign agent.

Although Judge Jackson did not directly criticize Judge Ellis for his light sentence of Manafort and puzzling remark that he believed Manafort "lived an otherwise, blameless life" she specifically blasted Manafort for his questionable lobbying career, saying it "infects our policymaking."

Jared Kushner

It is now known that Jared Kushner and Michael Flynn met with Russian Ambassador Kislyak at Trump Tower on December 1 or 2, 2016, shortly after the 2016 elections. Apparently, neither Kushner nor Flynn disclosed the meeting on their security clearance forms.[109] Not only was the meeting undisclosed, but the reason for it was highly unorthodox. According to an intercepted communication between the Ambassador and the Kremlin, Kushner had requested that the Russians give him access to a backchannel communications facility at the Russian embassy.[110] His apparent intent was that he wanted to communicate directly with Moscow, free from the prying eyes and ears of the FBI and U.S. intelligence agencies.

Kushner's request for a "back channel" line of communications with the Russians during the transition period, when he, Flynn and Trump himself were still technically private citizens, was extraordinary and unprecedented in and of itself. But then again, Kushner had so many titles and responsibilities heaped on him in only a few short weeks since the election, he was starting to be referred to in the press as "Secretary of Everything."[111] Whether it be peace in the Middle East to technology to the opiate addiction epidemic, Jared was Trump's "go to" man, so why wasn't it plausible that Trump would also want to circumvent the existing intelligence and diplomatic structures and ask Jared (with some help from Flynn) to be in charge of communications with the Russians?

Kushner had another undisclosed meeting during the Transition period with Sergey Gorkov, a KGB graduate and head of Vnesheconombank (VEB), the Russian state-owned bank that has been subject to U.S. sanctions.[112] This bank has also been linked to Russian spy operations in the U.S.[113]

While Kushner's apparent level of trust in the Russians demonstrated by his meeting with Kislyak and Gorkov may be surprising, it was not wholly unexpected. Kushner has strong business relationships with Russian individuals and companies tied to Russia and Vladimir Putin. In some cases, these relationships have been in place for many years.

In May 2015, Kushner's real estate company paid $295 million for the majority share in the former New York Times Building on West 43rd Street in Manhattan as part of a deal with Lev Leviev, the Uzbek-Israeli "King of Diamonds" with close ties to Vladimir Putin.[114] Leviev was the chairman of Africa Israel Investments Ltd., which has a Russian subsidiary, AFI Development PLC, a public company traded on the London Stock Exchange which is one of the largest real estate development companies in Russia.[115] Leviev is also chairman of the Federation of the Jewish Communities of the CIS (former Soviet republics), and is closely associated with Rabbi Berel Lazar, the Chief Rabbi of Moscow who is often referred to in the Jewish press as "Putin's rabbi."[116]

In November 2014, Kushner and his brother Joshua also formed a real estate investment company – Cadre – which attracted substantial venture capital from Russian high-tech billionaire Yuri Milner.[117] As founder of the investment firms, Digital Sky Technologies (now called Mail.Ru Group) and DST Global, Milner's net worth went from zero to $12 billion in two years as a result of his investments in Facebook and other social media platforms.[118] Milner also owned the largest internet providers in Russia and elsewhere in eastern and central Europe. Russian and Chinese investors who invested in Cadre and other Kushner companies were rewarded with U.S. visas as part of the EB-5 program. The program gives investors putting at least $500,000 into American companies a two-year visa and a pathway to U.S. citizenship.

Kushner and his wife, Ivanka, were also close friends with Russian billionaire and Putin crony Roman Abramovich and his wife, Dasha Zhukova. Ivanka invited her close friend Dasha to the Trump Inauguration in January 2017, [119] and they have been frequently spotted together at the U.S. Open tennis tournament and other events.[120]

Abramovich, who is perhaps best known as the owner of the legendary Chelsea Football Club in London, was reported by BBC to have given a $35 million yacht to Putin as a "gift." [121] He also has a one-third interest in Evraz PLC,[122] one of the world's largest steel manufacturing companies.[123] Through one of its Canadian subsidiaries, Evraz supplied about 40% of the steel used for the construction of the controversial Keystone XL pipeline in North Dakota.[124] One of Trump's first actions in office was to sign an executive order expediting the approval of the Keystone pipeline. Construction of the pipeline had been halted by the Obama Administration in November 2015 based on environmental and other concerns. One of Trump's campaign promises was to reverse this Obama order and to finish construction of the pipeline. Owned by TransCanada, the pipeline is intended to move Canadian tar sands oil southward through the Dakotas to Illinois, Oklahoma, and Texas. On January 24, 2017, Trump also signed another executive order requiring that the steel for all U.S. pipelines had to be made in the U.S. to the "maximum extent possible."[125] Two days later, TransCanada filed a presidential permit application for the Keystone pipeline with the U.S. Department of State, which was granted.[126]

Ironically, much of the steel to be used for the Keystone pipeline had already been manufactured outside the U.S. by Abramovich's company Evraz and was sitting in a field in North Dakota waiting to be used once Trump "green-lighted" the project.[127] Evraz had lobbied heavily against provisions that would have mandated that all of the Keystone steel be made in the U.S., and they got their wish when Trump's executive order contained enough "wiggle room" to ensure that all of Evraz's foreign-manufactured steel was used on the pipeline. Just to be doubly sure, Trump spokesperson Sarah Huckabee Sanders announced on March 3, 2017 that Trump's executive order requiring that U.S. steel be used on U.S. pipelines only applied to new pipelines, not those already under construction.[128] This "clarification" meant that the Keystone pipeline was exempted entirely from the executive order.

In March 2017, Jared and Ivanka took a ski vacation to Aspen, Colorado.[129] There was some grumbling emanating from the White House to the effect that Kushner, as one of Trump's senior advisors, should not have been off skiing in Aspen while Trump's health care agenda was going up in flames in Congress.[130] As it turned out, however, Kushner's trip to Aspen was not wholly unrelated to business. Abramovich and his wife Dasha just happen to own a chalet in Aspen, and the two couples just happened to arrive in Aspen on the same day (March 18th).[131] Although there were no photographs of the two families together in Aspen, it is reasonable to assume that — given the closeness of the relationship between the two couples — Jared and Roman found some quality time together to close the Keystone pipeline steel deal and cover other business matters of mutual interest.

Thus Kushner, like his father-in-law, has a longstanding history and close affinity for Russian oligarchs who operate within Putin's inner circle. At the same time, Kushner has had a longstanding suspicion (if not outright hostility) to federal law enforcement agencies and the media who, in his view, hounded his father out of the family business and into prison.[132] It must have seemed perfectly natural, therefore, for Kushner to want to communicate directly with the Russians, out of sight from the media and unfettered by federal law enforcement/intelligence agency "interference."

Ever since Jared Kushner bought 666 Fifth Avenue in December 2006 on his 27th birthday, it has been an albatross hanging around his neck. Kushner overpaid for the property at the height of the real estate bubble, just before it burst, paying $1.8 billion, or $1200 per square foot for this 41-floor tower. At that time equivalent properties in Manhattan, such as the Met Life Building on Park Avenue, were going for 50% less, or $600 per square foot.[133] Jared had bought himself a white elephant, and it was slowly bleeding him dry.

During the 2016 Presidential campaign, Jared actively wooed China's Anbang Insurance Group, but the deal fell apart.[134] He became increasingly desperate to find a lender, but there are just not that many banks out there willing to lend $4 billion on a troubled building, even in the center of Manhattan. What could be done? Then Donald Trump was elected as President, and Jared had his opening. If the Chinese were unwilling to do the deal, then maybe the Russians would be willing to bail him out. After all, weren't they desperate enough to have the crippling U.S. sanctions lifted in return for a mere $4 billion investment in a Manhattan building?

On December 1, 2016, Michael Flynn and Jared Kushner had their now infamous meeting with Russian Ambassador Kislyak at Trump Tower, and neither one of them reported the meeting on their security clearance forms.[135] Moreover, since none of the surveillance cameras or reporters who were camped out at Trump Tower during the transition period have any record of Kislyak's arrival or departure, he must have been smuggled in through a service elevator that was not under surveillance. Clearly, such subterfuge was done so for a reason, and as a federal prosecutor could (and probably will) argue, people who are trying to hide something usually have something to hide.

We now know from reports of intercepts of Kislyak's conversations with the Kremlin that Kushner and Flynn were asking the Russians to open up a back-channel communications line to Moscow.[136] They requested that the channel be in the Russian embassy or consulate, an extraordinary request no matter what the intended subject matter of the conversations. We do not know what the conversations were to be about, but it is unlikely that they were willing to go through all this "cloak and dagger" subterfuge just to talk about the weather.

Whatever their intentions, Kislyak appears to have referred Kushner to Sergei Gorkov, the Chairman of Vnesheconombank ("VEB"), a major Russian state-owned bank, who also met with Kushner at Trump Towers on December 13, 2016, during the transition period.[137] However, according to Gorkov, the meeting with Kushner was in Kushner's capacity as the head of Kushner Companies, not as a member of the Trump transition team.[138] In other words, the meeting was about business, not transition matters or affairs of state. Gorkov has added that the trip was part of a global strategy to meet with business and financial leaders in Europe, the U.S., and Asia, but neither Gorkov or the Russians have disclosed the identities of any other "business or financial leaders" that Gorkov met with during this time frame.

So what did Kushner and the Russian banker discuss on December 13, 2016? Well, it is reasonable to assume that they discussed the real estate business and banking. After all, *The Wall Street Journal* had already uncovered that VEB had provided financing for the purchase of a Ukrainian steel mill from a part owner who was simultaneously developing the Trump International Hotel and Tower in Toronto.[139] So, Kushner and Trump well knew that VEB was willing to do business with Trump associates and partners. Trump and Kushner also knew that the bank was generally understood to be "Putin's private slush fund."[140] It must have seemed perfectly logical for Kushner to make a financing pitch to this Russian banker, especially since Kushner (through Trump) held most of the cards regarding the lifting of sanctions.

As of the time of the Kushner-Gorkov meeting, both of them were well aware that VEB, like most major Russian financial institutions and businesses, was under severe U.S. sanctions. They knew, therefore, that it was unlikely – and indeed impossible – that any fruitful discussion could have taken place between the two of them about a Russian banking investment in 666 Fifth Avenue or any other Kushner properties could have taken place without some discussion as to how the incoming Trump Administration could lift the U.S. sanctions on the bank. Trump's consistent position on Russian sanctions ranged from lukewarm to hostile, so the issue of lifting such sanctions would have been a perfectly natural subject matter to discuss with Gorkov (and with Kislyak earlier in the month) except for the fact that Kushner in December 2016 was still a private citizen, and any discussions with representatives of a hostile foreign power – especially discussions which ran directly contrary to the existing Obama Administration's policy favoring increased sanctions against Russia for its annexation of Crimea and interference with the 2016 U.S. elections – violated the criminal provisions of the Logan and Espionage Acts and arguably constituted treason.

With so many questionable and sketchy contacts and relationships with Russians with significant Kremlin connections, as well as with Chinese and other foreign nationals, many knowledgeable commentators and former government officials, including myself, who had to undergo intense scrutiny in order to get their security clearances, began wondering out loud as to how Kushner could possibly have obtained a level of security clearance sufficient to serve as senior advisor to the President of the United States. As it turned out, those of us who were now outside of government and looking in were not the only ones who were concerned.

On January 24, 2019, NBC News reported that Trump senior advisor and son-in-law was rejected for a security clearance by two White House security specialists after his FBI background check raised concerns, but their supervisor overruled them and approved Kushner's top secret clearance.[141] Kushner application for the top secret security clearance was initially denied because of several red flags that were raised by the FBI background check regarding potential foreign influence, including his family's business activities, his foreign contacts, his foreign travel and meetings he had with Russians and other foreign representatives during the campaign.[142] The FBI supervisor who overruled the decision and approved the clearance was identified as Carl Kline, who apparently had done the same thing with regard to at least 30 other cases in the Trump White House and Administration.[143] The CIA, however, apparently balked at providing Kushner with an even higher clearance known as "sensitive compartment information" (SCI), and CIA officers reviewing Kushner's background information were reported to have wondered how Kushner could have received a top secret clearance in the first place.[144]

Representative Elijah Cummings, Chairman of the House Committee on Oversight and Reform, launched an investigation into the White House's security clearance process, citing "grave breaches of national security at the highest levels of the Trump Administration."[145]

We will have to see how the Mueller Investigation plays out, but a good working hypothesis is that Kushner and Gorkov were laying the groundwork for a $4 billion-plus investment by the Russians in one or more of the Kushner Company buildings or projects. The investment would represent about 7% of the $59 billion in assets that VEB had on hand, a substantial amount, but a small price to pay for the lifting of economic and financial sanctions that were slowly choking the Russian economy. Putin's favorite bank (VEB) had mostly wasted the $50 billion-plus that was sunk into the Sochi Winter Olympics, which was generally reported to be riddled with waste and corruption,[146] so the payment of a mere $4 billion to make the sanctions problem go away must have looked extremely attractive to the Kremlin.

In short, Jared Kushner was not only a trusted son-in-law to Trump, he also had a direct pipeline of contacts with powerful Russian oligarchs and bankers, and was well-positioned to help Trump in his quest for lucrative business deals with the Russians.

George Papadopoulos

Shortly after George Papadopoulos joined Donald Trump's Presidential campaign as a foreign policy advisor in early March 2016, he was approached by Joseph Mifsud, a London-based professor originally from Malta, who had substantial connections with Russian intelligence.[147] Mifsud told him that during a recent trip to Russia, he had learned that the

Russians were in possession of thousands of stolen emails that were politically damaging to Hillary Clinton. This disclosure was significant since it occurred before there was public knowledge that the DNC computers and John Podesta's emails had been hacked, both of which U.S. intelligence agencies believed were carried out by Russia intelligence operatives.

Papadopoulos met with Mifsud on March 14, 2016, in Rome, and March 24 and April 26 in London.[148] At the March 24 meeting, Mifsud brought along Olga Polonskaya, a 30-year-old Russian woman from St. Petersburg.[149] Papadopoulos later received an email from Mifsud indicating that Polonskaya was trying to contact him. On April 10th and 11th, Papadopoulos reached out to Polonskaya asking about a meeting with Russian Ambassador Kislyak, and Polonskaya responded that she had "already alerted my personal links to our conversation and your request...as mentioned we are all very excited by the possibility of a good relationship with Mr. Trump. The Russian Federation would love to welcome him once his candidature would be officially announced."[150] Papadopoulos immediately sent emails concerning a possible meeting between Trump and Putin to at least seven campaign officials and, after being told that Russia had "dirt" on Hillary Clinton it wanted to share with the Trump, the national campaign's co-chair Sam Clovis encouraged Papadopoulos to fly to Russia to meet with agents of the Russian Foreign Ministry.[151]

In May 2016, Papadopoulos revealed Russia's possession of Clinton-related emails at a chance "romantic encounter" with a woman who knew the top Australian diplomat to the United Kingdom, Alexander Downer.[152] Papadopoulos later passed on the tip directly to Downer, and over numerous glasses of wine, Papadopoulos confirmed to Downer the existence of these emails with "Clinton dirt" in them. After DNC emails stolen by Russia were published by Russian-intermediary Wikileaks, Australian officials relayed Papadopoulos' statements to their U.S. counterparts on July 22, 2016. The revelation of Papadopoulos' inside information about Russia's stolen DNC emails then became a driving factor in the FBI July 2016 opening an investigation into the Russian interference in the 2016 United States elections.

After flying back from Europe, Papadopoulos was arrested at Washington Dulles Airport on July 27, 2017, and agreed to cooperate with Special Counsel Mueller's investigation.[153] On October 5, 2017, Papadopoulos pleaded guilty in the U.S. District Court for the District of Columbia to making false statements to FBI agents relating to contacts he had with agents of the Russian government while working for the Trump campaign.[154] Papadopoulos's arrest and guilty plea became public on October 30, 2017, when court documents showing the guilty plea were unsealed, and on September 7, 2018, he was sentenced to 14 days in jail.[155]

Carter Page

In addition to Flynn, Cohen, Manafort, Gates, Kushner, and Papadopoulos, the Russia-friendly Trump Team had another senior adviser who was an enthusiastic and unabashed booster of Russian President Vladimir Putin's policies. This was Carter Page. As reported by *The Washington Post,* Page's praise for Putin and Trump at a June 2016 gathering of Washington foreign policy experts meeting with the visiting prime minister of India stunned the assembled group.[156] Page apparently lauded Putin as stronger and more reliable than President Obama and lectured on the benefits that a Trump presidency would have on U.S.-Russian relations. The following month, Page gave a similar speech in Moscow during an address at the New Economic School commencement.[157] Page criticized the U.S. and other Western countries for "imped[ing] potential progress through their often hypocritical focus on ideas such as democratization, inequality, corruption and regime change."

Before his affiliation with the Trump campaign, Page – a graduate of the Naval Academy at Annapolis, Maryland – worked for Merrill Lynch in Moscow from 2004 to 2007 and claimed to have an investment stake in Gazprom, the Russian-owned energy giant. He also claimed to be an adviser "on critical transactions for Gazprom." In a two-hour interview with *Bloomberg News* in late March 2016, Page said he advised Gazprom on some of its most significant deals, including the acquisition of a stake in an oil and natural gas field near Russia's Sakhalin Island.[158]

Page was extremely critical of the Obama Administration's decision to add Igor Sechin, a Russian official, to its sanctions list in 2014. Page praised the Russian official, who is considered to be one of Putin's closest allies over the past 25 years.[159] Page wrote, "Sechin has done more to advance U.S.-Russian relations than any individual in or out of government from either side of the Atlantic over the past decade."[160]

It is now clear that Page was a target of Russian intelligence operatives, at least as of 2013, when he was contacted in New York by Victor Podobnyy, a Russian U.N. team member who was using his U.N. diplomatic posting as a cover for his work as a Russian intelligence officer. According to a 2015 federal indictment of Podobnyy and two other Russian intelligence officers, these Russian agents dealt with an American citizen described only as "Male-1" in the indictment, but who Page later confirmed was himself.[161] Poldobnyy painted an unflattering picture of Page in conversations that were surreptitiously recorded by the FBI, describing him as extremely gullible, flatly stating in a recorded transcript: "I think he is an idiot…He got hooked on Gazprom thinking that if they have a project, he could rise up,"[162] the Russian officer told his colleagues, according to the FBI transcript. He said he planned to "feed [Page] empty promises" and "get documents from him."[163]

Page's financial interests were apparently severely damaged by the U.S. imposed economic sanctions placed on Russia after its annexation of Crimea and incursions into eastern Ukraine, as well as for its persistently poor record in the human rights area. According to *Bloomberg News*, Page's investment firm, Global Energy Capital, which had offices in New York close to Trump Tower, failed in its attempt to raise sufficient funds to invest in oil and gas deals in Russian and neighboring Turkmenistan.[164]

Page was bitterly incensed by U.S. sanctions, which he held responsible for the inability of his company to move ahead with its business plans in that part of the world. He told *Bloomberg News*: "So many people who I know and have worked with have been so adversely affected by the sanctions policy."[165] He also acknowledged that his own personal investments had suffered. "There's a lot of excitement regarding the possibilities for creating a better situation [under President Trump]," he added.[166]

Despite his limited academic or foreign policy credentials, Page's unabashedly pro-Russian views and frequent criticism of the U.S.'s Russian sanctions, as well as his extensive contacts with Russian government officials and intelligence operatives, made him a natural candidate for a position as a foreign policy advisor to the Trump Campaign. Thus, during a meeting at *The Washington Post* in March 2016, Trump identified Page as one of his foreign policy advisers.[167]

The adverse reaction by foreign policy experts to Page's blatantly anti-U.S. comments and Trump's sharp tilt towards Russia was swift, as reported by *The Washington Post*. "It scares me," said David Kramer, who was responsible for Russia and Ukraine at the State Department during the George W. Bush administration. He called Page's comments and those by Trump on the possibility of lifting sanctions against Moscow "deeply unsettling."[168]

While working on the Trump campaign during the summer of 2016, Page was invited to speak at an event in Moscow, which he attended after getting clearance from senior campaign officials.[169] In a memo to campaign colleagues, he said that along with making a speech, he had a "private conversation" with then-Russian Deputy Prime Minister Arkady Dvorkovich. He also wrote in a July 8, 2016, email to two campaign staff members that he received "incredible insights and outreach" from senior Russian officials.[170]

Of course, Trump and his White House spokespersons later tried to downplay the role that Carter had played during the campaign. However, there can be little doubt that Page was one of a number of key points of contact between the Trump and Russian teams.

Boris Epshteyn

When it comes to Trump advisors with a direct pipeline to the Kremlin, Trump Senior Advisor Boris Epshteyn's credentials were impeccable.[171] Having been born in Russia and emigrating to this country from Moscow in 1993, Epshteyn quickly rose in the ranks of the Trump Campaign to become one of Trump's key "go-to" surrogates on cable television. Whenever the press started asking about Trump's "soft" stance on Russia with regard to its annexation of Crimea or any of the other embarrassing topics involving Russia, Epshteyn would sally forth to defend the Trump Campaign's reputation, as well as that of Russia.[172]

As an attorney and investment advisor, Epshteyn has spent much of his professional career promoting investments in Russia in general, and the city of Moscow in particular. In an October 2013 conference in New York City called "Invest in Moscow!," Epshteyn put together panels that were mainly comprised of Moscow city government officials, like Sergey Cheremin, who heads up Moscow's foreign economic and international relations department.[173]

Unlike the way that business is conducted in the U.S., foreign investments in Russian companies rarely take place without the green light and involvement of the Russian leadership, right up to the top. Kathryn Stoner, an expert in U.S.-Russian relations at Stanford University, was quoted as explaining: "In Russia, where business and the state are so closely linked, business dealings automatically imply ties to people high up in government as well."[174] In other words, Epshteyn would not have been given such access to Russian officialdom without having high-level contacts in the Kremlin.

If there was any doubt remaining that Epshteyn was the officially-designated Russian apologist in the Trump camp, such doubts were dispelled after he started speaking as Trump's surrogate on all Russia-related matters.[175] Epshteyn adopted wholesale the propaganda being disseminated by Russian news outlets about that country's annexation of Crimea, which was and under international law, still is, part of Ukraine. This illegal and forceful taking of the entire Crimean Peninsula was strongly denounced by the U.S. and its allies. Nevertheless, appearing on CNN on July 31, 2016, Epshteyn took the position that "Russia did not seize Crimea." He added: "We could talk about the conflict that happened between Ukraine and the Crimea, it's an ongoing battle, but there was no seizure by Russia. That is an incorrect statement, characterization, of what happened."[176] In other words, Epshteyn was merely parroting the Russian party line and RT talking points, which was that the poor suffering Russian-speaking people of Crimea invited unmarked Russian troops to cross the border and occupy this entire section of Ukraine.

Epshteyn's refusal to even consider the possibility that Russia could have erred attracted the intense attention of the House Intelligence Committee, which subpoenaed him to testify behind closed doors on September 28, 2017.[177]

Roger Stone

Another Trump advisor who bragged that he had an inside track to Clinton documents stolen by Russia was Roger Stone, a former consulting partner of Paul Manafort. Stone was a legendary "dirty tricks" political operative and a specialist in opposition research. Stone was always a big Richard Nixon fan and felt that he had been unfairly railroaded into resigning the Presidency after the Watergate Scandal broke. In 2007, Stone had Richard Nixon's face tattooed on his back.[178]

Although he officially left the Trump campaign in August 2015, just two months after the campaign began, Stone continued to be in frequent contact with Trump and continued to provide critical assistance with Trump's pro-Russian campaign. Although Trump was never widely known for his discretion, Roger Stone had the unique ability to voice the kind of wild and crazy views that even Trump avoided explicitly stating. In other words, Stone was the consummate political hit man.[179] For example, as reported by *The Hill* on August 27, 2016, Stone told the *Financial Times* in an interview: "If Hillary wins, we're done as a nation. We'll be overrun by hordes of young Muslims, like Germany and France, raping, killing, violating, desecrating."[180]

Stone enlisted the support of some of his key associates in his quest to obtain damaging information on Hillary Clinton from the Russians and various organizations that were closely associated with Russian intelligence operations. For example, in May 2016, at Stone's request, Michael Caputo – senior Trump campaign communications adviser who has had deep business ties to Russia – arranged for Stone to meet in Sunny Isles, Florida with a Russian national, "Henry Greenberg" (a.k.a. Henry Oknyansky), who said that he had damaging information on Hillary Clinton. Stone later told *The Washington Post* that he met with Greenberg but rejected the man's proposal because he asked for $2 million.[181]

Sam Nunberg was another political advisor to the 2016 Trump campaign who was a longtime associate of Roger Stone, who was enlisted by Stone in his efforts to obtain stolen emails and other "dirt" that could be used to help the Trump campaign and to damage Hillary Clinton. On August 4, 2016, one day after Stone had a long conversation with Trump, Stone sent an email to Nunberg saying, "I dined with my new pal Julian Assange last nite."[182] It is likely that Stone meant he had an online meeting with Assange, since there is no record of Stone leaving the United States around that time, and Assange was in the Ecuadorian Embassy in London.

Four days later, on August 8, 2016, Stone further confirmed that he had been in touch with Assange and that Assange had given him advance warning that more stolen Clinton campaign documents were about to be publicly dumped on the internet. In a video interview, Stone stated that he had been in communication with Assange, and that "I believe the next tranche of his documents pertains to the Clinton Foundation, but there's no telling what the October surprise may be." [183]

Like clockwork, four days after Stone "predicted" that more stolen documents would be released in short order, one of Russian intelligence's online services known as "Guccifer 2.0" released documents that it said had been taken from a breach of the Democratic Congressional Campaign Committee (DCCC). On the same day, August 12, 2016, Guccifer 2.0 tweeted Stone, thanking him for his faith in their hacking operation.[184] The following day, on August 13, 2016, after Twitter had suspended its account, Stone tweeted at @wikileaks @GUCCIFER_2, stating that it was "outrageous" that *Twitter* had suspended Guccifer's account.[185] After all, publishing stolen emails and damaging the Clinton Campaign in the process was, in Stone's view, nothing more than a public service.

Later that same month, on August 21, 2016, Stone posted on Twitter a prediction that Clinton's then campaign manager, John D. Podesta, would soon be the primary subject of Wikileak's next data dump: "Trust me, it will soon [be] Podesta's time in the barrel." On October 7, 2016, about six weeks later, Wikileaks began releasing 50,000 stolen emails that had been collected by Russian agents on the same day that the Hollywood Access tape was released, in which Trump bragged to Billy Bush about his ability to grab women's genitals with impunity.[186]

As part of his efforts on behalf of the Trump Campaign to get damaging information on Hillary Clinton from Wikileaks or other Russian propaganda outlets, Stone also enlisted the support of Jerome Corsi, a rightwing author and "birther" conspiracy theorist regarding President Obama's birthplace. Stone asked Corsi to contact Julian Assange, the founder and driving force behind Wikileaks who was hiding out in the Ecuadorian Embassy in London to avoid extradition. As part of a proposed plea deal with Corsi, the Special Counsel's Office claimed it was Mr. Corsi's understanding that Stone was "in regular contact with senior members of the Trump campaign, including with then-candidate Donald J. Trump" when he asked Corsi in late July 2016 to "get to" Julian Assange, the founder of WikiLeaks.[187] When confronted by the FBI, Corsi apparently lied about Stone's request, but later admitted to the press that he expected to be indicted for lying to federal investigators because he had, in truth and in fact, passed the information on to Assange.[188] According to Corsi, the federal prosecutors were especially interested in an email he sent to Stone on Aug. 2, 2016, saying "Word is friend in embassy plans 2 more dumps," he wrote. "Impact planned to be very damaging." Corsi's "friend in the embassy" was Julian Assange.

Corsi's testimony before a federal grand jury about his interactions with Stone, as well as his email exchanges with Stone, put Stone in increased legal jeopardy. Stone had testified under oath to the House Intelligence Committee during 2017 that he had no "advance knowledge of the source or actual content of the WikiLeaks disclosure." Based on Corsi's testimony to the Special Counsel and the Grand Jury, it appears, then, that Stone lied under oath to Congress, which we know from one of the charges against Michael Cohen, is a crime that Mueller is not hesitant to pursue by way of criminal indictment.

Sure enough, on Friday, January 25, 2019, Stone was arrested in a pre-dawn raid by FBI at Stone's home in Ft. Lauderdale, Florida. According to court documents, the federal prosecutors had requested that Stone's indictment be sealed over concerns that public disclosure would increase the risk of Stone fleeing or destroying or tampering with evidence.[189]

The indictment of Stone alleged that a top Trump campaign official during the 2016 presidential campaign "was directed" to dispatch Stone to get information from WikiLeaks about the thousands of hacked Democratic emails.[190] Although the indictment did not specifically name Trump as an unindicted co-conspirator with Stone, it is highly likely that Trump, who was notorious for micro-managing the details of his business as well as his campaign, was the only one senior enough in the campaign to have "directed" a senior campaign official to take this action, rather than just "consulting with" or "discussing" this option. The only other two senior campaign officials who could have possibly had this degree of seniority to "direct" another senior campaign official to do this would be Donald Trump Jr. or possibly Jared Kushner. After his arrest, Stone appeared briefly in Federal District Court in Fort Lauderdale on the morning of his arrest, wearing ankle and waist shackles. After posting a $250,000 bond and surrendering his passport, he was released from federal custody and gave the crowd outside the courthouse their money's worth by flashing an iconic Nixon-esque waive of both arms with a "V" for Victory sign.[191] Stone defiantly announced that he would not "swear false witness" against Trump, which begged the question as to what truthful testimony he was prepared to give the prosecutors and grand jury about Trump's involvement in the apparent massive coordination between Trump Campaign operatives and the Russian/WikiLeaks hacking and data dumping operation. He also accused the FBI of terrorizing his wife and two Yorkies. If attention was what Stone wanted, he most definitely captured the spotlight, at least for a day or two until the next revelation regarding Trump/Russian collusion became public. "I have always said, the only thing worse than being talked about is not being talked about," Stone quipped to the assembled reporters.[192]

The seven-count indictment of Stone charges obstruction of an official proceeding, making false statements and witness tampering. According to the indictment, between June and July of 2016, Stone told "senior Trump campaign officials" about the stolen emails in WikiLeaks' possession that could be damaging to the Hillary Clinton campaign.[193] On July 22,2016, WikiLeaks released its first batch of Democratic emails, and the Trump Campaign wanted more.[194] This is when "a senior Trump Campaign official was directed to contact Stone about any additional releases and what other damaging information [WikiLeaks] had regarding the Clinton Campaign."[195]

Based upon the information disclosed by the Special Counsel's office in the indictment of Roger Stone and others, as well as now publicly available information, it appears reasonably clear now that the Trump Campaign had prior knowledge and a "heads up" that a treasure trove of damaging information about Hillary Clinton was about to be unleashed by WikiLeaks. For example, on October 3, 2016, Donald Trump Jr. exchanged Twitter messages with the WikiLeaks Twitter account and asked, "What's behind this Wednesday leak I keep reading about."[196] The following day, on October 4, 2016, Stone and Trump Campaign official Steve Bannon exchanged emails where Stone promised that WikiLeaks disclosures would be forthcoming "a load every week going forward."[197] As promised, a few days later, on October 7, 2016, WikiLeaks released more than 6000 emails, most of which had been hacked from the computer of John D. Podesta, Clinton's campaign chairman.[198] The WikiLease release appeared to be an attempt to distract from the public disclosure of the "Access Hollywood" tapes involving Trump 30 minutes earlier.

In short, with the indictment of Roger Stone, there appears to be a critical mass of evidence of active collusion with the Russians and their agents, such as Assange, WikiLeaks and Guccifer 2.0, by senior campaign officials in the Trump Campaign – and likely Candidate Trump himself. In addition to the Stone indictment, the government inadvertently disclosed in November 2018 that Julian Assange had been indicted under seal.[199] In other words, there is now significant evidence that the Trump Campaign was filled with treasonous schemers whose treachery temporarily succeeded in gaining them possession of the White House – the Holy Grail that every former KGB agent such as Putin could never even dare to imagine was possible in their most vodka induced dreams. However, the opportunity to enjoy the ill-gotten fruits of their labor may be short-lived. As Henry Wadsworth Longfellow paraphrased from the original Greek text in his poem "*Retribution*," "Though the mills of the gods grind slowly, yet they grind exceedingly [fine]." Truth will out. Justice will eventually be done.

*   *   *

After taking a close look at the rogue's gallery of advisors surrounding Trump, one thing is eminently clear: Trump intentionally surrounded himself, his Campaign, his Transition Team, and his Administration with a phalanx of Russian and Russian-leaning foreign policy advisors, including Manafort, Flynn, Page, Kushner, Epshtyn, and Stone. In making these appointments, Trump clearly sent a signal to Putin and his friends in the Kremlin that, if elected President of the United States, he was prepared to lift the sanctions on Russia, and even if he lost, he would at least have given Russia the benefit of having a Republican presidential candidate take a strong pro-Russian stance on various issues of critical importance to Putin and his Kremlin cronies.

All Trump expected in return from Putin was some "dirt" on Hillary and her closest advisors and some other help during the election. And then once the election was over, with Hillary Clinton winning but with her reputation irrevocably tarnished by the exquisitely executed disinformation campaign carried out by the Trump-Russia team. Putin would then put the long-awaited Trump Moscow Tower project on a "fast track" for approval, and even on the outside chance that the Trump-Russia campaign succeeded to the point that Trump was actually elected, the Moscow project could still be pursued in four or eight years after Trump vacated the White House and was ready to reap the rewards for his years of loyal service to Russia and Trump's common interests and shared worldview. NATO would have been weakened, perhaps fatally, Western democracies would plagued by Trumpist-style rightwing movements, and wavering countries in Eastern Europe such as Ukraine would have begin returning to the Russian/Soviet fold. Putin and Russia would owe Trump big time, and he would be there to collect.

After all, what are friends for?

CHAPTER 10

TRUMP AND THE PRO-RUSSIAN REPUBLICAN PLATFORM

During the July 2016 Republican National Convention in Cleveland, the Republican Platform was mysteriously watered down to make it more favorable to Russia. According to the L.A. Times, which published one of the first stories on this issue, this platform change marked a seismic shift in the Republican Party's foreign policy views. "For decades," they wrote, "Republican doctrine has viewed Russia as a power to mistrust. But in Donald Trump's GOP, Moscow's sins seem to matter less."[1]

Specifically, the GOP platform eliminated references that would require the U.S. to provide arms to Ukraine in its ongoing fight with Russia, which had seized the Crimean Peninsula in 2014 and was supporting armed separatists in eastern Ukraine. Originally, the draft of the GOP platform provided for the U.S. to supply Ukraine with weapons in addition to the substantial non-lethal aid the U.S. was already providing. However, after Trump surrogates reportedly intervened, the final passage supported the "providing appropriate assistance" to Ukraine, but eliminated any mention of providing arms to the government in Kiev. The platform also weakened language criticizing Russia for intervening in Ukraine.

Rachel Hoff, a member of the platform committee, was quoted by The Washington Post as saying: "It was troubling to me that they would want to water down language that supports a country that has been invaded by an aggressive neighbor."[2] She added: "I think the U.S. should properly come to Ukraine's aid in that struggle. In the past, that would not be considered a controversial Republican position."

Suspicion as to the origin of this critical revision immediately fell on Paul Manafort, Trump's then Campaign Manager, who well knew that an explicit call for the U.S. to provide defensive military equipment to Ukraine could tip the scales in Ukraine's favor in its ongoing confrontation with Moscow in Crimea and eastern Ukraine.

When asked by host Chuck Todd about this GOP platform revision on "Meet the Press" on July 31, 2016, Manafort emphatically denied that anyone in the Trump campaign organization had any role in changing the language of the Republican Party platform relating to Ukraine.[3] "It absolutely did not come from the Trump campaign," Manafort said. He also denied taking a personal role in altering the platform, saying "I had none. In fact, I didn't even hear of it until after our convention was over."

However, a few days later, *The Daily Beast* reported that Manafort's categorical denial as to having had any involvement in this policy change was false and that the Trump campaign went out of its way to dramatically alter the Republican Party's official and longstanding position on Ukraine.[4] Manafort's account was contradicted by four sources in the room, both for and against the language. Eric Brakey, a Maine delegate who identifies as a non-interventionist, said he supported the change, which was pushed in part by the Trump campaign. "Some staff from the Trump campaign came in and… came back with some language that softened the platform," Brakey told *The Daily Beast*.[5] "They didn't intervene in the platform in most cases. But in that case, they had some wisdom to say that maybe we don't want to be calling… for very, very clear aggressive acts of war against Russia."[6]

"They substantively changed it," Washington, D.C., delegate Rachel Hoff told *The Daily Beast*, who was present during the meeting. "It absolutely was my understanding that it was Trump staff." According to two Republican delegates, the Trump campaign's efforts were led in part by J.D. Gordon, a Trump campaign official and a former spokesman at the Pentagon.[7]

The Daily Beast further reported that records for the meeting seem to have disappeared. A co-chair for the national security platform subcommittee stated that the minutes for the meeting had been discarded, and the RNC had no comment when asked whether this was standard procedure for all the subcommittees.[8]

During the platform committee meeting where this Ukraine provision was being considered, pro-Ted Cruz delegate Diana Denman proposed language that called for "providing lethal defensive weapons" to Ukraine. Her amendment was put on hold so that Republican staff could work with Denman on the language. What followed was a back and forth between Denman and the Trump campaign, according to Denman. "They were over sitting in chairs at the side of the room," Denman said of two men who stated that they working for the Trump campaign, one of whom was Gordon. "When I read my amendment, they got up and walked over and talked to the co-chairmen and they read it. That's when I was told that it was going to be tabled."[9]

Denman says the two men took a copy of her amendment back to their chairs, then made calls on their cell phones. Later, she said the two members of Trump's team claimed to have called the campaign's New York headquarters, and that her amendment needed to be changed. *The Daily Beast* further reported that when the language came back up, after consultation with Trump's staff, and in direct contradiction to Manafort's insistence to the contrary, the section was watered down to call merely for "appropriate assistance" to Ukraine.

This change in wording was particularly controversial, given the fact that Manafort had previously worked for pro-Putin Ukrainian President Viktor Yanukovych, who was forced out of the country in February 2014 and is now in Moscow plotting a return to power in Ukraine. Putin subsequently annexed Crimea and encouraged an ongoing conflict in eastern Ukraine.

The Daily Beast further reported that it was also an unusual move for a Trump aide to be hovering over the committee's deliberations on Ukraine. That's something that did not occur in other subcommittees, or on very many other issues.

Trump's Approval Of Russian Aggression In Ukraine

Trump's admiration for Putin and all things Russian was also reflected in that way that he viewed Russian aggression in Ukraine and elsewhere. Following Russia's annexation of Crimea in March 2015, Trump must have given his Russian contacts a temporary scare by making statements that were in line with then prevailing U.S. and Western European foreign policy, which firmly condemned Russia for failing to respect Ukraine's territorial integrity in Crimea and in eastern Ukraine. For example, in September 2015, Trump sharply rebuked the entire Western response to Russian aggression in Ukraine as wholly inadequate. "So far we have all lip service," Trump said. Later, on March 13, 2016, while appearing on NBC's "Today" show, he denounced the Russian land grab in Ukraine, saying that it "should never have happened." Speaking to a Conservative Political

Action Conference, Trump darkly pronounced that Putin had seized "the heart and soul" of Ukraine. He predicted that if the U.S. and its allies did not take bold action, "that means the rest of Ukraine will fall."

However, by mid- 2016, after naming Paul Manafort as his Campaign Manager and Carter Page as his foreign policy advisor, Trump was firmly back in Russia's corner, reciting talking points that could well have been drafted by the Russians. He took the position that his Administration might well recognize Crimea as Russian territory and lift punitive U.S. sanctions against Russia. For example, during an appearance on ABC's "This Week," Trump used language that was virtually identical to that used by Putin and others in the Kremlin to justify Russia's land grab of Ukrainian territory. "The people of Crimea, from what I've heard, would rather be with Russia than where they were," Trump said. To be sure, in March 2014, 95.5% of Crimean voters did cast ballots to join Russia. But the opposition groups and a significant portion of the Crimean residents, including most Crimean Tatars who are native to the area, boycotted the referendum, which the European Union declared "illegal and illegitimate."[10]

The Trump campaign's dramatic policy shift regarding Ukraine was not terribly surprising given the fact that Trump and his private attorney/ fixer Michael Cohen were still secretly pursuing a Trump Moscow Tower project that required the Kremlin's approval, and which when completed, would bring hundreds of millions of dollars into the Trump's pocket and that of the Trump Organization. In fact, in addition to softening his public rhetoric towards Russia to the point of complete obsequiousness, it was later reported that Putin was offered a $50 million penthouse apartment in the Trump Moscow Tower,[11] which was a small price for Trump to pay for Putin's approval of the project and Russian assistance in the Presidential campaign.

Trump's uncritical adoption of Russian talking points with regard to Ukraine and Russia's annexation of Crimea has become inextricably mixed with a massive degree of ignorance regarding basic geopolitical facts in that region. For instance, Trump seemed to be ignorant of where Crimea exactly was located, and that it was part of Ukraine, at least prior to its occupation by the Russians in 2014. On July 31, 2016, in an interview with ABC News, Trump stated that Russian President Vladimir Putin was "not going to Ukraine…you can mark it down." This caused widespread consternation, since Russia was already clearly "in Ukraine," having already annexed Crimea. Indeed, about one week earlier, Trump stated during a press conference that, as President, he would probably withdraw U.S. objections to the annexation of Crimea. Also, at a Group of Seven (G-7) summit in Quebec, Canada in early June of 2018, Trump apparently expressed the view that Crimea should be part of Russia because most of the people there speak Russian.[12]

In short, the July 2016 pro-Russian modification of the Republican Party platform reflected the same deceptive pattern as did the Trump Team's meetings and conversations with Russian Ambassador Kislyak and all of the other Russian agents and representatives that Trump's handpicked senior advisors met with. Trump and his team were trying to chart a clearly pro-Russian foreign policy but were trying to do it by stealth, rather than being transparent about it. For example, an argument could have been made that the U.S. was taking an unnecessary national security risk by sending offensive and defense weapon systems to Ukraine, since Russia would view this as a provocation requiring an aggressive counter-move against the U.S. somewhere else. While I personally do not think that this argument is a persuasive one, and U.S. policy has almost always been biased in favor of helping embattled European democracies who are threatened by Russia, such an isolationist argument would at least been consistent with a discussion as to what is best for America, not what is best for Russia.

But this is not what Trump and his team did. When they changed the Republican platform or met with the Russians at Trump Tower and elsewhere, they tried to do it in secret, obsessed with establishing "back-channel communications" with the Russians so that U.S. intelligence and law enforcement officers would not know about their dealings with the Russians. And almost universally, when they met with the Russians, they denied it on their official disclosure forms, as well as to the press and to Congress, as if they had the nagging and overarching feeling that what they were doing was wrong and that this was not the kind of conduct that loyal and patriotic Americans should engage in. In other words, they acted as if they were guilty because they knew that, at its core, their self-serving was fundamentally contrary to the interests of their own country --- that it was treasonous.

CHAPTER 11

TREASON AT TRUMP TOWER

In Michael Wolff's book, *Fire and Fury*, Steve Bannon, former White House Senior Advisor, is quoted as saying that the June 2016 Trump Tower meeting between the president's eldest son Donald Jr. and a Russian lawyer was "treasonous" and "unpatriotic."[1] Bannon is also quoted as saying there was "zero" chance that then-candidate Trump did not meet with the attendees later that same day, or soon after that.[2]

Numerous examples come to mind as to how the actions of senior members of the Trump Team, or President Trump himself, could be viewed as treasonous, or at the very least, ready willing and able to betray their own country's interests for their own self-aggrandizement and that of Mother Russia. Evidence of the June 9, 2016 meeting at Trump Tower between members of Trump's team and high-level Russian operatives, plus the ensuing attempted cover-up of the substance of that meeting, provide excellent examples of possible grounds for an indictment of key members of the President's team. In the case of the President, impeachment on the grounds of treason is also a real possibility.

The basic facts are not seriously in question: Donald Trump Jr. received an email from publicist Rob Goldstone on June 3, 2016, promising dirt on Hillary Clinton. The information, which Don Jr. must have known were part of the stolen emails and other documents that Russian hackers had stolen from the DNC and the Clinton Campaign, was described as being part of Russia's support for Trump Sr's presidential bid. It was also made clear to Don Jr. that the purloined documents were coming from a senior Russian government official.[3]

Don Jr.'s immediate and ecstatic response was as follows: "If it's what you say I love it especially later in the summer."[4]

On June 9, 2016, at 4 p.m., the meeting took place at Don Jr.'s office at Trump Tower. In attendance was Natalia Veselnitskaya, a Russian lawyer and government agent well known in the United States for lobbying against the Magnitsky Act, which imposed severe sanctions against numerous Russian officials for human rights and other violations. Also in attendance was Rinat Akhmetshin, a Russian-American lobbyist and former Soviet counterintelligence officer suspected of having ongoing ties to Russian Intelligence and various Kremlin insiders. Ike Kaveladze, a Georgian-born American, was also present.

In addition to Don Jr., the Trump Team was represented at the meeting by Paul Manafort, Trump's campaign manager, and Jared Kushner, Trump's son-in-law, who was responsible for the administration's digital, online and social media campaigns. All three of these Trump campaign operatives may be presumed to have known that Russia had a highly developed and active cyber and digital campaign ongoing that – with the assistance of its *de facto* agents Julian Assange and his company Wikileaks – were disseminating thousands of embarrassing emails stolen from the NDC and the Clinton Campaign and using fake websites, *Facebook*, *Twitter* and other social media platforms to disrupt the 2016 elections to the maximum extent possible and to influence the election results in favor of Trump (or at least away from Clinton).

For the next 13 months – from June 9, 2016, to July 8, 2017 – this high-level Russia/Trump Team meeting remained a secret. Neither Don

Jr., Manafort, nor Kushner informed the FBI or other U.S. law enforcement officers that they had been approached by Russian operatives with a proposal to interfere in the U.S. presidential election by providing obviously stolen email "dirt" on Hillary Clinton to the Trump Team. Nor did any of the Americans on the Trump Team that attended the meeting disclose that the tacit agreement or understanding between the parties at the meeting was that, if – as they were promising -- the Russians helped Trump get elected through Hillary Clinton "dirt" and disinformation disseminated by WikiLeaks and on social media, then Tump would support the cancellation of the Magnitsky Act and other related sanctions against Russia once he took office. This was the essence of the corrupt *quid pro quo* collusion agreement between them. In other words, by not disclosing to U.S. law enforcement that, at the very least, they had been told by high-level Russian operatives that they had the fruits of a cyber-hacking crime, *i.e.*, the stolen Clinton and DNC emails, the Trump Team was aiding and abetting the concealment by the Russians of these cybercrimes. This amounted to providing "aid and comfort" to this country's enemies, which is punishable as treason.

On July 8, 2017, *The New York Times* first reported the meeting between Don Jr., Kushner, and Manafort with "a Russian lawyer who has connections to the Kremlin."[5] The information was attributed to "people familiar with the documents" and confirmed by representatives of Don Jr. and Kushner. On the same day (July 8, 2017), Don Jr. released a statement saying that the June 2016 meeting had been a "short introductory meeting" about adoptions and "not a campaign issue".[6]

Significantly, it was later disclosed that President Trump himself, aboard Air Force One on his way back from the G-20 meeting in Hamburg, Germany, was the primary draftsperson for the false and misleading statement released by Don Jr. on July 8, 2017.[7]

The New York Times also later reported that, during that fateful flight back from Europe aboard Air Force One and the ensuing days, there was an extensive discussion between the President and his aides concerning the potential risks and ramifications of the false statement that the President had drafted and directed Don Jr. to release.[8] One participant in at least some of these conversations was Mark Corallo, who was the spokesman for Trump's legal team at the time. The *Times* further reported that, during these conversations, White House Communications Director, Hope Hicks (who later resigned), stated that the Don Jr. emails setting up the Russia meeting "will never get out."[9] Corallo resigned shortly thereafter, based upon his concerns that he was being drawn into an obstruction of justice.[10]

When this false cover story quickly unraveled, Don Jr. acknowledged a few days later that he went into the meeting expecting to receive opposition research from Veselnitskaya that could hurt Clinton's campaign, adding that none was presented and that the conversation instead focused on the Magnitsky Act.

President Trump's own legal liability for this episode is extremely significant. As of July 2017, when President Trump drafted the false and grossly misleading "talking points" about the June 9, 2016 meeting, President Trump and the rest of his team knew that it had already been confirmed by U.S. intelligence agencies that Russia had intentionally attacked the U.S. during the 2016 presidential election cycle. They also knew that this cyberattack constituted a *de facto* declaration of cyber-war by Russia, which is one of the most damaging forms of assault on a country in this modern era. By drafting the phony "talking points" and by working to cover-up the true substance and intent of the June 9, 2016 meeting, Trump turned himself into an aider and abettor of high-level Russian agents. This constituted an act of treason since he was giving "aid and comfort" to the enemy.

Trump is also liable for obstruction of justice since the false statement he drafted for public dissemination was clearly intended to obstruct Special Counsel Mueller's investigation into allegations of collusion between the Trump Team and the Russians. It also shows that, although he was a sitting President with, presumably, more important matters of state to attend to, he micro-managed every detail relating to the White House. The micro-management extended to the Trump family response to public disclosures relating to the Russia investigation. All these acts point to Trump having the requisite *mens rea*, "guilty mind" and intent, to both obstruct justice as well as to aid Russia's own effort to cover-up its multitude of contacts and meetings with members of the Trump Team.

After learning that *The New York Times* was about to publish the series of emails setting up the meeting, Don Jr. posted the email chain via *Twitter* and explained that he considered the meeting to be "political opposition research." He summarized the meeting as "such a nothing... a wasted 20 minutes".[11] Eventually, however, Trump Jr. issued another statement in which he acknowledged that he had gone to the meeting expecting information about Hillary Clinton.

Veselnitskaya initially denied the allegation that she was or is connected to the Russian government, but later admitted that she was in regular contact with the Russian Prosecutor General's office and, specifically, with Prosecutor General Yuri Chaika about sharing information she acquired in her investigation relating to the Magnitsky Act.[12] Veselnitskaya was eventually indicted on January 8, 2019 by federal prosecutors in Manhattan for obstruction of an earlier money laundering investigation of Prevezon Holdings, a large real estate company with ties to the Kremlin, and its owner, Denis Pikatsyv.[13]

On April 6, 2017, long after the meeting had taken place, Jared Kushner belatedly filed a revised security clearance form in which he reported the meeting with Veselnitskaya, a Russian agent.[14] Kushner's failure to disclose this and other meetings with Russian operatives on security clearance forms is compelling evidence that Kushner well knew that the discussion with the Russians on June 9, 2016, was, in essence, a proposal by the Russians for the Trump Team to enter into a criminal conspiracy with them to violate the U.S. election laws and to use stolen data to improperly influence the election.[15] By not disclosing this meeting on security clearance forms and by not immediately informing the FBI that these Russians had admitted to him that they were in possession of stolen Clinton emails and that they made a corrupt proposal to the Trump Team, Kushner – as well as Don Jr. and Manafort – were participating in the Russian's cover-up of their illegal acts and schemes to improperly influence the 2016 elections and American democracy. There is a name for this: treason.

As a further apparent effort by the Trump White House to distance Trump from the June 9th meeting with the Russians, on July 13, 2017, Corey Lewandowski, Trump's former campaign manager (prior to Paul Manafort), was interviewed on MSNBC's Meet the Press, claiming that he and Trump were at a rally in Florida on the date of the June 9, 2016, meeting.[16] However, as it turned out, there was no rally in Florida on that date. In fact, Trump had been at a Trump Victory fundraising lunch at the Four Seasons Hotel in New York that day, two blocks from Trump Tower. At 1:02 PM, Trump left the lunch and returned to Trump Tower, "where he remained for the rest of the afternoon."[17] According to emails, the Don Jr. meeting started at 4:00 PM.

On July 31, 2017, The Washington Post confirmed that the bogus talking points regarding the meeting that had been released by Trump Jr. on July 8th was actually written (or at least approved) by his father on Air Force One, on the way back to the U.S. from the G-20 summit meeting in Germany.[18] The report said that President Trump had "overruled the consensus" of Trump Jr, Kushner, aides, and lawyers, who favored issuing "transparent" reports "because they believed the complete story would eventually emerge." The Post reported that Trump personally dictated, worked on, and released a version in Don Jr's name with claims which "were later shown to be misleading."[19] Some advisors reportedly feared "that the president's direct involvement leaves him needlessly vulnerable to allegations of a coverup."[20] At least one key advisor on the plane with Trump immediately resigned.

On July 10, 2017, the Vice Chairman of the Senate Intelligence Committee, Democratic Senator Mark Warner, stated that "This is the first time that the public has seen clear evidence of senior-level members of the Trump campaign meeting Russians to try to obtain information that might hurt the campaign of Hillary Clinton."[21] Warner also stated that the incident was part of a "continuing pattern" in which Trump officials and members of the Trump campaign have "conveniently forgotten meetings with Russians only when they are then presented with evidence, they have to recant and acknowledge those kind of meetings."[22]

On July 21, 2017, Mueller asked the White House to preserve all documents related to the Russian meeting in June 2016, and by August 3, 2017, Mueller had impaneled a grand jury in the District of Columbia that issued subpoenas concerning the meeting.[23]

In short, the June 9th meeting between Trump campaign officials and high-level Russian operatives, where the Trump Team enthusiastically welcomed the opportunity to obtain stolen Clinton emails that could then be used to further poison the already toxic political atmosphere and to swing the election to Trump, constituted by itself, and along with other similar communications,[24] substantial evidence of a criminal conspiracy. This is especially true where the Russians were overtly -- or at least tacitly -- letting it be known that they expected the Trump team to return the favor by lifting the onerous Russian sanctions that had been imposed by President Barack Obama. In other words, this is substantial evidence of a Conspiracy Against the United States in violation of Title 18, United States Code, Section 371. This also constituted evidence of treason, since Trump and his inner circle were, on many different levels, providing and promising to provide substantial aid and comfort to an enemy of the U.S. on matters directly contrary to the interests of this country.

Most significantly, Trump himself is liable for treason – or at least impeachment on the grounds that he betrayed America's trust – as well as for Obstruction of Justice, Conspiracy Against the United States and numerous other violations, in that he either personally drafted or approved the bogus "talking points" memo intended to throw the press and the Special Counsel's office off the scent at to the real purpose of the June 9, 2016 meeting. Trump also set as one of his primary goals during the Presidential campaign to encourage WikiLeaks, a known Russian front organization, to hack into Hillary Clinton's server and to obtain and release the "missing" emails that she either could not find or was otherwise unable to turn over to the FBI. The fact, therefore, that the Russians would have "dirt" on Clinton to hand over to the Trump campaign team was, in a sense, a positive response by the Russians to Trump's clear signal that he did not care whether U.S. laws were broken in the process, as long as the email "dirt" was somehow obtained and made public.

These actions by Trump relating to the June 9, 2016, meeting are, however, only a small piece in the vast mosaic about Trump's efforts, both during the campaign and transition periods, as well as during Presidency, to provide Russia with aid and comfort at every turn. Most significantly, he has refused to impose additional sanctions against Russia, despite the overwhelming and bi-partisan resolution of Congress directing that he do so.

Bluntly speaking, for the first time in American history, a sitting President has sold out his country and betrayed America. The label of "traitor" is, therefore, entirely appropriate.

CHAPTER 12

THE GATHERING STORM: DEMOCRACY IN CRISIS

Although the Trump Presidency is unquestionably a toxic and dangerous threat to American democracy, Trump himself is clearly not the sole precipitating cause of America's current crisis. The storm clouds had been gathering for decades before Trump took the fateful ride down the escalator at Trump Tower on June 16, 2015 and announced that he was running for President of the United States in order to keep illegal Mexican rapists from terrorizing the American countryside. American society and its democratic institutions were in deep distress prior to the 2016 presidential election, and well before Trump burst onto the national political stage and the Russian government concocted its wildly successful scheme to disrupt our democratic and electoral processes through a well-planned and coordinated cyberwarfare and disinformation campaign. The Trump phenomenon merely accelerated the erosion of our democratic institutions and norms.

For well over two centuries, America has been that Great City on a Hill, that beacon of hope for the poor and oppressed throughout the world who believed in America's promise that all people are created equal and have certain inalienable rights to life, liberty and the pursuit of happiness, and that in this land of opportunity anything and everything was possible. It was a country where immigrant families arriving in this country with little more than their hopes and dreams as they passed under the gaze of Lady Liberty in New York Harbor on their way to Ellis Island and American citizenship. All they wanted or needed was the same opportunity as every other American to make a good life for themselves and their families, armed with the benefits of universal education. Indeed, even during our own lifetimes we have seen immigrants such as Elon Musk, from South Africa, rise to the top of the American ladder based upon their technological expertise and audacious dream that a private American company could become the world leader in space technology and make realistic plans for the colonization of Mars.

To be sure, there have been other dark periods in American history, where our democratic experiment was imperiled, and the light of liberty was in extreme danger of being extinguished. Indeed, the country got off to a false democratic start with the Articles of Confederation on March 1, 1781, which proved to be unworkable since it did not create a proper balance between the states and their new federal government. The Constitutional Convention in 1787 in Philadelphia was convened to fix these structural problems, producing the U.S. Constitution that survived and generally thrived for over 243 years, but not without substantial stresses and strains along the way.

In 1860 and 1861, the Northern states and the U.S. government could have just sat on their hands and wished the seceding Southern states good riddance, thus sharply reducing the size of the United States and inhibiting its ability to develop into the economic and political world power that it seemed destined to become. But they didn't. After a series of mediocre Presidents who avoided the issue of slavery or tried to compromise on an issue so fundamental that it was not susceptible of compromise, almost miraculously, a courageous and inspiring leader emerged in the form of

Abraham Lincoln, who guided the country through the darkest days of the Civil War.

During the Great Depression of the 1930s, with the U.S. economy seeming to be fatally wounded, and unemployment and poverty holding much of the country in its vice-like grip, Franklin Delano Roosevelt of New York emerged as another great leader with the vision and foresight to remake the federal government through the New Deal into an instrument for reconstruction and reinvigoration of the economy and the restoration of the democratic spirit of the American people. Of course, it took the Japanese attack at Pearl Harbor on December 7, 1941 to totally galvanize the citizenry of the country into a common goal of defending American democracy and fellow democracies around the world from the onslaught of fascism, authoritarianism and despotism.

During the post-war era, the American constitutional system of government generally worked with relative efficiency and fairness, with the opposing political parties committed to the unwritten covenant that first and foremost, we were all Americans, and that our political differences should not permit us to throw off all restraints and to try to bludgeon our political opponents to death at the slightest provocation. The "norms of political opposition" were followed, which includes the understanding that those Americans who hold and express different political views that you do are not the "enemy" or "traitors," but that we are all in the same boat together, on a journey called the American democratic experiment, and that this noble enterprise is greater than all of us and worth protecting and preserving.

Even during the Watergate crisis of the early 1970s, Richard Nixon drew back from the brink of a full-blown constitutional crisis by, for example, respecting the decision of the Supreme Court in *U.S. v. Nixon,*[1] that he had to turn over the Watergate tapes to the Watergate special prosecutor. Nixon complied with the order and handed over the Watergate tapes, thus sounding his political death knell once they were publicly released. The Watergate tapes detailed Nixon's direct involvement and micro-management of the greatest political cover-up in recent political history – at least until the current President's direct attempts to derail the FBI's and Special Counsel Mueller's investigation of his campaign's collusion with the Russians. Nixon probably had the authority to fire the Watergate special prosecutor, and tried to do so by directing his Attorney General to do so in the now infamous Saturday Night Massacre. Nothing in the Constitution prohibited him from firing the federal prosecutor that was investigating him, although it most certainly could have been (and was) considered as an attempted obstruction of justice warranting impeachment.

The primary reason why Nixon's ham-handed attempt to kill the investigation of him by firing federal prosecutors and trying to manipulate his CIA director into telling the FBI to back off for "national security reasons" is that it violated the unwritten norm in American democracy that no man is above the law and that it is fundamentally wrong for a citizen – even the President of the United States – to interfere with a legitimate investigation of his own wrongdoing. If Nixon had not backed-off and then finally abandoned his obstruction campaign by resigning, then we truly would have had a constitutional crisis on our hands. But we didn't, and American democracy survived the Watergate crisis. It did so once again after Bill Clinton tarnished the office of the presidency and was impeached by the House of Representatives on December 19, 1998, only to be narrowly acquitted at the trial in the Senate.

However, we now find ourselves in a much more dangerous predicament than during the Watergate era since the norms of legitimate opposition, and almost every other norm, have fallen by the wayside at an increasingly accelerated pace. The inherent inefficiencies of a finely crafted American democracy, which was founded upon a constitutional system of checks and balances between the three branches of government -- the Executive, Legislative and Judicial branches – have turned into an unending nightmare of political paralysis and gridlock.

We can't say that our Founders didn't warn us. When Washington gave his Farewell Address in September 1796, he had a strong premonition that someone like Donald J. Trump would come along to threaten America's democracy and lead it towards authoritarianism and despotism. Washington's eight years as President had been filled with factionalism and partisan disputes, and he feared that, if this trend continued, the country would be eventually torn apart when one faction, "sharpened by the spirit of revenge," gained domination over another, resulting in "a more formal and permanent despotism."[2] He foresaw the rise of a despot, who would attain and hold power over the country by creating a permanent state of chaos, with constant "disorders and miseries" that would lead citizens "to seek security and repose in the absolute power of an individual." Washington also expressed the fear that partisanship would open the door "to foreign influence and corruption" such that "the policy and the will of one country are subjected to the policy and will of another."

Washington was probably thinking about England, Spain, France or some other western European power when he warned about the dangers of foreign corrupting influence. It is unlikely that he would have foreseen that more than two centuries later, Russia would be the first country in American history to obtain such a position of such "foreign influence and corruption" that Trump – as one of Washington's successors – refused to accept the conclusion of his own FBI and intelligence services that Russia had, in fact, attacked America with a cyber and disinformation campaign that may have significantly influenced the results of an extremely tight and razor-thin presidential election.

The erosion of democratic forms and norms has been paralleled by an erosion of the American people's faith in our economic system, which used to provide the promise of prosperity for all, but has now become the reality of extraordinary prosperity only for the very few. The pre-eminent position that American has enjoyed in the world since the end of World War II has been largely based upon the strength of its mighty economic engine and its ability to provide leadership and direction to the rest of the Free World that enjoyed democratic forms of government. Especially during the last two decades since the fall of the Berlin Wall on November 9, 1989 and the dismantling of the Soviet bloc, America has enjoyed an unprecedented global leadership position, as the NATO alliance and liberal democracies spread eastward in Europe, and democratically-elected governments throughout Central and South America, as well as parts of Asia, seemed to be flourishing.

The September 11th attacks of 2001 on the United States and the ensuing War on Terror tested the strength and resiliency of American democracy and that of our democratic allies around the globe, but even with the necessary restrictions on our privacy and freedom of travel imposed by greater airport security, FISA warrants and the establishment of a vast Department of Homeland Security, the threat of radical Islamist terrorism became largely manageable, even as homegrown domestic terrorists and mass murderers were increasingly able to spread mayhem on a regular basis here.

Over the past decade, however, America had become less the land of opportunity and beacon of democracy, and more the land of growing economic inequality, where the rich got richer and the middle class got poorer, and the dream of a financially secure middle-class life quickly faded for most Americans trying to advance up the economic ladder. The income gap between the rich and poor in this country continued growing for at least the past decade, with the wealthiest top 1% of Americans controlling over 40% of the country's wealth.[3]

The collapse of the U.S. financial system in 2008 so shocked the U.S. economy that only massive financial intervention by the government was able to stem the economic free-fall, which was the greatest downturn since the Great Depression. Powerful corporations convinced Congress and the White House that they were "too big to fail,"[4] and that they were entitled to huge bailouts with taxpayer monies. Meanwhile, countless Americans who had been lured into student debt with the promise that a higher education would open the doors of opportunity to them were stuck in low-paying jobs or unemployed, unable to meet their monthly student loan payments and unable to even discharge that debt in bankruptcy.

To be sure, there were some continuing flashes of brilliance and optimism in American society, exemplified by the extraordinary successes of tech companies in Silicon Valley and small pockets of creativity and innovation throughout the U.S. But for most Americans, these success stories did not touch their own lives, where unemployment, underemployment, low and stagnant wages and opiate addiction seemed to predominate. Countless American communities seemed to be condemned to an ever-increasing death spiral of neglect, hopelessness, lack of upward mobility and generations of entrenched poverty.

Just as our country's largest corporations are generally unaccountable for their actions, free to close down factories and engaging in massive lay-offs when they feel that they could cut expenses by hiring cheaper labor overseas, Congress has developed the same kind of lack of accountability and the same kind of gridlock that commuters experience each day on the highways surrounding our great cities, unable to compromise or even talk meaningfully to each other. Our political leaders seemed all too ready to plunge the country into one fiscal crisis after another by threatening a government shutdown if they don't get everything are asking for, willing to play Russian roulette with the economy and the American people.

Trump's surprising political success in the 2016 elections was based in large measure on his uncanny ability to exploit these economic fears and to mine those deep divisions in the country along racial and ethnic lines. During the campaign, he also was able to enflame the prejudices and fears of white working-class Americans that the continuing waves of foreign immigrants into the country were threatening to take away their jobs and the diminishing slice of America that they could still call their own.

Most commentators thought that once Trump had won the election, he would inevitably "tack" towards the center of the political spectrum, appealing to all Americans to come together as one people to face the formidable challenges facing the country. Remember President Obama's refrain in his November 4, 2008 victory speech in Grant Park in Chicago, that "we have never been just a collection of individuals or a collection of red states and blue states. We are, and always will be, the United States of America"?

Trump would have none of that. He was no great "Healer-In-Chief;" instead, he continued to prefer his more comfortable role as "Divider-In-Chief." Although he initially gave some lip service to the concept that he was the President of all Americans, he quickly slipped back into his more comfortable campaign mode, which was to cater to only his hard-core base by baiting and antagonizing all Democrats, the media, and the liberal bi-coastal elite that his base so loved to hear about at his campaign rallies. His message was clear: political correctness and concern about offending other Americans was a thing of the past, and that it is OK for white Americans to let out all those pent-up fears and anger, and to act upon those racist, misogynistic, homophobic and xenophobic prejudices that they had been told for so long they were supposed to suppress.

Moral and ethical relativism has taken hold in the Trump White House and all across Trumplandia, which included his hard-core base, Fox News and other "official" news outlets favored by the Administration, and the neo-Nazi, alt-right and Nativist organizations who responded to Trump's clarion call to come out from the shadows and enter the mainstream of American political discourse by storm.

When neo-Nazis and white supremacists marched in Charlottesville, Virginia with their tiki-torches, to the cadence of racist and anti-Semitic chants, President Trump announced that there were good and bad people "on both sides," so who are we to assign blame for the fact that one of the anti-protesters was crushed to death by a neo-Nazi using a car as an assault weapon. Lies, disinformation and the dissemination of "alternative facts" became such commonplace fare from Trump and the rest of the White House surrogates and sycophants surrounding him, that it has become the "new normal." What would have shocked and surprised us in prior years and in prior Administrations no longer has the same effect, since we have become so shell shocked and anesthetized by Trump and his dysfunctional team occupying the White House that many of us seemed to have depleted our human capacity for continuing outrage, partially shutting down in the interest of self-preservation.

For example, when Trump referred to the Democratic Congressional members as "treasonous" for having failed to applaud him during his first State of the Union address on January 30, 2018, America's capacity for outrage only lasted for a day or so. The term "treason" is defined in the U.S. Constitution as giving "aid and comfort to the enemy," such as when a sitting President is advised by the entire U.S. intelligence community that the country sustained a cyber attack by Russia and is being subjected to an ongoing disinformation campaign, but does nothing in response.

The economic gulf between rich and poor has continued to rapidly widen following the 2016 election, and Trump and his Republican enablers in Congress have accelerated this process to an alarming degree. A UN special commission felt compelled to conduct a fact-finding mission in the United States, visiting rural counties in Georgia, Alabama and West Virginia that had voted for Donald Trump.[5] The members of this UN commission, who were veteran diplomats who has spent considerable time studying poverty and the deprivation of fundamental human rights in Afghanistan, Sri Lanka and various African countries, were shocked by what they found in America, which is both one of the richest and one of the poorest countries on this earth, depending on where you are looking at any given moment.

The resulting UN report painted a devastating picture of the dismal conditions facing one of eight Americans, where all of the badges of generational and entrenched poverty were on display for all to see – from the rotting teeth, to the crushing debt, chronic unemployment, hopelessness, drug addiction, chronic untreated illnesses, criminalization of poverty and the evisceration of communities and the social safety net that Americans have rightfully come to depend on when all else fails.

The UN report, which was issued at about the same time as the December 2017 Republican tax cut was being passed, concluded that the American dream was a thing of the past, not the present, and that "a child born into poverty has almost no chance of getting out of poverty in today's United States, statistically." The Report further commented: "The proposed tax reform package stakes out America's bid to become the most unequal society in the world."

With Trump's signing of the Republican tax bill on December 22, 2017, it was now official: the richest 1 percent of Americas will see over 82 percent of its benefits. At the same time, this massive redistribution of wealth upwards will add $1.5 trillion to the deficit, which conservative Republicans used to rail against, but are now strangely quiet. As predicted, the mounting deficit caused by the tax cuts were used by the Republican leadership and the White House as a good excuse for gutting Medicare, Social Security and other longstanding and successful social programs. On October 16, 2018, Senate Majority Leader Mitch McConnell announced that the only way to offset the $1.5 trillion tax cut and $675 billion budget for the Department of Defense was to reduce the massive deficit by cutting entitlement programs such as Medicare, Medicaid and Social Security.[6]

How did it come to pass that Congress passed a tax bill that less than a quarter of Americans supported, and which was clearly designed to benefit the top 1% and large corporations, not the middle class? Almost every major newspaper and virtually every respected economist opposed the bill. The Republicans changed longstanding procedures in the Senate to avoid a filibuster, the hearings on the bill were almost non-existent, and the town hall style of discussions throughout the country that had so effectively saved the Affordable Care Act from repeal were by-passed.

The experience with the tax bill graphically demonstrated that Republican members of Congress and Senators were largely immune and insulated from the normal political considerations that we have come to expect from a well-functioning democracy. Our elected representatives proved time and time again that they were no longer primarily responsive to the will of the electorate – their fellow citizens. Rather, the only class of persons they respond to is the donor class. As Representative Chris Collins blurted out in a moment of candor as he was voting for the tax bill: "My donors are basically saying, 'Get it done or don't ever call me again.'"[7] In other words, our elected representative are, by and large, bought and paid for by their wealthy donors, so it should not be particularly surprising that they follow their marching order if they want to stay in power, which is almost universally the case.

In short, American democracy is undergoing an extreme stress test, and shows signs that it is cracking. The downward trajectory of our electoral system has been due to a combination of factors – including a biased census, the gerrymandering of electoral districts, and disenfranchisement of voting rights – that has successfully marginalized the poor and the minorities, accentuated the tribalism and divisions in our society, and thereby undermined the very foundations of our democracy.

On the brighter side, the midterm elections held on November 6, 2018 represented a substantial repudiation of the Trump Presidency and unified Republican control of both branches of Congress as well as the White House. In the House of Representatives, Democrats made a net gain of at least 40 seats, and at least 33 of these seats involved the unseating of the incumbent Republican member of Congress. In the Senate elections, Republicans expanded their majority by two seats, but the 116th United States Congress represents the first Congress since the 99th United States Congress in 1985-87 in which the Democrats control the House and the Republicans control the Senate. A record number of women (128) were sworn in to the House of Representatives on January 3, 2019 during the opening proceedings, and diversity in general was the clear winner. Such signs of democratic vitality are a welcome breath of fresh air, even as there was persistent evidence that our political system remains under extreme duress. Indeed, the end of 2018 and the start of a new year was marred by the purely manufactured crisis of the longest government shutdown in American history, precipitated by Trump's petulant reaction to Democratic refusal to agree to $5.7 billion in funding for a wall on our southern border.

CHAPTER 13

DRIFTING TOWARDS "ILLIBERAL DEMOCRACY"

"The tree of liberty must be refreshed from time to time
with the blood of patriots and tyrants."

Thomas Jefferson, 1787

In a 2014 speech, Viktor Orban, the President of Hungary, explained that his vision for Hungary was an "illiberal democracy." He pointed to Russia and Turkey as models of his vision for the new Hungary, where strongmen Vladimir Putin and Recep Tayyip Erdogan have vice-like grips on the political and judicial systems of their respective countries, and have largely cowed the press into submission. Another name for this model of one-party rule combined with a relatively free market system is "authoritarian capitalism," according to Hungarian economist Gabor Scheiring, calling it "the new political model."[1]

Orban's right-wing Fidesz party has controlled the Hungarian parliament since it assumed power in 2010 with only 53 percent of the popular vote, and has changed the constitution and legal system to assure its continued dominance.[2] Orban and his party also staffed the electoral commission and the state television stations with his cronies, and taken other steps to make it virtually impossible for the opposition to oust him from power. This was a bloodless coup that took place over time, so it is difficult to pinpoint exactly when Hungary ceased being a real democracy. Orban and his party now control all three branches of government, including the judiciary. Orban changed the constitution to provide for the appointment of judges by a single person, instead of an all-party committee and re-placed independent and experienced judges with his own political hacks.[3] He also converted all non-partisan and independent government agencies, such as the state auditor's and the state prosecutor's offices, into virtual arms of the Fidesz party.

Orban's strategy for winning total power was similar to that which Trump is now employing. Fear was the major ingredient. He exploited nationalism and fear of foreigners, using the government controlled and friendly media to mount a massive propaganda campaign depicting Hungary as a country under siege by Muslims and other dark-skinned immigrants, as well as by EU bureaucrats in Brussels who were scheming to eliminate Hungary's sovereignty.[4] In fact, Orban frequently reminds his fellow Hungarian citizens that Hungary was at the center of the struggle in the 15th Century between Christendom and the Ottoman empire, and that it was Hungarian forces that resisted the threatening hoards from the East. Vald III (popularly known as Vlad the Impaler) is often cited as one of the Hungarian historical figures who imposed an effective central government on his people through force of will and large doses of fear (hence his nickname). Orban and his party also enacted media laws imposing heavy fines on any press outlet that was deemed to be biased against the government, which quickly silenced any critics. Orban also urged friendly oligarchs to buy up local TV and radio stations, as well as local newspapers. In particular, Orban has demonized the Hungarian-American billionaire George Soros, who has heavily funded organizations in Hungary and throughout Central Europe advocating more-democratic civil societies, and who is also funding the Central European University in Budapest that largely champions democratic principles, human rights and the rule of law. The Hungarian government's propaganda campaign against Soros, who is Jewish, is heavily tinged with thinly-veiled anti-Semitic slogans and code words. Orban often defines Hungary's "enemies" as being "crafty," "speculating with money," and not having their "own homeland" but feeling like they "own the whole world."[5]

Trump, in his closing ad of the 2016 campaign, jumped on the "blame Soros for everything" conspiracy theorist bandwagon by featured the 88-year old Soros and two other American Jews as part of a "global power structure" acting in cahoots with Clinton against America.[6] More recently, he suggested that the Brett M. Kavanaugh protesters were "paid for by Soros," and said he "wouldn't be surprised" if Soros were behind the caravan.[7] "A lot of people say yes," he added.

Orban's Hungary is closer to Putin and to Russia than perhaps any other European country, and has actively supported pro-Russian positions. Hungary also awarded Russia a no-bid contract to expand Hungary's nuclear plant capability, effectively giving Russia control of most of Hungary's energy supplies. Orban has also praised President Trump's nationalist "America First" agenda, using Trumpian rhetoric to support his own nationalist agenda for Hungary. "We have received permission from, if you like, the highest position in the world," Orban has said.[8]

Although Orban has not, to my knowledge, gone so far as to advocate the actual construction of a physical Wall on the eastern borders of Hungary, he has imposed measures that have largely sealed Hungary off from the wave of more than one million migrants fleeing Syria, Afghanistan and Iraq. Orban simply ordered that Hungary's borders be closed, and further ordered the construction a 100-mile barbed wire fence ("a big beautiful fence") along the portions of the border most susceptible to illegal migration. Then, with much publicity and fanfare, he had it electrified. There are no reports of any migrants being impaled, but they seem to have gotten the message, notwithstanding the negative human rights implications.

Of course, Hungary's democratic roots are not as deep as America's, having been under Soviet and Warsaw pact domination until 1989, but its slide towards authoritarianism is still a cautionary tale for America. Just as the melting of the polar icecaps does not necessarily mean that our coastal cities will be under water within the next few months, in the long term, the consequences are likely to be catastrophic.

Hungary's closest European ally is Poland's *de facto* leader, Jaroslaw Kaczynski, who is clearly using Hungary as a model for his consolidation of state power in the executive branch, the politicization of the judicial system, and his suppression of a free press.

Italy is another European country where democracy is on the ropes, with no recovery in sight. Silvio Berlusconi first came to power there riding a wave of populism that was fed up with a ruling elite that was widely considered to be corrupt and out of touch. Once in office, Berlusconi – like Trump – only served to further weaken the structures of government through his corruption and coarse behavior that flouted basic concepts of public and private decency. Although Berlusconi eventually lost power, the Italian democratic system of government never recovered, with the recent elections in Italy propelling the populist Five Star Movement to prominence, which was originally started by a comedian and is now led by a 31-year-old who never held a full time job.[9] Other parties that cater to racism and extreme nationalism have also prospered in Italy's debased and compromised political environment.

In their ground-breaking book, *"How Democracies Die,"* authors Steven Levitsky and Daniel Ziblatt, both of whom are Harvard professors, details how numerous elected leaders have succeeded in subverting the democratic process in order to increase and perpetuate their power, and that in the process they have transformed otherwise democratic countries into virtual authoritarian dictatorships.[10] Levitsky and Ziblatt identify four warning signs that can identify whether a democratically-elected political leader is engineering a move towards authoritarianism: (1) the leader has a weak commitment to democratic rules; (2) he or she denies the legitimacy of opponents; (3) he or she tolerates violence; and (4) he or she shows some willingness to curb civil liberties or the media.[11]

This downward slide has already weakened or completely crippled democratic institutions in Russia, Hungary, Poland, Turkey, Venezuela, Ecuador, Nicaragua, Sri Lanka, Ukraine and Peru, among others. For example, when populist leader Hugo Chavez was elected President of Venezuela in 1998, the Venezuelan public overwhelmingly believed that democracy was the best form of government; nevertheless, this did not stop the country from sliding into autocracy. To put this in historical perspective, the authors assert that no more than two percent of Germans or Italians joined the Nazi or Fascist Parties before Hitler and Mussolini gained power, and yet those two fascist leaders adeptly consolidated and expanded their power once they were in office, to the point where they had dictatorial powers and could only be removed by military defeat. So little solace can be taken from the fact that Trump has the support of "only" about 35 to 40% of the public. That is more than enough of a "base" of support for the permanent seizure of the levers of power if the important American institutions fold under pressure.

To date, Trump has met all of the criteria for the identification of an autocratic demagogue. He has denounced journalists as the "enemy of the people;" called for the jailing of his political opponent, Hillary Clinton, and enlisted his key supporters such as Michael "Lock Her Up" Flynn to lead the chants at "Triumph of the Will"-type rallies calling for her incarceration; promised to pay the legal fees for any supporter who "beats the crap" out of protesters; and called for the rooting out of "deep state" career government employees in the Justice Department.

During the 2015 presidential primary campaign and the 2016 presidential campaign, Trump consistently came to the defense of his kindred spirit Vladimir Putin whenever questions were raised about Russia's abysmal record on human rights and the killing journalists and political opponents.[12] During an appearance on MSNBC's Morning Joe show, for example, after Putin praised Trump as "brilliant" and "talented," Trump responded by saying that it was an "honor" to be complimented by someone so "respected" around the world.[13] Trump added: "He's running his country and at least he's a leader." "But again, he kills journalists that don't agree with him," Joe Scarborough remarked, putting Trump on the spot. Trump refused to back down: "I think our country does plenty of killing also, Joe," adding: "There's a lot of stuff going on in the world right now, Joe. A lot of killing going on and a lot of stupidity and that's the way it is." Finally, only when Scarborough pressed him to directly condemn Putin's "disappearing" of journalists who criticized him, Trump weakly responded, "Sure."

Petty dictators around the globe have been emboldened by the new "Trump Doctrine" of contempt for human rights and glorification of brutality. President Rodrigo Duterte of the Philippines rose to power largely on his policy and practice of summary execution of drug users and dealer, a campaign that has claimed at least 12,000 lives. Small wonder that

Trump was warmly embraced by Duterte on his visit to the Philippines in November 2017. Trump's reaction: he complimented him for having done an "unbelievable job on the drug problem." Trump also got a good laugh when Duterte referred to reporters as "spies." Trump must have known that in the Philippines, as in Russia and other authoritarian countries, a reporter who asks too many questions or digs too deep will never live to enjoy old age.

The leaders of Myanmar have also apparently decided that this is a convenient time to carry out a genocide of the Rohingya ethnic Muslim minority in that country.[14] Prime Minster Hun Sen of Cambodia has justified his closing of radio stations and a leading newspaper, Cambodia Daily, by citing to Trump's attacks on "fake news."[15] In fact, Trump met with Hun Sen in November 2017, smiling broadly as the Cambodian Prime Minister praised him for his lack of interest in human rights.[16] Trump signaled the king of Bahrain that the hectoring of him by the Obama Administration over human rights issues would stop, promising "there won't be [any] strain with this administration."[17] Within a few days, the Bahrain government killed five protestors and, shortly thereafter, sentenced a human rights activist to five years in prison for tweeting about it.[18] Trump has also spoken approvingly of the Chinese Government's killing of pro-democracy protesters in Tiananmen Square in 1989, as well as Sadaam Hussein's brutal tactics in dealing with "counterterrorism," or any other form of dissent for that matter.[19] At a Republican fundraiser in early March 2018 at Mar-a-Lago, Trump praised President Xi Jinping of China, who had recently consolidated his power and was positioned to effectively become "emperor for life."[20] "He's now president for life. President for life. No, he's great," Trump said, adding that he would like to emulate Xi: "Maybe we'll have to give that a shot some day."[21]

Trump has also insisted on providing reassurances to the leadership of Saudi Arabia, despite the critical mass of evidence establishing that a Saudi government-sponsored hit squad had tortured, killed and dismembered journalist Jamal Khashoggi, a US-based columnist for The Washington Post, inside the Saudi consulate in Istanbul. Turkey and the US intelligence community quickly concluded that Saudi Crown Prince Mohammed bin Salman ordered the assassination because of Khashoggi's critical coverage of the regime. Trump's response was to shrug off the entire episode, hoping that it would blow over. When asked whether he believed the denials, Trump responded, "I want to believe them. I really want to believe them."[22] While Trump did give some lip-service to there being "very severe" consequences if the allegations of Saudi involvement proved to be true, he categorically ruled out a block on arms sales to Saudi Arabia and highlighted the country's role as a US ally against Iran and Islamist militants.[23] He also, at one point, said that the Saudi claims that Khashoggi had died in a "fist fight" were credible, despite evidence that one of the member of the Saudi team sent to Istanbul to "greet" Khashoggi arrived with a bone saw.

On December 19, 2018, Trump also recently set off a storm of protest by announcing via twitter an abrupt reversal of U.S. policy on Syria, where a relatively small U.S. military presence of about 2000 troops have been supporting the U.S.-backed, Kurdish-led Syrian Democratic Forces, which has scored a number of major victories against the remaining ISIS forces in Syria.[24] Trump's decision to withdraw American troops from Syria was apparently made hastily, without even consulting his national security team or allies and over strong objections from virtually everyone involved in the fight against ISIS.[25] The decision came about one week after a phone conversation with Turkish President Recep Tayyip Erdogan, who was threatening to start a major offensive against the Kurdish forces in northern Syria, which Turkey considers to be a terrorist organization but which the U.S. – at least until now – has considered as a close ally.[26] Leaving aside the human rights implications of a precipitous withdrawal of U.S. troops from Syria, the breach of commitment to a longstanding U.S. ally in the face of a threat by Turkey's virtual dictator is bound to have disastrous repercussions for the indefinite future. The major beneficiaries of this precipitous move (in addition to Turkey and ISIS) are the embattled and repressive Syrian government, Iran and, of course, Russia, which considers Syria to be its only client state in the Middle East and wishes to consolidate its power there. Similarly, Trump announced that he was considering a partial or total withdrawal of U.S. troops from Afghanistan, which could only be viewed as good news for ISIS and other terrorist groups, as well as welcome news for Russia.

On December 20, 2018, one day after Trump's abrupt announcement of the withdrawal of troops from Syria, Defense Secretary Jim Mattis resigned, citing policy differences with Trump.[27] In a two-page letter to the president, Mattis emphasized the value of U.S. leadership in strategic alliances, including NATO and the coalition to defeat Islamic State:

One core belief I have always held is that our strength as a nation is inextricably linked to the strength of our unique and comprehensive system of alliances and partnerships. While the US remains the indispensable nation in the free world, we cannot protect our interests or serve that role effectively without maintaining strong alliances and showing respect to those allies…NATO's 29 democracies demonstrated that strength in their commitment to fighting alongside us following the 9-11 attack on America. The Defeat-ISIS coalition of 74 nations is further proof.

Remarkably, this was the first time that a Secretary of Defense has resigned over policy differences with the president, and the fact that Mattis decided to publicly disseminate by letter his reasons for resigning underscored his sharp rebuke of Trump and his "America First" isolationist approach to foreign affairs. Mattis further noted that his "views on treating allies with respect …[were] informed by over four decades of immersion in these issues [and that] we must do everything possible to advance an international order that is most conducive to our security, prosperity and values…." Notably, Mattis did not thank Trump for the opportunity to serve him as his Secretary of Defense; rather, he thanked the country for the privilege "to serve alongside our men and women of the Department in defense of our citizens and our ideals." His letter also suggested differences with Trump over the president's handling of strategic challenges posed by Russia and China.[28]

The resignation drew an unusually sharp rebuke from Senate Majority Leader Mitch McConnell, who expressed "distress" over the Mattis resignation and publicly criticized Trump.[29] McConnell urged the president to replace Mattis with someone who shares the view that it's essential to maintain post-World War II alliances and has "a clear-eyed understanding of friends and foes," identifying Russia as an antagonist.[30]

"This is scary," Senator Mark Warner, the top-ranking Democrat on the Intelligence Committee, said in a tweet posted shortly after the announcement. "Secretary Mattis has been an island of stability amidst the chaos of the Trump administration." House Democratic Leader Nancy Pelosi also said she was "shaken" by his resignation.

The Mattis resignation marked the departure of the last of a trio of generals that Trump had placed in key national security posts, and which

Congress and the American public had come to rely on – perhaps naively – to be "the adults in the room" and capable of keeping the ship of state from careening off course. H.R. McMaster was appointed national security adviser one month into the Trump administration and then was ousted in April of 2018. John Kelly was Homeland Security Secretary and then White House chief of staff, a job he left in early January, 2019.

This abandonment of allies and sole reliance on America's unilateral power has been characterized by one White House official as the "We're America, Bitch" doctrine.[31] When asked to elaborate on this concept, this Trump Administration official explained: "Obama apologized to everyone for everything. He felt bad about everything." President Trump, in contrast, "doesn't feel like he has to apologize for anything America does."[32]

In other words, Trump has announced that America is better off by abandoning the our traditional alliances with like-minded democracies, such as NATO, demoralizing freedom-loving peoples around the world that have traditionally looked to America as its shining beacon of light and hope, and emboldening China, Russia and other authoritarian regimes to expand their influence in regions where American withdrawal creates a power vacuum. Isolationism or a "go-it-alone" policy is a dangerous and radical departure from the policies that have kept America safe and prosperous for the past 74 years. To now change that policy based upon the whim or caprice of an erratic and untested chief executive would be reckless and foolhardy, especially since there is mounting evidence that Trump's real objective is to tear down America while cozying up to a brutal and authoritarian dictator in Moscow who has, one way or another, compromised the President of the United States.

Trump demonstrated his new doctrine at the G-7 summit held in Canada in early June 2018, where he threatened our closest allies with a trade war and rejected the rules-based international order that has largely maintained world piece since World War II.[33] He insulted Canadian Prime Minister Trudeau and then, a few days later, directed effusive praise on Kim Jong-un, the world's most brutal dictator.[34] Inexplicably, the putative leader of the Free World acted as if he wanted to destroy it.[35] Trump complained, "We're like the piggy bank that everyone's robbing, and that ends." The conference was the annual meeting of the leaders of the seven most industrialized nations—Canada, France, Germany, Italy, Japan, the U.K. and the U.S.—come together to discuss foreign affairs. The meeting's official agenda focused on job growth, advancing gender equality, climate change and peacebuilding, but Trump came with his own agenda item: He wanted to invite Russia back into these meetings, which had been called the G-8 before Russia was booted out for invading and annexing Crimea, as well as for other human rights and international law outrages.[36] Trump, who arrived later than the other leaders, also made an early exit from the summit and skipped discussions on climate change.[37]

Just before arriving at the conference, Trump had imposed new tariffs, with a 25 percent tax on imported steel and a 10 percent tax on imported aluminum. These tariffs were particularly designed to hurt Canada, a major supplier of steel and aluminum to the U.S. markets. Canadian Prime Minister Justin Trudeau called them "totally unacceptable," describing them as "an affront to the long-standing security partnership between Canada and the United States, and in particular to the thousands of Canadians who have fought and died alongside American comrades-in-arms."[38] Trump's reaction was to announce that his Administration was looking into the possibility of imposing new tariffs "on automobiles flooding the U.S. Market!," he tweeted, personally insulting the Canadian Prime Minister by describing

Trudeau as "Very dishonest & weak."

On September 25, 2018, the United Nations General Assembly spontaneously laughed at Trump claimed his "administration has accomplished more than almost any administration in the history" of the United States.[39] Trump later argued that "they were laughing with me," not at him.[40]

Unsurprisingly, the U.S.'s approval ratings around the world have collapsed; a Gallup poll showed that approval of the U.S. had fallen to a record low of 30 percent, which puts us behind China (who knew that it was such a great bastion of human rights!) and just ahead of Russia.[41]

If Putin's secret mission for Trump is to cripple America and destroy its reputation, he is doing an excellent job of it. The question is: What are we going to do in response in order to preserve our basic democratic values, institutions and liberties.

CHAPTER 14

CAN A SITTING PRESIDENT BE INDICTED FOR TREASON OR OTHER CRIMES?

Since "Treason" is both a criminal offense that can be prosecuted in the federal district courts[1] as well as one of the three constitutionally-defined grounds for impeachment,[2] the question inevitably arises as to whether a federal prosecutor or federal grand jury can indict Trump while he is still occupying the White House, or whether prosecutors must bide their time until he leaves office before prosecuting him for treason or other criminal charges.

The Constitution explicitly provides for the indictment of the President, as well as all other civil officers and federal judges, *after* impeachment and removal from office, so why is it silent on the issue of whether a President can be indicted and tried for violations of the criminal law while he is still holding office? By remaining silent on the issue, did the founders intend to infer that a sitting President *could not* be indicted, or was it so obvious to them that a President *could be* indicted that they just did not feel it necessary to explicitly say so in so many words?

Since the issue of whether a sitting president can be indicted appear to be an "open" constitutional question that has never been squarely addressed by the Supreme Court, and no sitting president has actually been indicted, there has been much speculation – and indeed confusion – over whether Special Counsel Mueller can ask a federal grand jury to return an indictment against President Trump.[3] The only thing that we know for certain is that there is nothing in the Constitution clearly prohibiting it. All that the Constitution says about the prosecution of the President is that, in Article 1, Section 3, he (or she) is subject to prosecution after being impeached by the House of Representatives, and then convicted and removed from office by a two-thirds vote of the Senate.[4]

Even if there is no constitutional bar to the indictment of a sitting President, Special Counsel Robert Mueller may be bound to follow the policies and procedures of the U.S. Department of Justice, including a 2000 opinion of the Justice Department's Office of Legal Counsel stating that a sitting president should not be indicted.[5] However, this opinion is primarily based on the argument that the indictment of a sitting President would unnecessarily interfere with the functioning of the office of the Chief Executive, not that it is categorically mandated by the Constitution.

In addition, the Office of Legal Counsel at the Justice Department has been known to change or modify its opinions from time to time, and there is no reason to believe that it might not do so in the case of President Trump if he engaged in criminal behavior – such as a treasonous act or course of conduct, or refusal, for example, to follow an explicit order of the Supreme Court.

It should also be noted that the current Justice Department policy against the indictment of a sitting president is directly contrary to the position reached by government lawyers in both the Nixon and Clinton investigations, as discussed below. The closest the Supreme Court came to addressing the question was 1997 case of Clinton v. Jones, 520 U.S. 681 (1997), in which the Court considered the issue of whether a president could delay until the end of his term a civil suit by a private individual. The

Court unanimously rejected the argument of President Clinton's counsel that a civil trial would unduly impair a president's ability to carry out his duties, concluding that the mere inconvenience or even significant burden imposed by the defense of a civil suit did not rise to the level of a constitutional violation. It is, therefore, likely that the Court would reach the same conclusion in the context of a criminal indictment of the President, just as it did in the context of a civil suit.

The Watergate Memo

This was exactly the question faced by the Watergate Special Prosecutor in February 2014, when Special Prosecutor Leon Jaworski asked his legal staff to prepare a memorandum as to whether the Watergate Grand Jury could return an indictment against the then-sitting President Richard M. Nixon, or whether it would be limited to making a "Presentment" or public report documenting Nixon's criminal transgressions, to be forwarded to Congress for consideration as part of impeachment proceedings.

Not only is the Constitution silent on the question of whether a President could be simultaneously subject to indictment and impeachment, but the Supreme Court had never addressed the question. To be sure, the Supreme Court had ordered that President Nixon was required to turn over the infamous Watergate tape recordings that he had secretly made at the White House, as decided in United States v. Nixon. However, it did not specifically address the issue of whether Nixon could be indicted by the Special Prosecutor or the Justice Department.[6]

The Watergate memo got right to the point: "The facts described to you in a separate memorandum, in our view constitute clear and compelling prima facie evidence of the President's participation in a conspiracy

221

to obstruct justice."[7] The memo noted that "the Grand Jury – which exists wholly apart from these arrangements and indeed 'is a constitutional fixture in its own right," quoting Nixon v. Sirica, 487 F. 2d 700 – is obligated under the oath of office taken by each of its members 'diligently, fully and impartially [to] inquire into and true presentment make of all offenses which come to [its] knowledge....'"[8]

Invoking the fundamental legal principle that "No man is above the law," the Watergate memo noted that there is "the necessity for vindicating the integrity of the law. No principles are more firmly rooted in our traditions, or more at stake in the decision facing this office and the Grand Jury, than that there shall be equal justice for all and that "No man in this country is so high that he is above the law."[9] It also observed that by exempting a sitting President from the ordinary criminal processes to which all of the rest of us are subject would set a dangerous precedent, especially since "we are dealing with the very man in whom the Constitution reposes not only the most power in our society but also the highest and final obligation to ensure that the law is obeyed and enforced. Thus, failure to deal evenhandedly with the President would be an affront to the very principle on which our system is built."[10]

The Watergate memo further noted the irony of immunizing a sitting President from the possibility of indictment would be particularly acute where "the crime in question, a conspiracy to obstruct justice the purpose of which was to place certain individuals beyond the reach of the law."[11] The memo also discusses the fundamental difference between indictments and impeachments, which is that "impeachment is an avowedly 'political' process by which the people's representatives can remove a sitting President before the end of his term based upon a 'political' judgment about his fitness to govern."[12] Impeachment, of course, is not limited to situations where the President has committed a crime. The Constitution allocates to Congress the responsibility of determining whether a president should be impeached or not, while it allocates to grand and petit juries the task of deciding who should be indicted and convicted.[13]

The Watergate memo also makes reference to the plea bargain reached with Vice President Spiro Agnew, which was publicly criticized by some as having given him favorable treatment than others.[14] However, it is noted that the plea bargain was reached primarily to ensure that he was removed from public office, which, in essence, meant that the Executive Branch took it upon itself the function normally reserved for Congress, which is to decide whether a federal public officer should continue to hold office or not.

The memo from the Watergate Special Prosecutor's office cautioned that if it stood by and did not proceed with an indictment of the President when the evidence warranted such an indictment would be abrogating its proper function, and ceding to the Legislative Branch the decision as to whether the President should be "punished" by removal from office, which was basically a political, not a law enforcement, decision.[15] The memo did, however, acknowledge an awareness that an indictment of a sitting President "would be equivalent to substantially disabling, if not functionally removing, the President from office – a decision that is Constitutionally allocated to Congress and not to a prosecutor's office and Grand Jury."[16]

Ultimately, the Watergate Special Prosecutor's memo came down in favor of indictment of a sitting president when warranted by the evidence, since it will "assure that the criminal justice process fulfills its historic responsibilities, thus reaffirming the principle that the President, like everyone else, is subject to prosecution for commission of serious crimes."[17]

The memo further suggested that if a sitting president were to be indicted, convicted and sentenced to jail time, the 25th Amendment would come into play, since the Vice President "can govern the country should the President become 'unable to discharge the powers and duties of his office.'"[18]   An alternative to indictment suggested by the Watergate Memo would be for the Grand Jury to "recommend a Grand Jury presentment setting out in detail the most important evidence and the Grand Jury's conclusions that the President has violated certain criminal statutes and would have been indictment were he not President."[19] A Presentment would offer the additional advantage "of focusing the issues that must be resolved by Congress without infringing on Congress' constitutional prerogatives."[20]

Special Prosecutor Jaworski also made the same argument in a court brief, namely, that a sitting president could be indicted.[21] Ultimately, however, the Watergate Special Prosecutor either decided not to indict President Richard Nixon, or Nixon pre-empted the entire impeachment and indictment processes by resigning from office on August 9, 1974.

However, on October 10, 1973, Nixon's Vice President, Spiro Agnew, pleaded guilty to tax evasion charges and resigned his office as Vice President of the United States.[22] His resignation was part of a plea agreement with the U.S. Department of Justice, whereby Agnew avoided imprisonment in return for pleading "nolo contendere" (no contest) to the tax evasion charges alleging that he had failed to report $29,500 of income received in 1967, when he was Governor of Maryland.

Judge Walter E. Hoffman of the United States District Court sentenced Agnew to three years probation and fined him $10,000, but only after declaring from the bench that he would have sent Mr. Agnew to prison had not Attorney General Elliot L. Richardson personally interceded, arguing that leniency was justified.[23]

Agnew's resignation automatically set in motion, for the first time, the provisions of the 25th Amendment to the Constitution, under which the President was required to nominate a successor who will be subject to confirmation by a majority vote in both houses of Congress. Until a successor was confirmed and sworn in, the Speaker of the House, Carl Albert, a Democrat of Oklahoma, remained first in line of succession to the Presidency. Congress quickly confirmed the nomination of Gerald Ford, the Republican House Minority Leader from Michigan, as Nixon's new Vice President. Of course, when Nixon resigned, Gerald Ford assumed the office as the country's 38th President.[24]

Agnew's plea agreement and resignation followed an unsuccessful attempt by his lawyers to convince the federal district court that a sitting Vice President -- like a sitting President -- could not be indicted, arguing that, for example, the Constitution, at Article 3, Section 3, Clause 7, only mentions the indictment of a President or Vice President in connection with their potential criminal liability after impeachment and removal from office.[25] In their memorandum of law to the United States District Court for the District of Maryland, Agnew's lawyers noted that, at the Constitutional Convention in 1787, Alexander Hamilton had laid out a "plan" for the Constitution, which included the provision that the President could be impeached, convicted and removed from office, and that "he may be afterwards tried and punished in the ordinary course of law."[26] Vice President Agnew's lawyers argued that if the Founders did not intend for a sitting President to be indicted, then it surely followed that they would consider a sitting Vice President in the same light.

During the investigation of President Bill Clinton by Kenneth W. Starr, the Independent Counsel to the Department of Justice, the issue of the indictability of the President arose again. At that time, President Clinton was under investigation for various matters, starting with the "Whitewater" scandal involving Clinton's involvement in a particular real estate deal involving land development in Arkansas. There was also an investigation relating to the White House Travel Office and the misuse of FBI files by political operatives working in the White House.[27] Perhaps most famously, the Independent Counsel's investigation was expanded to include various allegations surrounding Monica Lewinsky, the White House intern alleged to have had an affair with the President, and this investigation involved multiple charges of obstruction of justice, witness tampering, perjury and subornation of perjury.

During the investigation, President Clinton refused to testify before a Grand Jury, and pled executive privilege to block his aides from testifying.[28] Professor Ronald D. Rotunda of the University of Illinois College of Law was asked Independent Counsel Kenneth Starr to study and report on this issue, which he did by letter to Mr. Starr dated May 13, 1998. He framed the legal issue as follows: "Does the Constitution immunize a President from being indicted for criminal activities while serving in the office of the President?" Or, to put it even more succinctly, "is a sitting President above the criminal law?"[29]

Professor Rotunda's answer was unequivocal: "I conclude that, in the circumstances of this case, President Clinton is subject to indictment and criminal prosecution, although it may be the case that he could not be imprisoned (assuming that he is convicted and that imprisonment is the appropriate punishment) until after he leaves that office."

In reaching that opinion, Professor Rotunda relied, in part, on the decision of the Circuit Court for the District of Columbia in Nixon v. J. Sirica,[30] where the court noted that a criminal prosecution and conviction (with imprisonment delayed) does not "compete with the impeachment device by working a constructive removal of the President from office."[31]

At the time that the memo was written, the Office of the Independent Counsel was investigating allegations involving witness tampering, document destruction, perjury, subornation of perjury, obstruction of justice, conspiracy, and illegal pay-offs, none of which related to President Clinton's official duties, even though some of the alleged violations occurred after he became President.

Professor Rotunda's memo reaffirmed the view expressed in various Supreme Court opinions, that the President "does not embody the nation's sovereignty. He is not above the law's commands ...."[32] To put it another way, the people "do not forfeit through elections the right to have the law construed against and applied to every citizen. Nor does the Impeachment Clause imply immunity from routine court process."[33] The memo to the Clinton Independent Counsel thus forcefully concluded: One looks in vain to find any textual support in the Constitution for any Presidential immunity (either absolute or temporary) from the commands of the criminal laws. If the framers of our Constitution wanted to create a special immunity for the President, they could have written the relevant clause. They certainly knew how to write immunity clauses, for they wrote two immunity clauses that apply to Congress.[34] But they wrote nothing to immunize the President. Instead, they wrote an Impeachment Clause treating the President and all other civil officer the same way. Other civil officers, like judges, have been criminally prosecuted without being impeached. Sitting Vice Presidents have been indicted even though they were not impeached.[35]

There is a middle ground between indicting a sitting a president versus just waiting until a sitting president leaves office and then indicting and prosecuting him (or her at some point in the hopefully not so distant future). This "middle ground" legal compromise would permit a prosecutor or grand jury to return an indictment against a sitting president, but to seal the indictment and stay the prosecution until the president left office.[36] Of course, Congress would have to amend and modify the speedy trial rules[37] to create an exception for an indictment of a sitting president.

Such a strategy would answer one of the most frequently raised arguments against the proposition that a sitting President may be indicted, which is that the indictment of a sitting President would interfere with the many weighty affairs of state that a sitting president must deal with on a daily basis. Leaving aside for the moment the fact that President Trump has spent about one-third of his Presidency on golf courses and other leisure resort properties he owns, leading to the inference that he seems to have a great deal of spare time on his hands, the "indict now but stay the prosecution and trial" approach would permit the President to go about his daily activities, e.g., hours of tweeting and watching Fox News, until such time as he resigned, was impeached, was voted out of office or (perish the thought) finished up a second term.

An indictment of a sitting President would serve the critically important purpose of not letting the five-year statute of limitations for most federal crimes elapse, rather than, in effect, immunize a sitting President from criminal indictment as long as he held onto the White House.[38] Thus, unless a sitting President waived the statute of limitations defense while he still held office in order to avoid indictment while he was still serving out his term – an unlikely event in the case of Trump – the only effective way of avoiding the elevation of the President above the law would be to provide for his indictment by a grand jury if the evidence so warranted, and then to stay the trial of the matter until after he left office.[39]

Leon Jaworski, the Special Watergate Prosecutor, tried to chart a different "middle ground" course by asking the Watergate grand jury to name President Nixon as an "unindicted co-conspirator" in an indictment naming other defendants, who were tried and convicted of their crimes. At the time this decision was made, the House was actively considering impeachment proceedings, which Mr. Jaworski – perhaps wisely – decided not to interfere with or short-circuit with a criminal indictment of the President.

The downside of such a halfway measure, however, is that the naming a sitting President as an unindicted co-conspirator exposes the President to the public condemnation of being "almost charged" in a criminal indictment without affording him the opportunity to defend those charges in open court, and without affording the federal prosecutors the opportunity to prove their case and convict a presidential felon. It also tends to undermine the concept that "No man is above the law," since the only reason for naming the President as an "unindicted co-conspirator" rather than as a defendant is that he is the sitting President and therefore arguably different from all other merely mortal Americans, who are subject to indictment and convicted for any and all crimes they may have committed.

*   *   *

This question of whether a sitting President can be indicted is as urgent today as it was back in 1974 during the Watergate era, and in 1998 during the Clinton Investigation, since the growing evidence that President Trump engaged in both treasonous acts designed to provide "aid and comfort" to the Russians in their efforts to disrupt and improperly influence the 2016 Presidential Campaign, as well as mounting evidence that he engaged in an Obstruction of Justice by, for example, firing FBI Director Comey and denigrating both the FBI and the prosecutors in the Special Counsel's Office conducting the investigation into Russia's attack on our electoral system and the Trump Team's encouragement and assistance in helping Russia carry out this hugely successful venture.

CHAPTER 15

AMERICA STRONG

It is not yet possible to write a conclusion to this unfolding saga of Russia's attack on the U.S. electoral system and the U.S. Department of Justice's investigation and prosecutions relating to the collusion and cooperation between Russian and American actors in that attack. The battle, or at least the war, is not yet over. Russia succeeded beyond its wildest dreams in attacking and damaging the U.S. electoral process. And they will be back. What we do about it is another matter.

I strongly believe, however, that America will survive this formidable stress test, and may even emerge from the ordeal stronger than ever. Americans have proved in the past that we are a fiercely patriotic and resilient people whenever our country has been threatened by an enemy, either foreign or domestic. And although our country is strong, it is not a cruel and heartless one. Every time that we have succumbed to the base impulses of hatred, prejudice, division and paranoia, our democratic and egalitarian spirit has eventually reasserted itself and we have emerged from the crisis with renewed strength.

Just as in June 1953 the "Red Scare" fever that Senator Joe McCarthy had been spreading like a virulent strain of influenza across the country finally broke, when his cruelty and callousness was exposed during Congressional hearings aired on national TV, this country too will soon tire of the crassness, venality and mindless cruelty of its current president. We will feel a profound and collective shame at having turned over the awesome power if the White House to a man with authoritarian and an-ti-democratic instincts who -- for psychological, financial, kompromat or just plain gratitude for having helped deliver this country's highest office to him -- has fundamentally betrayed and severely damaged his country for his own financial benefit and for the benefit of a hostile foreign power: Russia.

In the case of Senator McCarthy, the precipitating factors for his demise were the Congressional Army hearings themselves, as well as a documentary exposing the Senator and his tactics by the legendary journalist Edward R. Morrow. In Trump's case, maybe the resignation letter by Defense Secretary Mattis, alerting us to the dangers of turning our backs on our allies and international treaty commitments, will be the clarion call that finally shook us into action. Or maybe it will just be the cumulative effect of one disastrous decision after another by Trump favoring Russia and damaging America.

But this is just a belief on my part, not yet a reality. Hopefully, it is not just wishful thinking. While hope is important, it is not enough to shake our fellow Americans and elected representatives from their collective stupor. Only a unified resolve can make it happen. It will require all Americans to come together and work together to right this terrible wrong. Given the deep divisions in our country, between the red and the blue states, between rich and poor, between those who are already aware of the intense danger our uniquely American system faces, and those who would not even begin to worry until mandatory Russian language training was required in all of our public schools and Trump declares himself to be "President for Life."

Nothing like this has ever happened before in this nation's history, and it is high time that our fellow citizens realized that we have a traitor in our midst who must be ousted as soon as constitutionally possible, either through indictments and convictions, impeachment and removal, or if necessary, at the polls in 2020. Trump's resignation is also an option, although a full pardon by a President Pence would – in my humble opinion -- be a gross miscarriage of justice. Crimes of this magnitude cannot be forgiven or forgotten with the mere stroke of a pen. No man is above the law, and the countless American men and women who have made the ultimate sacrifice to defeat the forces of tyranny that have dared to threaten and attack our country deserve better. They deserve a full accounting.

Although I personally feel that former FBI Director Comey did this country a great disservice by insisting on publicly castigating presidential candidate Hillary Clinton for what he concluded were non-indictable offenses, while remaining mute on the far more serious investigation of then candidate Trump as to possible collusion with the Russians, I also feel that Director Comey partially redeemed himself by refusing to comply with Trump's strong request that he "go easy" on the FBI's investigation of Michael Flynn and the rest of the "Russia investigation." In the end, Comey proved himself to be a true patriot, and hopefully feels some remorse regarding his not-insubstantial role in permitting a traitor to illegitimately seize the White House. Comey also exhibited a firm grasp on the seriousness of the Russian attack on our democratic institutions, which is continuing. On June 8, 2017, in testimony before the Senate Intelligence Committee, Comey eloquently stated:

> The reason this is such a big deal, is that we have a big messy wonderful country where we fight with each other all the time. But nobody tells us what to think, what to fight about, what to vote for except other Americans. And that's wonderful and often painful. But we're talking about a foreign government that [is] using technical intrusion, lots of other methods and tried to shape the way we think, we vote, we act. That is a big deal. And people need to recognize it. It's not about Re-

publicans or Democrats. They're coming after America, which I hope we all love equally. They want to undermine our credibility in the face of the world. They think that this great experiment of ours is a threat to them. So they're going to try to run it down and dirty it up as much as possible. That's what this is all about. And they will be back. Because we remain — as difficult as we can be with each other, we remain that shining city on the hill. And they don't like it.[1]

Similarly, former CIA Director John Brennan has proved to be a modern-day Paul Revere, warning his countrymen (and women) of the dangers posed by the foreign attack on our soil and calling us to action. At a hearing of the House Intelligence Committee Russia Investigation Task Force on May 23, 2017, Brennan testified as follows:

Well, for the last 241 years, the nation and the citizens have cherished the freedom and liberty upon which this country was founded upon. Many brave Americans have lost their lives to protect that freedom and liberty and lost their lives to protect the freedom and liberties of other peoples around the world. Our ability to choose our elected leaders, as we see fit, is, I believe, an inalienable right that we must protect with all of the resources and authority and power.

… And the fact that the Russians tried to influence that election so that the will of the American people was not going to be realized by that election, I find outrageous and something that we need to, with every last ounce of devotion to this country, resist and try to act to prevent further instances of that. And so, therefore, I believe, this is something that's critically important to every American. Certainly, it's very important for me, for my children and grandchildren to make sure that never again will a foreign country try to influence and interfere in the foundation stone of this country, which is electing our democratic leaders.[2]

Yes, we have met the enemy, and they are us.[3] The Russians could not possibly have so successfully meddled with this "foundation stone" of our great republic if our divisions were not so deep, if our democratic institutions were not so weakened and dysfunctional, and if they did not have substantial assistance from Trump and his team of Russia-friendly operatives.

Our response to this attack has been impeded because a self-interested White House has continually attacked the FBI and the Special Counsel's office for their investigation and prosecution of numerous malfeasants as a "Witch Hunt," and at least two of the three Congressional investigations into these matters by the Republican-controlled Congress prior to the 2018 mid-term election have foundered on the shoals of petty partisanship. Whether the Democratic majority in the House can now do a better job of ferreting out the whole truth of the matter and taking appropriate action remains to be seen.

Maybe this will actually bring us together, rather than drive us further apart. The phrase "Boston Strong" first emerged after the terrorist bombing of the Boston Marathon on Patriot's Day, April 15, 2013. It was soon emblazoned on the "Green Monster" wall at Boston's Fenway Park, and the Boston Bruins displayed the slogan on their helmets at their game two days after the bombings. At the first Red Socks baseball game in Fenway Park after the bombings, the stadium announcer spoke the word that the entire crowd already felt: "We are one. We are strong. We are Boston. We are Boston strong."[4]

Perhaps at some time in the future we will be able to look back on this ordeal and say, "Yes, it was a terrible ordeal, but we were able to finally bring these traitors to justice and prove once again that we are 'America Strong.'"

EPILOGUE
THE MUELLER REPORT

Overview

Although the Mueller Report was released on April 18, 2019, shortly after the original publication of the hardcover version of *Treason & Betrayal*, the overwhelming portion of the evidence cited in the Report was already covered in this book. No, I did not have an advance copy of the Mueller Report (in case you were wondering). Instead, the reason for this is that most of the evidence referenced in the Report was already part of the public record compiled by countless journalists and news organizations over the past several years. It is a testament to the effectiveness and professionalism of the media that the Special Counsel's team -- with all of its subpoena power, a vast array of investigative tools and resources to investigate Russia's cyberattack on American democracy -- largely confirms prior press reporting. Despite a near-constant barrage of charges of "Fake News" by the White House, the report confirms Mr. Trump's enthusiastic encouragement of Russia's illegal activities, which significantly helped his campaign eke out a slim victory in the Electoral College.

Perhaps the most vivid tidbit of new information provided by the Mueller Report is an accounting by Attorney General Session's top aide, Jody Hunt, of a meeting in the Oval Office on May 17, 2017. According to contemporaneous notes taken by Hunt, when Trump received word from Jeff Sessions that Deputy Attorney General Rod Rosenstein had just appointed Robert Mueller as Special Counsel, Mr. Trump slumped into his chair, candidly confiding to the group surrounding him: "Oh my God. This is terrible. This is the end of my presidency," adding "I'm f***ed, underscoring his visceral understanding that any thorough investigation of his campaign's dealings with the Russians would be fatal to his presidency.

In one fleeting moment of clarity and honesty, Trump must have realized that, as the Mueller Report recounted in excruciating detail, Trump and his team welcomed Russia's massive attack on the foundations of American democracy. The fruits of the Russian hacking-and-dumping campaign, as well as its disinformation campaign on social media, provided the Trump Campaign with a substantial boost. While the first response of any responsible presidential candidate who was approached by a Russian agent with offers of stolen Clinton and other Democratic emails and additional illegally obtained information would have been to notify the FBI, the thought of alerting U.S. law enforcement or intelligence agencies to these overtures by the Russians never occurred to Trump or his minions. Instead, Jared Kushner, Michael Flynn and other Trump operatives discussed with Russian Ambassador Kislyak and others the possibility of setting up a "backchannel" communications link between the Trump Campaign and, later, the Transition Team, and the Kremlin so that they could communicate with each other without fear that U.S. law enforcement or intelligence agencies would be monitoring their discussions. Trump encouraged Roger Stone and others to find out more about when WikiLeaks – a de facto arm of Russian intelligence operations – would be dumping additional stolen data that would be embarrassing to Hillary Clinton and helpful to Trump. According to Michael Cohen, Trump's attorney, Stone reported to Trump by telephone that he had spoken with Julian Assange of WikiLeaks and that they would be making another huge data dump of anti-Clinton stolen documents within the next few days, which proved to be reliable information.

Indeed, as the Mueller Report explains, Trump and Paul Manafort specifically discussed how the information obtained by the Russians through its illegal hacking operations – which was then disseminated through Russian-controlled outlets such as Guccifer 2.0, DC Leaks and WikiLeaks – could become the centerpiece of the Trump Campaign strategy. In return for Russian help in tipping the almost evenly balanced scales of the election ever so slightly in Trump's favor, the Trump team reciprocated. When Paul Manafort and Rick Gates – the Campaign Chairman and Deputy Chairman of the Trump Campaign – repeatedly met with Konstantin Kilimnik, a known Russian GRU military intelligence operative and longstanding associate of Manafort, they transferred to him key polling data from precincts in critical Midwestern battleground states. Both Trump and his senior campaign operatives were intent on maximizing – or "weaponizing" – the public impact of the illegal data obtained and disseminated by the Russians by both using that data to shape Trump's campaign message and to assist the Russians in their efforts to selectively target key battleground states with the help of sensitive polling data. Fortunately for Trump, Manafort was in a position to expertly analyze and interpret the polling data for the Russians.

The clear takeaway from the Mueller Report is that, in order to gain some unfair political advantage in the 2016 presidential campaign, Trump and his team were willing without hesitation to betray the core interests of the United States. They were not interested in maintaining the integrity of our democratic and electoral systems. They were willing to provide aid and comfort to the efforts of a hostile foreign power to attack America and to shake its democratic foundations to its core.

The stark portrait of a presidential candidate and a campaign organization was their willingness to jeopardize fundamental U.S. interests for short term political gain. There is overwhelming evidence that they solicited and utilized data that they knew had been hacked and stolen by the Russians, and then compounded their wrongdoing by publicly repudiating their own country's intelligence agencies and siding with the a former KGB agent and autocratic president of this hostile foreign power when he denied any responsibility for this massive attack. These series of actions by Trump amounted to a fundamental betrayal of the U.S. on a scale never before experienced by our country.

Moreover, the Mueller Report's recitation of Mr. Trump's repeated attempts to obstruct and derail the Special Counsel's investigation was intended to provide a detailed road map for impeachment proceedings by Congress. A simple reading of the text belies Attorney General Barr's protestations to the contrary regarding Mueller's intentions in that regard. The report makes it clear that if anyone other than a sitting president had committed the acts outlined in Volume 2 of the Report, dealing with the ten episodes involving obstruction of justice, Mueller would have asked a federal grand jury to return a criminal indictment against the wrongdoer. He did just that in the cases involving Paul Manafort, Michael Cohen and others who had lied to the FBI, tampered with witnesses or other evidence, or otherwise attempted to obstruct and interfere with the Special Counsel's criminal investigation.

The Mueller Report took great pains to protest that the Special Counsel's office reached no factual conclusions as to whether or not Mr. Trump did, in fact, obstruct justice. Indeed, Mueller had to walk back some of his early morning Congressional testimony before the House Judiciary Committee on July 24, 2019. During his early testimony that day before

Congress, Mueller suggested that the only reason Trump had not been indicted was that he felt constrained by the Dept. of Justice's Office of Legal Counsel's (OLC) opinions that a sitting president cannot be indicted (a conclusion that is nowhere to be found in the U.S. Constitution itself). If he were being totally candid, Mueller would have let this testimony stand as an eminently appropriate supplement to his Report. But he did not. In the afternoon session of his testimony to Congress, he meekly withdrew his earlier testimony on this point and, instead, confirmed the totally unsatisfactory and rather disingenuous official conclusion of his Report, which is that he reached no conclusion on the obstruction issue, despite the overwhelming evidence of obstruction.

However, the Mueller Report also made it clear that if the evidence had shown that Trump had not obstructed justice, he would have said so, which he did not. This statement received considerable criticism from those who correctly pointed out that a prosecutor's job is to either indict or not to indict, not to exonerate the subject or target of an investigation, and certainly not – in any case dealing with an ordinary citizen – that there was some evidence of guilt. Mueller thus bit his tongue and refrained from explicitly stating the obvious and inevitable conclusion that any conscious being would reach after reviewing all the damning evidence amassed by the Mueller team, namely, that yes, indeed, Trump obstructed justice on multiple occasions and that Congress should impeach him for such blatant high crimes and misdemeanors. This is the same conclusion that was reached by over 1000 former federal prosecutors, who concluded based upon the evidence laid out in the Mueller Report, anyone other than a sitting president would have been quickly indicted on multiple felony counts.

Summary of Mueller Report Conclusions

Officially entitled "Report on the Investigation into Russian interference in the 2016 Presidential Election," the Mueller Report is divided into two volumes.

Volume I, which deals with the evidence of Russian interference, concludes that this interference in the 2016 presidential election occurred "in a sweeping and systematic fashion" and "violated U.S. criminal law."[1] Two methods are listed by which the Russians attempted to influence the election. The first method was the social media disinformation campaign by Russia's Internet Research Agency (IRA) which flooded U.S. social media platforms with materials supporting the Trump presidential campaign and disparaging Hillary Clinton, aiming to "provoke and amplify political and social discord."[2] The second method used by the Russians were the efforts by the GRU, Russian military intelligence, to conduct computer hacking operations yielding hundreds of thousands of documents. This hacking was followed by the strategic release of the stolen materials that were damaging to the Clinton campaign and the Democratic Party through online front organizations, such as "DC Leaks," "Guccifer 2.0," or through WikiLeaks.[3]

The Report further found that the Trump campaign "welcomed" these ongoing illegal efforts by the Russians, "expected [to] benefit electorally from information stolen and released through Russian efforts," and maintained multiple links between Trump campaign officials and numerous individuals with ties to the Russian government.[4] Despite the

---

1   Mueller Report, Vol. 1, p. 1.
2   Vol. 1, p. 4.
3   Id.
4   Id., at p. 66.

plethora of evidence that multiple Trump campaign operatives knowingly dealt with agents of the Russian government, the Mueller Report concluded it did not find sufficient evidence that the Trump campaign "coordinated or conspired with the Russian government in its election-interference activities." The only charges that the Special Counsel's office pursued were against U.S. citizens under federal statutes relating to conspiracy or violations of the Foreign Agent Registration Act (FARA). These charges were filed against Paul Manafort and Rick Gates, in conjunction with their lobbying work for Ukraine's Party of Regions.[5]

So how could the Special Counsel have possibly concluded that there was insufficient evidence of a conspiracy or coordination between the Trump campaign and the Russians? Trump and his associates actively encouraged the Russians to illegally hack Clinton and Democratic Party databases and formulated a campaign strategy which placed the strategic use of this stolen data at its epicenter. There are several reasons for the Special Counsel's anomalous conclusions on this point. First, the potential goals of the conspiracy were so narrowly defined as to make a finding of participation by the Trump campaign in that conspiracy virtually impossible. Second, the highest legal standard of "proof beyond a reasonable doubt" was improperly applied to an essentially fact-finding exercise, not a prosecutorial decision. Third, the campaign of lies, obfuscation, destruction of records and use of encryption technology so successfully obstructed the investigation that the "smoking gun" evidence that Mueller was looking for never came to light. Fourth and finally, Mueller let Trump off the hook by not forcing him to testify under oath which, based on Trump's demonstrably false written responses, would have added considerable weight to the perjury and obstruction charges that Trump should be facing once he leaves office.

---

5   See Mueller Report, Vol. 1, p. 180.

Narrowly defined scope of the "conspiracy."

Mueller and his team were "investigating" a narrowly defined and hypothetical criminal scenario that no one ever alleged or even suspected had taken place, namely, that the Trump team had actively participated in the Russian hacking and dissemination of the stolen data.

If the Special Counsel's office had examined the evidence on a broader – and more realistic -- conspiracy theory, then it may well have reached a different conclusion. Under longstanding and well-established law of conspiracy, a party may be held responsible as a co-conspirator even though he or she does not overtly participate in the underlying crime. In this case, the crime was the illegal hacking of databases and dissemination of stolen documents. As long as the party subscribes to the overall goals of the underlying criminal conspiracy and commits some overt act in furtherance of that conspiracy, they can be held criminally liable.[6] Examples of overt acts include, but are not limited to:

1. Trump's vocal encouragement of the Russians to hack Clinton's emails;

2. Don Jr.'s decision to meet with a high-level Russian delegation on the premise that they had substantial "dirt" on Hillary Clinton;

3. Jared Kushner's meetings with the Russian Ambassador in an effort to open up a "back channel" communications link between the Kremlin and the Trump Team;

---

6   Conspiracy is defined as follows: An agreement between two or more people to commit an illegal act, along with an intent to achieve the agreement's goal. U.S. statutes also require an overt act toward furthering the agreement. See *Whitfield v. United States,* 453 U.S. 209 (2005). Conspiracies allow for derivative liability where conspirators can also be punished for the illegal acts carried out by other members, even if they were not directly involved. Thus, where one or more members of the conspiracy committed illegal acts to further the conspiracy's goals, all members of the conspiracy may be held accountable for those acts. See https://www.law.cornell.edu/wex/conspiracy

4. Paul Manafort's provision of a known or suspected Russian agent (Konstantin Kilimnik) with critical polling data and confidential Trump campaign strategy blueprints;

These acts and a host of other actions provides more than enough evidence for a conclusion that Trump and his operatives both conspired and coordinated with the Russians, notwithstanding their non-involvement in the actual hacking and dissemination operations through DC Leaks, Guccifer 2.0 and other Russian front organizations such as WikiLeaks.

To use an analogy, if someone is aware that a bank robbery is being committed by others, and then participates in the laundering or distribution of the stolen bank funds after the fact, then that person is liable under state and federal criminal laws for aiding and abetting. They are accessories in furtherance of the conspiracy to rob the bank and to successfully disseminate the fruits of that crime.

Inappropriate Use of "Beyond a Reasonable Doubt" Standard

Another reason why the Mueller Report reaches the rather startling conclusion that there was insufficient evidence of a conspiracy or coordination between the Trump and Russian camps is that he chose to apply a virtually impossibly high "beyond a reasonable doubt" standard for evaluating the available evidence. He could have reasonably determined a more realistic "preponderance of the evidence" (also referred to as the "more-likely-than-not" standard) or "probable cause" standard that is generally applied in fact-finding investigation such as the one that Mueller's team engaged in, and is consistent with the lesser standard applicable to grand jury indictments.[7]

---

7   Grand juries generally apply a "probable cause" standard, *i.e.*, the grand jury believes that there is probable cause to believe that the indicted defendant committed a crime. As explained in the U.S. Dept. of Justice Guidelines for grand juries, "[t]he grand jury listens to the prosecutor and witnesses, and

The use of a standard of proof other than the "beyond a reasonable doubt" standard applicable to criminal trials would have been particularly compelling in this investigation since Mueller apparently made the decision at the outset that the investigation could never, under any circumstances, result in the indictment of Trump while he was still a sitting president. Therefore, the investigation into Trump's activities was purely a fact-finding exercise from the start, so standards of proof applicable in a criminal trial context should have never been applied. In its introductory statement on evidence, the Mueller Report seems to be saying that it applied a "preponderance of the evidence"-type standard in deciding what evidence it felt the Special Counsel could rely upon, stating:"[W]hen substantial, credible evidence enabled the Office to reach a conclusion with confidence, the report states that the investigation established that certain actions or events occurred."

The Starr Report, which was issued on September 11, 1998,[8] was a referral by Special Prosecutor Kenneth W. Starr to Congress, recommending that the then-sitting president, William Clinton, should be impeached. It applied the lower standard of proof of "substantial and credible information" and entitled each one of its eleven grounds of impeachment in these terms, even when the impeachment charge dealt with criminal conduct, such as "lying under oath" or "obstruction of justice."[9] If Mueller and his team had taken a similar approach, they would likely have had little trouble concluding that Trump and his campaign operatives conspired and coordinated with the Russians to use stolen documents and a disinformation social media campaign to tip the 2016 election scales in Trump's favor improperly.

---

then votes in secret on whether they believe that enough evidence exists to charge the person with a crime." See ttps://www.justice.gov/usao/justice-101/charging.

8   See https://www.washingtonpost.com/wp-srv/politics/special/clinton/icreport/icreport.htm

9   Id.

The Trump Team's Obstruction of the Mueller Probe Succeeded In Hiding Critical Evidence From the Investigators

The Mueller Report candidly admits that one of the reasons why the Special Counsel's team did not get huge chunks of relevant evidence was that critical witness lied to the federal investigators, and destroyed or covered up crucial evidence. These actions prevented the Special Counsel from reaching any conclusion on the "conspiracy and coordination" issue without knowing the full picture.[10] As the Mueller Report laments:

> Even when individuals testified or agreed to be interviewed, they sometimes provided information that was false or incomplete, leading to some of the false-statements charges described above. And the Office faced practical limits on its ability to access relevant evidence as well-numerous witnesses and subjects lived abroad, and documents were held outside the United States. Further, the Office learned that some of the individuals we interviewed or whose conduct we investigated-including some associated with the Trump Campaign— deleted relevant communications or communicated during the relevant period using applications that feature encryption or that do not provide for long-term retention of data or communications records. In such cases, the Office was not able to corroborate witness statements through comparison to contemporaneous communications or fully question witnesses about statements that appeared inconsistent with other known facts.[11]

Mueller Inexplicably Closed Down the Investigation Without Getting Trump's Sworn Testimony

From the very beginning of the Mueller probe, President Trump repeatedly and publicly stated that he was fully willing to testify in the Special Counsel's investigation under oath.[12] He is quoted as saying: "I'm looking forward to it actually."[13] Nevertheless, the Special Counsel's

---

10   See Vol. 1, p. 10.

11   Vol. 1, p. 10.

12   See, e.g., ttps://www.usatoday.com/story/news/politics/2018/01/24/trump-says-he-would-testify-under-oath-muellers-russia-probe/1063745001/

13   *Id.*

investigation concluded with a finding of "no conspiracy" between the Russians and the Trump campaign without ever questioning Trump under oath. Despite the fact, they had full knowledge that he lied in several material respects concerning his sworn written answers to the Special Counsel's interrogatories, or at the very least, gave answers that were incredible and/ or inconsistent with the sworn testimony of other witnesses.

Now we will never know what Trump's sworn testimony would have been when questioned under oath as to what he knew and when he knew it about Russia's dissemination of stolen Clinton emails and other information, both directly through DC Leaks and other Russian front organizations, and indirectly through WikiLeaks. Trump also was never required to directly answer the difficult questions as to his active encouragement of Russia to find Clinton's "missing" emails or the Trump Campaign's active solicitation of "dirt" on Clinton that the Russians said they were holding.

The Mueller Report contains extensive details regarding the attempts by Trump and his minions to get their hands on these illegally obtained documents but provides no credible explanation as to why the investigation was brought to an abrupt and premature halt without questioning the man at the top: Trump himself. Mueller may well have failed to assemble a critical mass of evidence pointing to a conspiracy and coordination between the Trump team and the Russians because members of the Trump team lied to the investigators or failed to disclose all relevant evidence. Because the Special Counsel's office failed to use all of the investigative and law enforcement tools available to it to obtain that evidence, including the sworn testimony of Trump himself, they were unable to prove a conspiracy.

Mueller gave up on the idea of issuing a subpoena to Trump because he calculated that it would take too much time and resources litigating the issue. But given the importance of the issues involved the federal courts would likely have given the matter their highest priority, and the issue would quickly rocket its way to the Supreme Court, where based on the Nixon Watergate tapes precedent, Mueller would have likely prevailed, and Trump would have been forced to testify under oath.

Small wonder, then, that, with an incomplete investigation, Mueller meekly concluded that there was insufficient evidence of a conspiracy and coordination with the Russians. Now that the Special Counsel's investigation has been shut down, it is likely that we will never know the full extent of the largest and most damaging of conspiracies in American political history between a presidential candidate and a hostile foreign power.

Volume II of the Mueller Report covers obstruction of justice, but the Special Counsel took the position from the beginning of the investigation that Trump could never be charged and prosecuted while he was still in office, no matter how damning the evidence amassed against him regarding obstruction of justice. Mueller based this conclusion that he could not indict a sitting president on the opinions of the DOJ's Office of Legal Counsel (OLC),[14] and constitutional concerns that the indictment of a sitting president would interfere with the president's ability to carry out his duties.[15]

---

14   See Mueller Report, Vol. II, p. 1: "The Office of Legal Counsel (OLC) has issued an opinion finding that 'the indictment or criminal prosecution of a sitting President would impermissibly undermine the capacity of the executive branch to perform its constitutionally assigned functions' in violation of the constitutional separation of powers. [...] this Office accepted OLC's legal conclusion for the purpose of exercising prosecutorial jurisdiction."

15   See Vol. II, pp. 1–2: "[...] apart from OLC's constitutional view, we recognized that a federal criminal accusation against a sitting President would place burdens on the President's capacity to govern and potentially preempt constitutional processes for addressing presidential misconduct. *Footnote: See U.S. CONST. Art. I § 2, cl. 5; § 3, cl. 6; cf. OLC Op. at 257–258 (discussing relationship between im-*

Consequently, Volume II of the Mueller Report found that the investigation "does not conclude that the President committed a crime," but "it also does not exonerate him,"[16] since the Special Counsel's office had no confidence in Trump's innocence after carefully examining his intent and actions.[17]

The Report cites ten examples where Trump could have been found to obstruct justice while president, and one episode before he was elected. Among other things, Trump "launched public attacks on the investigation and individuals involved in it who could possess evidence adverse to the President, while in private, the President engaged in a series of targeted efforts to control the investigation."[18]

The episodes of arguable obstructions of justice by Trump during the 2016 campaign and while he was in office may be summarized as follows:

• Trump Campaign's Response to Russian Support

As detailed in Section A of Volume II of the Report, Trump denied that he had any dealings whatsoever with Russia during the campaign. However privately he and various campaign operatives were persistently trying to obtain information about "any further planned WikiLeaks

---

peachment and criminal prosecution of a sitting President). [...] Even if an indictment were sealed during the President's term, OLC reasoned, 'it would be very difficult to preserve [an indictment's] secrecy,' and if an indictment became public, '[t]he stigma and opprobrium' could imperil the President's ability to govern."

16   See Vol. II, p. 7: "while this report does not conclude that the President committed a crime, it also does not exonerate him."

17   See Vol. II, p. 2: "Fourth, if we had confidence after a thorough investigation of the facts that the President clearly did not commit obstruction of justice, we would so state. Based on the facts and the applicable legal standards, however, we are unable to reach that judgment. The evidence we obtained about the President's actions and intent presents difficult issues that prevent us from conclusively determining that no criminal conduct occurred. Accordingly, while this report does not conclude that the President committed a crime, it also does not exonerate him."

18   Vol. 2, p. 185.

releases"[19] The Report also infers that Trump was given a "heads up" in advance of a WikiLeaks data dump that it was coming. According to the report, shortly after a WikiLeaks release, Deputy Campaign Manager Rick Gates was going to LaGuardia Airport in New York City with Trump when Trump took a phone call. After the call, "candidate Trump told Gates that more releases of damaging information would be coming." Indeed, according to Gates, the Trump campaign was planning its entire strategy around the data dumps of stolen documents from WikiLeaks and other Russian front organizations.[20] The report also notes that Trump consistently said that he had no business connections to Russia, despite the Trump Organizations continuing efforts well into the presidential campaign cycle to build a Trump Tower in Moscow.

• President's conduct in Michael Flynn investigation

In Section B of Volume II, the Report outlines the contacts that Michael Flynn, Trump's first National Security Advisor, had with Russian Ambassador Sergey Kislyak in December 2016 after the Obama Administration imposed sanctions against Russia on December 29, 2016.[21] Flynn called Kislyak and requested that Russia not escalate the matter with reciprocal sanctions. He then briefed K.T. McFarland, who was slated by Trump to be his Deputy National Security Advisor. On December 30, 2016, Russian President Putin announced that Russia "would not take

---

19   Vol. II, p. 15: "Trump also expressed skepticism that Russia had hacked the emails at the same time as he and other Campaign advisors privately sought information about any further planned WikiLeaks releases."

20   Vol. I, p. 54: "According to Gates, by the late summer of 2016, the Trump Campaign was planning a press strategy, a communications campaign, and messaging based on the possible release of Clinton emails by WikiLeaks."

21   Vol. II, p. 25: "Flynn, who was in the Dominican Republic at the time, and K.T. McFarland, who was slated to become the Deputy National Security Advisor and was at the Mar-a-Lago resort in Florida with the President-Elect and other senior staff, talked by phone about what, if anything, Flynn should communicate to Kislyak about the sanctions."

retaliatory measures in response to the sanctions at that time and would instead 'plan . . . further steps to restore Russian-US relations based on the policies of the Trump Administration.'"

The Mueller Report describes a November 2017 voicemail Flynn's attorneys received from Trump's "personal counsel", reportedly John Dowd, who stated, "[I]f...there's information that implicates the President, then we've got a national security issue,...so, you know, ...we need some kind of heads up",[22] reiterating the president's "feelings toward Flynn and, that still remains."[23]

• President's reaction to FBI's Russia investigation being publicized

Section C of Volume II describes that, after Trump learned that then-Attorney General Jeff Sessions planned to recuse himself from the Special Counsel investigation, Trump sought to prevent Session's move. After Sessions announced his recusal on March 2, 2017, Trump expressed anger at Sessions for the decision and then privately asked Sessions to "unrecuse" himself.[24] On March 20, 2017, Comey publicly disclosed that the FBI was conducting the Russian investigation, and in the days that followed, Trump contacted Comey and other intelligence agency leaders and asked them to publicly deny that the President had any connection to the Russian election-interference effort in order to 'lift the cloud' of the ongoing investigation."[25]

• Dismissal of James Comey

Section D of Volume II of the Report describes that "[i]n the week leading up to Comey's May 3, 2017, Senate Judiciary Committee testimony,

---

22   Vol II, p. 121.
23   Id.
24   Vol. I, p. 148.
25   Vol. II, p. 48.

the President told Don McGahn that it would be the last straw if Comey did not set the record straight and publicly announce that the President was not under investigation, despite repeated requests that Comey make such an announcement."[26] Trump told his aides that he was going to fire Comey on May 5, and did so on May 9, 2017. The report notes: "Substantial evidence indicates that the catalyst for the President's decision to fire Comey was Comey's unwillingness to publicly state that the President was not personally under investigation, despite the President's repeated requests that Comey make such an announcement."[27] The following day, Trump boasted about the firing of Comey to the Russian foreign minister and Russian Ambassador Kislyak in an Oval Office meeting, saying: "I just fired the head of the F.B.I. He was crazy, a real nut job. I faced great pressure because of Russia. That's taken off."[28]

• **President's efforts to remove the Special Counsel**

In Section E of Volume II, the Report describes that when Jeff Sessions recused himself from the Special Counsel investigation, Trump said something along the lines of: "that it was the end of his presidency and that Attorney General Sessions had failed to protect him and should resign. Sessions submitted his resignation, which the President ultimately did not accept".[29] On June 14, 2017, "the press reported that the President was under investigation for obstruction of justice and the President responded with a series of tweets criticizing the Special Counsel's investigation."[30] The following weekend, Trump called White House Counsel Don McGahn and "directed him to have the Special Counsel removed because

---

26   Vol. II, p. 75.

27   Id.

28   Id.

29   Vol. II, p. 77.

30   Vol. II, pp. 77-78.

of asserted conflicts of interest."[31] McGahn did not act on the request "for fear of being seen as triggering another Saturday Night Massacre and instead prepared to resign."[32] However, McGahn stayed on as White House Counsel until October 17, 2018.

• **President's efforts to curtail the Special Counsel investigation**

Section F of Volume II of the Report describes that, on June 19, 2017, two days after Trump ordered Don McGahn to fire the Special Counsel, Trump had a meeting in the Oval Office with Corey Lewandowski, the former Trump campaign manager who was not working for the government. Trump asked Lewandowski to deliver a message to Sessions that would "have had the effect of limiting the Russia investigation to future election interference only."[33] The report relays that Trump told Lewandowski "that Sessions was weak and that if the President had known about the likelihood of recusal in advance, he would not have appointed Sessions."[34] Trump dictated the following message to Lewandowski, who wrote it down: "I know that I recused myself from certain things having to do with specific areas. But our POTUS . .. is being treated very unfairly. He shouldn't have a Special Prosecutor/Counsel b/c he hasn't done anything wrong. I was on the campaign w/ him for nine months, there were no Russians involved with him. I know it for a fact b/c I was there. He didn't do anything wrong except he ran the greatest campaign in American history."[35] The message also directed Sessions to meet with the Special Counsel and limit his jurisdiction to future election interference.[36] " Trump reportedly said

---

31   Vol. II, p. 78.
32   Vol. II, p. 78.
33   Vol. II, p. 90.
34   Vol. II, p. 91.
35   Vol. II, p. 91.
36   Id.

that "if Sessions delivered that statement he would be the 'most popular guy in the country.'"[37] Lewandowski arranged a meeting with Sessions, but it was canceled "due to a last-minute conflict."[38]

On July 19, 2017, Trump again met Lewandowski in the Oval Office and inquired if Lewandowski passed the message to Sessions. Lewandowski replied that it would be done "soon." The Report further states: "Lewandowski recalled that the President told him that if Sessions did not meet with him, Lewandowski should tell Sessions he was fired."[39] Immediately after this second meeting, Lewandowski passed the message to White House official Rick Dearborn to relay to Sessions. Dearborn was uncomfortable with this, and chose not to pass the message, although the Report quotes Dearborn as telling Lewandowski that he had "handled the situation."[40]

• President's efforts to prevent disclosures on Trump Tower meeting

Section G of Volume II of the Report cites to three different occasions between June 29 and July 9, 2017, when Trump directed Hope Hicks, former White House Communications Director, and others not to disclose emails and other information about the June 9, 2016, Trump Tower meeting. That was the meeting Don Jr. and other senior Trump campaign officials anticipated receiving "dirt" on Hillary Clinton from Russian government representatives.

• President's efforts to have Attorney General control investigation

Section H of Volume II of the Report states that during 2017–2018, Trump tried to convince Jeff Sessions to reverse his recusal over the Special

---

37   Vol. II, p. 92.
38   Vol. II, p. 91.
39   Vol. II, p. 93.
40   Vol. II, p. 91-92.

Counsel investigation and to launch an investigation into Hillary Clinton.[41] "On multiple occasions in 2017, the President spoke with Sessions about reversing his recusal so that he could take over the Russia investigation and begin an investigation of Hillary Clinton.[42] According to the Report, there was evidence that at least one purpose of the President's conduct toward Sessions was to have Sessions assume control over the Russia investigation and supervise it in a way that could restrict its scope. [...] A reasonable inference from those statements and the President's action is that an unrecused Attorney General would play a protective role and could shield the President from the ongoing Russia investigation."[43]

• President orders McGahn to deny press reports

In Section I of Volume II of the Report, Trump again obstructed justice by pressuring McGahn to deny press reports in late January 2018 that Trump had ordered him to fire the Special Counsel in June 2017. "After the story broke, the President, through his counsel and two aides, sought to have McGahn deny that he had been directed to remove the Special Counsel," according to the Report.[44] Trump told then-White House Staff Secretary Rob Porter to tell McGahn to create a false record that made clear Trump never directed McGahn to fire the Special Counsel.[45] "Porter thought the White House communications office should handle the matter, but the President said he wanted McGahn to write a letter to the file 'for our records' and wanted something beyond a press statement to demonstrate that the reporting was inaccurate. The President referred to McGahn as a 'lying bastard' and said that he wanted a record from

---

41   Vol. II, pp. 112-113.

42   Id.

43   Id.

44   Vol. II, p. 113.

45   Vol. II, p. 115.

him."[46] Porter recalled Trump "saying something to the effect of 'If he doesn't write a letter, then maybe I'll have to get rid of him.'"[47] Ultimately, Trump did not fire McGahn, who left the White House on October 17, 2018.

• President's conduct towards Flynn, Manafort, and "redacted name"

Section J of Volume II of the Report details that Trump took actions "directed at possible witnesses in the Special Counsel's investigation," including Flynn and Manafort.[48] The Report notes that actions were taken by Trump and his counsel "could have had the potential to affect Flynn's decision to cooperate, as well as the extent of that cooperation."[49] Concerning Manafort, the Report finds that "there is evidence that the President's actions had the potential to influence Manafort's decision whether to cooperate with the government."[50]

• President's conduct involving Michael Cohen

Section K of Volume II of the Report describes the final episode of Trump's potential obstruction, which concerned Michael Cohen, his former personal lawyer. "There is evidence that could support the inference that the President intended to discourage Cohen from cooperating with the government because Cohen's information would shed adverse light on the President's campaign-period conduct and statements," the Report states.[51] The Report further recounts that Trump encouraged Cohen to "stay strong," and that "[a]fter the FBI searched Cohen's home and

---

46	Id.
47	Vol. II, pp. 115-116.
48	Vol. II, p. 120.
49	Id.
50	Vol. II, p. 131.
51	Vol. II, p. 155.

office in April 2018, the President publicly asserted that Cohen would not 'flip' and privately passed messages of support to him."[52] "Cohen also discussed pardons with the President's counsel and believed that if he stayed on message, he would get a pardon or the President would do 'something else' to make the investigation end. But after Cohen began cooperating with the government in the summer of 2018, the President publicly criticized him, called him a 'rat', and suggested that his family members had committed crimes."[53]

Remaining Questions Unanswered By the Mueller Report

Although the Mueller Report was reasonably comprehensive in several respects, particularly concerning its detailed discussion about how the Russians went about successfully interfering in the 2016 election and how Trump and some of his cohorts attempted to obstruct the investigation, it was virtually silent on other relevant topics. For example, the Report is utterly silent on two critical aspects of the investigation, namely, the investigation of Trump's financial ties with Russia, and the FBI's counterintelligence investigation to determine whether Trump was (and still is) compromised by Russia to such a degree that he is no longer fit to defend America's interests and carry out the duties of his office.

We know from reliable reporting that the Special Counsel's office was deeply involved in the counterintelligence aspect of the FBI investigation that was triggered by Trump's firing of then FBI Director James Comey, and yet the Mueller Report is entirely silent on that point. Do we or do we not have a sitting President in the White House who has been so co-opted and compromised by the Russians that he is, for all intents and

---

52   Vol. II, p. 6.

53   Id.

purposes, a Russian agent acting in the best interests of a hostile foreign power to the detriment of the country he is supposed to be leading? We don't know – and may never know -- because Mueller and others in the Justice Department will not tell us. Surely, an investigation of such critical importance to the well-being of the nation could not have vanished into thin air. And yet Mueller announced that he would not answer any questions about this or any other topic outside the four corners of his Report, and then when he appeared before the House Committees and was asked about it under oath, he demurred and declined to answer.

Nor does the Mueller Report tell us anything about the treasure trove of financial data on Trump that the Special Counsel's office inevitably collected in its wide investigative net during the two years of its investigation. Mueller was reticent or apprehensive about crossing the line in the sand that Trump drew, warning Mueller away from pursuing subpoenas of Deutsche Bank and other financial institutions who are sitting on ticking fiscal time bombs that could reveal the extent of Trump's ties with Russian oligarchs and Russian interests. It is a virtual certainty that vast amounts of raw financial data relating to Trump and the Trump Organization have been amassed during the investigation. Mueller seemed content with shutting down his investigation without any in-depth analysis of this data and its critical significance to any understanding as to why Trump is enamored with Putin and all things Russian. The Mueller Report completely ignores this "follow the money" trail, and yet Mueller inexplicably refused "to go beyond the Report" and give Congress and the American people any of the valuable information that his team must have amassed.

And that is not the worst of it. The obstruction of justice aspect of the investigation gathered virtually conclusive proof that Trump committed at least ten different obstructions of justice. However, he stopped short of stating the inescapable conclusion that Trump violated the federal criminal code. As previously mentioned, Mueller felt constrained by Department of Justice policy, which reached the dubious conclusion that the Vice President and every other member of the Executive Branch could be indicted while in office, but that a sitting President was somehow above the law and could not be indicted. In his short speech that accompanied the actual release of the redacted Report, Mueller mistakenly stated that the indictment of a sitting president was "unconstitutional," even though the Constitution is entirely silent on that issue. However, the Founding Fathers have a well-deserved reputation for explicitly stating in the Constitution what they thought should be included in it, and omitting any language that they thought should not be included. The Constitution doesn't say that a sitting president cannot be indicted. Period. Department of Justice policy is simply that: a policy. Policies can be changed when they prove, as in this case, to be obsolete or when a sitting president is flagrantly violating the criminal laws, and when those violations of criminal laws helped get him elected in the first place.

But Mueller went far beyond the Department of Justice guidelines. These guidelines set forth Dept. of Justice policy not to indict and prosecute a sitting president. The policy does not say that a fact-finding investigation such as that which was conducted by the Special Counsel cannot state the obvious conclusion that yes, in fact, the sitting president did obstruct justice and that the only reason he cannot be prosecuted for those crimes is that he is still in office.

In other words, not only did Mueller conclude that he could not indict Trump, but he went far beyond the requirements of DOJ policy by formulating the dubious "Mueller Doctrine." This doctrine says that a Special Counsel cannot even conclude that a sitting president violated the criminal laws by obstructing justice because he could not defend and seek to vindicate himself in a court of law. As if Trump's twitter feed and unlimited access to the press would not give him an adequate forum to defend himself from a Special Counsel's conclusion that he violated the law. In other words, the logical premise of Mueller's failure to reach a conclusion as to the obstruction investigation – namely, that it would be "unfair" to a sitting president for the Special Counsel to conclude that an obstruction or obstruction had, indeed, taken place if the Special Counsel did not also have the power to indict the president – was fundamentally absurd.

As a result, Mueller left the door wide open for Attorney General Barr to concoct the outlandish "conclusion," after a 48-hour incomplete review, that "the President has not obstructed justice," despite the overwhelming evidence collected by the Mueller team to the contrary.

In short, the Mueller investigation, while thorough and comprehensive in some respects, fell woefully short in other significant areas due to a misguided commitment to excessive "fairness" to a sitting president, without taking into proper consideration the obligations of "fairness" to the American people to have a rogue president and his machinations totally exposed and denounced for what they are. Sad to say, Mueller fumbled the ball on the 3-yard line, and America is paying a high price for it.

Mueller's failure to state the logical conclusions of his obstruction of justice investigation left the field wide open for Attorney General Barr to weigh in with a four-page letter to Congress on March 24, 2019 that completely distorting the findings and conclusions of the Mueller Report, which was not publicly released until several weeks later. In addition to falsely stating that Mueller had found "no collusion" between the Trump campaign and the Russians, Barr took advantage of Mueller's misguided "no conclusion" approach to the obstruction question by criticizing Mueller for failing to reach a conclusion.[54] Barr then stated his own totally unfounded "conclusion" that Trump had not, in fact, obstructed justice.

On March 27, 2019, Mueller wrote to Barr, stating in classically understated prose, that the Barr March 24th letter "did not fully capture the context, nature, and substance of this office's work and conclusions," and that this led to "public confusion."[55] Mueller asked Barr to release the report's introduction and executive summaries ahead of the full report, which Barr declined to do, saying he preferred to avoid "piecemeal" release of part of the report before releasing a redacted version of the entire document.

Mueller's "Farewell Speech" and Congressional Testimony

For those of us who thought that Robert Mueller would be a knight in shining armor, who would slay the Trump dragon and save American democracy, his Report, followed by his "farewell" speech on May 29, 2019, and Congressional testimony on July 24, 2019, were deeply disappointing. In particular, both his speech and his Congressional testimony were little more than painful reminders that the Mueller Report left many vital questions unanswered, and that its principal author has no intention of answering them.

---

54   See Barr letter of 03 24 19, p. 3: "The Special Counsel's decision to describe the facts of his obstruction investigation without reaching any legal conclusions leaves it to the Attorney General to determine whether the conduct described in the report constitutes a crime."

55   Mueller, Robert S. (March 27, 2019). "Special Counsel Mueller's letter to Attorney General Barr". The Washington Post.

Special Counsel Mueller's primary job was to determine whether and to what extent the Russians carried out a massive cyberattack on our democratic electoral processes in 2016. His investigation and indictment of those foreign agents who interfered with our last presidential election should generally be counted as a success, although none of the Russian trolls and operative who were indicted were ever arrested or otherwise brought to justice, and it is unlikely that they ever will be. Still, the Mueller team's ability to unravel the elements of the complex and robust cyberattack and disinformation campaign the Russians launched during the 2016 presidential campaign was impressive. The investigation confirmed that the U.S. intelligence agencies were right when they concluded that Russia was behind this assault on our electoral and democratic processes, something that Trump himself has never been able to bring himself to admit.

There can be no question Mueller is a great patriot and an extraordinary exemplar of honor and integrity who has dedicated decades of his life to public service. Nevertheless, his obstinate insistence that all of the evidence, analysis and conclusions of his Special Counsel team can be found within the four corners of his Report demonstrates a lack of awareness on his part as to how, in this digital age, the public's perception of his Report would be received. It would not be based on reading it (which a shrinking percentage of the public actually engages in), but, rather, on visual images on a TV or a computer screen of Mueller and others explaining the contents of the Report at Congressional hearings, such as the ones that took place before the House Judiciary and Intelligence Committees on July 24, 2019.

Despite his somewhat dry, terse, halting and sometimes slightly confusing answers to questions that were posed to him, the Democrats on the Judiciary and House Intelligence Committees were able to present a compelling case that Trump had, at the very least, engaged in repeated attempts to obstruct justice. They were also able to provide testimony that Trump had interfered with the Special Counsel's ongoing investigation of his conduct and that of his campaign vis-a-vis Russia's interference with the 2016 election.

Perhaps the most effective portion of Mueller's testimony before the House Judiciary Committee on the morning of July 24, 2019 came when Mueller, in response to questioning by Committee Chair Jerry Nadler, testified that his investigation did not "totally exonerate" Donald Trump, as the president has repeatedly stated. Mueller further contradicted Trump, and impliedly chastised Attorney General Barr, by saying that he did *not* find that the president had not obstructed justice. Nadler asked:

"The president has repeatedly claimed your report found there was no obstruction and it completely and totally exonerated him. That is not what your report said, is it?"

"Correct, not what the report said," Mueller replied.

"The report did not conclude he did not commit obstruction of justice? Is that correct?" Nadler followed up.

"That is correct," Mueller said.

In addition, Mueller seemed to surprise at least one Republican member of the Committee by stating that, although it was Dept. of Justice policy not to indict a sitting president, Trump could be charged for federal crimes once he left the office. No wonder Trump is leaving the door open to help again from Russia and perhaps other foreign powers in the 2020 election, now that he realizes that this is the only way he can extend his "stay out of jail" free card.

During the July 24th hearings, Democrats were also able to highlight some of the more egregious episodes of obstruction of justice by Trump.

These included Trump's June 2017 direction to White House counsel McGahn to fire the Special Counsel following news reports that he was investigating the president for obstruction of justice, and Trump's later insistence that McGahn manufacture a false internal memorandum that would contradict reporting about this order.

Another highlight of the hearings was the reference to Trump's instructions during the summer of 2017 to Corey Lewandowski, his former campaign manager, to tell Attorney General Jeff Sessions to limit the Mueller investigation to "prevent further investigative scrutiny of the president and his campaign conduct."

Democrats also highlighted Trump's repeated instructions that Sessions "unrecuse" himself from running the investigation, which the Mueller Report said led to a "reasonable inference" that the president wanted his attorney general to act as a shield from the investigation.

Mueller's testimony at the House Committee hearings also touched on Trump's efforts, in part through his private attorneys, to influence the cooperation and testimony of several possible witnesses, including former campaign chairman Paul Manafort and his former personal attorney, Michael Cohen, by holding out the possibility of pardons and by making public and private threats.

Whether the contents of the Mueller Report, when combined with the Congressional hearing testimony, can unite Democrats and public opinion behind a concerted impeachment effort seems unlikely. However, there was some additional clarity brought to the Mueller Report and the results of the investigation, which sorely needed correction after Trump and Barr's repeated false mantra of "no collusion, no obstruction."

The Mueller Report Makes Out a Strong Case That Trump Committed Treason and Has Consistently Betrayed His Sworn Duty to His Country

Leaving aside for the moment the question of whether Trump and his cohorts engaged in a criminal conspiracy with the Russians to unlawfully interfere with the 2016 presidential election and to undermine our democratic institutions, or whether Trump obstructed justice, the evidence contained in the Mueller Report paints a very vivid portrait of a candidate and then president who remained ever ready, willing and able to sell out the interests of his own country, and to provide aid and comfort to a hostile foreign power whenever it served his own personal or political interests. This is the textbook definition of "treason" as defined by the U.S. Constitution and by federal statute.

The evidence of Trump's treason and betrayal is overwhelming. Time and time again, President Trump called for the Russians to hack into Hillary Clinton's email server illegally and to find the "missing" 30,000 emails. He praised WikiLeaks for its multiple data dumps of stolen documents that were damaging to the Clinton Campaign and helpful to Trump. Multiple surrogates and agents, including Roger Stone, George Papadopoulos, Carter Page, Paul Manafort and others, were encouraged to obtain as much information as possible regarding the Russian stolen documents, and how and when they would be publicly released. There is evidence from Michael Cohen that Trump was given advanced warning of at least one WikiLeaks data dump. Never once did Trump or any other member of his team hesitate for one second in their dealings with the Russians to consider alerting the FBI to the fact that their Russian contacts were giving them critical evidence of Russia's ongoing criminal conspiracy against the United States. Instead, they blatantly encouraged, aided and abetted, and benefitted from the illegal fruits of the Russian conspiracy. Then they consistently lied about it after the fact, since they knew what the Russians were doing was illegal, and that they were complicit in that conspiracy by remaining silent and failing to alert U.S. law enforcement to what they knew about the Russian cyberattack on America.

Significantly, one important fact in the public record that does not appear to be covered by the Mueller Report is that Trump consistently impeded the investigation of Russia's massive cyberattack on our electoral system by refusing to accept the unanimous conclusion of all U.S. intelligence agencies that it was Russia who was behind the illegal hacking and disinformation campaign on U.S. social media platforms, and instead accepting the denials by Russian President Vladimir Putin. Moreover, when reports started appearing in the media about Don Jr.'s meetings with the Russians at Trump Tower on June 9, 2016, Trump himself actively intervened to rewrite a press release for Don Jr., omitting any reference to the purpose of the meeting. As we now know, that purpose was to obtain some benefit from the Russians for the Trump Campaign. Instead, Trump inserted a false and fabricated statement that the meeting was all about "Russian adoptions."

The 1941 equivalent of Trump's conduct would have been for President Franklin D. Roosevelt to have raised doubts after the attack on Pearl Harbor on December 7, 1941, as to whether it was the Japanese navy that had attacked us. Trump's continued questioning of the conclusions by U.S. agencies that Russia was the culprit behind the cyberattacks and his attempt to cover up the fact the Russians had made a direct overture to Don Jr. gave Russia substantial political cover. This cover severely impeded the ability of the U.S. to mount a coordinated and effective response to this act of Russian aggression. In other words, it gave substantial "aid and comfort" to our primary geopolitical enemy, and amounted to treason.

In short, the underlying facts laid out in the Mueller Report, as well as those already in the public record, make out a compelling case for the conclusion that Trump and his cohorts gave "aid and comfort" to a hostile foreign power's efforts to illegally hack into Democratic databases and to improperly influence the 2016 presidential election. Trump's conduct meets the classic definition of "treason" under the U.S. Constitution and criminal laws, and since no man is above the law, he should be held accountable either by way of impeachment, or a criminal indictment and prosecution as soon as he vacates the White House on January 20, 2021.

* * *

Although he was typically cryptic about it, Mueller has now passed the baton to Congress on the issue of what to do with Trump. Without actually using the "I" word, Mueller essentially concluded that the only way to get rid of a criminal sitting president is to impeach him. Now it is up to our elected representatives to do their constitutional duty.

It is, therefore, now up to Congress to decide whether it should just continue to investigate Trump's misdeeds until November 2020 and then let the American electorate (or more precisely, the Electoral College) decide, or to formally commence impeachment proceedings against an unfit president who has clearly sided with a hostile foreign power against his own country. Also, he then used all of the tools of his office to obstruct an investigation of his highly questionable actions. Whichever route Congress takes, one thing is clear: never before has this Republic had a president in the White House whose loyalty and patriotism to the country and its democratic ideals been so compromised. There is still a counterintelligence investigation ongoing by the U.S. Justice Department as to whether or not the Russians have so effectively compromised him that he can no longer fulfill his oath of office "to preserve, protect and defend the Constitution of the United States." And yet Trump still has no shame.[56]

The Democrats may think that it is politically advantageous just to investigate Trump for the next two years and hope that the American electorate ousts him from office in 2020, and they may be correct in that assessment. But the crisis in the presidency is real and immediate, and the clear and present danger to our country posed by an unfit and possibly compromised president in the White House requires immediate action. Those in Congress who preach political caution and expediency will be judged harshly by history if – God forbid -- their hesitation and political expediency leads America into a genuine national or international crisis over the next two years with a virtual madman at the helm.

---

56   See Appendix for article by the author that was originally published in the *Morning Consult* on April 19, 2019 See https://morningconsult.com/opinions/mr-president-have-you-no-shame/

APPENDIX

MR PRESIDENT: HAVE YOU NO SHAME[1]

President Trump reached a new low in his interview with George Stephanopoulos of ABC News over 30 hours aboard Air Force One on June 11-12, 2019. During the interview, Trump admitted that he was willing to listen to a foreign government if they approached him with information on a political rival. "I think I'd want to hear it...I think you might want to listen, there isn't anything wrong with listening," he said. He also said he might not tell the FBI about it, even though Director Christopher Wray said that such offers of foreign assistance should be reported.

Yes, Mr. President, there is something wrong with listening to an agent of a foreign country – especially Russia – when the clear intention on providing you, Don Jr. or anyone else on Team Trump with useful "dirt" on an actual or potential Democratic rival is to curry favor with you and your Administration, knowing that you will thereafter feel obligated and politically indebted to that foreign power. In other words, you will be even more compromised than you already are based upon the numerous favors that Russia did for you both before, during and after the 2016 election. Although he will never admit it, Trump and virtually every other thinking American knows, deep down, that the 2016 presidential election was so close in several key battleground states, such as Michigan, New Hampshire, Wisconsin and Pennsylvania, that Russia's criminal efforts to tilt the

1   This article by the author was originally published in the *Morning Consult* on April 19, 2019, See https://morningconsult.com/opinions/mr-president-have-you-no-shame/

electoral scales in Trump's favor may have made all the difference. So why wouldn't he just hang out another "Open for business" sign as we move closer to the 2020 election? It worked last time – both for Trump and for Russia – so why not use the same winning formula again!

When hours and then more than a day went by without the White House, the Justice Department or any senior Administration official "correcting" Trump's statement and clarifying that such a receipt of a "thing of value," namely opposition research, from a foreign national is as much clear violation of Federal Election Law as the receipt of an unreported cash contribution from a foreign entity, finally Federal Election Commission chief Ellen Weintraub was forced to step up to the plate and say the obvious: "Anyone who solicits or accepts foreign assistance risks being on the wrong end of a federal investigation," she said in her statement. "Any political campaign that receives an offer of a prohibited donation from a foreign source should report that offer to the Federal Bureau of Investigation."

Meanwhile, Mitch McConnell and virtually every other Republican in the Senate kept their collective mouths shut and looked the other way, with the exception of Mitt Romney and a few others who began to mumble their disagreement with the President's approach, which seemed to be inviting Russia, China, North Korea and every other hostile foreign power to find "dirt" on Joe Biden and every other leading Democratic candidate, so that it could be delivered on a silver platter to a grateful Donald Trump, who would reward them generously if only they helped him cling to power for another four years.

Where are the Republicans who are finally willing to join with their Democratic colleagues in Congress and finally say: "Enough is enough.

You cannot go on like this, breaking every legal and political norm in our carefully balanced democratic system. We are a country where the Rule of Law is king, not some crafty demagogue such as yourself who rules solely through the exercise of fear and raw power."

Where is our Joe Welch? On June 9, 1954, a Boston lawyer named Joseph Nye Welch confronted the most powerful demagogue of his time – Senator Joseph McCarthy of Wisconsin -- who was the chief proponent of the "Red Scare" conspiracy theory that the U.S. federal agencies, military branches and Hollywood had become so infiltrated with card-carrying Communists and their "fellow travelers" that American was in imminent danger of a Communist coup. Senator McCarthy destroyed countless lives and reputations with his reckless accusation, but he went too far when he attacked a young lawyer in Welch's law firm.

"Until this moment, Senator," Welch said, I think I have never really gauged your cruelty or your recklessness... If it were in my power to forgive you for your reckless cruelty I would do so, [but I cannot]... Let us not assassinate this lad further, Senator. You've done enough. Have you no sense of decency, sir? At long last, have you left no sense of decency?"

With these few words, and with millions of Americans watching the televised hearings, the McCarthy "Red Scare" fever seemed to break, almost instantaneously, and on December 2, 1954, the Senate, by a vote of 67-22, voted to censure him, making him one of only a very few senators in American history to ever be so disciplined. He died on May 2, 1957 at the age of 48, most likely of complications brought on by his alcoholism.

President Trump, like Senator Joe McCarthy, has repeatedly crossed the line of civility and propriety so many times over the last few years that we have trouble some times of remembering how presidents use to act and how they use to speak, inspiring us to accomplish great things, providing us with hope and solace in times of crisis, mass shootings and natural disasters, and defending democratic institutions and ideals whenever they are threatened, whether at home or elsewhere in the world. Perhaps now, after years of Trump's boorishness and open invitations to Russia and other hostile foreign powers to meddle with our democratic processes, we have finally had enough. Mr. President, at long last have you no shame? If you do not, then it is time for you give up the great office that you have demeaned and diminished – either voluntarily or, if necessarily, involuntarily by way of impeachment or at the ballot box. Either way, you must know that there is a growing chill in the air, that your days are numbered, and that you silent Republican colleagues will pay a great price for their Mephistophelean bargain that they have struck these past two or three years.

TRUMP - RUSSIA TIMELINE

1987	In his ghostwritten book *The Art of the Deal*, Trump says that he spoke with then-Soviet Ambassador Yuri Dubinin "about building a large luxury hotel across the street from the Kremlin in partnership with the Soviet government." Trump actually traveled to the country that year to scout locations.[1]
1996	The Trump Organization explores a potential Moscow real estate deal, but it proves fruitless.[2]
AUGUST 1998	Russia defaults on its debt and Russian stock market collapses. Russian millionaires and billionaires frantically search for a safe-haven outside of Russia to invest their money. The Trump Organization starts specifically marketing to the Russian financial elite and attracts tens and hundreds of millions of dollars from Russia and other former Soviet Union countries into Trump real estate projects in New York City and elsewhere.
OCTOBER 1998	Trump begins construction of the Trump World Tower near the U.N. headquarters on the East Side of Manhattan, and begins selling units

to Russians and other Eastern European and Central Asian buyers, even though the building is not scheduled to open until 2001. By 2004, one-third of buyers of the units on the top floors of the building (76th through 83rd floor) involve people or entities from Russia or neighboring countries.

2005   The Trump Organization signs a one-year deal with the Bayrock Group for a construction project in Moscow. One of the Bayrock Group's principal owners is Felix Sater, a Russian-born businessman with links to Russian organized crime. Working with Russian investors, Sater finds an old pencil factory in Moscow he believes could be the site for a Trump luxury skyscraper.[3] Sater handles the negotiations, but gives Trump regular updates on the project, visiting Trump's office at Trump Tower in Manhattan to tell him that, for example, they were "Moving forward on the Moscow deal." The deal never materializes, but Trump and Sater stay in close touch.

JUNE 2005   Paul Manafort proposes to Russian oligarch Oleg Deripaska that he be retained to develop a strategy for influencing politics, business dealings and news coverage inside the United States, Europe and former Soviet republics to benefit

274

the Deripaska and the Russian government.

2006

Donald Trump Jr. and Ivanka Trump travel with Sater to Moscow, where Sater takes Trump's children on a tour of the Kremlin. Ivanka gets to sit and spun around in Putin's chair when the Russian president isn't around.[4]

2007

At a 2007 deposition, Trump testifies that "Russia is one of the hottest places in the world for investment," adding: "We will be in Moscow at some point."[5]

SEPTEMBER 19, 2007

Trump launches his Trump SoHo project in downtown Manhattan, which he is developing largely with money from Russia and its neighboring countries, with the assistance of Russian-born financier and former felon Felix Sater and Kazakhstan-born developer Tevfik Arif, who are financing the project through their company, Bayrock.

OCTOBER 15, 2007

In an interview with Larry King, Trump says: "Look at Putin – what he's doing with Russia – I mean, you know, what's going on over there. I mean this guy has done – whether you like him or don't like him – he's doing a great job."

JULY 2008

Trump sells a Florida mansion to a Russian

oligarch for $95 million (Trump says it was $100 million), despite the fact that the Florida real estate market had begun to crash. Trump had bought the home at auction for $41 million three years earlier. This was reported to be the most expensive home sold in the U.S., at least as of this date.

The Russian buyer-billionaire, Dmitry Rybolov-lev, never lived in the home, which was reported to be "unlivable" at the time Trump sold it, and had to be demolished.[6] The property was appraised for only $78.2 million in 2009.

SEPTEMBER 2008
At a real estate conference, Donald Trump Jr. states that money had been "pouring in" to the Trump Organization from Russia and former Soviet states, and since that date, a significant amount – or most -- of the funding for Trump Organization projects is financed by such monies.

JAN. 2010 - JAN. 2011
After leaving Bayrock, Felix Sater becomes senior adviser to Donald Trump, according to his Trump Organization business card. He also has a Trump Organization email address and office.

APRIL 8, 2013
Three Russians whom the FBI later accused of spying on the United States are recorded dis-

cussing efforts to recruit Carter Page. According to *The Washington Post*, "[T]he government's application for the surveillance order targeting Page included a lengthy declaration that laid out investigators' basis for believing that Page was an agent of the Russian government and knowingly engaged in clandestine intelligence activities on behalf of Moscow, officials said."

JUNE 18, 2013

Anxiously anticipating the Miss Universe Pageant later in the year, Trump tweets: "Do you think Putin will be going to The Miss Universe Pageant in November in Moscow - if so, will he become my new best friend?"

JULY 8, 2013

After a BBC reporter questions Trump about Felix Sater's alleged prior connections to organized crime, Trump ends the interview.

OCTOBER 17, 2013

When David Letterman asks Trump, "Have you had any dealings with the Russians?" Trump answers, "Well I've done a lot of business with the Russians..." Letterman then asks, "Vladimir Putin, have you ever met the guy?" Trump says, "He's a tough guy. I met him once."

OCTOBER 2013

Boris Epshteyn, who has spent much of his professional career promoting investments in Russia, particularly the City of Moscow, organizes a conference in New York City called "Invest in Moscow!" He puts together panels that were mainly comprised of Moscow city government officials, like Sergey Cheremin, who heads up Moscow's foreign economic and international relations department.[7]

NOVEMBER 2013

Trump attends Miss Universe Pageant Competition in Moscow, where he meets various wealthy Russian oligarchs with close ties to Putin, including Aris Agalarov, who claims to have introduced Trump to various well-connected business and real estate people while he is in Moscow.[8] Trump makes a cameo appearance in a video with Agalarov's pop-star son, Emin Agalarov.[9] On November 11, 2013, Trump expresses his appreciation to Agalarov by tweeting: "I had a great weekend with you and your family. You have done a FANTASTIC job. TRUMP TOWER-MOSCOW is next. EMIN was WOW!"[10]

NOVEMBER 2013

Two real estate developers with close ties to Putin's inner circle — Alex Sapir and Rotem Rosen — also join Trump in Russia and work to make a real estate deal happen.[11] Putin does not attend the Pageant, but sends his regrets and a small gift to show his appreciation for Trump.

NOVEMBER 2013

While in Moscow for the Miss Universe Pageant, Trump spends two nights at the Ritz-Carlton in Moscow, the site of some salacious allegations by former British MI-6 agent Christopher Steele in his Dossier, later made public by Buzzfeed on January 10, 2017, in which Steele suggests that Trump was compromised by Russian intelligence and that it is possible that the Russians have surveillance tapes and recordings of Trump's alleged escapades while in Moscow.

NOVEMBER 2013

Upon his return from Moscow, Trump tells Real Estate Weekly: "The Russian market is attracted to me," adding, "I have a great relationship with many Russians, and almost all of the oligarchs were in the room."

NOVEMBER 5, 2013

In a deposition, an attorney asks Trump about Felix Sater. "If he were sitting in the room right now, I really wouldn't know what he looked like," Trump answers. When asked how many times he had ever spoken with Sater, Trump says, "Not many." When asked about his July 2013 BBC interview during which he was questioned about Sater's alleged connections to organized crime, Trump says he didn't remember it.

FEBRUARY - MARCH 2014   Paul Manafort's primary client, pro-Russian Ukraine President Viktor Yanukovich, flees Ukraine after a popular uprising known as the Maidan and seeks refuge in Russia under the protection of Putin and the Kremlin leadership. Manafort continues to represent the pro-Russian forces in Ukraine with the help of Rick Gates and a Russian-Ukrainian GRU military intelligence officer by the name of Konstantin Kilimnik. In their haste to flee Kiev, the pro-Russian Ukraine government leaders leave behind incriminating evidence, including a Black Ledger linking Manafort to the payment of $12.7 million in off-the-books payments from the pro-Russian Party of Regions.

MARCH 6, 2014   At the 2014 Conservative Political Action Conference, Trump says: "You know, I was in Moscow a couple of months ago. I own the Miss Universe Pageant and they treated me so great. Putin even sent me a present, a beautiful present." On the same day, President Obama signs an executive order imposing sanctions on Russia for its unlawful annexation of Crimea.

NOVEMBER 2014   Jared Kushner and his brother Joshua form a real estate investment company – Cadre – which attracts substantial venture capital from Russian high-tech billionaire Yuri Milner.[12] Other Russian and Chinese investors who invest in Cadre and other Kushner companies are rewarded with U.S. visas as part of the EB-5 program.

JANUARY - JUNE 2015   Carter Page meets and gives documents relating to U.S. sanctions against Russia to Victor Podobnyy, a Russian intelligence operative in New York City. An indictment unsealed in January 2015 show that Podobnyy tried to recruit Page ("Male-1") "as an intelligence source." Pobodnyy refers to Page as an "idiot," but considered him to be useful.

MAY 2015   Trump son-in-law Jared Kushner's real estate company pays $295 million for the majority share in the former New York Times Building on West 43rd Street in Manhattan as part of a deal with Lev Leviev, the Uzbek-Israeli "King of Diamonds" with close ties to Vladimir Putin.[13] Leviev is the chairman of Africa Israel Investments Ltd., which has a Russian subsidiary, AFI Development PLC, a public company traded on the London Stock Exchange which is one of the largest real estate development companies in Russia.[14] Leviev is also chairman of the Federation of the Jewish Communities of the CIS (former Soviet republics), and is closely associated with Rabbi Berel Lazar, the Chief Rabbi of Moscow who is often referred to as "Putin's rabbi."[15]

JUNE 16, 2015

Trump announces that he is a running for President.

JULY 2015

As Felix Sater later told BuzzFeed News on May 17, 2018, Sater decides that he and Trump should capitalize on all the press attention that Trump was receiving to push the Moscow Trump Tower deal forward. "I figured, he's in the news, his name is generating a lot of good press," Sater says. "A lot of Russians weren't willing to pay a premium licensing fee to put Donald's name on their building. Now maybe they would be."

STARTING JULY 2015

Russian military intelligence (GRU) gains access to the Democratic National Committee (DNC) computer network and continues to access this until at least June 2016, as part of a computer hacking and cyber warfare plan by the Russian government to disrupt U.S. democratic and electoral processes, and to influence the 2016 presidential election in Trump's favor.

AUGUST 16, 2015

Trump Campaign announces it is firing Roger Stone after negative news reporting on Stone; Stone says he quit. Either way, Stone remains a trusted confident of Trump and regular surrogate on cable TV and other media outlets.

SEPTEMBER 2015

Sater organizes a meeting with Michael Cohen, Trump's personal attorney and "fixer," to discuss having Trump license his name on a Russian-built building in Moscow. The plan is that the Trump Organization wouldn't actually construct the Moscow tower, but it would put his name on the structure and receive a portion of the revenue that was generated.[16] Sater goes to work finding a builder and financing for the project.

SEPTEMBER 21, 2015

On Hugh Hewitt's radio program, Trump says, "The oligarchs are under [Putin's] control, to a large extent. I mean, he can destroy them, and he has destroyed some of them... Two years ago, I was in Moscow . . . I was with the top-level people, both oligarchs and generals, and top-of-the-government people. I can't go further than that, but I will tell you that I met the top people, and the relationship was extraordinary."

SEPTEMBER 29, 2015

Trump tells Bill O'Reilly: "I will tell you in terms of leadership he [Putin] is getting an 'A,' and our president is not doing so well."

OCTOBER 12, 2015

Sater emails Cohen that Putin and a "top deputy" would meet with a surrogate for Sater in Moscow. He also advises that a Russian bank — VTB Bank — would fund the project.[17]

OCTOBER 13, 2015   Felix Sater sends an email to Michael Cohen, executive VP of the Trump Organization and Trump's personal lawyer, attaching a letter of intent signed by Andrey Rozov, owner of L.C. Export Investment Co., of Moscow, for the development of "Trump World Tower Moscow" for Trump's signature. The Tower is planned to be 100 stories tall with a pointy top, with a spa and fitness area to be branded 'The Spa by Ivanka Trump." The agreement calls for the payment of a $4 million upfront fee to the Trump Organization, plus no upfront costs, a percentage of the sales, and control over marketing and design." The email suggests that this deal would cement relations between the Trump Organization and Russian President Vladimir Putin.

OCTOBER 28, 2015   According to Michael Cohen's statement to congressional investigators on August 28, 2017, Donald Trump signs the letter of intent for Trump World Moscow Tower. This is the same day as the third Republican presidential debate. Later, on December 18, 2018, CNN obtains the signed copy of the letter. On behalf of Trump, Cohen afterwards wrote to Sater and Rozov that "we are truly looking forward to this wonderful opportunity."

NOVEMBER 3, 2015   Sater emails Cohen, referring to the Moscow real estate project: "Michael we can own this story. Donald doesn't stare down, he negotiates and understands the economic issues and Putin only wants to deal with a pragmatic leader, and a successful business man is a good candidate for someone who knows how to negotiate. "Business, politics, whatever it all is the same for someone who knows how to deal."[18]

Sater further writes to Cohen: "I will get Putin on this program and we will get Donald elected," adding:"Buddy our boy can become President of the USA and we can engineer it. I will get all of Putins [sic] team to buy in on this."[19] In addition, Sater writes: "Everything will be negotiated and discussed not with flunkies but with people who will have dinner with Putin and discuss the issues and get a go-ahead... "My next steps are very sensitive with Putin's very, very close people. We can pull this off."

NOVEMBER 10, 2015   At a Republican primary debate, Trump says: "I got to know [Putin] very well because we were both on 60 Minutes. We were stablemates, and we did very well that night."

NOVEMBER 30, 2015   An Associated Press reporter asks Trump about Felix Sater. Trump answers, "Felix Sater, boy, I have to even think about it. I'm not that familiar with him."

DECEMBER 10, 2015

Retired Lt. Gen. Michael Flynn attends gala dinner and 10th Anniversary celebration in Moscow for RT (Russia Today), a Russian government propaganda arm. Flynn is photographed sitting at the same table next to Vladimir Putin. Flynn, who later becomes a foreign policy advisor and then National Security Advisor to Trump, gives a speech that is critical of the Obama administration's foreign policy towards Russia. He is paid $45,000 for his appearance by the Russian news agency, which he later fails to report as income on his government financial disclosure forms.

JANUARY 2016

Michael Cohen writes to Putin's spokesman, Dmitri S. Peskov, asking for help restarting the Trump Tower project, which had stalled. But Mr. Cohen did not appear to have Mr. Peskov's direct email, and instead wrote to a general inbox for press inquiries.[20]

FEBRUARY 17, 2016

As Trump begins to realize that not every American voter loves Russia as much as he does, Trump uncharacteristically walks back his story about his relationship with Russia: He tells the press: "I have no relationship with [Putin], other than he called me a genius."

FEBRUARY 29, 2016   Paul Manafort submits a five-page, single-spaced, proposal to Trump, outlining his primary qualifications that were of interest to Trump, which is assisting rich and powerful oligarchs and dictators in Russia, Ukraine and other parts of the world. Trump sees real value in Manafort's Russia connections and accepts Manafort's offer to work without compensation. Shortly thereafter, on March 29, 2016, Manafort is hired by the Campaign and, within a few weeks, on April 20, 2016, is named Campaign Chairman.

MARCH 17, 2016   Jeff Sessions climbs aboard Trump's pro-Russia campaign express train by saying, "I think an argument can be made there is no reason for the US and Russia to be at this loggerheads. Somehow, someway we ought to be able to break that logjam. Strategically it's not justified for either country."

MARCH 2016   By March of 2016, Russian intelligence operatives already have established close ties with Wikileaks and Assange, and with the acquisition of a treasure trove of documents from the hacked emails from the Clinton Campaign and the Democratic Congressional Campaign Committee in late March and early April 2016, U.S. intelligence agencies are able to confirm that Wikileaks had essentially become an arm of Russian intelligence.

MARCH 2016

According to a report by *The Guardian* on November 27, 2018, Manafort meets with Julian Assange of Wikileaks inside the Ecuadorian embassy in London in 2013, 2015, and then again in March of 2016.[21] If accurate, this information provides further proof of the links – through WikiLeaks -- between the Trump Campaign and the Russian intelligence operatives who were collecting illegally hacked documents used to badly damage the Hillary Clinton Campaign.

Papadopoulos sends emails concerning possible meeting with Putin to at least seven campaign officials, and Trump national campaign co-chairman Sam Clovis encourages Papadopoulos to fly to Russia to meet with agents of the Russian Foreign Ministry, after being told that Russia had "dirt" on Hillary Clinton it wanted to share with Trump's campaign.

MARCH 21, 2016

At an editorial board meeting with the Washington Post, Trump announces that Carter Page was a member of his foreign policy team. It is later learned that the FBI was monitoring Page's communications as part of an already ongoing investigation of Russian influence on the presidential campaign and election. Page had been identified by the FBI and U.S. intelligence as a Russian agent as early as 2013 in an investigation that led to the arrest and imprisonment of a Russian agent posing as a Russian banker.

MARCH 21, 2016

At the same Trump meeting with the Washington Post editorial board, Trump names George Papadopoulos as another one of his foreign policy advisors, calling him "an excellent guy." Papadopoulos later discloses to an Australian diplomat that the Russians had "dirt" on Hillary Clinton, and when the FBI is informed by an Australian diplomat, the Russia probe is initiated. Papadopoulos later pleads guilty to lying to FBI agents about his contacts with Russian operatives; his conversations are monitored for a period of at least several months as part of a FISA warrant, which was renewed three times for 90-day periods.

APRIL 2016

Manafort emails Russian agent (and his "handler") Konstantin Kilimnik to ask of the "OVD [Oleg V. Deripaska] operation" had seen the positive press that Manafort was receiving for his work with the Trump Campaign. "How do we use [this positive press and Manafort's position atop the Campaign] to get whole?"

Manafort emailed Kilimnik.

LATE APRIL 2016

The Democratic National Committee's IT department notices suspicious computer activity, contacts the FBI, and hires a private security firm, CrowdStrike, to investigate.

MAY 2016

CrowdStrike determines that highly sophisticated Russian intelligence-affiliates are responsible for the DNC hack.

MAY 2016

At the request of Roger Stone, Michael Caputo -- senior Trump campaign communications adviser who has deep business ties to Russia --arranges for Stone to meet in Sunny Isles, Florida with a Russian national, "Henry Greenberg" (a.k.a. Henry Oknyansky), who says that he had damaging information on Hillary Clinton. Stone later says that he rejected the proposal from Greenberg because he asked for $2 million.

MAY 7, 2016

Russian agent Konstantin Kilimnik later tells the Washington Post that he came to the U.S. on May 7, 2016 to discuss "business issues." One of these "issues" was how to monetize their relationship with Oleg Deripaska, a Russian oligarch close to Putin by offering him "private briefings" on the Trump Campaign.

MAY 21, 2016

George Papadopoulos emails Paul Manafort, a Trump advisor and later (as of June 20, 2016) Trump Campaign Chairman, stating: "Russia has been eager to meet Mr. Trump for quite sometime and have been reaching out to me to discuss."

Also in May 2016, Papadopoulos tells a woman who knows the top Australian diplomat to the United Kingdom, Alexander Downer, that Russia had email "dirt" on Hillary Clinton, and Papadopoulos confirms to Downer the existence of these emails. After the DNC emails stolen by Russia were published by Wikileaks, on July 22, 2016, Australian officials relayed Papadopoulos' statements to American officials. This triggers the FBI to open an investigation into the Russian interference in the 2016 United States elections.

JUNE 3, 2016

Don Jr. receives an email from publicist Rob Goldstone saying that the Russians had information that could be damaging to the Clinton campaign that was purportedly "part of Russian and its government's support for Mr. Trump." The email also states that Russian pop star Emin Agalarov was reaching out on behalf of his father, Aras Agalarov, a Russian real estate developer who had ties to Donald Trump Sr.

with regard to the 2013 Miss Universe pageant in Moscow run by Trump. Goldstone further writes that "the Crown prosecutor of Russia met with his father Aras this morning and in their meeting offered to provide the Trump campaign with some official documents and information that would incriminate Hillary and her dealings with Russia and would be very useful to your father. This is obviously very high level and sensitive information but is part of Russia and its government's support for Mr. Trump – helped along by Aras and Emin." Don Jr. responds: "[I]f it's what you say I love it especially later in the summer."

JUNE 9, 2016

Donald Trump Jr., Paul Manafort and Jared Kushner meet at Trump Tower with Natalia Veselnitskaya, a Russian lawyer close to the Russian leadership and other Russian operatives to discuss a proposal that the Russians provide stolen emails and other "dirt" on Hillary Clinton in return for the agreement from the Trump Campaign that, if elected president, Donald Trump would ease the U.S. sanctions on Russia. Also present are Ike Kaveladze, a vice president of a Russian real estate company, Rinat Akhmetshin, a Russian-American lobbyist, and Anatoli Samochornov, a translator. The meeting takes place on the floor below Donald Trump's office in Trump Tower. Mr. Trump was in New York on that day. Steve Bannon, who was not present at the meeting, has publicly described the meeting as "treasonous" and that there was "zero" chance that Candidate Trump did not know about the meeting.

JUNE 12, 2016   Julian Assange of Wikileaks publicly confirms during a BBC interview that he had damning emails relating to Clinton.

JUNE 15, 2016   Guccifer 2.0, a Russian intelligence front, takes credit in a blog post for hacking the DNC computers and releases some documents, including the DNC's 200-page opposition research report on Donald Trump. The blog further discloses that the bulk of the stolen files and emails were given to Wikileaks, which had become, for all intents and purposes, an arm of Russian intelligence. Trump releases a statement accusing the DNC as behind the hacking.

JUNE 20, 2016   Trump names Paul Manafort as his Campaign Chairman, knowing that Manafort had been a key advisor to Viktor Yanukovich, the former pro-Russian President of Ukraine, and a close associate of several Ukrainian and Russian oligarchs close to Vladimir Putin. Manafort had

been named in a civil RICO lawsuit brought
by former Prime Minister Yulia Tymoshenko,
alleging money laundering by Manafort and
other on behalf of Ukraine President Yanukovich and Ukraine oligarch Dimitri Firtash. The
civil RICO case and the exhibits submitted as
part of that case, which was handled by the law
firm of McCallion & Associates LLP, triggered
an FBI investigation that was supervised by the
U.S. Attorney's Office for the Southern District
of New York. When U.S. Attorney Preet Bha-
rara was fired by Trump as head of that office,
and after Trump fired FBI Director Comey, the
Manafort investigation was transferred to Special Counsel Mueller's office.

JULY 5, 2016

FBI Director James Comey holds a press conference announcing that the FBI has closed
its investigation into Hillary Clinton's use of a
private email server while she was secretary of
state. Comey says Clinton had been "extremely
careless" in handling "very sensitive, highly classified information," but does not recommend
prosecution.

JULY 6, 2016

A second batch of hacked DNC documents
appears on the Guccifer 2.0 website.

JULY 7, 2016

Paul Manafort offers to give "private briefings"

to Russian billionaire Oleg Deripaska regarding the 2016 presidential campaign. See Washington Post article, Sept. 20, 2017. Manafort uses Konstantin Kilimnik, a Russian military (GRU) intelligence agent as an intermediary.

JULY 7-8, 2016

Carter Page visits Moscow after informing Jeff Sessions and some other members of the campaign's national security team about his Moscow visit. In his Moscow speech at the New Economic School, Page is critical of U.S. policy toward Russian. Russian Deputy Prime Minister Arkady Dvorkovich also speaks at the event, and Page later admits that he spoke to two Russian government officials during his visit. The FBI later discloses that, in addition to the Papadopoulos information, Page's speech in Moscow "was a catalyst for the FBI investigation into the connections between Russia and President Trump's campaign."

JULY 18-21, 2016

Republican National Convention takes place in Cleveland, Ohio, and nominates Donald J. Trump as Republican presidential candidate. Mike Pence is nominated as Vice Presidential candidate. Michael Flynn leads delegates in "Lock Her Up" chant, referencing Democratic presidential candidate Hillary Clinton. Flynn assures the adoring delegates that he knows the national security business far better than Hillary Clinton, and that "if I did a tenth, a tenth of what she did, I would be in jail today."

JULY 18, 2016

The Washington Post reports that the Trump campaign worked at the Republican Convention to water down a plank of the 2016 Party Platform that gutted the GOP's longstanding support for Ukrainian resistance to Russia's 2014 annexation of Crimea and intervention in eastern Ukraine.

JULY 18, 2016

At a Heritage Foundation event during the Republican Convention, Jeff Sessions speaks individually with Russian ambassador Sergey Kislyak. Sessions later testifies during his confirmation hearing as Attorney General that he had not met or spoken with any Russian officials. Carter Page and J.D. Gordon, another Trump foreign policy advisor, also meet with Kislyak at the Republican Convention.

JULY 22, 2016

WikiLeaks releases nearly 20,000 DNC emails, and eventually released 44,000 emails and 17, 000 attachments. Some of these data dumps were done within hours of the release of the Access Hollywood tape where Trump can be overheard bragging to Billy Bush as to what he, as a celebrity, could do to women.

JULY 22, 2016   Immediately following the Wikileaks release of damaging Clinton emails, Australian officials relay Papadopoulos' statements about Russian involvement in those stolen emails to American officials. This triggers the FBI to open an investigation into the Russian interference in the 2016 United States elections.

JULY 24, 2016   When ABC News' George Stephanopoulos asks whether there were any connections between the Trump campaign and Putin's regime, Trump campaign chair Paul Manafort answers, "No, there are not. And you know, there's no basis to it."

JULY 25, 2016   Trump tweets: "The new joke in town is that Russia leaked the disastrous DNC emails ... because Putin likes me."

JULY 27, 2016   At a press conference, where it was raised that Trump had bragged about a "relationship" with Putin in 2013, Trump states that he doubted that Russia was responsible for hacking the DNC computer network, but invited Russian to find the 30,000 personal emails that Clinton's staff deleted when she left office as U.S. Secretary of State. "Russia, if you're listening, I hope you're able to find the 30,000 emails that are missing."

At the same press conference, he insists: "I never met Putin. I've never spoken to him." In an interview with CBS News, he reiterates: "But I have nothing to do with Russia, nothing to do, I never met Putin, I have nothing to do with Russia whatsoever."

END OF JULY 2016 The FBI has opened an investigation into possible collusion between members of the Trump campaign and Russian operatives.

LATE JULY 2016 Roger Stone asks Jerome Corsi, a conservative writer, to "get to" Julian Assange, the founder of WikiLeaks. Corsi lies about this to the FBI but later admits passing Stone's request on to an intermediary with Assange. According to Corsi, the federal prosecutors were especially interested in an email he sent to Stone on Aug. 2, 2016, saying "Word is friend in embassy plans 2 more dumps," he wrote. "Impact planned to be very damaging." Corsi's "friend in the embassy" is Julian Assange.

Corsi's testimony places Stone in legal jeopardy since testified under oath to the House Intelligence Committee during 2017 that he had no "advance knowledge of the source or actual content of the WikiLeaks disclosure."

JULY 29, 2016

Kilimnik emails Manafort, saying that he had met that day with the man who had given Manafort "the biggest black caviar jar several years ago." The "black caviar jar" is reliably believed to be a reference to a large sum of money. Kilimnik further told Manafort that he and "the man" had talked for five hours and that he had important messages to relay to Manafort as a result. Kilimnik wanted to set up a meeting with Manafort.

JULY 31, 2016

During an ABC News interview, Trump says: "You know, the people of Crimea, from what I I've heard, would rather be with Russia than where they were." In other interviews with the New York Times and in public statements in July 2016, Trump also questioned the U.S. commitment to defending its NATO allies, and promised to "look into" recognizing Russia's de-facto annexation of Crimea.

JULY 31, 2016

Boris Epshteyn, who has been appearing on cable TV programs as Trump's surrogate on Russia-related matters, takes the position on CNN that "Russia did not seize Crimea." This and other statements made by Epshteyn are identical to talking points used by Russian government spokespersons on RT and other Russian government propaganda outlets.

On the same day, Manafort denies knowing anything about the change in the Republican platform regarding Ukraine.

AUGUST 2, 2016

Paul Manafort, Rick Gates and Russian agent Konstantin Kilimnik meet at Grand Havana Room located at 666 Fifth Avenue, a few blocks away from Trump Campaign headquarters in Trump Tower.

Earlier the same day, Manafort asked Gates by email to print out some material for the meeting. At the meeting, the three discussed various matters "very much to the heart of what the special counsel's office is investigating," according to what prosecutor Andrew Weissmann of Mueller's office told Judge Amy Berman Jackson later in early February 2019.[22] It is believed that the topics discussed included (a) the so-called "Ukrainian peace plan" which would effectively concede Russia's annexation of Crimea and lift U.S. sanctions on Russia, and (b) the turn-over from Manafort, then-Trump Campaign Chairman, to Kilimnik (a Russian agent) U.S. polling data, presumably for use by Russia as part of its cyber-criminal disinformation campaign designed to swing the 2016 election away from Clinton and towards Trump. It is reported that this meeting between the three was considered so secret that the three left through separate doors, as later noted by Judge Jackson at a hearing in early February 2019. Weissman further elaborated at the February 2019 court hearing that one of the special counsel's main tasks was to examine "contacts between Americans and Russia" during the 2016 election and to determine whether Trump associates conspired with the Russian-backed interference campaign.[23] "That meeting – and what happened at that meeting – is of significance to the special counsel," Weissman noted.

AUGUST 3, 2016

Flight records show that a private plane belonging to Russian oligarch Oleg Deripaska landed at Newark International Airport shortly after midnight, a few hours after the meeting between Manafort, Gates and Kilimnik. The plane returned to Moscow after being on the ground for only a few hours.

AUGUST 4, 2016

One day after Stone says that he had a conversation with Trump, Stone sends an email to his longtime associate, Sam Nunberg, saying, "I dined with my new pal Julian Assange last nite." It is likely that Stone meant he had an online meeting with Assange, since there is no record of Stone leaving the United States around that time, and Assange was in the Ecuadorian

Embassy in London.

AUGUST 5, 2016   In response to Carter Page's ongoing public criticism of US sanctions against Russia over its annexation of Crimea and his praise for Putin, Trump campaign spokesman Hope Hicks describes Page as an "informal policy adviser" who "does not speak for Mr. Trump or the campaign." Later that month, the FBI obtains a Federal Intelligence Surveillance Act ("FISA") warrant to monitor Page's communications. The initial 90-day warrant is renewed more than once.

AUGUST 8, 2016   Roger Stone, a friend and informal advisor to Trump, says that he had "communicated with [Julian] Assange," referring to the founder of WikiLeaks. He also predicts that "the next tranche of his documents [will] pertain to the Clinton Foundation but there's no telling what the October surprise may be."

AUGUST 9, 2016   Paul Manafort quits or is fired from Trump Campaign, after a series of articles appear disclosing further details regarding the extent of Manafort's ties with the pro-Russian Yanukovich Administration and the millions that he had received. His deputy, Rick Gates, stayed on, presumably to maintain the close working relationship between the Trump campaign and the pro-Putin forces in Russia and Ukraine.

AUGUST 12, 2016

A Russian intelligence online service known as "Guccifer 2.0" releases documents taken from a breach of the Democratic Congressional Campaign Committee (DCCC). On the same day, Guccifer 2.0 tweets Stone, thanking him for his faith in their hacking operation ("thanks that u believe in the real #Guccifer2").

AUGUST 13, 2016

After Twitter had suspended Guccifer2's account, Stone tweets at @wikileaks @GUCCI-FER_2, stating that it was "Outrageous" that Twitter had suspended Guccifer's account.

AUGUST 14, 2016

The New York Times reports that a secret ledger had been discovered in Kiev, Ukraine linking Manafort to $12.7 million in "off the books" payments from a pro-Russian party in Ukraine from 2007 to 2012.

AUGUST 15, 2016

Sam Clovis, Trump's national campaign co-chair, encourages Trump campaign national security advisor George Papadopoulos to make a trip to Russia. This exchange was disclosed as part of court documents relating to the Papadopoulos' plea agreement reached with the Justice Dept. on October 30, 2017.

AUGUST 14-17, 2016   Roger Stone exchanged Twitter messages with
                        Guccifer 2.0. Guccifer tells Stone: "Please tell
                        me if I can help u anyhow."

AUGUST 17, 2016   The Associated Press reports that, in 2012,
                        Manafort secretly routed more than $2 million
                        from Ukraine President Yanukovych's gov-
                        erning pro-Russia Party of Regions to two US
                        lobbying firms working to influence American
                        policy toward Ukraine.

AUGUST 19, 2016   Manafort resigns from the Trump campaign.

AUGUST 21, 2016   Roger Stone predicts that Wikileaks will be pub-
                        licly dumping more stolen emails relating to the
                        Clinton campaign, tweeting: "Trust me, it will
                        soon [be] Podesta's time in the barrel," referring
                        to Clinton campaign chairman John Podesta.
                        It was revealed shortly thereafter that Podes-
                        ta's emails had been hacked, and were publicly
                        released.

SEPTEMBER 8, 2016   Jeff Sessions meets Russian Ambassador Kis-
                        lyak in his Senate office.

SEPTEMBER 23, 2016   Yahoo News reports that U.S. intelligence
                        agencies are investigating whether Page engaged
                        in private communications with senior Russian
                        officials, including talks about a potential lifting

of economic sanctions if Trump is elected president. The report also discloses that Page's activities have been discussed with senior members of Congress during briefings about suspected Russian attempts to influence the election, and that Sen. Reid wrote his August letter to Comey after one of those briefings.

OCTOBER 3, 2016

Roger Stone tweets: "I have total confidence that @wikileaks and my hero Julian Assange will educate the American people soon #Lock-HerUp."

OCTOBER 3-4, 2016

WikiLeaks sends a twitter message to Donald Trump Jr.: "Hiya, it'd be great if you guys could comment on/push this story," referring to comments that Hillary Clinton allegedly made about Julian Assange as to whether the U.S. could "just drone" Assange. Trump Jr. responded: "Already did that earlier today. It's amazing what she can get away with." He also asked WikiLeaks: "What's behind this Wednesday leak I keep reading about?"[24] The following day, on October 4, 2016, Stone and Trump Campaign official Steve Bannon exchanged emails where Stone promised that WikiLeaks disclosures would be forthcoming "a load every week going forward."[25]

OCTOBER 7, 2016   The Department of Homeland Security and the Office of the Director of National Intelligence issue a statement saying the Russian government "directed" the hacking "to interfere with the US election process."

OCTOBER 7, 2016   The Access Hollywood tape on Trump is made public. About 30 minutes later, after the release of the damaging Access Hollywood tapes, WikiLeaks begins to release about 6000 John Podesta's emails.26

OCTOBER 9, 2016   During presidential debate with Democratic presidential nominee Hillary Clinton, Trump says "maybe there is no hacking." That was two days after the U.S. intelligence community issued a statement confirming that the Russian government "directed" the hacking.
Trump: "But I notice, anytime anything wrong happens, they like to say the Russians are [doing the hacking]. Maybe there is no hacking. But they always blame Russia."

OCTOBER 11, 2016   Trump tweets: "I hope people are looking at the disgraceful behavior of Hillary Clinton as exposed by WikiLeaks. She is unfit to run."

OCTOBER 12, 2016   WikiLeaks asks Don Jr. in a twitter message to have his father tweet a link to WikiLeaks-disclosed Democratic emails: "Hey Donald, great to see you and your dad talking about our publications. Strongly suggest your dad tweets this link if he mentions us wisearch.tk. i.e you guys can get all your followers digging through the content. There's many great stories the press are missing and we're sure some of your follows will find it."

OCTOBER 12, 2016

Roger Stone tells NBC News, "I have back-channel communications with WikiLeaks."

OCTOBER 19, 2016

During the third presidential debate, Trump dismisses the Oct. 7, 2016 U.S. intelligence findings: "[Clinton] has no idea whether it is Russia, China or anybody else ... Our country has no idea." Trump adds: "I don't know Putin. I have no idea ... I never met Putin. This is not my best friend."

OCTOBER 21, 2016

The FBI receives approval from the Foreign Intelligence Surveillance Court (the FISA court) to monitor the communications of Carter Page.

OCTOBER 28, 2016

In a letter to key leaders in the House and Senate, which is quickly leaked to the press, FBI Director Comey says that in connection with the FBI's closed investigation into Hillary Clinton's private email server, it was reviewing emails on a computer belonging to Clinton adviser Huma Abedin. Comey says nothing about the ongoing FBI investigation into connections between the Trump campaign and Russia.

OCTOBER 30, 2016   According to MSNBC's Rachel Maddow, the $100 million plane belonging to the Russian oligarch who had bought a Florida residence from Trump in 2008 was in Las Vegas on the same day Trump was holding a rally there.

NOVEMBER 5, 2016   In a letter to key leaders in Congress, Comey confirms that the FBI has completed its review of the additional Abedin emails and has not changed its earlier recommendation not to recommend prosecuting Clinton for her use of a private email server.

NOVEMBER 8, 2016   Trump is elected as President based upon Electoral College tally, despite losing by about 3 million votes.

NOVEMBER 9, 2016   After Putin announces Trump's election victory, Russia's Parliament erupts in applause.

NOVEMBER 10, 2016   Russia's deputy foreign minister admits that the Kremlin had continuing communications with Trump's "immediate entourage" during the campaign.

NOVEMBER 10, 2016   President-elect Trump meets with President
                     Obama, who warns him not to hire Michael
                     Flynn for any significant position in his admin-
                     istration.

NOVEMBER 18, 2016   President-elect Trump appoints Michael Flynn
                     as his national security adviser.

NOVEMBER 2016   Felix Sater, Michael Cohen and a pro-Russian
                     Ukrainian politician present a "peace plan"
                     relating to Ukraine to the White House, which
                     basically took a pro-Russian view that Russia's
                     annexation of Crimea should be recognized by
                     the U.S. and that the U.S. should not interfere in
                     pro-Russian efforts to occupy additional por-
                     tions of eastern Ukraine.

DECEMBER 1-2, 2016   Jared Kushner, Trump's son-in-law and advisor,
                     and Michael Flynn meet with Russian ambas-
                     sador Kislyak at Trump Tower. Kushner and
                     Kislyak discuss the possibility of setting up a
                     secret and secure communications channel be-
                     tween Trump's transition team and the Kremlin.
                     See Washington Post article, May 2017. Kush-
                     ner confirms to congressional investigators on
                     July 24, 2017: "I asked if they had an existing
                     communications channel at his embassy we
                     could use where they would be comfortable
                     transmitting the information they wanted to re-

lay to General Flynn." Kushner and Flynn were apparently concerned that the FBI or other U.S. intelligence operatives would intercept these communications.

DECEMBER 8-13, 2016   Page visits Moscow again, telling state-operated RIA Novosti news service, "I am meeting with business leaders and thought leaders." Kremlin spokesman Dmitry S. Peskov tells journalists that Russian officials had no plans to meet with Page and Russian Deputy Foreign Minister Sergei Ryabkov says that foreign ministry officials also had no plans to meet Page. Page says he had "the opportunity to meet with an executive from Rosneft," the Russian oil giant, while in Moscow.

Page confirms to Sputnik News on December 12, 2016 that he had attended numerous meeting with Trump.

DECEMBER 9, 2016   Trump questions the U.S. intelligence community's track record — citing its intelligence work prior to the Iraq war in 2003.

Trump: "These are the same people that said Saddam Hussein had weapons of mass destruction." Trump added: "The election ended a long time ago in one of the biggest Electoral College victories in history. It's now time to move on…"

DECEMBER 11, 2016

In an interview on Fox News, Trump says the U.S. intelligence community did not know who was behind the hacking.

Trump: "They have no idea if it's Russia or China or somebody. It could be somebody sitting in a bed some place. I mean, they have no idea."

DECEMBER 11, 2016

Trump praises Rex Tillerson, chairman of ExxonMobil and receipient of Russia's "Order of Friendship" Medal from Vladimir Putin in 2013, as "much more than a business executive" and a "world-class player." Trump says that Tillerson "knows many of the players" and did "massive deals in Russia" for Exxon.

DECEMBER 13, 2016

Trump nominates Rex Tillerson to be Secretary of State. Former Russian Energy Minister Vladimir Milov tells NBC news that Tillerson was a "gift for Putin." Rumors swirl that Putin had "vetoed" Mitt Romney for the post because he was a hardline anti-Russian.

DECEMBER 13, 2016

Jared Kushner meets with Sergey N. Gorkov, the chief of Vnesheconombank (VNB), a Russian state-owned bank that was sanctioned by the Obama administration in 2014 after Russia annexed Crimea. These sanctions prohibit any U.S. citizen from dealing with the bank. In a statement released by the bank after the meeting became publicly known, it is stated that Gorkov met with Kushner in his capacity as the then-chief executive officer of Kushner Companies, a real estate development company looking for capital.

Kushner, however, told Congressional investigators in an 11-page letter on or about July 24, 2017, emphatically insisting that the meeting had nothing to do with his work as a businessman. He said the men did not discuss sanctions against Russia or anything about "my companies, business transactions, real estate projects, loans, banking arrangements or any private business of any kind."[27]

DECEMBER 22, 2016   Michael Flynn asks Ambassador Kislyak if Russia would delay or defeat the upcoming U.N. Security Council resolution vote that sought to condemn Israel's building of settlements in the West Bank and East Jerusalem. The Obama administration had agreed to allow the resolution to come up for a vote.

DECEMBER 29, 2016   The Obama administration announces a num-

ber of punitive actions and sanctions "in response to the Russian government's aggressive
harassment of U.S. officials and cyber operations aimed at the U.S. election in 2016."

DECEMBER 29, 2016   Later that same day, Michael Flynn, with the
knowledge and consent of Trump and national
security advisor K.T. McFarland, who are at
Trump's resort at Mar-A-Lago in Florida, calls
Russian Ambassador Kislyak and requests that
Russia not retaliate in response to the additional
sanctions imposed on Russia earlier that day, explicitly or implicitly implying that Russia should
wait until after Trump's inauguration, so that
the Trump Administration could make good on
its promise to have closer relations with Russia
by lifting the sanctions.

DECEMBER 30, 2016   Russian President Putin issues a statement saying that Russia will not retaliate against the U.S.
for imposing sanctions, expressing his hope that
the incoming Trump administration will pave
the way "toward the restoration of Russia-Unit-
ed States relations...." Trump praises Putin in a
tweet, calling him "very smart!"

JANUARY 3, 2017   Trump questions the motives and integrity
of the U.S. intelligence community by tweet-
ing: "The 'Intelligence' briefing on so-called

313

"Russian hacking" was delayed until Friday, perhaps more time needed to build a case. Very strange!"

JANUARY 4, 2017   Trump favorably quotes WikiLeaks founder Julian Assange to cast doubt on the intelligence community's findings about Russia's involvement in the election. According to the U.S. intelligence report, Russian military intelligence used WikiLeaks to publicly release hacked emails that were damaging to Clinton, a claim Assange denied and which denial Trump accepted. Trump: "Julian Assange said "a 14 year old could have hacked Podesta" - why was DNC so careless? Also said Russians did not give him the info!"

JANUARY 6, 2017   The Office of the Director of National Intelligence releases a declassified intelligence report, subscribed to by all 17 U.S. intelligence agencies, concluding: "Russian President Vladimir Putin ordered an influence campaign in 2016 aimed at the US presidential election." It describes the cyberattack on the U.S. Trump never acknowledges the accuracy of this report, and repeatedly characterizes it as "fake news."

JANUARY 6, 2017   On the same day, Trump is briefed by FBI Director Comey on a two-page synopsis of the

Dossier prepared by Christopher Steele, a former British intelligence (MI-6) officer, regarding Trump's and the Trump Campaign's ties with Russian operatives, and compromising information that the Russians allegedly had on Trump.

JANUARY 10, 2017   At his confirmation hearings, U.S. Attorney General-designee Jeff Sessions denies any contact between the Trump campaign and the Russians: "I have been called a surrogate at a time or two in that campaign and I didn't have – did not have communications with the Russians." Sessions later acknowledges that he had two meetings with Kislyak during the campaign.

JANUARY 10, 2017   BuzzFeed publishes the full 35-page Steele Dossier.

JANUARY 11, 2017   Trump accuses U.S. intelligence agencies of leaking a two-page synopsis of the Steele Dossier, which concluded that Russia had damaging information on Trump. According to multiple CNN sources, one reason the nation's intelligence chiefs took the extraordinary step of including the synopsis in the briefing documents was to make the President-elect aware that such allegations involving him were circulating among intelligence agencies, senior members of Congress and other government officials in

Washington. These senior intelligence officials also included the synopsis in the briefing of President-elect Trump to demonstrate that Russia had compiled information potentially harmful to both political parties, but only released information damaging to Hillary Clinton and Democrats.

Trump claims the leak of the two-page synopsis of the Steele Dossier was done to take "one last shot at me, comparing it to "living in Nazi Germany." Trump tweets: "Intelligence agencies should never have allowed this fake news to 'leak' into the public. One last shot at me. Are we living in Nazi Germany?"

JANUARY 11, 2017   UAE Crown Prince Mohammed bin Zayed Al-Nahyan ("MBZ"), Erik Prince, the founder of private military contractor Blackwater, and Kirill Dmitriev, a Russian banker, meet in the Seychelles, an island nation in the Indian ocean. It is believed that Eric Prince told the House Intelligence Committee that the meeting with Dmitriev was a chance business meeting and that nothing of substance was discussed. However, according to Lebanese-American George Nader, who is cooperating with the Mueller investigation, the meeting was pre-arranged so that Prince, a Trump supporter and brother of

Betsy DeVos, Trump's Education Secretary, and Dmitriev could discuss a "back channel" communications link between the Trump team and the Kremlin. Nader has already testified before the Grand Jury.

JANUARY 12, 2017

White House press secretary Sean Spicer denies that Trump knows who Carter Page is.

JANUARY 13, 2017

In response to The Washington Post's article about Flynn's Dec. 29 conversations with the Russian ambassador Kislyak, press secretary Sean Spicer says it was only one call, and that they "exchanged logistical information" for an upcoming call between Trump and Putin after the inauguration.

JANUARY 15, 2017

Trump tells the Times of London: "We should trust Putin." Trump further says that he is skeptical about NATO, and sharply criticizes German Chancellor Angela Merkel.

JANUARY 15, 2017

Vice President Mike Pence, on CBS's Face the Nation, says: "What I can confirm, having to spoken with [Flynn] about it, is that those conversations that happened to occur around the time that the United States took action to expel diplomats had nothing whatsoever to do with those sanctions."

JANUARY 20, 2017

Trump sworn in as 45th President of the United States. He gives his "American Carnage" speech, portraying America, in essence, as a wasteland that only he can save.

JANUARY 20, 2017

Ivanka Trump attends inauguration with her good friend, Dasha Zhukova, the wife of Putin crony and Russian oligarch Roman Abramovich.[28]Ivanka and Dasha are also photographed together at the U.S. Open tennis tournament and other events.[29]

JANUARY 21, 2017

On his first full day as president, Trump visits the CIA headquarters in Langley, Virginia. In his remarks, Trump promised to support the intelligence community, but then blames the media for distorting his past statements about U.S. intelligence.

"And the reason you're my first stop is that, as you know, I have a running war with the media. They are among the most dishonest human beings on Earth. And they sort of made it sound like I had a feud with the intelligence community. And I just want to let you know, the reason you're the number-one stop is exactly the opposite — exactly.

JANUARY 22, 2017

Mike Flynn is sworn in as national security advisor.

JANUARY 23, 2017

Notwithstanding National Park Service and other photos showing that Trump's inaugural crowd was substantially smaller than that of President Obama at either one of his inaugurations, White House Press Secretary Sean Spicer erroneously states: "This was the largest audience to ever witness an inauguration, period, both in person and around the globe." White House counselor Kellyanne Conway defends Spicer's false statement by claiming that Spicer was using "alternative facts."

JANUARY 24, 2017

Two days after he was sworn in as Trump's national security adviser, Flynn is interviewed by FBI agents, who ask him about two conversations that he had with Ambassador Kislyak in December 2016. Flynn lies to them, stating that he did not ask Kislyak in the December 29, 2016 conversation to have Russia refrain from retaliating in response to the Obama administrations Russia sanctions announced that same day for interfering in the 2016 elections. He also falsely denies having asked Kislyak in the December 22, 2106 conversation for Russia to delay or defeat the U.N. Security Council resolution condemning Israel.

JANUARY 24, 2017

One of Trump's first actions in office is to sign an executive order expediting approval of the

Keystone XL pipeline, which was designed to transport Canadian tar sands oil southward through the Dakotas to Texas. 40% of the steel for the pipeline is manufactured by the Canadian subsidiary of a Russian company, Evraz PLC, partially owned by Roman Abramovich. Construction of the pipeline had been halted by the Obama Administration in November 2015 based on environmental and other concerns. One of Trump's campaign promises was to reverse this Obama order and to finish construction of the pipeline. Owned by TransCanada, the pipeline is intended to move Canadian tar sands oil southward through the Dakotas to Illinois, Oklahoma, and Texas. On January 24, 2017, Trump also signs another executive order requiring that the steel for all U.S. pipelines had to be made in the U.S. to the "maximum extent possible."[30] On March 3, 2017, however, Trump basically exempts the Russian/Canadian steel piping from this "buy American steel" requirement by "clarifying" that that the requirement only applies to new pipelines, not those like the Keystone pipeline already under construction.[31]

JANUARY 26, 2017   Acting Attorney General Sally Yates meets with White House counsel Donald McGahn at the White House, telling McGahn that high-ranking administration officials, including Vice President Pence, had made statement about Flynn's conduct that the Justice Dept. knew to be untrue. In response, the White House takes no action to prevent Flynn from continuing to access top secret documents until the FBI investigation of him later became public knowledge. Trump also orders that Yates be fired.

JANUARY 27, 2017   During a dinner at the White House, President Trump asks for a pledge of "loyalty" from then FBI Director James Comey, who was overseeing the investigation of alleged collusion between the Trump Campaign and Russian operatives. According to Comey's later congressional testimony, Trump said: "I need loyalty, I expect loyalty." Comey replied: "You will always get honesty from me." Trump responded: "That's what I want, honest loyalty."

JANUARY 27, 2017   The FBI interviews Papadopoulos, who makes false statements to the effect that he did not have contact with Russians during the campaign. He later pleads guilty to lying to FBI agents, and cooperates with the Special Counsel's investigation.

JANUARY 30, 2017   Trump fires Acting Attorney General Yates for not enforcing the Muslim travel ban. In a statement, Trump says that she had 'betrayed the Department of Justice" by refusing to defend the travel ban in court.

LATE JANUARY 2017
Felix Sater and Andrii Artemenko, a pro-Russian legislator from Ukraine meet with Michael Cohen and give him a pro-Russian "peace plan" for Ukraine whereby Russia would "lease" portions of Ukraine for 50 or 100 years and the U.S. would ease or eliminate sanctions on Russia. Cohen says that he will give the plan to Michael Flynn.

FEBRUARY 2017
During an interview, Russian agent Konstantin Kilimnik described to Radio Free Europe the key role polling date had played in Manafort's political consulting work. "I've seen him work in different countries, and he really just does, you know, take very seriously his polling and, you know, he can stand, you know, two weeks going through the data, and he'll come with the best strategy you can ever have, and he'll put it on the table of the candidate," Kilimnik said.

FEBRUARY 10, 2017
On the Friday before Trump spends a weekend at Mar-A-Lago, a plane belonging to the Russian oligarch who had bought a Palm Beach, Florida residence from Trump in 2008 flies from the south of France to Miami International Airport.

FEBRUARY 13, 2017   Flynn resigns (or is fired), acknowledging that he misled VP Mike Pence and others about his conversations with Russian Ambassador Kislyak.

FEBRUARY 14, 2017   Trump privately meets with FBI Director James Comey in the Oval Office, after asking all those present to leave the room. Trump then asks Director Comey to, in words or substance, make sure that the FBI drops the investigation of former National Security Advisor Michael Flynn. According to Comey, Trump says: "I hope you can let this go, you can see your way clear to letting this go, to letting Flynn go. He is a good guy. I hope you can let this go," referring to the Flynn investigation.

FEBRUARY 14, 2017   Trump directs several officials to leave a White House briefing so that he can speak privately with Daniel Coats, the Director of National Intelligence, and Mike Pompeo, the CIA Director. Trump then asks them to persuade Comey to "back off" the investigation of Michael Flynn.

FEBRUARY 16, 2017   During a press conference, Trump says: "I own nothing in Russia. I have no loans in Russia. I don't have any deals in Russia... Russia is fake news. Russia — this is fake news put out by the media." When asked whether anyone else from his Campaign or Administration was involved with the Russians, Trump says: "No," Trump says. "Nobody that I know of."

FEBRUARY 17, 2017

FBI Director Comey meets privately with members of the Senate Intelligence Committee to discuss the Russia investigation. Immediately thereafter, the Committee sends a letter asking more than a dozen agencies, organizations and individuals, including the White House, to preserve all communications related to the Senate panel's investigation into Russian interference in the 2016 election.

MARCH 2017

Jared and Ivanka Kushner vacation in Aspen, Colorado. Their close friends Roman Abramovich and his wife are there at the same time, while Trump signs an executive order exempting Russian/Canadian steel manufactured by companies partially owned by Abramovich from the "buy US steel" requirements relating to the Keystone XL pipeline.

MARCH/APRIL 2017

Trump tells Comey in phone calls that he wanted Comey to "lift the cloud" of the Russia investigation.

MARCH 2017

Trump makes separate appeals to the Director of National Intelligence, Daniel Coats, and to

Adm. Michael S. Rogers, the director of the National Security Agency, urging them to publicly deny the existence of any evidence of collusion during the 2016 election.

MARCH 2, 2017

Attorney General Jeff Sessions acknowledges at a press conference that he met with the Russian ambassador and failed to disclose those meetings to the Senate. He recuses himself from any involvement in the Special Counsel's investigation.

MARCH 2, 2017

In a reversal of his previous comments, Carter Page tells MSNBC's Chris Hayes that "I do not deny that [I met with Russian Ambassador Sergey Kislyak]," adding, "I'm not going to deny that I talked with him. ... I will say that I never met him anywhere outside of Cleveland, let's just say that much."

MARCH 4, 2017

Trump accuses Obama in a series of tweets of illegally "tapping my phones in October" during the "very sacred election process." He compares Obama's actions to Watergate and called him a "bad (or sick) guy!" No evidence is ever produced by Trump or anyone else supporting this claim.

MARCH 20, 2017

Comey confirms the existence of the FBI investigation at a hearing of the House Intelligence Committee. Comey states that the investigation includes "investigating the nature of any links between individuals associated with the Trump campaign and the Russian government and whether there was any coordination between the campaign and Russia's efforts."

MARCH 30, 2017   Trump calls Comey and asks him what could be done to "lift the cloud" of the Russia investigation from his administration. Trump stresses that "the cloud" is interfering with his ability to make deals for the country and that "he hoped [Comey] could find a way to get out that he wasn't being investigated."

MARCH 31, 2017   Trump tweets: "Mike Flynn should ask for immunity in that this is a witch hunt (excuse for big election loss), by media & Dems, of historic proportion!"

APRIL 11, 2017   Trump calls Comey, asking him for a response to his request for a statement that he (Trump) was not personally under investigation. Trump states, according to Comey: "Because I have been very loyal to you, very loyal; we had that thing you know."

APRIL 26, 2017   WikiLeaks messages Don Jr. with a video attached entitled, "Fake News."

MAY 5, 2017

In an interview airing May 5, 2017 on Boston's public radio station, Golf writer James Dodson describes a conversation he had in 2014 with Eric Trump. When Dodson asked him how the Trumps financed their golf courses, Eric answered: "Well, we don't rely on American banks. We have all the funding we need out of Russia." Dodson responded, 'Really?' And he said, 'Oh, yeah. We've got some guys that really, really love golf, and they're really invested in our programs. We just go there all the time."

MAY 9, 2017

Trump fires Director Comey, initially stating that the reason for his dismissal was his mishandling of the email investigation of Hillary Clinton. Deputy Attorney General Rod Rosenstein wrote a memo critical of Comey, citing his holding of a press conference on July 5, 2016 to publicly announce his recommendation to not charge Clinton with any offenses relating to her misuse of a private email server for official government business while she was the Secretary of State under Obama, and disclosing on October 28, 2016 that the FBI had reopened its investigation of Clinton.

MAY 10, 2017

Trump asks his staff and all other Americans to leave the Oval Office so he could speak there privately with Russian Ambassador Kislyak and

Russian Foreign Minister Sergei Lavrov. He then tells Russian officials in the Oval Office that the firing of Comey, who he described as a "nut job," had "taken off" the "great pressure" of the Russia investigation. Trump explains to the Russians: "I just fired the head of the FBI. He was crazy, a real nut job." He also states: "I faced great pressure because of Russia. That's taken off." Trump also discusses during this meeting with the Russian officials classified information about an ISIS terrorist threat involving laptop computers on commercial airlines. Later, on May 16, 2017, it is disclosed that this classified information came from Israeli intelligence.

MAY 11, 2017

Trump tells NBC's Lester Holt during an interview on national TV that he decided to fire Comey because of "the Russia thing." Trump states: "He [Rosenstein] made a recommendation [to fire Comey], but regardless of [the] recommendation I was going to fire Comey, knowing there was no good time to do it. And, in fact, when I decided to just do it, I said to myself, I said, 'You know, this Russia thing with Trump and Russia is a made-up story. It's an excuse by the Democrats for having lost an election that they should have won."

MAY 2017

U.S. Department of Justice and FBI open counterintelligence investigation of Trump to determine whether he is a Russian agent who is acting in a manner that is a danger to U.S. national security.[32]

MAY 17, 2017

Rod Rosenstein appoints former FBI Director Robert S. Mueller III as Special Counsel to investigate possible collusion between Russian and the Trump campaign. The Special Counsel's office immediately took over the ongoing federal investigation of Manafort and Gates being conducted for the past several years which was being handled primarily by the FBI and the U.S. Attorney's Office for the Southern District of New York (SDNY).

MAY 17, 2017

Shortly after hearing that the Justice Department had appointed Robert Mueller as Special Counsel to take over the Russia investigation, Trump berates Attorney General Jeff Sessions, accusing him of "disloyalty" for having caused the Trump Administration to lose control over the investigation.

MAY 18, 2017

Trump tweets that the Mueller investigation "is the single greatest witch hunt of a politician in American history!" Trump denies at a press conference with the president of Colombia that day that he had asked Comey to close down the FBI's investigation of Flynn. "No, No. Next Question."

MAY 22, 2017

The Washington Post reports that in March 2017, Trump made separate appeals to the Director of National Intelligence, Daniel Coats, and to Adm. Michael S. Rogers, the director of the National Security Agency, urging them to publicly deny the existence of any evidence of collusion during the 2016 election.

MAY 23, 2017

Former CIA Director John O. Brennan testifies before the House Intelligence Committee that he is concerned about contacts between Russian officials and Trump campaign operatives.

JUNE 12, 2017

Christopher Ruddy, a friend of President Trump, tells the press that Trump was considering firing Mueller. During that same month (June 2017), Trump orders White House counsel Don McGahn to fire Mueller, but backs off when McGahn threatens to quit.

JULY 7, 2017

Trump meets with Putin at the G20 Summit, where Putin denies meddling in the 2016 U.S. election.

JULY 8, 2017

Aboard Air Force One, Trump helps draft a

false public statement for his son, Don Jr., claiming that a June 9, 2016 meeting with a Russian lawyer at Trump Tower was about "adoption policy." In a statement to the New York Times, Don Jr. states: We primarily discussed a program about the adoption of Russian children that was active and popular with American families years ago and was since ended by the Russian government, but it was not a campaign issue at the time and there was no follow up."

JULY 9, 2017

Don Jr. retracts his "adoption policy" story issued the preceding day and acknowledges that the June 9, 2016 Trump Tower meeting with the Russians was to discuss damaging information that the Russian government said it had about Hillary Clinton. Don Jr. states: "The woman stated that she had information that individuals connected to Russia were funding the Democratic National Committee and supporting Mrs. Clinton."

JULY 11, 2017

Don Jr. releases email exchanged relating to June 9, 2016 Trump Tower meeting. He received an email from one of his father's Russian business partners on June 3, 2016, which promised dirt on Hillary Clinton. Don Jr. replied: "I love it."

JULY 12, 2017   Regarding the June 9, 2016 meeting with the
                     Russians at Trump Tower, Trump says," I only
                     heard about it two or three days ago," and "it
                     was attended by a couple of other people,"
                     Jared and "the other one, [who]was playing with
                     his iPhone."

JULY 24, 2017   Jared Kushner confirms to congressional inves-
                     tigators: "I asked if they had an existing com-
                     munications channel at his embassy we could
                     use where they would be comfortable trans-
                     mitting the information they wanted to relay to
                     General Flynn."

JULY 26, 2017   In a tweet, Trump calls for the firing of FBI
                     Deputy Director Andrew McCabe, a potential
                     corroborating witness for Comey's conversa-
                     tions with Trump.

JULY 26, 2017   The FBI executes a search warrant at the home
                     of Paul Manafort in Alexandria, Virginia.

JULY 27, 2017   George Papadopoulos is arrested at Dulles
                     International Airport and charged with lying to
                     FBI agents. He decides to cooperate.

AUGUST 1, 2017   White House Press Secretary Sarah Sanders
                     confirms that Trump was involved in draft-
                     ing the statement for Don Jr. issued on July

8th about the June 9, 2016 meeting at Trump Tower. According to the emails released by Don Jr. on July 11, 2017, the statement was, at best, misleading since it failed to disclose that Don Jr. hade been promised "some official documents and information that would incriminate Hillary [as] part of Russia and its government's support for Mr. Trump."

AUGUST 28, 2017

Michael Cohen sends a a two-page letter to the House and Senate intelligence committees, lying about three critical things:

1. The Trump Tower Moscow project ended in January 2016 and was not discussed extensively with others in the Trump Organization.

2. Cohen "never agreed" to travel to Russia in connection with the Moscow project and "never considered" asking Trump to travel for the project.

3. Cohen "did not recall any Russian government response or contact about the Moscow Project."

Cohen admits in open court at his sentencing hearing on November 29, 2018 that these were lies.[33] "I made these statements to be consistent with Individual-1's political messaging and to be loyal to Individual-1," Cohen said in court.

SEPTEMBER 6, 2017

Facebook announces that it had identified about 3000 politically related ad buys connected to 470 fake accounts linked to Russia. The ads were placed through International Research Agency, a Russian intelligence-linked troll farm.

SEPTEMBER 22, 2017

Trump tweets: "The Russia hoax continues, now it's ads on Facebook. What about the totally biased and dishonest Media coverage in favor of Crooked Hillary?"

OCTOBER 5, 2017

George Papadopoulos pleads guilty to making false statements to FBI agents relating to contacts he had with agents of the Russian government while working for the Trump campaign.

OCTOBER 24-25, 2017

Michael Cohen appears before the House Intelligence Committee, and appears the following day before the Senate Intelligence Committee. As he later admitted, he lied under oath about the extent of his contacts with Russians during the 2016 campaign, and about when he and Trump stopped working on the Trump Moscow Tower deal. He testified that they basically dropped the plan around the time of the Iowa caucuses in or about February 2016, but in fact

the negotiations and plans for this Moscow
tower continued well into June 2016.

OCTOBER 27, 2017   Michael Cohen testifies before the House and
                     Senate Intelligence Committees, falsely stating
                     that he stopped working on the Trump Moscow
                     Tower deal before the Republican presidential
                     caucus in Iowa in or about February 1, 2016,
                     when in truth and in fact, as he later admitted
                     to, the project continued well into June of 2016,
                     and that Trump had signed a letter of credit
                     with the Russians relating to the project where-
                     by a Russian bank that had been on the U.S.
                     sanction list would provide the financing.

OCTOBER 27, 2017   Paul Manafort and Rick Gates, Manafort's busi-
                     ness associate and Deputy Campaign Manager
                     of the Trump campaign, are indicted on mon-
                     ey laundering and tax evasion charges related
                     to their work for the pro-Russian Ukrainian
                     party. Manafort is accused of laundering "more
                     than $18 million" that he used to buy property,
                     goods and services in the United States without
                     paying federal taxes. The indictment contains 12
                     counts, including conspiracy against the United
                     States, conspiracy to launder money, unregis-
                     tered agents of a foreign principal, false and
                     misleading statements relating to the Foreign
                     Agents Registration Act, false statements, and

seven counts of failure to file reports of foreign bank and financial accounts.

OCTOBER 30, 2017

The Manafort and Gates indictments are unsealed, and both are arraigned in federal court. Court documents are also unsealed in the Papadopoulos case, disclosing his contacts with individuals with connections to the Russian government while he was involved in the Trump Campaign.

NOVEMBER 2, 2017

The *New York Times* reports that Page, in testimony before the House Intelligence Committee, reveals he met with Russian officials during his July 2016 trip to Moscow. Page also reportedly emailed at least one Trump campaign adviser about his discussions with Russian government officials, legislators, and businessmen.

NOVEMBER 11, 2017

Trump tells reports on Air Force One that at his recent meeting with Putin at the Asia-Pacific Economic Cooperation summit, Putin denied meddling in the U.S. election. Trump concluded, "He did not do what they are saying he did."

NOVEMBER 13, 2017

The Atlantic reports that Don Jr. corresponded with WikiLeaks in a series of direct Twitter messages.

DECEMBER 1, 2017

Michael Flynn pleads guilty to making false statements to the FBI about his two discussions with Ambassador Kislyak in December 2016.

DECEMBER 14, 2017

Putin says that accusations of Russian collusion "inflicted damage to the domestic political situation" in the U.S.

JANUARY 3, 2018

An excerpt of Michael Wolff's new book, "Fire and Fury," is released, in which Steve Bannon is quoted as describing the June 9, 2016 meeting in Trump Tower between Don Jr. and other Trump team members with Russians about getting "dirt" on Hillary Clinton as "treasonous" and "unpatriotic."

JANUARY 9, 2018

Dianne Feinstein, the top Democrat on the Senate Foreign Relations Committee, releases the transcript of the August interview with Glen Simpson, founder of Fusion GPS, the company that hired Christopher Steele, the author of the Dossier, to investigate possible Russian/Trump connections.

JANUARY 25, 2018

The *New York Times* reports that Trump ordered the firing of Special Counsel Mueller in June 2017, but backed down after White House counsel Donald F. McGahn II threatened to resign.

JANUARY 29, 2018

The White House says it will not implement sanctions required by bipartisan legislation, because the threat of sanctions already acts as a "deterrent."

JANUARY 31, 2018

The New York Times reports that former Trump legal spokesperson Mark Corallo plans to tell the Special Counsel that White House Communications Director Hope Hicks could have committed obstruction of justice after a conference call in which she told Trump that the Don Jr. emails "will never get out."

FEBRUARY 2, 2018

The House Intelligence Committee releases the "Nunes memo" claiming   the FBI abused its authority by seeking FISA court approval for the surveillance on Carter Page based on the Steele Dossier, although the memo concedes that the Papadopoulos information received by the FBI triggered the Russia investigation.

FEBRUARY 6, 2018

Secretary of State Rex Tillerson tells Fox News that Russia is already attempting to influence the 2018 midterm elections and that it will be difficult to "pre-empt" the meddling.

FEBRUARY 13, 2018

DNI Dan Coats tells the Senate Intelligence Committee at a hearing that the U.S. is "under attack" on the cybersecurity front, and that it is likely that Russia will continue its cyberattacks on the U.S. by "using elections as opportunities to undermine democracy, sow discord and undermine our values."

FEBRUARY 16, 2018   The Special Counsel indicts 13 Russians for illegally interfering in the 2016 election, alleging that some of the Russians traveled to the U.S. under false pretenses to collect intelligence and to "reach significant numbers of Americans for purposes of interfering with the US political system, including the presidential election of 2016."

FEBRUARY 20, 2018   A criminal information and plea agreement is filed in federal court relating to Alex van der Zwaan, the Dutch attorney working for the Skadden Arps law firm that had lied to FBI agents interviewing him in London on November 3, 2017. He admitted that he falsely told the agents that his last communication with Rick Gates had been in mid-August 2016, that it consisted of only an innocuous text message, and that his last communication with "Person A" -- who is independently identified as Konstantin Kilimnik, the Manafort associate and GRU Russian intelligence agent.

FEBRUARY 22, 2018   On February 22, 2018, a federal grand jury in

Alexandria, Virginia filed a new set of charges against Manafort and Gates, charging them with 32 counts of tax, financial, and bank fraud charges. Buried among the many other charges was the allegation that the chief executive of a Chicago bank (which was later disclosed to be CEO Steve Calk of Federal Savings Bank) "expedited" approval of $16 million in loans for Paul Manafort after Manafort had discussed with him a possible role for the executive in the Trump campaign and ultimately in President Donald Trump's administration.

FEBRUARY 23, 2018

Rick Gates pleads guilty to one count of conspiracy against the United States and one count of making false statements to the FBI. In exchange for agreement to plead guilty and to cooperate with federal prosecutors, the government agreed that other charges relating to money laundering, acting as an unregistered foreign agent, and making other false statements would be dropped. On November 14, 2018, Special Counsel Mueller's office pushed back the sentencing of Gates, representing in federal court that Gates was still cooperating on "several ongoing investigations."

FEBRUARY 28, 2018

NBC News reports that the Special Counsel's office is asking witnesses whether Trump knew that Democratic emails were being stolen before the public knew about it, and if he had advance knowledge of WikiLeak's plans to publish the stolen information. Also of interest was the relationship between Roger Stone and Julian Assange.

MARCH 7, 2018

The *New York Times* reports that the Special Counsel's office has evidence that Trump had conversations with two key witnesses —White House counsel Don McGahn II and former chief of staff Reince Priebus -- about their discussions with investigators. Trump reportedly told McGahn to issue a statement denying an article about Trump's request to McGahn that Mueller be fired, and he also asked Priebus as to how his interview had gone with the federal investigators.

MARCH 7, 2018

The *Washington Post* reports that the Special Counsel has evidence of a secret meeting in the Seychelles on January 11, 2017 involving George Nadar, and advisor to the de facto leader of the United Arab emirates, Erik Prince, a Trump backer and founder of Blackwater, and Kirill Dmitriev, manager of a Russian sovereign wealth fund. They apparently discussed the establishment of a backchannel between the incoming Trump Administration and the Kremlin.

MARCH 14, 2018   The New York Times reports that the Special
                      Counsel's office has subpoenaed the Trump
                      Organization and demanded the production of
                      documents relating to Russia and other matters.

MARCH 27, 2018   In a court filing, the Special Counsel's office
                      states that Manafort and Gates were in touch
                      with a Manafort associate identified as "Person
                      A," who is reliably believed to be Konstantin
                      Kilimnik, the Russian intelligence agent working
                      for Manafort in Ukraine and Russia.

APRIL 3, 2018   Alex van der Zwaan is sentence to a prison
                      term of 30 days a $20,000 fine. He had plead-
                      ed guilty to lying about his contacts with Rick
                      Gates and "Person A" (Konstantin Kilimnik).

APRIL 9, 2018   Facebook releases information on whether user
                      data was compromised by Cambridge Analytica,
                      a "data mining" company with links to both
                      the Trump Campaign and WikiLeaks. Facebook
                      says that it could have affected more than 87
                      million accounts, and 2.2 billion Facebook users
                      receive a notice regarding "Protecting Your
                      Information."

APRIL 9, 2018   FBI and other federal agents execute a search
                      warrant of Cohen's home, office and hotel
                      room, carting off box-loads of sensitive docu-
                      ments and tape recordings.

APRIL 17, 2018

Former FBI Director James Comey's memoir, "A Higher Loyalty," is released. Comey discloses that his decision to go public with disclosure that the Hillary Clinton email investigation had been re-started shortly before the 2016 election was motivated by a concern that he would be making Clinton "an illegitimate president by concealing the restarted investigation....," suggesting that a major factor in his thinking was that Clinton was way ahead in the polling so anything he said would probably not affect the results. Comey does not address the question of whether he ever considered that he might be making Trump an illegitimate president by not disclosing the FBI's ongoing investigation into possible collusion between the Trump Campaign and the Russians during the 2016 campaign.

MAY 2, 2018

Rudy Giuliani reveals on Fox News that Trump repaid his attorney Michael Cohen the $130,000 payment that he made to Stormy Daniels at Trump's request about 2 weeks before the 2016 election.

MAY 16, 2018

The Senate Judiciary Committee releases over 2500 pages of documents relating to its investigation of the June 9, 2016 meeting between Trump team members and the Russians who promised to help the Campaign by providing dirt on Hillary Clinton. The documents generally confirm that Don Jr. and his Trump associates had, in fact, sought "dirt" on Hillary Clinton, but that they were never actually directly provided with that information by the Russians.

MAY 22, 2018

The White House announces that Republican House Intelligence Chairman Devin Nunes and Republican House Oversight Chairman Trey Gowdy would receive classified briefings from Justice Dept. and intelligence officials regarding the confidential FBI source in the Russia investigation.

JUNE 4, 2018

Federal prosecutors accuse Paul Manafort of witness tampering while he is on pretrial release.

JUNE 8, 2018

Paul Manafort and Russian-Ukrainian GRU agent Konstantin Kilimnik are indicted by the Special Counsel's office on obstruction of justice charges relating to witness tampering.

JUNE 15, 2018

The Special Counsel's office convinces a federal judge to revoke Paul Manafort's bail and remand him to jail, accusing him of witness tampering.

JUNE 18, 2018

Roger Stone and Michael Caputo acknowledge

that they failed to tell investigators about their contact with Henry Greenberg, a Russian national who offered to give them dirt on Hillary Clinton for $2 million.

JULY 13, 2018   Deputy Attorney General Rod Rosenstein announces the indictment of 12 Russian nationals on charges of computer hacking and the spreading of disinformation and false conspiracy theories during the 2016 election.

JULY 26, 2018   NBC News reports that Michael Cohen has asserted that Trump knew in advance about the meeting at Trump Tower on June 9, 2016 involving Don Jr., Manafort and Jared Kushner, and a group of Russians, and that this knowledgeable source's information contradicts Don Jr's congressional testimony in May 2017. It is also reported that Cohen is willing to testify that Don Jr. told his father about the meeting.

AUGUST 10, 2018   Andrew Miller, an associate of Roger Stone, is held in contempt after refusing to appear before the grand jury hearing testimony by the Special Counsel's office relating to the Russia investigation.

AUGUST 19, 2018   Trump lawyer and former New York City Major Rudy Giuliani states on Meet the Press that he is worried about a Mueller interview of Trump since Trump might be "trapped in a perjury." Giuliani explains that Trump's version of the truth may be different than Mueller's, and that "Truth isn't truth."

AUGUST 19, 2018

The *New York Times* reports that White House counsel Don McGahn has been cooperating with the Special Counsel's investigation that that he has been interviewed at least three times for a total of 30 hours over a 9-month period. The article suggests that McGahn was worried that Trump might try to make him a scapegoat and that he would be asked to take the fall for Trump.

AUGUST 21, 2018

A federal jury in Alexandria, Virginia finds Manafort guilty of 8 of 18 counts of financial fraud. He continues to face the additional charges pending in federal court in Washington, D.C., as well as the 10 counts in the Virginia federal case where the jury was unable to reach a verdict.

AUGUST 21, 2018

Government prosecutors announce a plea agreement with Michael Cohen, whereby Cohen agrees to plead guilty to charges of federal tax evasion, making false statements to a federally-insured bank, and campaign finance violations. The plea is entered followed the filing of an eight-count criminal information, alleging that Cohen concealed more than $4 million in personal income from the IRS, made false statements to a federally-insured financial institution in connection with a $500,000 home equity loan, and, in 2016, caused $280,000 in payments to be made to silence two women – Stormy Daniels and Karen McDougal -- who otherwise planned to speak publicly about their alleged affairs with a presidential candidate and "Individual-1," Donald J. Trump, thereby intending to influence the 2016 presidential election. Cohen pled guilty today before U.S. District Judge William H. Pauley III. Trump is, therefore, essentially charged as an unindicted co-conspirator. Cohen confirmed that he conspired with Trump by telling the federal judge under oath in open court on the record that it was Trump who had directed him to make the hush money payments to the two women that Trump wanted to silence, at least until after the November 2016 presidential election.

SEPTEMBER 7, 2018   George Papadopoulos is sentenced to 14 days in jail.

SEPTEMBER 14, 2018   Paul Manafort enters into a plea agreement whereby he agrees to plead guilty to two of the many counts in the indictment charging him with having engaged in a conspiracy involving money laundering, tax fraud, failing to report foreign bank accounts, violating rules requiring registration of foreign agents, lying and witness tampering. Manafort also agrees to forfeit to the government his $7.3 million mansion in the Hamptons and his $3 million Trump Tower condo, and to fully cooperate with the Special Counsel's ongoing investigation.

OCTOBER 10, 2018

Richard Pinedo is sentenced to six months in prison and six months of home confinement for engaging in a scheme to sell fake online identities that were used by the 13 Russians indicted by the Special Counsel's office for interfering with the 2016 elections.

OCTOBER 19, 2018

Federal prosecutors charge Elena A. Khusyaynova, a Russian woman working for a Russian oligarch close to Putin, is charged with attempting to interfere in the 2018 midterm elections through the use of social media platforms creating thousands of phony social media and email accounts designed to appear as if they were owned by Americans.

OCTOBER 23, 2018

The Special Counsel's office is reported to have obtained information indicating that Jerome

Corsi, a right-wing commentator and conspiracy theorist, had advance knowledge of the stolen emails from the Clinton Campaign that were forwarded by Russian intelligence operatives to WikiLeaks for dissemination.

NOVEMBER 7, 2018   Jeff Sessions resigns as Attorney General. Matthew Whitaker, a critic of the Mueller investigation, is named as Acting Attorney General.

NOVEMBER 16, 2018   Reporters locate a court document mistakenly filed by the Justice Department charging Julian Assange of WikiLeaks, saying that the charges and arrest warrant "would need to remain sealed until Assange is arrested...."

NOVEMBER 26-27, 2018   The Special Counsel's office files a report with the U.S. District Court in Washington, D.C., stating that Manafort had lied to federal investigators and violated his plea agreement. The prosecutors conclude in this report that, based upon Manafort's breach of the plea agreement, the Special Counsel's office was no longer bound to recommend a reduced sentence for him based upon his cooperation and "acceptance of responsibility." Shortly thereafter, it is reported that Manafort had been secretly communicating with the White House during the time period that he was supposedly cooperating with the government investigation, and was thereby passing on valuable information about the nature and direction of the investigation into collusion between the Trump Team and the Russians.

NOVEMBER 29, 2018   Michael Cohen pleads guilty in federal court, admitting that he lied to the Congressional Committee in August 2017 and that, in fact, the Trump Tower Moscow project had not ended in January 2016 and was, in fact, discussed extensively with others in the Trump Organization. Cohen further admits that he had agreed to travel to Russia in connection with the Moscow project and had considered asking Trump to travel for the project. Cohen further admitted that he had lied when he stated that he "did not recall any Russian government response or contact about the Moscow Project."

Cohen states in court: "I made these statements to be consistent with Individual-1's political messaging and to be loyal to Individual-1." With Cohen's November 29, 2018 plea agreement, the public learns for the first time that Cohen that Trump were still actively seeking the Kremlin's approval for the Trump Moscow project well into the 2016 Presidential primaries, and that Cohen discussed the status of the project with Trump on at least three occasions and briefed Trump's family members about it. Cohen also admitted to agreeing to travel to Russia for meetings on the project, and confirmed that the "Individual 1" described in the court doc uments filed in connection with Cohen's plea agreement was, in fact, Trump.

NOVEMBER 2018

Federal prosecutors inadvertently disclosed that Julian Assange had been indicted under seal.[34] Trump also meets with Putin at G20 meeting in Buenos Aires without any U.S. notetaker or translator.

DECEMBER 4, 2018

Special Counsel's office releases sentencing memo for Michael Flynn. In the sentencing memo, Mueller assessed Flynn's cooperation as "substantial," and wrote that "a sentence at the low end of the guideline range—including a sentence that does not impose a term of incarceration—is appropriate and warranted."

DECEMBER 7, 2018

The Special Counsel's office files a sentencing memo claiming Paul Manafort lied about his contacts with Trump Administration officials and his interactions with Russian intelligence agent Konstantin Kilimnik.

DECEMBER 7, 2018

The Special Counsel's office files a sentencing

memo regarding Michael Cohen, saying that he had provided relevant and useful information regarding Trump's efforts to build a Moscow Trump Tower and other matters.

DECEMBER 12, 2018   Michael Cohen is sentenced by a federal judge to a three-year prison term and over $1 million in fines, for having violated federal Campaign Finance laws and for having lied to a Congressional Committee about Trump's Moscow project. Trump was described in the government's sentencing memo as the "Individual-1" who had conspired with Cohen to violate federal law. The only reason Trump himself was not indicted was that the Justice Department guidelines barred the indictment of a sitting president.

DECEMBER 12, 2018   On the same day that Cohen is sentenced, federal prosecutors also disclose that they had entered into a "non-prosecution" agreement with AMI, the parent company to the National Enquirer, which admitted that it made a $150,000 to Karen McDougal "in concert with" the Trump presidential campaign, in order to ensure that McDougal did not make public her damaging allegations about Trump before the 2016 presidential election. NBC News reports that Trump was in the room in 2015 when Michael Cohen and David Pecker discussed ways

TRUMP · RUSSIA TIMELINE

that Pecker and AMI could counter negative
stories about Trump's alleged affairs.

DECEMBER 17, 2018   Bijan Kian and Kamil Ekim Alptekin, two
former associates of Michael Flynn, are charged
with conspiracy to act as agents of a foreign
government by trying to influence American
politicians in a plot to extradite a Turkish cleric
living in the U.S.

DECEMBER 19, 2018   A federal judge agrees to delay the sentencing
of Michael Flynn, but reacts negatively to sen-
tencing memo submitted by Flynn's attorneys,
who suggested inferentially that Flynn may have
been tricked or coerced into lying to FBI agents
about his contacts with Ambassador Kislyak
and the Russians. The judge tells Flynn, "You
sold your country out." Flynn admits to the
judge that he was well aware that lying to a federal agent was a crime when he was interviewed
by the FBI agents in the White House.

DECEMBER 19, 2018   The Trump Administration announced that it
intended to lift sanctions against several huge
Russian aluminum companies owned by Oleg
v. Deripaska, one of the most powerful Russian oligarchs who had close ties to both Paul
Manafort and Vladimir Putin.[35] The companies,
including Rusal – the world's second-largest

aluminum companies – had been hit with U.S. Treasury Department sanctions in April 2018 after U.S. intelligence services had concluded that Russia was behind the efforts to interfere with the 2016 elections.[36] However, Deripaska himself remained on the sanctions list, which prevented or interfered with his efforts to gain access to the funds generated from his sale of some of his shares in these companies.[37] Representative Lloyd Doggett of Texas described the lifting of the sanctions amounted to Mr. Trump "sliding another big gift under Vladimir Putin's Christmas tree."[38] He called for a rigorous congressional review of the deal, and said that if it "is what it appears — a Rusal ruse — then we should reject this latest Trump scam."[39]

DECEMBER 20, 2018

Defense Secretary James Mattis resigns in response to Trump's announcement that he planned to withdraw U.S. troops from Syria and Afghanistan, issuing public letter of resignation implicitly criticizing Trump for undermining America's alliances, including NATO.

JANUARY 8, 2019

A court filing by Paul Manafort's legal team inadvertently discloses that Manafort gave proprietary internal polling data to Konstantin Kilimnik, a Manafort associate and Russian intelligence operative. The Special Counsel's office is reported to be investigating whether the Trump team was colluding with the Russians by feeding them proprietary polling data that could be used to target key battleground states and demographics for Facebook and other social media campaigns using disinformation and phony websites. It is also reported that the Special Counsel's office interviewed Tony Fabrizio, the Trump Campaign's chief pollster, in February 2018.

JANUARY 8, 2019

Natalia Veselnitskaya, the Russian lawyer and government operative who attended the June 9, 2016 Trump Tower meeting with Don Jr., Manafort and Kushner, is indicted by federal prosecutors in Manhattan for obstruction of an earlier money laundering investigation of Prevezon Holdings, a large Russian real estate company with close ties to the Kremlin.

JANUARY 11, 2019

The *New York Times* reports that immediately after Trump fired FBI Director Comey on May 9, 2017, the U.S. Department of Justice officials authorized the FBI to open up a Counterintelligence investigation into whether "the president's own actions constituted a possible threat to national security" and whether he was "working on behalf of Russia against American interests."40 One of the goals of the investigation was to determine "whether Mr. Trump was knowingly working for Russia or had unwittingly fallen under Moscow's influence." The FBI investigation of Trump also had a criminal aspect, which was whether the firing of Comey constituted an obstruction of justice.

JANUARY 17, 2019   BuzzFeed News reports that Trump directed his attorney Michael Cohen to lie to Congress about negotiations to build the Moscow Tower Project, citing two unnamed federal law enforcement officials. The BuzzFeed article further reports that Trump supported a plan, set up by Cohen, to visit Russia during the 2016 presidential campaign so that Trump could personally meet with Putin and jump-start the tower negotiations. It is further reported that" even as Trump told the public he had no business deals with Russia ... Trump and his children Ivanka and Donald Trump Jr. received regular, detailed updates about the real estate development from Cohen, whom they put in charge of the project."[41]

JANUARY 18, 2019   In a rare public statement, the Special Counsel's office disputed the BuzzFeed Report of the prior day that Trump had told Michael Cohen to lie to Congress about the Moscow Tower project. According to the statement made by the

Special Counsel's office, "BuzzFeed's description of specific statements to the Special Counsel's Office, and characterization of documents and testimony obtained by this office, regarding Michael Cohen's Congressional testimony are not accurate."

JANUARY 19, 2019

Trump tells reporters: "I appreciate the special counsel coming out with a statement," referring to the Special Counsel's office statement disputing the January 17, 2018 BuzzFeed story alleging that Trump told Cohen to lie to Congress. "I think it was very appropriate that they did so. I very much appreciate that."

JANUARY 21, 2019

It is further disclosed that, when the Trump Administration lifted the sanctions against three of Deripaska's companies, it entered into a binding confidential document signed by both sides that was far less tough on Deripaska than the Trump Administration said it was.[42] Instead of extracting "painful concessions" from him, the deal contained provisions that essentially benefitted him to the tune of hundreds of millions of dollars, freeing him from hundreds of millions in debt while leaving him and his allies with a majority ownership of one of his most important companies.[43]

JANUARY 24, 2019

NBC News reports that Trump senior advisor and son-in-law Jared Kushner was rejected for a security clearance by two White House security specialists after his FBI background check raised concerns, but their supervisor overruled them and approved Kushner's top secret clearance.[44] Kushner application for the top secret security clearance was initially denied because of several red flags that were raised by the FBI background check regarding potential foreign influence, including his family's business activities, his foreign contacts, his foreign travel and meetings he had with Russians and other foreign representatives during the campaign.[45] The CIA, however, apparently balked at providing Kushner with an even higher clearance known as "sensitive compartment information" (SCI), and CIA officers reviewing Kushner's background information were reported to have wondered how Kushner could have received a top secret clearance in the first place.[46]

Representative Elijah Cummings, Chairman of the House Committee on Oversight and Reform, launched an investigation into the White House's security clearance process, citing "grave breaches of national security at the highest levels of the Trump Administration."[47]

JANUARY 25, 2019

Longtime Trump advisor Roger Stone is arrested in a pre-dawn raid by FBI at Stone's home in Ft. Lauderdale, Florida.[48] The indictment of Stone alleges that a top Trump campaign official during the 2016 presidential campaign "was directed" to dispatch Stone to get information from WikiLeaks about the thousands of hacked Democratic emails.[49] Although the indictment did not specifically name Trump as an unindicted co-conspirator with Stone, it is highly likely that Trump was the only one senior enough in the campaign to have "directed" a senior campaign official to take this action. Based upon the information gathered by the Special Counsel's office, as well as now publicly available information, it appears reasonably clear that the Trump Campaign had prior knowledge and a "heads up" that a treasure trove of damaging information about Hillary Clinton was about to be unleashed by WikiLeaks.

JANUARY 29, 2019

The Financial Times discloses that Trump met with Putin in November 2018 at the G20 meeting in Buenos Aires without any U.S. translator or notetaker present. It is also disclosed that, with regard to prior private meetings that he had with Putin, Trump had ordered the U.S. notetakers to keep their notes secret, and when

Congressional committees started discussing whether to subpoena the notes of translators or note keepers who attended any Trump/Putin meetings, Trump had their notes confiscated.

FEBRUARY 7, 2019

A redacted transcript of a February 4, 2019 court hearing was released relating to Paul Manafort's criminal case in the U.S. District Court for the District of Columbia, in which Andrew Weissmann, one of the prosecutors on the Special Counsel's team told Judge Amy Berman Jackson that Manafort's lies about his meetings with Russian agent Konstantin Kilimnik were significant because they related to "what we think is going on, and what we think the motive here is."[50] The redacted transcript refers to multiple lies by Manafort about the number of his meetings with Kilimnik and the topics they discussed, which – while redacted – are likely to be the references in prior court filings to the topic of a "Ukrainian peace plan" that would basically encompass most of the Kremlin's objectives in Ukraine, including international acceptance of Russian annexation of Crimea and the lifting of U.S. sanctions on Russia. Manafort also lied about his meeting with Kilimnik and Gates at the Grand Havana Club on August 2, 2016, as well as Ukraine-related issues in December 2016 and twice in early 2017. One of these meetings was when Kilimnik was in Washington in January 2017 for Trump's inauguration. The transcript further revealed that Manafort had continued to work for a client in Ukraine in 2018 after his indictment.

FEBRUARY 13, 2019

Judge Amy Berman Jackson of the U.S. District Court for the District of Columbia ruled that Manafort intentionally lied to Special Counsel Mueller's office after agreeing to cooperate with its investigation into interference by Russia into the 2016 presidential election.[51] Judge Jackson relied to a memorandum submitted by the Justice Department setting forth Manafort's falsehood, including lies about payments and his dealings with Konstantin Kilimnik, a Russian GRU agent who was indicted during 2018 along with other Russian intelligence agents. The Judge set sentencing for March 13, 2019.

FEBRUARY 14, 2019

In a pre-released recording of a CBS "60 Minutes" interview scheduled for a full release on Sunday, February 17, 2019, former deputy director Andrew G. McCabe told CBS's Scott Pelley that Rob Rosenstein and other top Justice Department officials became so alarmed by Trump's decision in May 2017 to fire then FBI Director James Comey that they discussed

whether to recruit cabinet members to involve
the 25th Amendment of the Constitution to
remove Trump from office.[52] McCabe also
confirmed that he had ordered the FBI team investigating Russia's election interference to look
into whether Trump had obstructed justice in
firing Comey, and to open a counter-intelligence
investigation into whether Trump, while occupying the oval office, was working on behalf of
Russia against American interests, i.e., whether
Trump was a traitor in the White House. "I
was very concerned that I was able to put the
Russia case on absolutely solid ground, in an
indelible fashion," McCabe said. "That were I
removed quickly, or reassigned or fired, that the
case could not be closed or vanish in the night
without a trace."

FEBRUARY 15, 2019   Special Counsel Mueller's office files a Sentencing Memo for Paul Manafort in the the U.S.
District Court for the Eastern District of Virginia seeking a prison sentence of between 19.6
and 24.4 years in prison and a fine of between
$50,000 and $24 million. The prosecutors write
that "there was nothing ordinary about the
millions of dollars involved in the defendant's
crimes, the duration of his criminal conduct or
the sophistication of his schemes." In support

of the relatively harsh recommended sentence, the sentencing memo further argued: "Manafort did not commit these crimes out of necessity or hardship. He was well-educated, professionally successful and financially well off. He nonetheless cheated the United States Treasury and the public out of more than $6 million in taxes at a time when he had substantial resources."[53]

FEBRUARY 15, 2019

In a filing in the Roger Stone case, Special Counsel Mueller's office said that search warrants had uncovered communications between Stone and "Organization-1" [WikiLeaks], and between Stone and "Guccifer 2.0" (an online presence of Russian intelligence (GRU), something that Stone adamantly denied ever doing directly, insisting that he always used a "back-channel" such as radio host Randy Credico or conspiracy theorist Jerome Corsi.[54] Credico and Corsi are referred to in Stone's indictment as "Person 1" and "Person 2." he communications were uncovered as a result of search warrants executed on accounts in the investigation of Russian hackers, who were also indicted. Stone's attorneys objected to his case being considered as "related" to the Russian hackers indictment, but Judge Jackson overruled the objection, which means that the Stone case will continue to be assigned to her. The Clinton Campaign hacked emails were given by the Russians to WikiLeaks, and the new evidence indicates that Stone communicated with WikiLeaks about these stolen emails. Judge Jackson also issues a gag order restricting Stone and his attorneys from discussing the case publicly.

FEBRUARY 17, 2019

Former FBI Deputy Director Andrew McCabe tells CBS's Scott Pelley during a "60 Minutes" interview that he and Deputy Attorney General Rob Rosenstein discussed invoking the 25th Amendment to remove Trump from office after the firing of then-Director James Comey of the FBI, and Rosenstein also considered wearing a wire to the White House so that he could record his conversations with Trump. McCabe also confirms that he opened a counterintelligence investigation of Trump after Comey's firing to determine whether Trump was working for the Russians and acting contrary to U.S. interests.

FEBRUARY 18, 2019

Trump accuses McCabe and Rosenstein of treason and of "planning an illegal act" by considering invoking the 25th Amendment to remove him as President. Constitutional law scholar Laurence Tribe ridicules understanding of the word "treason" as "ignorant and constitutionally illiterate."[55] Maya Wiley, a legal analyst at MSNBC, pointed out the irony of Trump's description of McCabe and Rosenstein's activities as "treasonous" when the 25th Amendment is enshrined in the Constitution.

FEBRUARY 19, 2019

The *New York Times* publishes the results of its investigation of Trump's two-year attempt to obstruct and discredit the Special Counsel's Russia investigation into interference with the 2016 election and possible collusion with the Trump Campaign. In stark detail, the article "reveals an extraordinary story of a president who has attacked the law enforcement apparatus of his own government like no other president in history, and who has turned the effort into an obsession."[56] The investigation documented 1100 instances that Trump attacked the investigation. For example, it is reported that in late 2018, Trump called Matthew G. Whitaker, his newly installed attorney general, asking whether Geoffrey S. Berman, the United States attorney for the Southern District of New York and a Trump ally, could be put in charge of the widening investigation. Mr. Whitaker told a different story under oath before the House Judiciary Committee, testifying that Trump had never pressured him over the various investigations.

The House Democrats, under the leadership of Jetrold "Jerry" Nadler, the member of Congress who is chairman of the House Judiciary Committee, announced that the Committee was placing Mr. Whitaker's testimony under scrutiny for possible perjury.

FEBRUARY 21, 2019   CNN reports that the Senate Intelligence Committee is seeking to question David Geovanis, a Moscow-based American businessman with longstanding ties to Trump. The Committee is reported to be following up on the testimony of other witnesses, who told Committee members that Geovanis could shed light on Trump's personal and commercial activities in Russia dated back to the 1990s.[57] Geovanis helped organize the 1996 trip to Moscow by Trump, who was pursuing what became one of his life-long obsessions, which was to build a Trump Tower in Moscow. Also on the 1996 trip were real estate moguls Bennett LeBow and Howard Lorber, who later became substantial contributors to Trump's 2016 campaign, and who were personally acknowledged by Trump from the podium after Trump won the 2016 New York Republican primary. Lober is reported by the New York Times as being one of the Trump family associates who spoke with Donald Trump Jr. from blocked numbers around the time of the infamous June 9, 2016 Trump Tower meeting with Russian operatives peddling "dirt" on Hillary Clinton to Manafort, Kushner and Don Jr. of the Trump campaign.

FEBRUARY 27, 2019

Michael Cohen publicly testifies before the House Committee on Oversight and Reform, portraying Trump as a con man, a cheat and a racist.[58] Cohen provided the Committee with documentary evidence supporting his testimony that Trump reimbursed him for the $130,000 he had laid out from a personal line of credit to pay $130,000 in hush money to Stormy Daniels, the porn star with whom Trump had an affair, and for which Cohen was indicted and plead guilty to federal Campaign Finance Law violations. Cohen produced a check for $35,000 dated August 1, 2017 drawn on Trump's personal bank account that bore Trump's distinctive signature. He also produced another $35,000 from Trump's trust account signed by his son, Don Jr. and Allen Weisselberg, the Trump Organizations longstanding chief financial officer. Cohen testified that he discussed these reimbursement payments from Trump, that he says involved 11 installments, with Trump during his first visit to the Oval Office after Trump had been sworn in as president. Importantly, Cohen testified that Trump directed him to lie about Trump's knowledge of the payments to Daniels.

Cohen also suggested in his testimony that Trump knew about the infamous June 9, 2016 meeting at Trump Tower between Don Jr. and other senior officials in the Trump Campaign with Russians claiming that they could provide "dirt" on Hillary Clinton. Cohen also testified that Trump told him in "code" in a way to suggest that Cohen lie to Congress about the time period during the 2016 election campaign that Trump and Cohen were still negotiating on a possible Trump Tower project in Moscow. Cohen also testified that he was in Trump's office in July 2016 during the 2016 campaign when Roger Stone told Trump over a speaker-phone that he had just spoken to Julian Assange of WikiLeaks and that additional stolen emails and other "dirt" on Hillary Clinton would be released in the next few days. Cohen testified that Stone told Trump that Assange had told him that there would be a "massive dump of emails that would damage Hillary Clinton's campaign." This testimony strongly inferred that Trump had advance knowledge of the coordination between his campaign operatives and the Russian/WikiLeaks conspirators who were hacking/stealing information and then publicly disclosing it with the dual purpose of damaging the Clinton Campaign and helping Trump get elected. [59]

MARCH 4, 2019

The House Judiciary Committee, under the leadership of Committee Chairman Jerrold Nadler serves document request on 81 agencies, entities and individuals for information relevant to the Committee's investigation into alleged obstruction of justice, public corruption and abuse of power by Trump, his administration, and his associates.

MARCH 7, 2019

Judge T.S. Ellis of the U.S. District Court in Alexandria, Virginia sentences former Trump Campaign Manager Paul Manafort to a surprisingly lenient 47-month prison term, which is generally viewed as little more than a slap on the wrist, considering the fact that Manafort is clearly the highest profile and unrepentant white-collar criminals to be sentenced in federal court in recent memory. Manafort was facing up to 25 years in prison for having carried out several complex banking fraud schemes, which defrauded both banks and the U.S. government. Federal prosecutors had argued that Manafort deserved between 19 and 25 years in prison as well as millions of dollars in fines and restitution for his crimes, after a jury convicted him following a three-week trial in the summer of 2018. Judge Ellis's light sentence and radical downward departure under the federal sentencing guidelines was particularly surprising, given the fact that Manafort showed little or no remorse, and even lied under oath following a plea deal after the trial, which deal the federal prosecutors were permitted to cancel.

Judge Ellis also commented that he believed Manafort "lived an otherwise blameless life," which raised serious questions as to whether the Judge had been properly informed about Manafort's career over means to me at least that the Judge did not have any understanding whatsoever as to what Manafort has been doing over the past couple of decades.

Manafort made a very lucrative career as a political consultant and operative for the most autocratic and brutal dictators throughout the globe, including former Philippines President Ferdinand Marcos, former dictator of Zaire Mobutu Sese Seko, and Nigerian former President and General Seni Abacha. Manafort's clients have had so consistently been linked with systematic human rights abuses that they were commonly referred to in Washington as "the torturer's lobby."

In addition to human rights abusers, Manafort was inevitably drawn like a moth to the flame by the billionaire oligarchs such as Oleg Deripaska, who funded Manafort's lavish personal life style with tens of millions of dollars for his assistance in laundering hundreds of millions of dollars through offshore accounts in Cyprus, the Cayman Islands and other world money laundering centers. In fact, I headed up a team of lawyers who detailed some of the first publicly disclosed evidence of Manafort's money laundering activities here in the U.S., which were originally filed as part of a civil RICO suit that I brought on behalf of Yulia Tymoshenko, the former Ukrainian Prime Minister who was jailed in Ukraine on trumped-up politically-motivated charges by pro-Russian President Viktor Yanukovich with the invaluable assistance of Manafort and Rick Gates, two of his chief political advisors and strategists. This evidence was then turned over to the FBI and the U.S. Attorney's Office for the Southern District of New York, which launched an investigation of Manafort and his Ukrainian and Russian racketeering partners. This investigation was even-

tually turned over to Special Counsel Mueller's
Office.

MARCH 12, 2019   Letitia James, the New York State Attorney
General, announced that   her office had is-
sues subpoenas to Deutsche Bank and Investors
Bank in connection with civil investigations into
four major projects by the Trump Organization,
including Trump International Hotel in Washington, the Trump National Doral Golf Club
in Florida, the Trump International Hotel and
Tower in Chicago, and an effort to acquire the
Buffalo Bills NFL team in 2014.

MARCH 13, 2019   Judge Amy Berman Jackson of federal district court in Washington, D.C. sentences Paul
Manafort to an additional 43-month jail term,
bringing Manafort's combined sentence on both
of his federal cases to 7.5 years. Judge Jackson makes it perfectly clear at the sentencing
hearing that she was disgusted with Manafort's
deceptive behavior and his failure to accept
genuine responsibility for his crimes, noting that
it is "hard to overstate the number of lies, the
amount of fraud and the extraordinary amount
of money involved." She also suggested that he
was undermining American values and interests,
by acting as an unregistered foreign agent.

MARCH 13, 2019   Just moments after Paul Manafort was sentenced by Judge Amy Berman Jackson in federal court in Washington, D.C., the New York County District Attorney's Office announced that a state grand jury had returned an indictment of Manafort on 16 felony state counts relating to residential mortgage fraud, conspiracy, falsifying business records, and other charges.

MARCH 22, 2019   Attorney General William P. Barr sends a letter to congressional leadership announcing, "that Special Counsel Robert S. Mueller III has concluded his investigation of Russian interference in the 2016 election and related matters." Barr also advised them in this letter that there were no instances where the Attorney General or acting Attorney General had "concluded that a proposed action by a Special Counsel was so inappropriate or unwarranted under established Departmental practices that it should not be pursued." Barr further promised to advise as to the Special Counsel's "principal conclusions" once he had an opportunity to review the confidential report, and that he was consulting with Deputy Attorney General Rod Rosenstein and Special Counsel Mueller "to determine what other information from the report can be released to Congress and the public consistent with the law, including the Special Counsel regulations, and the Department's long-standing practices and policies." Barr further reiterated his promise made to Congress to provide "as much transparency as possible."

MARCH 24, 2019

Attorney General Barr releases a summary letter to Congress, stating that "the Special Counsel's investigation did not find that the Trump campaign or anyone associated with it conspired or coordinated with Russia in its efforts to influence the 2016 U.S. presidential election." On the issue of whether Trump obstructed justice, the Barr letter reports that Mueller "ultimately determined not to make a traditional prosecutorial judgment" on this important issue, and that "while [the Mueller Report] does not conclude that the President committed a crime, it also does not exonerate him." Barr also reports, however, that in his view and in that of Deputy Attorney General Rod Rosenstein, "the evidence developed during the Special Counsel's investigation is not sufficient to establish that the President committed an obstruction-of-justice offense."

APRIL 18, 2019

Redacted Mueller Report is publicly released by the U.S. Dept. of Justice. Congress gets a less redacted version.

APRIL 19, 2019   Chairman Nadler of the House Judiciary
                   Committee subpoenas the Justice Dept. for an
                   unredacted version of the Mueller Report.

APRIL 19, 2019   Elizabeth Warren becomes the first major
                   Democratic presidential candidate to call for
                   Trump's impeachment.

MAY 1, 2019   Attorney General Barr testifies before the Sen-
                   ate Judiciary Committee on the Mueller Report.

MAY 2, 2019   Attorney General Barr fails to appear at a
                   scheduled Congressional hearing after a dispute
                   as to the format. One Congressman ridicules
                   Barr by bringing a bucket of KFC and a statute
                   of a chicken to the hearing room.

ENDNOTES

PROLOGUE

1   Isikoff, Michael; Corn, David, *Russian Roulette*, p. 305 (Twelve 2018).

CHAPTER 1 - THE SIBERIAN CANDIDATE

1   "betray." *ahdictionary.com*. American Heritage Dictionary of the English Language, 2016. Web.

2   Cillizza, Chris. "Donald Trump just held the weirdest Cabinet meeting ever." *cnn.com*. CNN, 13 June 2017, https://www.cnn.com/2017/06/12/politics/donald-trump-cabinet-meeting/index.html.

3   Savransky, Rebecca. "Priebus thanks Trump for 'opportunity and the blessing' to serve his agenda." *thehill.com*. The Hill, 12 June 2017, https://thehill.com/homenews/administration/337427-priebus-thanks-trump-for-opportunity-and-the-blessing-to-serve-his.

4   Landler, Mark et al. "Trump Withdraws U.S. Forces From Syria, Declaring 'We Have Won Against ISIS'." nytimes.com. *New York Times,* 19 Dec. 2018, https://www.nytimes.com/2018/12/19/us/politics/trump-syria-turkey-troop-withdrawal.html.

5   "READ: James Mattis' Resignation Letter." *cnn.com*. CNN, 20 Dec. 2018, https://www.cnn.com/2018/12/20/politics/james-mattis-resignation-letter-doc/index.html.

6   Frum, David. "Why Is Trump Spouting Russian Propaganda?" *theatlantic.com*. The Atlantic, 3 Jan. 2019, www.theatlantic.com/ideas/archive/2019/01/trump-just-endorsed-ussrs-invasion-afghanistan/579361/.

7   The former Soviet Union invaded Afghanistan in 1979 to prop up Afghanistan's then- communist government, which was battling anticommunist guerrillas. The U.S. condemned the Soviet move and eventually helped the mujahideen rebel forces. See Shesgreen, Deirdre. "Trump says former Soviet Union was 'right' to invade Afganistan, prompting ridicule." *usatoday.com*. USA Today, 2 Jan. 2019, www.usatoday.com/story/news/world/2019/01/02/president-trump-former-soviet-union-right-invade-afghanistan/2466897002/.

ENDNOTES

8	This was not the first time that Trump had repeated Russian propaganda talking points. On July 17, 2018, shortly after meeting with Putin, Trump voiced his "concerns" on Fox News that defending the "tiny" and "aggressive" nation of Montenegro could theoretically result in World War III. See Macias, Amanda and Higgins, Tucker. "Trump says defending tiny NATO ally Montenegro could result in World War III." *cnbc.com*. CNBC, 18 July 2018, https://www.cnbc.com/2018/07/18/trump-defending-nato-ally-montenegro-could-result-in-world-war-3.html. Previously, this "concern" had only been expressed by Putin and others in the Kremlin, who desperately and unsuccessfully – tried to prevent Montenegro from joining NATO by supporting a failed plot to assassinate that country's leader, overthrow its western-leading government, and steer it back into the Russian orbit. See Farmer, Ben. "Russia plotted to overthrow Montenegro's government by . . .", The Telegraph, 19 Feb. 2017, https://www.telegraph.co.uk/news/2017/02/18/russias-deadly-plot-overthrow-montenegros-government-assassinating/.

9	@GlennKesslerWP, "Is it possible that Trump's remarks on Afghanistan –and that the Soviets invaded because of "terrorists" – reflect a conversation he had with Putin?" *Twitter,* 2 Jan. 2019, 3:03 p.m., twitter.com/GlennKesslerWP/status/1080600543133868032.

10	Benen, Steve. "Why did Trump endorse old Soviet talking points about Afghanistan?" *msnbc.com*. MSNBC, 3 Jan. 2019, http://www.msnbc.com/rachel-maddow-show/why-did-trump-endorse-old-soviet-talking-points-afghanistan.

11	Kaczynski, Andrew et al. "80 Times Trump talked about Putin." *cnn.com*. CNN, 2017, https://www.cnn.com/interactive/2017/03/politics/trump-putin-russia-timeline/.

12	Ibid.

13	Ibid.

14	Ibid.

15	Ibid.

16	Colvin, Jill. "Trump admitted to meeting Putin years ago, but now says G20 was the first time." *globalnews.ca*. Global News, 7 July 2017, https://globalnews.ca/news/3582302/trump-putin-first-meeting-g20-2/.

17	Bennett, Brian. "Trump says it's 'an honor' to meet Putin; Russian president 'delighted'." *latimes.com*. Los Angeles Times, 7 July 2017, https://www.latimes.com/politics/washington/la-na-essential-washington-updates-trump-says-its-an-honor-to-meet-1499440492-htmlstory.html.

18   Murray, Stephanie. "Putin: I wanted Trump to win the election." *politico.com*. Politico, 16 June 2018, https://www.politico.com/story/2018/07/16/putin-trump-win-election-2016-722486.

19   Fabian, Jordan. "Trump refuses to denounce Russian involvement in election at joint presser with Putin." *thehill.com*. The Hill, 16 June 2018, https://thehill.com/homenews/administration/397203-trump-denies-russian-involvement-in-election-at-joint-presser-with.

20   Ibid.

21   @SenBobCasey. "Instead of holding Vladimir Putin accountable in Helsinki, President Trump embraced him and in doing so diminished America's standing in the international community and shamed the office of the presidency." *Twitter*, 16 July 2018, 12:10 p.m., https://twitter.com/SenBobCasey/status/1018935809590943744.

22   @JohnBrennan. "Donald Trump's press conference performance in Helsinki rises to & exceeds the threshold of "high crimes & misdemeanors." It was nothing short of treasonous. Not only were Trump's comments imbecilic, he is wholly in the pocket of Putin. Republican Patriots: Where are you???" *Twitter*, 16 July 2018, 8:52 a.m., https://twitter.com/JohnBrennan/status/1018885971104985093.

23   Samuels, Brett. "Ryan: 'The president must appreciate that Russia is not our ally'." *thehill.com*. The Hill, 16 June 2018, https://thehill.com/homenews/house/397235-ryan-trump-must-appreciate-that-russia-is-not-our-ally.

24   Carney, Jordain. "McConnell: Russians are not our friends." *thehill.com*. The Hill, 16 June 2018, https://thehill.com/homenews/senate/397281-mcconnell-russians-are-not-our-friends.

CHAPTER 2 - TRAITORS IN THE WHITE HOUSE

1   Parker, Ashley and Rucker, Phillip. "President Trump faces his hardest truth: he was wrong." *washingtonpost.com*. The Washington Post, 20 Mar. 2017, www.washingtonpost.com/politics/president-trump-faces-his-hardest-truth-he-was-wrong/2017/03/20/af9cabfc-0d83-11e7-9b0d-d27c98455440_story.html?utm_term=.b250a518ae5.

2   Sharon LaFraniere, Kenneth P. Vogel and Maggie Haberman, *"Manafort Accused of Sharing Trump Polling Data With Russian Associate,"* The New York Times,

January 8, 2019, ttps://www.nytimes.com/2019/01/08/us/politics/manafort-trump-campaign-data-kilimnik.html

3   Adam Goldman, Michael S. Schmidt and Nicholas Fandos, "*F.B.I. Opened Inquiry Into Whether Trump Was Secretly Working on Behalf of Russia,*" The New York Times, January 11, 2019, https://www.nytimes.com/2019/01/11/us/politics/fbi-trump-russia-inquiry.html.

4   The closest that a previous presidential candidate may have come to treason and betrayal is probably when Richard M. Nixon, in the closing weeks of the 1968 presidential campaign, tried to get word to the South Vietnam leaders to persuade them not to agree to a proposed peace plan before the election. See Baker, Peter. "Nixon Tried to Spoil Johnson's Vietnam Peace Talks in '68, Notes Show." *nytimes.com.* The New York Times, 2 Jan. 2017, www.nytimes.com/2017/01/02/us/politics/nixon-tried-to-spoil-johnsons-vietnam-peace-talks-in-68-notes-show.html?module=inline.

5   Article II, Section 1 of the U.S. Constitution states, that with regard to the President: "Before he enter on the Execution of his Office, he shall take the following Oath or Affirmation: —"I do solemnly swear (or affirm) that I will faithfully execute the Office of President of the United States, and will to the best of my Ability, preserve, protect and defend the Constitution of the United States."

6   Article III, Section 3 states: "Treason against the United States, shall consist only in levying War against them, or in adhering to their Enemies, giving them Aid and Comfort. No Person shall be convicted of Treason unless on the Testimony of two Witnesses to the same overt Act, or on Confession in open Court."

7   "Traitor" is defined as "one who betrays another's trust or is false to an obligation or duty." *merriam-webster.com.* Merriam-Webster Dictionary, www.merriam-webster.com/dictionary/traitor.

8   While the President's Oath of Office requires that he "preserve, protect and defend the Constitution of the United States," it somewhat oddly does not include the specific language contained in the oath of office for the Vice President and all other federal office holders, employees and members of the armed services, who must swear to "support and defend the Constitution of the United States against all enemies, foreign and domestic; [and] that I will bear true faith and allegiance to the same." See U.S. Code § 3331 - Oath of office.

9   One of the threshold questions in deciding whether a person is guilty of Treason is whether he is "adhering" or "colluding" with an "enemy" of the

United States is whether there must be a formal declaration of war to be issued by Congress or the President for a hostile power to be considered as an "enemy" for purposes of determining whether Treason has been committed. As discussed in greater detail in Chapter 8, a strong case may be made that a country with interests that are substantially hostile or antagonistic to those of the U.S. – such as Russia – may be considered to be an "enemy" of the U.S. for purposes under the Treason clause of the Constitution or the Treason statute, even though there is no formal declaration of war against Russia. Since the end of World War II, the United States has avoided the use of formal declarations of war against enemies and hostile powers, and has engaged in numerous "hot" and "cold" wars against foreign hostile powers without any formal declarations of war.

10 Substantially the same definition of "treason" is found in Title 18, United States Code, § 2381, which states: "Whoever, owing allegiance to the United States, levies war against them or adheres to their enemies, giving them aid and comfort within the United States or elsewhere, is guilty of treason and shall suffer death, or shall be imprisoned not less than five years and fined under this title but not less than $10,000; and shall be incapable of holding any office under the United States."

11 Article II, Section 4 of the U.S. Constitution provides: "The President, Vice President and all civil Officers of the United States, shall be removed from Office on Impeachment for, and Conviction of, Treason, Bribery, or other high Crimes and Misdemeanors."

12 See Baylor, Chris. "A Key Reason The Founders Wanted the Electoral College: To Keep Out Demagogues and Bullies." *washingtonpost.com*. The Washington Post, 12 Dec. 2016, https://www.washingtonpost.com/news/monkey-cage/wp/2016/12/12/a-key-reason-the-founders-wanted-the-electoral-college-to-keep-out-demagogues-and-bullies/?utm_term=.6f6cf310ef6c.

13 *Marbury v. Madison*, 5 U.S. (1 Cranch) 137 (1803), which is arguably the most important constitutional law decision ever decided by the Supreme Court, established the principle of judicial review in the United States, meaning that American courts have the power to strike down laws, statutes, and some government actions that contravene the U.S. Constitution.

14 See Tribe, Laurence. "Yes, the Constitution Allows Indictment of a President." *lawfareblog.com*. Lawfare, 20 Dec. 2018, www.lawfareblog.com/yes-constitution-allows-indictment-president.

15 The Constitution's silence on the issue of whether a sitting president can be indicted is somewhat odd since the Founders were not reticent about explicitly giving immunity to members of Congress under certain circumstances.

For example, Article I of the Constitution explicitly immunizes from arrest all members of Congress "during their attendance at the Sessions of their respected Houses, and in going to and returning from the same."

16   See *Departures and Variances*. Office of General Counsel, U.S. Sentencing Commission, Apr. 2018, www.ussc.gov/guidelines/primers/departures-and-variances.

17   Ibid.

18   Nixon was named as an unindicted co-conspirator in February 1974, but the first public reports of this were made in June 1974. See Liptak, Adam and Rutenberg, Jim. "Cohen Implicates President Trump. What Do Prosecutors Do Now?" *nytimes.com*. The New York Times, 21 Aug. 2018, https://www.nytimes.com/2018/08/21/us/politics/cohen-trump-indicted.html. In all likelihood, Nixon was not indicted due to concerns by government prosecutors about whether the U.S. Constitution allows for the indictment of a sitting President, which they decided not to test in federal court prior to Nixon's resignation.

19   See Bump, Philip. "How the Campaign Finance Charges Against Michael Cohen Implicate Trump." *washingtonpost.com*. The Washington Post, 21 Aug. 2018; see also "Trump Called 'Unindicted Co-Conspirator' in Echoes of Watergate." thecrimereport.com. The Crime Report, 22 Aug. 2018, https://thecrimereport.org/2018/08/22/trump-called-unindicted-co-conspirator-in-echoes-of-watergate/; see also Illing, Sean. "What Does Michael Cohen's Plea Deal Mean for Trump? I asked 13 Legal Experts." *vox.com*. Vox News, 21 Aug. 2018, https://www.vox.com/2018/8/21/17765566/michael-cohen-plea-deal-trump-mueller.

20   Dickerson, John. "Of all the things Trump has been called, "Individual 1" may be the most damaging." *cbsnews.com*. CBS News, 22 Aug. 2018, www.cbsnews.com/news/donald-trump-individual-1-impact-of-michael-cohen-guilty-plea-agreement/.

21   Ibid.

22   See generally Cohen, M. Richard and Witcover, Julida. *A Heartbeat Away: The Investigation and Resignation of Vice President Spiro T. Agnew*. Viking Adult, 1974, pp. 342-350.

23   Notably, Harvard constitutional law professor Laurence Tribe recently tweeted, with regard to the allegations regarding Michael Flynn's dealings with the Russians and what Vice President Pence knew about it. See @tribelaw. "Don't forget Flynn may well have highly incriminating evidence against VPOTUS Mike Pence . . . And we know a sitting VP can be indicted and convicted." *Twitter*, 1 Dec. 2017, 10:12 a.m., https://twitter.com/tribelaw/status/936613922760790018?lang=en.

24   See Myers, D. James. "Bringing the Vice President Into the Fold: Executive Immunity and the Vice Presidency." 50 B.C.L.REV. 897, 924-26 (2009), citing Memorandum from Randolph D. Moss, Assistant Att'y Gen., Off. of Legal Couns., on A Sitting President's Amenability to Indictment and Criminal Prosecution 1 (Oct. 16, 2000), https://www.justice.gov/olc/opinion/sitting-president%E2%80%99s-amenabilityindictment-and-criminal-prosecution [https:// perma.cc/69XW-8VU4].

25   Ibid at 926.

26   *United States v. Nixon*, 418 U.S. 683 (1974).

27   See Chapter 8 herein.

28   Trump's Taj Mahal filed for bankruptcy six months after it opened in April 1990 in Atlantic City. In July 1991, Trump's Taj Mahal filed for bankruptcy, and two properties declared bankruptcy in 1992. A fourth property, the Plaza Hotel in New York, declared bankruptcy in 1992. PolitiFact found two more bankruptcies filed after 1992, totaling six. Trump Hotels and Casinos Resorts filed for bankruptcy again in 2004, after accruing about $1.8 billion in debt. Trump Entertainment Resorts also declared bankruptcy in 2009. See Lee, Michelle. "Fact Check: Has Trump Declared Bankruptcy Four or Six Times?" *washingtonpost.com*. The Washington Post, 26 Sep. 2016, http://www.washingtonpost.com/ politics/2016/live-updates/general-election/real-time-fact-checking-and-analysis-of-the-first-presidential-debate/fact-check-has-trump-declared-bankruptcyfour-or-six-times/; see also Qiu, Linda. "Yep, Donald Trump's companies have declared bankruptcy...more than four times." *politifact.com*. Politi Fact, 21 June 2016, https://www.politifact.com/truth-o-meter/statements/2016/jun/21/hillary-clinton/yep-donald-trumps-companies-have-declared-bankrupt/.

29   Langlois, Shawn. "CNN's Acosta Refuses to give up the mic during heating confrontation with Trump." *marketwatch.com*. The Market Watch, 7 Nov. 2018, https://www.marketwatch.com/story/cnns-acosta-refuses-to-give-up-themic-during-heated-confrontation-with-trump-2018-11-07.

30   At a press conference in July, 2016, Trump said: "Russia, if you're listening, I hope you're able to find the 30,000 emails that are missing," referring to emails Mrs. Clinton had deleted from the private account she had used when she was secretary of state. "I think you will probably be rewarded mightily by our press." See Schmidt, S. Michael. "Trump Invited the Russians to Hack Clinton. Were They Listening?" *nytimes.com*. The New York Times, 27 July 2016, https:// www.nytimes.com/2018/07/13/us/politics/trump-russia-clinton-emails.html.

31   "Trump Tower Russia Meeting: At Least Eight People in the Room."

cnn.com. CNN, 15 July 2017, www.cnn.com/2017/07/14/politics/donald-trump-jr-meeting/index.html.

32   Sanger, David. "Obama Strikes Back at Russia for Election Hacking." *nytimes.com.* The New York Times, 29 Dec. 2016, www.nytimes.com/2016/12/29/us/politics/russia-election-hacking-sanctions.html.

33   Schmidt, S. Michael. "Documents Reveal New Details on What Trump Team Knew About Flynn Calls With Russia's Ambassador." *nytimes.com.* The New York Times, 1 Dec. 2017, www.nytimes.com/2017/12/01/us/politics/flynn-russia-sanctions.html.

34   Hirscheld Davis, Julie. "Trump Presses NATO on Military Spending, but Signs Its Criticism of Russia." *nytimes.com.* The New York Times, 11 July 2018, www.nytimes.com/2018/07/11/world/europe/trump-nato-summit.html.

35   Sanger, David and Haberman, Maggie. "Donald Trump Sets Conditions for Defending NATO Allies Against Attack." *nytimes.com.* The New York Times, 20 July 2016, www.nytimes.com/2016/07/21/us/politics/donald-trump-issues.html.

CHAPTER 3 - POOR LITTLE RICH KID: THE EARLY YEARS

1   Kranish, Michael and Fisher, Marc. *Trump Revealed: the Definitive Biography of the 45th President.* Scribner, 2017.

2   Ibid.

3   Ibid.

4   Ibid.

5   Ibid.

6   Ibid.

7   Ibid.

8   Ibid.

9   Ibid.

10   The richest 1% in the United States now own more wealth than the bottom 90 percent. See Kristof, Nicholas, "An Idiot's guide to Inequality." *nytimes.com.* The New York Times, 23 July 2014, www.nytimes.com/2014/07/24/opinion/

nicholas-kristof-idiots-guide-to-inequality-piketty-capital.html.

The top 1% of Americans, in terms of wealth, have roughly doubled their share of America's wealth since 1980, from 11% in 1980 to 20% in 2014. See Rothwell, Jonathan. "Myths of the 1 Percent: What Puts People at the Top." *nytimes.com*. The New York Times, 1 Nov. 2018, www.nytimes.com/2017/11/17/upshot/income-inequality-united-states.html. In terms of income rather than wealth, the upper 1 percent of Americans is now taking in nearly a quarter (25%) of the nation's income every year, which is a doubling of the income figures over a 25-year period. Stiglitz, Joseph. "Of the 1%, By the 1%, For the 1%." *vanityfair.com*. Vanity Fair, May 2011, www.vanityfair.com/news/2011/05/top-one-percent-201105. "This trend, combined with slow productivity growth, has resulted in stagnant living standards for most Americans." See Rothwell, Jonathan, supra.

11   In The Captured Economy, authors Brink Lindsey and Steven Teles argue that regressive regulations and laws that benefit the rich are a primary cause of the huge income gains among elite professionals and financial managers in the United States and of a reduction in growth. See also Rothwell, Jonathan. "Myths of the 1 Percent: What Puts People at the Top." Richard Reeves, Joseph Stiglitz, Robert Reich and Luigi Zingales have also written extensively about how the political power elites in the U.S. have undermined markets and contributed to income inequality. These analysts have cited to the following problems caused or influenced by current laws and regulations, among others: subsidies for the financial sector's risk-taking; overprotection of software and pharmaceutical patents; the escalation of land-use controls that drive up rents in desirable metropolitan areas; favoritism toward market incumbents via state occupational licensing regulations. Ibid.

12   Barstow, David and Craig, Susanne et al. "Trump Engaged in Suspect Tax Schemes as He Reaped Riches From His Father." *nytimes.com*. The New York Times, 2 Oct. 2018, https://www.nytimes.com/interactive/2018/10/02/politics/donald-trump-tax-schemes-fred-trump.html.

13   Ibid.

14   Ibid.

15   Ibid.

16   "In lawsuit deposition, Trump repeatedly called out for exaggerating wealth." *cbsnews.com*. CBS News, 24, May 2016, www.cbsnews.com/news/elections-2016-donald-trump-worth-reveals-in-deposition-tim-obrien-lawsuit-2006/.

17   Ibid.

18   Barstow, David and Craig, Susanne et al. "Trump Engaged in Suspect Tax Schemes as He Reaped Riches From His Father," *nytimes.com*. The New York Times, 2 Oct. 2018, https://www.nytimes.com/interactive/2018/10/02/us/politics/donald-trump-tax-schemes-fred-trump.html.

19   Ibid.

20   Mayer, Jane. "Donald Trump's Ghostwriter Tells All." *newyorker.com*. The New Yorker, 25 July 2016, www.newyorker.com/magazine/2016/07/25/donald-trumps-ghostwriter-tells-all; See also Lind, Dara. "Wayne Barrett Covered Donald Trump for 40 years. Here's what he's learned," *vox.com*. Vox News, 1 June 2016, www.vox.com/2016/6/1/11690238/wayne-barrett-donald-trump.

21   Ibid.

22   Greenberg, Jonathan. "Trump lied to me about his wealth to get onto the Forbes 400. Here are the tapes." *washingtonpost.com*. The Washington Post, 20 Apr. 2018, https://www.washingtonpost.com/outlook/trump-lied-to-me-about-his-wealth-to-get-onto-the-forbes-400-here-are-the-tapes/2018/04/20/ac762b08-4287-11e8-8569-26fda6b404c7_story.html.

23   Mulchany, Susan. "Confessions of a Trump Tabloid Scribe." politico.com. Politico, May/June 2016, www.politico.com/magazine/story/2016/04/2016-donald-trump-tabloids-new-york-post-daily-news-media-213842.

24   Ibid.

25   Mayer, Jane. "Donald Trump's Ghostwriter Tells All."

26   Ibid.

27   Ibid.

28   Ibid.

29   Ibid.

CHAPTER 4 - A USEFUL IDIOT

1   While some psychiatric professionals and a large number of amateur armchair psychological profilers have suggested that Trump suffers from Narcissistic Personality Disorder (NPD), a Class B personality disorder, the prevailing view seems to be that a diagnosis of his condition is less important than an accurate description of Trump's thought processes and behavior, and whether what he says and what he does adversely affects the performance of his duties. See,

e.g., Marshall, John. "Is President Trump Mentally Ill? It Doesn't Matter." *talking pointsmemo.com.* TPM, 6 Jan. 2018, https://talkingpointsmemo.com/edblog/is-president-trump-mentally-ill-it-doesnt-matter. There appears to be a consensus that Trump is impulsive, erratic, driven by petty aggressions and paranoia, show-ing poor impulsive control, and an inability to moderate self-destructive behavior. "He is frequently either frighteningly out of touch with reality or sufficiently pathological in his lying that it is impossible to tell." Ibid. Both are very bad.

2   See, *e.g.,* Fessler, Pam. "Crafting a Mental Profile of a Terrorist." *npr.org.* NPR, 17 Aug. 2005, www.npr.org/templates/story/story.php?storyId=4804389; See also "Podcast: Psychology of Profiling in Terrorism." *inhomelandsecurity.com.* InHomeland Security, 12 July 2012, inhomelandsecurity.com/podcast-psycholo-gy-of-profiling-in-terrorism/.

3   Safire, William. "On Language." *nytimes.com.* The New York Times, 12 Apr. 1987, nytimes.com/1987/04/12/magazine/on-language.html.

4   Congressional Record, Vol. 105, 30 June 1959, p. A5653.

5   The Editorial Board. "Donald Trump's Denial About Russia." *nytimes.com.* The New York Times, 15 Dec. 2016, https://www.nytimes.com/2016/12/15/opinion/donald-trumps-denial-about-russia.html.

6   Morell, Michael. "I Ran the C.I.A. Now I'm Endorsing Hillary Clinton." *nytimes.com.* The New York Times, 5 Aug. 2015, www.nytimes.com/2016/08/05/opinion/campaign-stops/i-ran-the-cia-now-im-endorsing-hillary-clinton.html.

7   Ibid.

8   Ibid.

9   Ibid.

10   Wolff, Michael. "Donald Trump Didn't Want to Be President." *nymag. com.* The New York Magazine, 8 Jan. 2018, nymag.com/intelligencer/2018/01/michael-wolff-fire-and-fury-book-donald-trump.html.

11   Ibid.

12   "Trump: I'm 'Like, Really Smart,' a 'Very Stable Genius'." thedailybeast. com. The Daily Beast, Jan. 2018, www.thedailybeast.com/trump-im-like-really-smart-a-very-stable-genius.

13   Ibid.

14   Trump actually got the name of the school wrong; since 1972, it has

been named the Wharton School of the University of Pennsylvania, the Wharton Business School or just "Wharton." It was, however, named "Wharton School of Finance and Commerce" from 1902 to 1971. See Spinelli, Dan. "Trump Flaunts Wharton Degree, But his College Years Remain a Mystery." *thedp.com*. The Daily Pennsylvanian, 19 Aug. 2015, https://www.thedp.com/article/2015/08/donald-trump-wharton-classmates.

15   Ibid.

16   Ibid.

17   Ibid.

18   Ibid.

19   Ibid.

20   Ibid.

21   Ibid.

22   Ibid.

23   Rabin, Alex. "With a Penn Graduate in the Oval Office for the First Time, here's a Look at Former President William Henry Harrison's Time at the University." *thedp.com*. The Daily Pennsylvanian, 26 Jan. 2017, www.thedp.com/article/2017/01/william-henry-harrison-history.

24   "Bush Returns to Yale for Commencement Speech." *cnn.com*. CNN, 21 May 2001, www.cnn.com/2001/ALLPOLITICS/05/21/bush.speech/.

25   Pearl, Ayelet. "Obama's Politicized Commencement Speech." *cpreview.org*. Columbia Political Review, 15 May 2021, www.cpreview.org/blog/2012/05/obamas-politicized-commencement-speech.

26   Sadurni, Luis. "Donald Trump May Have Donated Over $1.4 million to Penn." *thedp.com*. The Daily Pennsylvanian, 3 Nov. 2016, www.thedp.com/article/2016/11/trumps-history-of-donating-to-penn.

27   Ibid.

28   Beam, Alex. "How smart is Donald Trump?" *bostonglobe.com*. The Boston Globe, 6 Aug. 2018, www.bostonglobe.com/opinion/2018/08/05/how-smart-donald-trump/hHGm2NU3cbeOgCQ9A92ehM/story.html.

29   Zorn, Eric. "Is Trump Smarter Than Those Whose Brainpower He Criticizes? Let's Find Out!" *chicagotribune.com*. The Chicago Tribune, 7 Aug. 2018, www.

chicagotribune.com/news/opinion/zorn/ct-perspec-zorn-trump-iq-lemon-lebron-0808-20180806-story.html.

30   Ibid.

31   Ibid.

32   Ibid.

33   Ibid.

34   Ibid.

35   Ibid.

36   Ibid.

37   Ibid.

38   Ibid.

39   Ibid.

40   Ibid.

41   Asghar, Rob. "Why Donald Trump Has Experts Redefining 'Smart' and 'Genius'." *forbes.com*. Forbes, 4 Mar. 2018, www.forbes.com/sites/robasghar/2018/03/04/why-donald-trump-has-experts-redefining-smart-and-genius/#1e78b4845ee9.

42   Ibid.

43   Ibid.

44   Ibid.

45   Ibid.

CHAPTER 5 - THE DONALD AND THE DRAFT

1   Martin, Jonathan and Rappeport, Alan. "Donald Trump Says John McCain Is No War Hero, Setting Off Another Storm." *nytimes.com*. The New York Times, 18 July 2015, www.nytimes.com/2015/07/19/us/politics/trump-belittles-mccains-war-record.html.

2   Ibid.

3   Lizza, Ryan. "John McCain Has a Few Things to Say About Donald Trump." *newyorker.com*. The New Yorker, 16 July 2015, www.newyorker.com/news/news-desk/john-mccain-has-a-few-things-to-say-about-donald-trump.

4   Mak, Tim. "Draft-Dodger Trump Said Sleeping Around Was My 'Personal Vietnam'." *thedailybeast.com*. The Daily Beast, 16 Feb. 2016, www.thedaily-beast.com/draft-dodger-trump-said-sleeping-around-was-my-personal-vietnam.

5   Ibid. See also Kaczynski, Andrew. "Trump Isn't Into . . . " *buzzfeed-news.com*. BuzzFeed News, 16 Feb. 2016, www.buzzfeednews.com/article/andrewkaczynski/trump-isnt-into-anal-melania-never-poops-and-other-things-he#.ldZMnyq0a.

6   Lee, Kurtis. "How Deferments Protected Donald Trump From Serving in Vietnam." *latimes.com*. The Los Angeles Times, 4 Aug. 2016, www.latimes.com/politics/la-na-pol-donald-trump-military-20160803-snap-htmlstory.html.

7   Ibid.

8   Ibid.

9   Ibid.

10   Ibid.

11   Ibid.

12   Ibid.

13   Eder, Steve and Philipps, Dave. "Donald Trump's Draft Deferments: Four for College, One for Bad Feet." *nytimes.com*. The New York Times, 1 Aug. 2016, https://www.nytimes.com/2016/08/02/us/politics/donald-trump-draft-record.html.

14   Ma, Alexandra. "Trump biographer examined his feet for bone spurs that helped him avoid Vietnam but 'didn't see anything'." *businessinsider.com*. Business Insider, 27 Dec. 2018, www.businessinsider.com/trump-tried-to-show-biographer-bone-spurs-that-helped-him-avoid-draft-2018-12.

15   Eder, Steve. "Did a Queens Podiatrist Help Donald Trump Avoid Vietnam?" *nytimes.com*. The New York Times, 26 Dec. 2018, www.nytimes.com/2018/12/26/us/politics/trump-vietnam-draft-exemption.html.

16   Ibid.

17   Ibid.

18   Ibid.

19   Ibid.

20   Bates, Daniel. "Exclusive: Donald Trump pictured in uniform as a cadet captain . . . " *dailymail.com.* The Daily Mail, 20 July 2015, www.dailymail.co.uk/ news/article-3168648/Donald-Trump-pictured-uniform-cadet-captain-dodged-Vietnam-draft-four-deferments-bone-spur.html.

21   Ibid.

22   Ibid.

23   Ibid.

24   Blair, Gwenda. *Donald Trump: Master Apprentice.* Simon & Schuster, 2007.

CHAPTER 6 - BOUGHT AND PAID FOR

1   Border Wall Could Cost 3 Times Estimates, Senate Democrats' Report Says." *nytimes.com.* The New York times, 18 Apr. 2017, www.nytimes. com/2017/04/18/us/politics/senate-democrats-border-wall-cost-trump.html.

2   "Joseph McCarthy: Debate with Welch During Senate Trials." *Speeches,* n.d.,<http://www.speeches-usa.com/Transcripts/joseph_mccarthy-debate. html.

3   Barrett, Wayne. *Trump: The Deals and the Downfall.* HarperCollins, 1992.

4   Ibid.

5   Robbins, Tom. "Trump and the Mob." *themarshallproject*.org. The Marshall Project, 27 Apr. 2016, <https://www.themarshallproject.org/2016/04/27/ trump-and-the-mob#.V9KFwUR3V>.

6   For more on Biff Halloran, see Rowan, Roy. "The Mafia's Bite Of The Big Apple Byzantine Building Codes and Horrendous Logistics Help the Mob Control New York City Construction -- at a Price That the Big Developers Have Been All Too Willing to Pay." Fortune Magazine, 6 June 1988; see also Raab, Selwyn. "Ex-Hotel Owner With Former Ties to Mobsters Disappears." *nytimes.com.* The New York Times, 29 Oct. 1998, <http://www.nytimes.com/1998/10/30/ nyregion/ex-hotel-owner-with-former-ties-to-mobsters-disappears.html>.

7   Robbins, Tom. "The Truth about Donald Trump and His Links to the Mob." *newsweek.com.* Newsweek, 1 May 2016, <http://www.newsweek.com/

truth-about-trump-mob-454053>. This piece was originally published by The Marshall Project.

8   "Only a handful of union workers from Union Local 95 were employed on the site; the vast majority were illegal Polish alien workers, who worked under inhumane conditions, and who were grossly underpaid." See Robbins, "Trump and the Mob."

9   Hays, Constance L. "Judge Says Trump Tower Builders Cheated Union on Pension Funds. " *nytimes.com*. The New York Times, 26 Apr. 1991, <http://www.nytimes.com/1991/04/27/nyregion/judge-says-trump-tower-builders-cheated-union-on-pension-funds.html>.

10   Ibid.

11   Glenny, Misha. *McMafia: A Journey Through the Global Criminal Underworld*. Alfred A. Knopf, 2008, pp. 72–73.

12   Koenigs, Michael. "The Controversial Residents of Trump Tower." *abcnews.go.com*. ABC News, 23 Feb. 2018, https://abcnews.go.com/Politics/controversial-residents-trump-tower/story?id=52577191.

13   O'Brien, Timothy L. *TrumpNation: The Art of Being the Donald*. Warner Business, 2005; See also Goodman, Peter S. "Trump Suit Claiming Defamation Is Dismissed." *nytimes.com*. The New York Times, 31 Aug. 2016, <http://www.nytimes.com/2009/07/16/business/media/16trump.html>.

14   Sallah, Michael, and Michael Vasquez. "Failed Donald Trump Tower Thrust into GOP Campaign for Presidency." *miamiherald*.com. The Miami Herald, 12 Mar. 2016, <http://www.miamiherald.com/news/politics-government/election/article65709332.html>.

15   "Eric Trump: 'We Have All The Funding We Need Out of Russia'." *The Moscow Project*, 2014, https://themoscowproject.org/collusion/eric-trump-funding-need-russia/.

16   Ibid.

17   Ibid.

18   Melby, Caleb and Geiger, Keri. "Behind Trump's Russia Romance, There's a Tower Full of Oligarchs." *bloomberg.com*. Bloomberg Businessweek, 16 Mar. 2017, www.bloomberg.com/news/articles/2017-03-16/behind-trump-s-russia-romance-there-s-a-tower-full-of-oligarchs.

19   O'Brien, Timothy. "Trump, Russia and a Shadowy Business Partnership."

bloomberg.com. Bloomberg Businessopinion, 21 June 2017, www.bloomberg.com/opinion/articles/2017-06-21/trump-russia-and-those-shadowy-sater-deals-at-bayrock.

20   Longman, Martin. "Trump's SoHo Project, the Mob, and Russian Intelligence." *washintgonmonthly.com*. Washington Monthly, 20 Feb. 2017, washingtonmonthly.com/2017/02/20/trumps-soho-project-the-mob-and-russian-intelligence/.

21   Champion, Marc. "How a Trump SoHo Partner Ended Up With Toxic Mining Riches From Kazakhstan." *bloomberg.com*. Bloomberg, 11 Jan. 2018, www.bloomberg.com/news/features/2018-01-11/how-a-trump-soho-partner-ended-up-with-toxic-mining-riches-from-kazakhstan.

22   Ibid.

23   "Corruption Trial Against Former Almaty Mayor Opens in Kazakhstan." *rferl.org*. Radio Free Europe, Radio Library, 26 July 2018, www.rferl.org/a/corruption-trial-against-former-almaty-mayor-opens-in-kazakhstan/29391601.html.

24   Mosk, Matthew and Ross, Brian et al. "From Russia With Trump: A Political Conflict Zone." *abcnews.go.com*. ABC News, 22 Sep. 2016, abcnews.go.com/Politics/russia-trump-political-conflict-zone/story?id=42263092.

25   Silverstein, Ken. "Miami: Where Luxury Real Estate Meets Dirty Money." *thenation.com*. The Nation, 2 Oct. 2013, https://www.thenation.com/article/miami-where-luxury-real-estate-meets-dirty-money/.

26   Unger, Craig. "Trump's Russian Laundromat." *newrepublic.com*. The New Republic, 13 July 2017, newrepublic.com/article/143586/trumps-russian-laundromat-trump-tower-luxury-high-rises-dirty-money-international-crime-syndicate.

27   Layne, Nathan et al. "Special Report: Russian elite invested nearly $100 million in Trump buildings, records show." *reuters.com*. Reuters, 17 Mar. 2017, https://www.reuters.com/article/us-usa-trump-property-specialreport/special-report-russian-elite-invested-nearly-100-million-in-trump-buildings-records-show-idUSKBN16O2F6.

28   Glaister, Dan. "Donald Trump Sells Florida Mansion For Record Sum." *theguardian.com*. The Guardian, 17 July 2008, www.theguardian.com/world/2008/jul/17/donaldtrump.usa.

29   Ibid.

30   Venook, Jeremy. "Trump's Been Talking About His Business Interests in Russia for 30 Years." *theatlantic.com*. The Atlantic, 10 May 2017, www.theatlantic.com/business/archive/2017/05/trump-lawyers-up-conflicts-of-interest/526185/.

31   Dorell, Oren. "Donald Trump's Ties to Russia Go Back 30 Years." *usatoday.com*. USA Today, 15 Feb. 2017, www.usatoday.com/story/news/world/2017/02/15/donald-trumps-ties-russia-go-back-30-years/97949746/.

32   Littlefield, Bill. "A Day (And A Cheeseburger) With President Trump." *wbur90,9*, 5 May 2017, www.wbur.org/onlyagame/2017/05/05/james-dodson-donald-trump-golf.

CHAPTER 7 - TREASON: A BRIEF HISTORY

1   "traitor." *merriam-webster.com*. Merriam-Webster Dictionary, 2019. Web.

2   The word "traitor" originated with Judas' handing over of Jesus to the chief priests, captains of the temple and elders (Luke 22:52); it is derived from the Latin *traditor*, which means "one who delivers." Christian theology and political thinking until after the Enlightenment considered treason and blasphemy as synonymous, as it challenged both the state and the will of God. Kings were considered chosen by God, and to betray one's country was to do the work of Satan.

3   Catholic dissident Guy Fawkes and 12 co-conspirators planned to blow up King James I of England during the opening of Parliament on November 5, 1605. Their assassination attempt failed when Fawkes was discovered the night before lurking in a cellar below the House of Lords next to 36 barrels of gunpowder. Londoners immediately began lighting bonfires in celebration that the plot had failed, and a few months later Parliament declared November 5 a public day of thanksgiving.

4   Article II, Section 4 states: "The President, Vice President, and all civil Officers of the United States shall be removed from Office on Impeachment for, and Conviction of, Treason, Bribery, or other High Crimes and Misdemeanors."

5   Sherfinski, David. "Michael McCaul on Hillary Clinton's private server, hacks: 'It's treason'." *washingtontimes.com*. The Washington Times, 3 Nov. 2016, https://www.washingtontimes.com/news/2016/nov/3/michael-mccaul-hillary-clinton-server-hacks-its-tr/.

6   On January 20, 2017 Gorka, born in the U.K. and of Hungarian her-

itage, appeared on Fox News on the evening of the U.S. presidential inauguration wearing a badge, tunic, and ring of the Order of Vitéz. See generally
Staff, Toi. "Top Trump aide wears medal of Hungarian Nazi collaborators."
timesofisrael.com. The Times of Israel, 14 Feb. 2017, www.timesofisrael.com/
top-trump-aide-wears-medal-of-hungarian-nazi-collaborators/; Fortin, Ja-
cey. "Who is Sebastian Gorka? A Trump Adviser Comes Out of the Shadows." *nytimes.com*. The New York Times, 17 Feb. 2017, https://www.nytimes.
com/2017/02/17/us/politics/dr-sebastian-gorka.html; Davies, Caroline. "'A
Fabulous Trump press conference': who are his British cheerleaders?" *theguardian.
com*. The Guardian, 17 Feb. 2017, https://www.theguardian.com/us-news/2017/
feb/17/a-fabulous-press-conference-who-are-trumps-british-cheerleaders. The
U.S. State Department lists this Order among organizations having been "under
the direction of the Nazi government of Germany" during World War II. See
*Foreign Affairs Manual and Handbook: Organizations Under the Direction of the Nazi
Government of Germany*. U.S. Department of State, 18 Nov. 2015. Various right-
wing anti-Semitic groups, such as the Hungary Guarda, have adopted symbols
of the Order to promote their cause and ideology. Possibly because of these
alleged affiliations – and various statements made by Gorka giving rise to claims
that Gorka himself is a Nazi sympathizer – Gorka resigned on August 25, 2017,
although Gorka claimed he resigned because he believed White House officials
were undermining the "Make America Great Again" platform. He quickly was
hired as a Fox News contributor.

7   Gorka stated: "If this had happened in the 1950s, there would be people up on treason charges right now. The Rosenbergs, OK? This is equivalent to
what the Rosenbergs did and those people got the chair." Gorka was referring to
the investigation House Republicans had announced into the circumstances surrounding the sale of Canadian mining corporation, Uranium One, which was approved in 2010 by the Obama administration. At the time, a committee involving
Hillary Clinton approved the sale to Rosatom, Russia's Atomic Energy Agency.

8   Landers, Elizabeth and Diamond, Jeremy. "Trump labels some Democrats 'treasonous' for their State of the Union reaction." *cnn.com*. CNN, 6
Feb. 2018, https://www.cnn.com/2018/02/05/politics/donald-trump-dem-
ocrats-treasonous/index.html. Trump has also referred to the Democrats as
"death and un-American."

9   See "Trump slams special counsel after retweeting image of Rosenstein
behind bars." 29 Nov. 2018, https://johnib.wordpress.com/tag/james-clapper/.

10   Harvard Law Dean Ervin Griswold described McCarthy's role as "judge,
jury, prosecutor, castigator, and press agent, all in one." See "Have you No Sense
of Decency?" U.S. Congress. Senate. https://www.senate.gov/artandhistory/his-
tory/minute/Have_you_no_sense_of_decency.htm.

11   Ibid.

12   Ibid.

13   Substantially the same definition of "treason" may be found in Title 18, United States Code, § 2381, which states: "Whoever, owing allegiance to the United States, levies war against them or adheres to their enemies, giving them aid and comfort within the United States or elsewhere, is guilty of treason and shall suffer death, or shall be imprisoned not less than five years and fined under this title but not less than $10,000; and shall be incapable of holding any office under the United States."

14   The issue of whether Russia can be considered as an "enemy" of the United States for purposes of the Constitutional or statutory definition of treason, or whether there must be a formal declaration of war for a state of war to exist between two countries, is fully explored in Chapter 8 *infra*. Specifically, the argument is made that Russia's cyber-warfare attack on the United States over the past several years, and particularly during the 2016 Presidential election, is the contemporary equivalent of an attack on the U.S. and constitutes a declaration of war by a hostile power against the U.S. just as much as the attack on Pearl Harbor on December 7, 1941 and the terrorist attack on the World Trade Center on September 11, 2001 immediately made Japan and Al-Quaada de facto enemies of the United States. Significantly, Russia considered its cyberwarfare capabilities to be an extension of Russia's military power. In February 2016, for example, senior Kremlin advisor and top Russian cyber official Andrey Krutskikh told the Russian national security conference in Moscow that Russia was working on new strategies for the "information arena" that was equivalent to testing a nuclear bomb and would "allow us to talk to the Americans as equals." Moreover, if, in fact, Russia may be considered to be an "enemy" under the definition of treason, then it naturally follows that any American citizen who gives "aid and comfort" to Russia in support of its efforts to manipulate the U.S. electoral process and undermine its democratic institutions is guilty of treason.

15   Madison, James. *The Federalist Papers* No. 43.

16   See The Crimes Act of 1790, Ch. 9, 1 Stat. 112. http://legisworks.org/congress/1/session-2/chap-9.pdf.

17   "If any person or persons, owing allegiance to the United States of America, shall levy war against them, or shall adhere to their enemies, giving them aid and comfort within the United States, or elsewhere..." they shall be guilty of treason.

18   "... and that if any person or persons, having knowledge of the com-

mission of any of the treasons aforesaid, shall conceal, and not, as soon as may be, disclose and make known the same … such person or persons, on conviction, shall be adjudged guilty of misprision of treason…."

19   Benedict Arnold's treason predated the drafting and ratification of the U.S. Constitution. After defecting to the British side, Arnold became a General in the British Army and died of old age after he returned to England following the end of the American Revolution.

20   The Whiskey Rebellion was a tax protest beginning in 1791 that was triggered by the first tax imposed on a domestic product by the newly formed U.S. government. The tax was intended to generate revenue for the war debt incurred during the Revolutionary War. Farmers of the western frontier resisted the tax on whiskey, which often served as a medium of exchange. Many of the resisters were war veterans who believed that the tax violated the principle of the American Revolution that there should be no taxation without local representation.

21   The U.S. House of Representatives broke an Electoral College tie by naming Thomas Jefferson as president, and Burr as his vice president.

22   Dr. Cooper's published letter stated: "General Hamilton and Judge Kent have declared in substance that they looked upon Mr. Burr to be a dangerous man, and one who ought not be trusted with the reins of government."

23   Dueling was illegal at the time, but gentlemen regularly engaged in this archaic practice on a generally harmless and ritualized basis. It was rumored that Hamilton had participated in 10 other duels, where either no shots were fired or shots were fired into the ground to indicate a man's courage, but without any risk of harm to hitting the other participant.

24   *U.S. v. Burr*, 25 Fed. Cas. 55, no. 14,693 C.C.D.Va. 1807.

25   Ibid at 3.

26   Marshall declared "that he who counsels, procures, or aids treason, is guilty accessorily, and solely in virtue of the common law principle that what will make a man an accessory in felony makes him a principal in treason." Ibid at 20.

27   Hoffer, Peter Charles. *The Treason Trials of Aaron Burr.* U. Press of Kansas, 2008.

28   Wertheim, Lewis J. "The Indianapolis Treason Trials, the Elections of 1864, and the Power of the Partisan Press." *Indiana Magazine of History,* 1989, pp. 236-260.

29   Notwithstanding this, some Northern leaders still tried to indict various Confederate leaders for treason, and Grant reminded President Johnson of the terms of surrender. See "Grant, Lee, Parole, and Treason." 16 Sep. 2009, https://www.aleksandreia.com/2009/09/16/grant-lee-parole-treason/.

30   Roy Franklin Nichols, Roy Franklin. "United States vs. Jefferson Davis, 1865-1869." *American Historical Review* vol. 31, no. 2, 1926, pp. 266-284.

31   The 1798 Alien and Sedition Acts and the Espionage Act of 1917 both have much broader definitions of offenses against the United States than the Constitution's Article III definition of treason. Another federal statute – 18 U.S. Code §798 – dealing with disclosure of classified information, may also relevant, since it states, in part, that whoever knowingly and willfully communicates to an unauthorized person any classified information (which would include information discussed at the relevant intelligence briefings) then that person shall be fined or imprisoned for not more than 10 years or both.

32   Baker, Peter and Rudoren, Jodi. "Jonathan Pollard, American Who Spied for Israel, Released After 30 Years." *nytimes.com.* The New York Times, 30 Nov. 2015, www.nytimes.com/2015/11/21/world/jonathan-pollard-released.html.

33   Ibid.

CHAPTER 8 - IS RUSSIAN AN ENEMY OF THE U.S.?

1   On August 17, 1787, the Convention voted to change the clause from "make" to "declare." See 2 *The Records of the Federal Convention of 1787,* at 318-19 (Max Farrand ed., rev. ed. 1966). A supporter of the change argued that it would "leav[e] to the Executive the power to repel sudden attacks." *Ibid.* at 318.

2   "As Lincoln later put it: "[Is] it possible to lose the nation and yet preserve the Constitution?"'"

Youngstown Sheet & Tube Co. v. Sawyer, 343 U.S. 579, 662 (1952) (Clark, J., concurring).

3   *The Federalist* No. 23, at 122 (Alexander Hamilton) (Charles R. Kesler ed., 1999). Hamilton further noted, "Energy in the executive is a leading character in the definition of good government. It is essential to the protection of the community against foreign attacks." *Ibid.* at 423. This is no less true in war. "Of all the cares or concerns of government, the direction of war most peculiarly demands those qualities which distinguish the exercise of power by a single hand." *Ibid.* No. 74, at 447.

4   Ibid.

5   *Harlow v. Fitzgerald*, 457 U.S. 800, 812 n.19 (1982).

6   *See Nixon v. Fitzgerald*, 457 U.S. 731, 749-50 (1982).

7   *Dep't of Navy v. Egan*, 484 U.S. 518, 529 (1988) (quoting *Haig v. Agee*, 453 U.S. at 293-94); see also *Ludecke v. Watkins*, 335 U.S. 160, 173 (1948) ("The Founders in their wisdom made [the President] not only the Commander-in-Chief but also the guiding organ in the conduct of our foreign affairs," possessing "vast powers in relation to the outside world")\; and *United States v. Curtiss-Wright Export Corp.*, 299 U.S. 304, 320(1936) (the foreign affairs power is "the very delicate, plenary and exclusive power of the President as sole organ of the federal government in the field of international relations—a power which does not require as a basis for its exercise an act of Congress").

8   *Nixon v. Adm'r of Gen. Servs.*, 433 U.S. 425, 443 (1977).

9   *Lichter v. United States*, 334 U.S. 742, 782 (1948); see also, Memorandum Opinion For the Deputy Counsel to the President, Opinions of the Office of Legal Counsel, Vol. 25, "The President's Constitutional Authority To Conduct Military Operations Against Terrorists and Nations Supporting Them," John C. Yoo, Dep. Attorney General (September 25, 2001), and cases cited therein (p. 190, ftnt.3), including *Johnson v. Eisentrager*, 339 U.S. 763, 789 (1950) (President has authority to deploy United States armed forces "abroad or to any particular region"); *Fleming v. Page*, 50 U.S. (9 How.) 603, 615 (1850) ("As commander-in-chief, [the President] is authorized to direct the movements of the naval and military forces placed by law at his command, and to employ them in the manner he may deem most effectual . . . ."); *Loving v. United States*, 517 U.S. 748, 776 (1996) (Scalia, J., concurring in part and concurring in judgment) (The "inherent powers" of the Commander in Chief "are clearly extensive."); *Maul v. United States*, 274 U.S. 501, 515-16 (1927) (Brandeis & Holmes, JJ., concurring) (President "may direct any revenue cutter to cruise in any waters in order to perform any duty of the service"); *Massachusetts v. Laird*, 451 F.2d 26, 32 (1st Cir. 1971) (the President has "power as Commander-in-Chief to station forces abroad"); *Authority to Use United States Military Forces in Somalia*, 16 Op.O.L.C. 6 (1992).

10   There was no declaration of war issued by Congress during the American Civil War, even though the Confederate States of America were recognized by the United States as a belligerent power, albeit not a sovereign nation.

11   Memorandum from John C. Yoo, Deputy Assistant Attorney Gen., U.S. Dep't of Justice, to the Deputy Counsel to the President, "The President's Constitutional Authority to Conduct Military Operations Against Terrorists and Na-

tions Supporting Them," Sept. 25, 2001. *lawfare.s3-us-west-2.amazonaws.com/ staging/ s3fs-public/ uploads/ 2013/ 10/ Memorandum-from-John-C-Yoo-Sept-25-2001.pdf*.

12 Ibid.; although the participation of the U.S. military in Afghanistan has been going on for the past 17 years, it is not the longest undeclared war in U.S. history. Arguably the U.S.'s longest war lasted 46 years, and was fought against the Apache Nation between approximately 1840 and 1886.

13 On December 8, 1941, Congress approved a resolution declaring war with Japan, with the Senate unanimously approved the resolution, 82-0. Three days later, on December 11, 1941, the Senate again unanimously declared war on both Germany and Italy. On June 4, 1942, Congress approved a resolution declaring war with Bulgaria, Hungary and Rumania. See *https:// www.senate.gov/ pagelayout/ history/ h.../ WarDeclarationsbyCongress.htm*

14 "U.S. Enters Korean Conflict." *archives.gov.* National Archives, 7 Sep. 2016, https://www.archives.gov/education/lessons/korean-conflict.

15 Wong, Edward. "Why Is the U.S. Wary of a Declaration to End the Korean War?" *nytimes.com.* The New York Times, 13 Aug. 2018, https://www.nytimes.com/2018/08/13/world/asia/korea-peace-treaty-trump-us.html.

16 "U.S. Involvement in the Vietnam War: the Gulf of Tonkin and Escalation, 1964." *history.state.gov.* Office of the Historian, https://history.state.gov/milestones/1961-1968/gulf-of-tonkin.

17 Kelleher, Kevin. "Microsoft Says Russia Has Already Tried to Hack 3 Campaigns in the 2018 Election." *fortune.com.* Fortune, 19, July 2018. http://fortune.com/2018/07/19/microsoft-russia-hack-2018-election-campaigns/.

18 Dlouhy, Jennifer A. and Riley, Michael. "Russian Hackers Attacking U.S. Power Grid and Aviation, FBI Warns." *bloomberg.com.* Bloomberg, 15 Mar. 2018, https://www.bloomberg.com/news/articles/2018-03-15/russian-hackers-attacking-u-s-power-grid-aviation-fbi-warns.

19 War Powers Resolution, Pub. L. No. 93-148, 87 Stat. 555 (1973), codified at 50 U.S.C. §§ 1541-1548.

20 Memorandum from John C. Yoo, Deputy Assistant Attorney Gen., U.S. Dep't of Justice, to the Deputy Counsel to the President, "The President's Constitutional Authority to Conduct Military Operations Against Terrorists and Nations Supporting Them," Sept. 25, 2001. *lawfare.s3-us-west-2.amazonaws.com/ staging/ s3fs-public/ uploads/ 2013/ 10/ Memorandum-from-John-C-Yoo-Sept-25-2001.pdf*

21 Botelho, Greg. "Adam Gadahn, American mouthpiece for al Qaeda,

killed." *cnn.com*. CNN, 23, Apr. 2015, https://www.cnn.com/2015/04/23/world/adam-gadahn-al-qaeda/index.html.

22   Ibid.

23   Savage, Charlie. "Attack Renews Debate Over Congressional Consent." *nytimes.com*. The New York Times, 21, Mar. 2011, https://www.nytimes.com/2011/03/22/world/africa/22powers.html.

24   Ibid.

25   "Why Obama's Libya strikes don't require congressional approval." *washingtonpost.com*. The Washington Post, 24 Mar. 2011, https://www.washington-post.com/opinions/why-obamas-libya-strikes-dont-require-congressional-approval/2011/03/24/AB9nxMQB_story.html.

26   Ibid.

27   Perez, Evan. "How the U.S. thinks Russians hacked the White House." *cnn.com*. CNN, 8 Apr. 2015, https://www.cnn.com/2015/04/07/politics/how-russians-hacked-the-wh/index.html.

28   Ibid.

29   Ignatius, David. "Russia's radical new strategy for information warfare." *washingtonpost.com*. The Washington Post, 18 Jan. 2017, https://www.washing-tonpost.com/blogs/post-partisan/wp/2017/01/18/russias-radical-new-strate-gy-for-information-warfare/.

30   Perlroth, Nicole and Sanger, David E. "Cyberattacks Put Russian Fingers on the Switch at Power Plants, U.S. Says." *nytimes.com*. The New York Times, 15 Mar. 2018, https://www.nytimes.com/2018/03/15/us/politics/russia-cyber-attacks.html.

31   Ibid.

32   Mazzetti, Mark and Benner, Katie. "12 Russian Agents Indicted in Mueller Investigation." *nytimes.com*. The New York Times, 13 July 2018, https://www.nytimes.com/2018/07/13/us/politics/mueller-indictment-russian-intelli-gence-hacking.html.

33   Garza, Alejandro De La. "Here's What Deputy Attorney General Rod Rosenstein Said. . ." *time.com*. Time, 13 July 2018, http://time.com/5338451/rod-rosenstein-russian-indictment-transcript/.

34   Indeed, shortly after the firing of FBI Director Comey, Deputy At-

torney General Rosenstein was reported to have considered secretly recording his conversations with Trump. Goldman, Adam and Schmidt, Michael S. "Rod Rosenstein Suggested Secretly Recording Trump and Discussed 25th Amendment." *nytimes.com*. The New York Times, 21 Sep. 2018, https://www.nytimes.com/2018/09/21/us/politics/rod-rosenstein-wear-wire-25th-amendment.html.

35   Korte, Gregory and Fritze, John. "Russian indictments come days before Trump's first summit with Putin." *usatoday.com*. USA Today, 13 July 2018, https://www.usatoday.com/story/news/politics/2018/07/13/trump-says-probe-harms-u-s-russian-relations/782487002/.

36   "Russia says U.S. indictment of 12 military agents is aimed at spoiling Trump-Putin summit." *pbs.org*. PBS, 13 July 2018, https://www.pbs.org/newshour/world/russia-says-u-s-indictment-of-12-military-agents-is-aimed-at-spoiling-trump-putin-summit.

37   As discussed in Chapter 14 herein, the issue of whether a sitting President may be indicted without being first impeached by the House and convicted by the Senate is an open one, but in the author's view, the arguments favoring indictment of a sitting president are more persuasive, especially where, as here, the crimes committed by the sitting president relate to the very electoral process by which he was elected, thus calling into question the legitimacy of his presidency. Does it really make sense that a president who illegally manipulated the electoral process with the help of a foreign power – and thereby committing treason – can claim immunity from prosecution for his crimes for the balance of a presidential term that is literally one of the "fruits" of that greatest crime committed in the history of our country? I think not.

CHAPTER 9 - ALL THE PRESIDENT'S (PRO-RUSSIAN) MEN

1   Crowley, Michael. "The Kremlin's Candidate." *politico.com*. Politico Magazine, May/June 2016, www.politico.com/magazine/story/2016/04/donald-trump-2016-russia-today-rt-kremlin-media-vladimir-putin-213833.

2   Windrem, Robert. "Guess Who Came to Dinner With Flynn and Putin." *nbcnews.com*. NBC News, 18 Apr. 2017, www.nbcnews.com/news/world/guess-who-came-dinner-flynn-putin-n742696.

3   Ibid.

4   Dilanian, Ken. "Russians Paid Mike Flynn $45k for Moscow Speech, Documents Show." *nbcnews.com*. NBC News, 16 Mar. 2017, www.nbcnews.com/news/us-news/russians-paid-mike-flynn-45k-moscow-speech-documents-show-n734506.

5   "Top Trump adviser defends payment for Russian speaking engage-ment." *yahoo.com*. Yahoo!, 18 July 2016, www.yahoo.com/news/trump-support-er-defends-payment-russian-175611942.html.

6   Priest, Dana. "Trump adviser Michael T. Flynn on his dinner with Pu-tin and why Russia Today is just like CNN." *washingtonpost.com*. The Washing-ton Post, 15 Aug. 2016, https://www.washingtonpost.com/news/checkpoint/wp/2016/08/15/trump-adviser-michael-t-flynn-on-his-dinner-with-putin-and-why-russia-today-is-just-like-cnn/.

7   Wright, Austin. "Lawmakers: Flynn likely broke law in not revealing Russia payments." *politico.com*. Politico, 25 Apr. 2017, www.politico.com/sto-ry/2017/04/25/lawmakers-flynn-did-not-disclose-russia-payments-in-securi-ty-clearance-application-237576.

8   Savage, Charlie. "How Michael Flynn May Have Run Afoul of the Law." *nytimes.com*. The New York Times, 25 May 2017, www.nytimes.com/2017/05/25/us/politics/michael-flynn-russia.html.

9   Fisher, Marc. "The Partisan Warrior." *washingtonpost.com*. The Washing-ton Post, 14 Dec. 2018, https://www.washingtonpost.com/graphics/2018/poli-tics/michael-flynn-partisan-warrior/.

10   Shear, Michael. "Obama Warned Trump About Hiring Flynn, Of-ficials Say." *nytimes.com*. The New York Times, 8 May 2017, www.nytimes.com/2017/05/08/us/politics/obama-flynn-trump.html.

11   Teague Beckwith, Ryan. "Michael Flynn Led a 'Lock Her Up' Chant at the Republican Convention . . ." *time.com*. Time, 1 Dec. 2017, time.com/5044847/michael-flynn-hillary-clinton-republican-convention-lock-her-up/.

12   Miller, Greg et al. "National security adviser Flynn discussed sanctions with Russian ambassador, despite denials, officials say." *washingtonpost.com*. The Washington Post, 9 Feb. 2017, https://www.washingtonpost.com/world/nation-al-security/national-security-adviser-flynn-discussed-sanctions-with-russian-am-bassador-despite-denials-officials-say/2017/02/09/f85b29d6-ee11-11e6-b4ff-ac2cf509efe5_story.html.

13   Entous, Adam et al. "Justice Department warned White House that Flynn could be vulnerable to Russian blackmail, officials say." *washingtonpost.com*. The Washington Post, 13 Feb. 2017, https://www.washingtonpost.com/world/national-security/justice-department-warned-white-house-that-flynn-could-be-vulnerable-to-russian-blackmail-officials-say/2017/02/13/fc5dab88-f228-11e6-8d72-263470bf0401_story.html.

14   Bertrand, Natasha. "Top Trump transition official in private email: Russia 'has just thrown' the election to Trump." *businessinsider.com*. Business Insider, 2 Dec. 2017, https://www.businessinsider.com/emails-kt-mcfarland-russia-thrown-election-to-trump-flynn-2017-12.

15   Harris, Shane and Barrett, Devlin. "Former Trop White House official revises statement to special counsel about Flynn's calls with Russian ambassador." *washingtonpost.com*. The Washington Post, 22 Sep. 2018, https://www.washingtonpost.com/world/national-security/former-top-white-house-official-revises-statement-to-special-counsel-about-flynns-calls-with-russian-ambassador/2018/09/21/77bb8a7c-bb50-11e8-bdc0-90f81cc58c5d_story.html.

16   Hemel, Daniel and Posner, Eric. "Why the Trump Team Should Fear the Logan Act." *nytimes.com*. The New York Times, 4 Dec. 2017, https://www.nytimes.com/2017/12/04/opinion/trump-team-flynn-logan-act.html.

17   MacFarquhar, Neil. "Vladimir Putin Won't Expel U.S. Diplomats as Russian Foreign Minister Urged." *nytimes.com*. The New York Times, 30 Dec. 2016, www.nytimes.com/2016/12/30/world/europe/russia-diplomats-us-hacking.html.

18   Groppe, Maureen. "Pence, Flynn and the Russia investigation: A Timeline of Key Events." *usatoday.com*. USA Today, 10 Dec. 2017, www.usatoday.com/story/news/politics/2017/12/10/pence-flynn-and-russia-investigation-timeline-key-events/935046001/.

19   LoBianco, Tom and Collinson, Stephen. "Sally Yates says she warned White House that Flynn was a blackmail risk." *cnn.com*. CNN, 9 May 2017, www.cnn.com/2017/05/08/politics/sally-yates-senate-testimony/index.html.

20   Entous, Adam et al. "Justice Department warned White House that Flynn could be vulnerable to Russian blackmail, officials say."

21   Perez, Evan and Diamond, Jeremy. "Trump fires acting AG after she declines to defend travel ban." *cnn.com*. CNN, 31 Jan. 2017, www.cnn.com/2017/01/30/politics/donald-trump-immigration-order-department-of-justice/index.html.

22   McCallion, Kenneth F. "Michael Flynn sentencing memo on Russia is a ticking time bomb for Team Trump." *usatoday.com*. USA Today, 6 Dec. 2018, www.usatoday.com/story/opinion/2018/12/06/michael-flynn-donald-trump-russia-redactions-hold-truth-column/2220071002/.

23   Hettena, Seth. "A Brief History of Michael Cohen's Criminal Ties." *rollingstone.com*. Rolling Stone, 10 Apr. 2018, www.rollingstone.com/politics/politics-

news/a-brief-history-of-michael-cohens-criminal-ties-628875/.

24   Ibid.

25   Ibid.

26   Ibid.

27   "Read the full transcript of Glenn Simpson's Senate testimony." *washingtonpost.com*. The Washington Post, 22 Aug. 2017, https://apps.washingtonpost.com/g/documents/politics/read-the-full-transcript-of-glenn-simpsons-senate-testimony/2700/.

28   Hamburger, Tom et al. "In 'Little Moscow,' Russians helped Donald Trump's brand survive the recession." *washingtonpost.com*. The Washington Post, 4 Nov. 2016, https://www.washingtonpost.com/politics/in-little-moscow-russians-helped-donald-trumps-brand-survive-the-recession/2016/11/04/f9db-d38e-97cf-11e6-bb29-bf2701dbe0a3_story.html.

29   Weiss, Brennan. "Trump's oldest son said a decade ago that a lot of the family's assets came from Russia." *businessinsider.com*. Business Insider, 21 Feb. 2018, www.businessinsider.com/donald-trump-jr-said-money-pouring-in-from-russia-2018-2.

30   Layne, Nathan et al. "Russian elite investigated nearly $100 million in Trump buildings." *reuters.com*. Reuters Investigates, 17 Mar. 2017, www.reuters.com/investigates/special-report/usa-trump-property/.

31   Ibid.

32   Ibid.

33   Feuer, Alan. "What We Know About Trump's $130,000 Payment to Stormy Daniels." *nytimes.com*. The New York Times, 27 Aug. 2018, https://www.nytimes.com/2018/08/27/nyregion/stormy-daniels-trump-payment.html.

34   Ward, Alex. "Trump Tower Moscow, and Michael Cohen's lies about it, explained." *vox.com*. Vox, 19 Dec. 2018, https://www.vox.com/world/2018/11/.../michael-cohen-trump-tower-moscow-mueller.

35   Haake, Garrett et al. "Democrats pounce after Cohen admits he lied to Congress about Trump Tower project in Russia." *nbcnews.com*. NBC News, 29 Nov. 2018, https://www.nbcnews.com/politics/congress/democrats-pounce-after-cohen-admits-he-lied-congress-about-trump-n941711.

36   Ward, Alex. "Trump Tower Moscow, and Michael Cohen's lies about it,

explained," supra, ftnt. 34.

37   Twohey, Megan and Shane, Scott. "A Back-Channel Plan for Ukraine and Russia, Courtesy of Trump Associates." *nytimes.com*. The New York Times, 19 Feb. 2017, https://www.nytimes.com/2017/02/19/us/politics/donald-trump-ukraine-russia.html.

38   Apuzzo, Matt. "F.B.I. Raids Office of Trump's Longtime Lawyer Michael Cohen; Trump Calls It 'Disgraceful'." *nytimes.com*. The New York Times, 9 Apr. 2018, https://www.nytimes.com/2018/04/09/us/politics/fbi-raids-office-of-trumps-longtime-lawyer-michael-cohen.html.

39   Mazzetti, Mark et al. "Cohen Pleads Guilty and Details Trump's involvement in Moscow Tower Project." *nytimes.com*. The New York Times, 29 Nov. 2018, www.nytimes.com/2018/11/29/nyregion/michael-cohen-trump-russia-mueller.html.

40   McCallion, Kenneth. "How much the borscht just thickened: The Trump-Russia connections are getting impossible to explain away." *nydailynews.com*. Daily News, 29 Nov. 2018, www.nydailynews.com/opinion/ny-oped-how-much-the-borscht-just-thickened-20181129-story.html.

41   "Michael Cohen pleads guilty to lying to Congress." *politico.com*. Politico, 29 Nov. 2018, www.politico.com/story/2018/11/29/michael-cohen-making-surprise-court-appearance-in-new-york-1026107.

42   McCallion, Kenneth. "How much the borscht just thickened: The Trump-Russia connections are getting impossible to explain away," supra, ftnt. 40.

43   Ibid.

44   Ibid.

45   Ibid.

46   Ibid.

47   Ibid.

48   Weiser, Benjamin and Rashbaum, William K. "Michael Cohen Sentenced to 3 Years After Implicated Trump in Hush-Money Scandal." *nytimes.com*. The New York Times, 12 Dec. 2018, https://www.nytimes.com/2018/12/12/nyregion/michael-cohen-sentence-trump.html.

49   Davidson, Adam. "The Michael Cohen Sentencing Memos are Damning For Trump." *newyorker.com*. The New Yorker, 7 Dec. 2018, https://www.newyo-

rker.com/news/swamp-chronicles/the-michael-cohen-sentencing-memos-are-damning-for-trump.

50   However, once a president leaves office, the Constitution makes it explicitly clear that he may be criminally prosecuted.

51   Weiser, Benjamin and Rashbaum, William K. "Michael Cohen Sentenced to 3 Years After Implicated Trump in Hush-Money Scandal."

52   Breuniger, Kevin and Pramuk, Jacob. "National Enquirer boss and long-time Trump friend David Pecker gets federal immunity in Michael Cohen case." *cnbc.com*. CNBC, 32 Aug. 2018, https://www.cnbc.com/2018/08/23/national-enquirer-david-pecker-told-prosecutors-trump-knew-of-cohen-payments-report.html.

53   See McCallion, Kenneth. "Prosecutors have a strong criminal case against Trump." *nydailynews.com*. Daily News, 12 Dec. 2018, https://www.nydailynews.com/opinion/ny-oped-prosecutors-have-a-criminal-case-against-trump-20181212-story.html.

54   "Berke, Barry et al. "What Cohen's Deal Means for Trump." *nytimes.com*. The New York Times, 29 Nov. 2018, https://www.nytimes.com/2018/11/29/opinion/cohen-deal-mueller-means-for-trump.html.

55   Tackett, Michael , "Five Takeaways From Cohen's Testimony to Congress," New York Times, Feb. 27, 2019 www.nytimes.com/2019/02/27/us/politics/cohen-testimony.html.

56   McCallion, Kenneth, "Cohen has just made Trump's crimes vividly clear," New York Daily News, Feb. 27, 2019 www.nydailynews.com/opinion/ny-oped-cohen-has-just-made-trumps-crimes-vividly-clear-20190227-story.html.

57   Brogan, Pamela. *The Torturers' Lobby: How Human Rights-Abusing Nations Are Represented in Washington*. The Center for Public Integrity, 1992, https://cloudfront-files-1.publicintegrity.org/legacy_projects/pdf_reports/THETORTURERSLOBBY.pdf.

58   Stone, Peter. "Trump's new right-hand man has history of controversial clients and deals." *theguardian.com*. The Guardian, 27 Apr. 2016, https://www.theguardian.com/us-news/2016/apr/27/paul-manafort-donald-trump-campaign-past-clients.

59   Kramer, Andrew et al. "Secret Ledger in Ukraine Lists Cash for Donald Trump's Campaign Chief." *nytimes.com*. The New York Times, 14 Aug. 2016, www.nytimes.com/2016/08/15/us/politics/paul-manafort-ukraine-donald-trump.html.

60   Higgins, Andrew and Kramer, Andrew E. "Archrival Is Freed as Ukraine Leader Flees." *nytimes.com*. The New York Times, 22 Feb. 2014, https://www.nytimes.com/2014/02/23/world/europe/ukraine.html.

61   Kramer, Andrew. "How a Ukrainian Hairdresser Became a Front for Paul Manafort." *nytimes.com*. The New York Times, 15, Sep. 2018, www.nytimes.com/2018/09/15/world/europe/ukraine-paul-manafort.html.

62   Horwitz, Jeff and Butler, Desmond. "AP Sources: Manafort tied to undisclosed foreign lobbying." *apnews.com*. AP News, 17 Aug. 2016, apnews.com/c01989a47ee5421593ba1b301ec07813.

63   Ibid.

64   Ibid.

65   Burns, Alexander and Haberman, Maggie. "Donald Trump Hires Paul Manafort to Lead Delegate Effort." *nytimes.com*. The New York Times, 28 Mar. 2016, www.nytimes.com/politics/first-draft/2016/03/28/donald-trump-hires-paul-manafort-to-lead-delegate-effort/.

66   Kilimnik was indicted with Manafort on June 8, 2018 on obstruction of justice charges relating to witness tampering. See Horwitz, Jeff and Danilova, Maria. "Russian Charged with Trump's Ex-Campaign Chief Is Key Figure." *usnews.com*. US News, 2 July 2018, https://www.usnews.com/news/world/articles/2018-07-02/russian-charged-with-trumps-ex-campaign-chief-is-key-figure; see also Prolop, Andrew. "Mueller just added more charges to Paul Manafort – and indicted Konstantin Kilimnik." *vox.com*. Vox, 8 June 2018, www.vox.com/2018/6/8/17442614/mueller-manfort-kilimnik-indicted-russia.

67   Dilanian, Ken and Winter, Tom. "Manafort Offered Private Briefings on 2016 Race to Russian Billionaire." *nbcnews.com*. NBC News, 20 Sep. 2017, www.nbcnews.com/news/us-news/manafort-offered-private-briefings-2016-race-russian-billionaire-n803246.

68   Harding, Luke and Collyns, Dan. "Manafort held secret talks with Assange in Ecuadorian embassy, sources say." *theguardian.com*. The Guardian, 27 Nov. 2018, www.theguardian.com/us-news/2018/nov/27/manafort-held-secret-talks-with-assange-in-ecuadorian-embassy.

69   McCallion, Kenneth. "How much the borscht just thickened: The Trump-Russia connections are getting impossible to explain away," supra, ftnt. 40.

70   Watson, Kathryn. "How did WikiLeaks become associated with Russia?" *cbsnews.com*. CBS News, 15 Nov. 2017, www.cbsnews.com/news/how-did-wikileaks-become-associated-with-russia/.

71   Tran, Mark. "WikiLeaks to publish more Hillary Clinton emails-Julian Assange." *theguardian.com*. The Guardian, 12 June 2016, www.theguardian.com/media/2016/jun/12/wikileaks-to-publish-more-hillary-clinton-emails-julian-assange.

72   Haberman, Maggie and Martin, Jonathan. "Paul Manafort Quits Donald Trump's Campaign After a Tumultuous Run." *nytimes.com*. The New York Times, 19 Aug. 2016, www.nytimes.com/2016/08/20/us/politics/paul-manafort-resigns-donald-trump.html.

73   Manafort's weakness for expensive clothing seemed to capture the public imagination, particularly the revelation that Manafort had bought a $15,000 ostrich jacket with his ill-gotten gains. See Givhan, Robin. "Paul Manafort's ostrich Jacket pretty much sums up Paul Manafort." *washingtonpost.com*. The Washington Post, 2 Aug. 2018, https://www.washingtonpost.com/news/arts-and-entertainment/wp/2018/08/02/paul-manaforts-ostrich-jacket-pretty-much-sums-up-paul-manafort/.

74   *Tymoshenko v. Firtash et al*, U.S.D.C., S.D.N.Y, Case 1:11-cv-02794-KMW.

75   Berthelsen, Christian and Farrell, Greg. "Robert Mueller Subpoenas Paul Manafort Bank Records in Russia Investigation." *time.com*. Time, 10 Aug. 2017, http://time.com/4895426/robert-mueller-paul-manafort-bank-account-subpoena/; see also Berthelsen, Christian and Farrell, Greg. "With Bank Subpoenas, Mueller Turns Up the Heat on Manafort." *Bloomberg.com*. Bloomberg, 10 Aug. 2017, https://www.bloomberg.com/news/articles/2017-08-10/with-bank-subpoenas-mueller-is-said-to-turn-up-heat-on-manafort.

76   "Manafort had $10 million loan from Russian oligarch: court filing." *reuters.com*. Reuters Politics, 27 June 2018, www.reuters.com/article/us-usa-trump-russia-manafort/manafort-had-10-million-loan-from-russian-oligarch-court-filing-idUSKBN1JN2YF; see also Baker, Stephanie and Voreacos, David. "Manafort Reported $10 Million Loan From Russian Oligarch in 2010." *bloomberg.com*. Bloomberg Politics, 28 June 2018, www.bloomberg.com/news/articles/2018-06-28/manafort-reported-10-million-loan-from-russian-oligarch-in-2010.

77   Vogel, Kenneth P. and Goldstein, Matthew. "How Skadden, the Giant Law Firm, Got Entangled in the Mueller Investigation." *nytimes.com*. The New York Times, 24 Feb. 2018, www.nytimes.com/2018/02/24/us/politics/skadden-law-firm-mueller-investigation.html.

78   See Kramer, Andrew R. "Prize Catch for Ukrainians at Boat Harbor: A Soggy Trove of Government Secrets." *nytimes.com*. The New York Times, 26 Feb.

2014, https://www.nytimes.com/2014/02/27/world/europe/a-prize-catch-for-ukrainians-at-a-boat-harbor-an-ousted-presidents-secrets.html.

79   Vogel, Kenneth P. and Kramer, Andrew E. "Skadden, Big New York Law Firm, Faces Questions on Work With Manafort." *nytimes.com*. The New York Times, 21 Sep. 2017, https://www.nytimes.com/2017/09/21/us/politics/law-firm-faces-questions-for-ukraine-work-with-manafort.html.

80   It is general knowledge in intelligence circles that no one ever really "retires" from the GRU. Once in the GRU, always in the GRU.

81   LaFraniere, Sharon and Vogel, Kenneth P. "Former Skadden Lawyer Pleads Guilty to Lying in Russia Investigation." *nytimes.com*. The New York Times, 20 Feb. 2018, https://www.nytimes.com/2018/02/20/us/politics/alex-van-der-zwaan-gates-russia-mueller.html.

82   Kahn, Matthew. "Documents: Alex Van Der Zwaan Information, Statement of Offense, and Plea Agreement." *lawfareblog.com*. LawFare, 20 Feb. 2018, https://www.lawfareblog.com/documents-alex-van-der-zwaan-information-statement-offense-and-plea-agreement.

83   Ibid.

84   Ibid.

85   LaFraniere, Sharon and Vogel, Kenneth P. "Former Skadden Lawyer Pleads Guilty to Lying in Russia Investigation."

86   Beauchamp, Zack. "What the latest Mueller indictment tells us about his strategy." *vox.com*. Vox, 20 Feb 2018, www.vox.com/world/2018/2/20/17031766/mueller-indictments-alex-van-der-zwaan-paul-manafort.

87   Filkins, Dexter. "Was There a Connection Between a Russian Bank and the Trump Campaign?" *newyorker.com*. The New Yorker, 15 Oct. 2018, https://www.newyorker.com/magazine/2018/10/15/was-there-a-connection-between-a-russian-bank-and-the-trump-campaign.

88   On August 21, 2018, a defamation case brought by German Khan and his two partners in Alfa Group was dismissed by a federal judge hearing the case. See Harding, Luke. "Author of Trump-Russia dossier wins libel case in US court." *theguardian.com*. The Guardian, 21 Aug. 2018, www.theguardian.com/us-news/2018/aug/21/author-of-trump-russia-dossier-wins-libel-case-in-us-court-christopher-steele.

89   Polantz, Katelyn and Stark, Liz. "Dutch lawyer is first person to be sen-

tenced in Mueller probe, gets 30 days in prison." *cnn.com*. CNN, 3 Apr. 2018, www.cnn.com/2018/04/03/politics/alex-van-der-zwaan-sentencing/index.html.

90   Schmidt, Michael S. and Goldman, Adam. "Manafort's Home Searched as Part of Mueller Inquiry." *nytimes.com*. The New York Times, 9 Aug. 2017, www.nytimes.com/2017/08/09/us/politics/paul-manafort-home-search-mueller.html.

91   "Full Text: Paul Manafort Indictment." *politico.com*. Politico, 30 Oct. 2017,   www.politico.com/story/2017/10/30/full-text-paul-manafort-indictment-244307.

92   The author and his law firm, McCallion & Associates LLP, served as U.S. counsel for Tymoshenko while she was incarcerated and tried on bogus, politically-motivated charges by the pro-Russian Yanukovich Regime. While still incarcerated in Ukraine, McCallion & Associates LLP filed a civil RICO complaint against Manafort, Gates and others in the U.S. District Court for the Southern District of New York on behalf of Tymoshenko and others. See *Tymoshenko v. Firtash et al*, 11-cv-02794 (KMW). The details of this complaint, and the document attached to it, became part of the source material for the federal investigation leading to the indictments of Manafort, Gates and van der Zwaan.

93   Kaytukov, Alan and Smith, Alexander. "Mistake in Manafort Indictment Shows Case Was 'Cooked Up,' Russia Says." *nbcnews.com*. NBC News, 31 Oct. 2017,   www.nbcnews.com/news/world/mistake-manafort-indictment-shows-case-was-cooked-russia-says-n815911.

94   Prokop, Andrew. "Read: Mueller's new indictment of Paul Manafort and Rick Gates." *vox.com*. Vox, 22 Feb. 2018, www.vox.com/2018/2/22/17042254/robert-mueller-paul-manafort-indictment.

95   Johnson, Kevin. "Paul Manafort trial: Bank fast-tracked loan as Trump chairman discussed cabinet posts for CEO." *usatoday.com*. USA Today, 10 Aug. 2018, www.usatoday.com/story/news/politics/2018/08/10/paul-manafort-trial-judge-jury-friday-update/956821002/.

96   Prokop, Andrew. "Robert Mueller just flipped his third former Trump aide." *vox.com*. Vox, 23 Feb. 2018, www.vox.com/2018/2/23/17045226/robert-mueller-flip-rick-gates-russia.

97   Ibid.

98   Samuelsohn, Darren. "Mueller delays sentencing for ex-Trump aide Gates over ongoing cooperation." *politico.com*. Politico, 14 Nov. 2018, www.politico.com/story/2018/11/14/rick-gates-sentencing-mueller-probe-990758.

99   Prokop, Andrew. "Mueller just added more charges to Paul Manafort — and indicted Konstantin Kilimnik," vox.com.

100   Johnson, Kevin et al. "Paul Manafort trial: Just finds former Trump campaign manager guilty on 8 counts in tax fraud case." *usatoday.com*. USA Today, 21 Aug. 2018, www.usatoday.com/story/news/politics/2018/08/21/paul-manafort-verdict/995713002/.

101   Gearan, Anna. "'Bada bing bada boom': Paul Manafort's attempt to smear a jailed Ukrainian Politician." *washingtonpost.com*. The Washington Post, 14 Sep. 2018, www.washingtonpost.com/politics/bada-bing-bada-boom-paul-manaforts-attempt-to-smear-a-jailed-ukrainian-politician/2018/09/14/c5ac93b6-b837-11e8-a2c5-3187f427e253_story.html?utm_term=.8a852d388bd8.

102   Kalatizadeh, Hadassa. "Govt to Seize Manafort's Hamptons Home & Trump Tower Condo in Plea Deal." *thejewishvoice.com*. The Jewish Voice, 10 Oct. 2018, thejewishvoice.com/2018/10/10/govt-seize-manaforts-hamptons-home-trump-tower-condo-plea-deal/.

103   Ibid.

104   Ibid.

105   Ibid.

106   Wang, Christine et al. "Ex-Trump campaign chief Paul Manafort broke plea deal, lied to prosecutors, Mueller says." *cnbc.com*. CNBC, 26 Nov. 2018, www.cnbc.com/2018/11/26/prosecutors-allege-paul-manafort-lied-to-investigators.html

107   Samuels, Brett. "Manafort attorney relayed info about Mueller probe to Trump lawyers: report." *thehill.com*. The Hill, 27 Nov. 2018, https://thehill.com/policy/national-security/418600-manaforts-attorney-relayed-info-about-mueller-investigation-to-trump.

108   LaFraniere, Sharon. "Judge Orders Paul Manafort Jailed Before Trial, Citing New Obstruction Charges." *nytimes.com*. The New York Times, 15 June 2018, https://www.nytimes.com/2018/06/15/us/politics/manafort-bail-revoked-jail.html.

109   Apuzzo, Matt. "Jared Kushner Gets Security Clearance, Ending Swirl of Questions Over Delay." *nytimes.com*. The New York Times, 23 May 2018, https://www.nytimes.com/2018/05/23/us/politics/jared-kushner-security-clearance.html; Wright, Austin. "Cummings: Why does Kushner still have a security clearance?" *nytimes.com*. The New York Times, 21 June 2017, https://www.politico.com/story/2017/06/21/elijah-cummings-jared-kushner-security-clearance-239815.

110   Craig, Susanne et al. "Jared Kushner, a Trump In-Law and Adviser, Chases a Chinese Deal." *nytimes.com*. The New York Times, 7 Jan. 2017,   https://www.nytimes.com/2017/01/07/us/politics/jared-kushner-trump-business.html; Nakashima, Ellen et al. "Russian ambassador told Moscow that Kushner wanted secret communications channel with Kremlin." *washingtonpost.com*. The Washington Post, 26 May 2017, https://www.washingtonpost.com/world/national-security/russian-ambassador-told-moscow-that-kushner-wanted-secret-communications-channel-with-kremlin/2017/05/26/520a14b4-422d-11e7-9869-bac8b446820a_story.html.

111   Liptak, Kevin. "Trump's Secretary of Everything: Jared Kushner." *cnn.com*. CNN, 3 Apr. 2017, www.cnn.com/2017/04/03/politics/jared-kushner-donald-trump-foreign-policy/index.html.

112   Filipov, David et al. "Explanations for Kushner's meeting with head of Kremlin-linked bank don't match up." *washingtonpost.com*. The Washington Post, 1 June 2017, https://www.washingtonpost.com/politics/explanations-for-kushners-meeting-with-head-of-kremlin-linked-bank-dont-match-up/2017/06/01/dd1bdbb0-460a-11e7-bcde-624ad94170ab_story.html.

113   Rosenberg, Matthew et al. "Investigation Turns to Kushner's Motives in Meeting With Putin Ally." *nytimes.com*. The New York Times, 29 May 2017, https://www.nytimes.com/2017/05/29/us/politics/jared-kushner-russia-investigation.html; *see also Sharkov, Damien. "Who Is Sergey Gorkov, The Russian Banker Jared Kushner Allegedly Met?" newsweek.com. Newsweek, 20 May 2017,* https://www.newsweek.com/sergey-gorkov-grad-russian-banker-kushner-617422.

114   Hayoun, Massoud. "Trump and His Advisers Are Connected to a Self-professed Friend of Putin." *psmag.com*. Pacific Standard Magazine, 12 Jan. 2017,   https://psmag.com/news/trump-and-his-advisors-are-connected-to-a-self-professed-friend-of-putin; *Madsen, Wayne. "Jared Kushner: A Suspected Gangster Within the Trump White House." strategic-culture.org. Strategic Culture Foundation, 17 Apr. 2017,* https://www.strategic-culture.org/news/2017/04/17/jared-kushner-suspected-gangster-within-trump-white-house.html.

115   Schreckinger, Ben. "The Happy-Go-Lucky Jewish Group That Connects Trump and Putin." *politico.com*. Politico Magazine, 9 Apr. 2017, https://www.politico.com/magazine/story/2017/04/the-happy-go-lucky-jewish-group-that-connects-trump-and-putin-215007; *see also* Hayoun, Massoud. "Trump and His Advisers Are Connected to a Self-professed Friend of Putin."

116   Gebert, Konstanty. "Putin's Jews." *momentmag.com*. Moment Magazine, 5 Nov. 2015, www.momentmag.com/putins-jews/; *"Putin on our side, says Russia's*

chief rabbi." jewishnews.timesofisrael.com. Jewish News, 28 Apr. 2017, jewishnews.timesofisrael.com/putin-on-our-side-says-russias-chief/.

117   Weiss, Lois. "Real estate startup Cadre raises whopping $50M." *nypost. com.* New York Post, 26 Jan. 2016, *nypost.com/2016/01/26/real-estate-startup-cadre-raises-whopping-50m/.*

118   Wolff, Michael. "How Russian Tycoon Yuri Milner Bought His Way Into Silicon Valley." *wired.com.* Wired, 21 Oct. 2011, https://www.wired.com/2011/10/mf_milner/.

119   Frates, Katie. "Ivanka Invites Russian Billionaire's Wife To Inauguration Weekend." *thedailycaller.com.* The Daily Caller, 20 Jan. 2017, https://dailycaller.com/2017/01/20/ivanka-invites-russian-billionaires-wife-to-inauguration-weekend/.

120   "Smart move! Princess Beatrice opts for office chic as she mingles with Ivanka Trump . . ." *dailymail.co.uk.* The Daily Mail, n.d., www.dailymail.co.uk/femail/article-3785193/Princess-Beatrice-opts-office-chic-mingles-Ivanka-Trump-Wendi-Deng-Karlie-Kloss-Men-s-Open-final.html.

121   Oliphant, Roland. "Vladimir Putin, Roman Abramovich, and the 25 million yacht." *telegraph.co.uk.* The Telegraph, 25 Jan. 2018, https://www.telegraph.co.uk/news/worldnews/vladimir-putin/12120710/Vladimir-Putin-Roman-Abramovich-and-the-25-million-yacht.html.

122   "Share Information." *Evraz,* 24 Dec. 2018, www.evraz.com/investors/information/.

123   "About." *Evraz,* 2019, https://www.evraz.com/about.

124   See generally "Keystone XL builders can use non-U.S. steel, White House says now." *reuters.com.* Reuters, 3 Mar. 2017, www.reuters.com/article/us-transcanada-keystone-steel-idUSKBN16A2FC; *Lance, Peter. "Trump Reverses Pledge To Mandate U.S. Steel For Keystone Pipeline . . . " huffingtonpost.com. The Huffington Post, 6 Mar. 2017,* https://www.huffingtonpost.com/entry/trump-reverses-pledge-to-mandate-us-steel-for-keystone_us_58bbae99e4b0fa65b844b451; *"Keystone pipeline won't use U.S. steel despite Trump pledge." pbs.org. PBS News, 4 Mar. 2017,* www.pbs.org/newshour/rundown/keystone-pipeline-us-steel-trump/; *"Keystone pipeline won't use US steel despite President Trump pledge." fox6now.com. Fox 6 News, 3 Mar. 2017,* https://fox6now.com/2017/03/03/keystone-pipeline-wont-use-us-steel-despite-president-trump-pledge/; *Scheyder, Ernest et al. "American steel unlikely to get Keystone boost despite Trump order." reuters.com. Reuters, 20 Jan. 2017,* www.reuters.com/article/us-usa-trump-pipeline-transcanada-idUSKBN15E22M.

125   Holland, Steve and Volcovici, Valerie. "Trump clears way for controversial oil pipelines." *reuters.com*. Reuters, 24 Jan. 2017, www.reuters.com/article/us-usa-trump-pipeline/trump-clears-way-for-controversial-oil-pipelines-idUSKB-N15820N.

126   U.S.D.C.   S.D.T.,   Case   4:16-cv-00036,   www.eenews.net/assets/2017/01/31/document_ew_01.pdf.

127   Newkirk, Margaret and Deaux, Joe. "Under Trump, Made in America is Losing Out to Russian Steel." *bloomberg.com*. Bloomberg Businessweek, 25 Oct. 2017, www.bloomberg.com/news/articles/2017-10-25/under-trump-made-in-america-is-losing-out-to-russian-steel.

128   "Press Gaggle by Principal Deputy Press Secretary Sarah Sanders En Route Orlando, Florida." *whitehouse.gov*. White House Press Briefings, 3 Mar. 2017, www.whitehouse.gov/briefings-statements/press-gaggle-principal-deputy-press-secretary-sarah-sanders-en-route-orlando-florida/.

129   Spargo, Chris. "Last day in paradise: Ivanka Trump and Jared Kushner enjoy final day on the slopes . . ." *dailymail.co.uk*. The Daily Mail, 24 Mar. 2017, https://www.dailymail.co.uk/news/article-4343956/Ivanka-Trump-Jared-Kushner-enjoy-final-day-Aspen.html.

130   Bennett, Kate. "Trump unhappy Jared Kushner took a powder on the ski slopes as health care bill floundered." *cnn.com*. CNN, 26 Mar. 2017, https://www.cnn.com/2017/03/24/politics/jared-kushner-aspen-ski-trip-obamacare/index.html.

131   Edwards, David. *"Jared Kushner flew to Aspen same day as 'one of Putin's closest confidants' whose wife is pals with Ivanka." rawstory.com. Raw Story, 27 Mar. 2017,* https://www.rawstory.com/2017/03/jared-kushner-flew-to-aspen-same-day-as-one-of-putins-closest-confidants-whose-wife-is-pals-with-ivanka/; *Keefe, Josh. "Did Ivanka Trump and Jared Kushner Meet A Putin-Connected Russian Oligarch in Aspen?" ibtimes.com. International Business Times, 27 Mar. 2017,* https://www.ibtimes.com/did-ivanka-trump-jared-kushner-meet-putin-connected-russian-oligarch-aspen-2515668.

132   Ward, Vicky. "Jared Kushner's Second Act." *esquire.com*. Esquire, 18 Aug. 2016, www.esquire.com/news-politics/a47697/jared-kushner-trump-campaign/; *see also Smith, Chris. "Jared Kushner and Donald Trump: Like Father, Like Son-in-Law." vanityfair.com. Vanity Fair, 26 May 2016,* https://www.vanityfair.com/news/2017/05/jared-kushner-and-donald-trump-like-father-like-son-in-law.

133   Bagli, Charles V. "A Big Deal, Even in Manhattan: A Tower Goes for $1.8 Billion." *nytimes.com*. The New York Times, 7 Dec. 2006, www.nytimes.

com/2006/12/07/nyregion/07building.html; *Chung, Jen. "666 Fifth Goes to the Kushners." gothamist.com. Gothamist, 7 Dec. 2006, gothamist.com/2006/12/07/666_ fifth_goes.php.*

134   Weiss, Lois. "Chinese investor backs out of Kushner Companies project." *nypost.com.* New York Post, 28 Mar. 2017, *nypost.com/2017/03/28/chinese-investor-backs-out-of-kushner-companies-project/.*

135   Tucker, Eric. "4 Meetings with Russians disclosed by Jared Kushner." *chicagotribune.com.* The Chicago Tribune, 24 July 2017, https://www.chicagotribune.com/news/nationworld/ct-jared-kushner-russian-meetings-20170724-story.html.

136   Haberman, Maggie et al. "Kushner Is Said to Have Discussed a Secret Channel to Talk to Russia." *nytimes.com.* The New York Times, 26 May 2017, https://www.nytimes.com/2017/05/26/us/politics/kushner-talked-to-russian-envoy-about-creating-secret-channel-with-kremlin.html.

137   Tucker, Eric. "4 Meetings with Russians disclosed by Jared Kushner," supra, ftnt. 133.

138   Grabar, Henry. "Does the Theory That Jared Kushner Met With the Russians to Get a Real Estate Loan Make Any Sense?" *slate.com.* Slate, 31 May 2017, https://slate.com/business/2017/05/why-did-jared-kushner-meet-with-the-russians.html.

139   Barry, Rob et al. "Russian State Run Bank Financed Deal Involving Trump Hotel Partner." *wsj.com.* The Wall Street Journal, 17 May 2017, https://www.wsj.com/articles/russian-state-run-bank-financed-deal-involving-trump-hotel-partner-1495031708; Voorhees, Josh. "Trump Hotel Project Reportedly Benefited from Russian State-Run Bank." *slate.com.* Slate, 17 May 2017, https://slate.com/news-and-politics/2017/05/trump-toronto-hotel-reportedly-got-some-help-from-a-big-russian-bank.html.

140   Groll, Elias. "Why Is Putin's 'Private Slush Fund' Courting Jared Kushner?" *foreignpolicy.com.* Foreign Policy, 7 Apr. 2017, https://foreignpolicy.com/2017/04/07/why-is-putins-private-slush-fund-courting-jared-kushner/; *see also "White House, Russian bank differ on Jared Kushner secret meeting." chicagotribune.com. The Chicago Tribune, 1 June 2017,* https://www.chicagotribune.com/news/nationworld/politics/ct-jared-kushner-russian-bank-meeting-20170601-story.html.

141   Grise, Katherine, "Kushner's top secret security clearance," CNN, January 25, 2019 https://www.cnn.com/2019/01/25/politics/jared-kushner-security-clearance-overruled/index.html

142   Ibid.

143   Ibid.

144   Ibid.

145   Ibid.

146   Weiss, Michael. "Jared Kushner Tempted by Russia's Bank of Spies." *thedailybeast.com*. The Daily Beast, 28 Mar. 2017, https://www.thedailybeast.com/jared-kushner-tempted-by-russias-bank-of-spies.

147   Kirkpatrick, David. D. "The Professor Behind the Trump Campaign Adviser Charges." *nytimes.com*. The New York Times, 31 Oct. 2017, https://www.nytimes.com/2017/10/31/world/europe/russia-us-election-joseph-mifsud.html.

148   Ibid.

149   LaFraniere, Sharon et al. "How the Russia Inquiry Began: A Campaign Aide, Drinks and Talk of Political Dirt." *nytimes.com*. The New York Times, 30 Dec. 2017, https://www.nytimes.com/2017/12/30/us/politics/how-fbi-russia-investigation-began-george-papadopoulos.html.

150   Reilly, Steve. "Timeline: The many times George Papadopoulos tried to connect the Trump campaign with Russia."*nytimes.com*. The New York Times, 2 Nov. 2017, https://www.usatoday.com/story/news/2017/11/02/timeline-many-times-george-papadopoulos-tried-connect-trump-campaign-russia/820951001/.

151   Helderman, Rosalind S. and Hamburger, Tom. "Trump officials encouraged George Papadopoulos to build 'partnership with Russia' with TV interview, emails reveal." *independent.co.uk*. Independent, 25 Mar. 2018, https://www.independent.co.uk/news/world/americas/george-papadopoulos-latest-you-should-do-it-donald-trump-russia-investigation-bryan-lanza-emails-a8272866.html.

152   LaFraniere, Sharon et al. "How the Russia Inquiry Began: A Campaign Aide, Drinks and Talk of Political Dirt."

153   Sullivan, Eileen and Thursh, Glenn. "George Papadopoulos, First to Plead Guilty in Russia Inquiry." *nytimes.com*. The New York Times, 30 Oct. 2017, https://www.nytimes.com/2017/10/30/us/politics/george-papadopoulos-russia-trump.html.

154   Mazzetti, Mark and LaFraniere, Sharon. "George Papadopoulos, Ex-Trump Advisor, Is Sentenced to 14 Days in Jail." *nytimes.com*. The New York Times,

7 Sep. 2018, https://www.nytimes.com/2018/09/07/us/politics/george-papado-poulos-sentencing-special-counsel-investigation.html.

155   Ibid.

156   Mufson, Steven and Hamburger, Tom. "Trump adviser's public comments, ties to Moscow stir unease in both parties." *washingtonpost.com*. The Washington Post, 5 Aug. 2016, https://www.washingtonpost.com/business/economy/trump-advisers-public-comments-ties-to-moscow-stir-unease-in-both-parties/2016/08/05/2e8722fa-5815-11e6-9aee-8075993d73a2_story.html?utm_term=.5241ea0c02e9.

157   Graham, David A. "What Carter Page's Testimony Revealed." *theatlantic.com*. The Atlantic, 7 Nov. 2017, www.theatlantic.com/politics/archive/2017/11/carter-page-international-man-of-mystery/545159/.

158   Mider, Zachary. "Trump's New Russia Adviser Has Deep Ties to Kremlin's Gazprom." *bloomberg.com*. Bloomberg, 30 Mar. 2016, www.bloomberg.com/news/articles/2016-03-30/trump-russia-adviser-carter-page-interview.

159   Mufson, Steven and Hamburger, Tom. "Trump adviser's public comments, ties to Moscow stir unease in both parties," supra, ftnt. 149.

160   Ibid.

161   Goldman, Adam. "Russian Spies Tried to Recruit Carter Page Before He Advised Trump." *nytimes.com*. The New York Times, 4 Apr. 2017, www.nytimes.com/2017/04/04/us/politics/carter-page-trump-russia.html.

162   Ignatius, David. "How Carter Page got tangled up in the Russian web." *washingtonpost.com*. The Washington Post, 7 June 2018, https://www.washingtonpost.com/opinions/how-carter-page-got-tangled-up-in-the-russian-web/2018/06/07/3fd9676c-6a73-11e8-9e38-24e693b38637_story.html.

163   Ibid.

164   Mider, Zachary. "Trump's New Russia Adviser Has Deep Ties to Kremlin's Gazprom."

165   Ibid.

166   Ibid.

167   Ryan, Missy and Mufson, Steven. "One of Trump's foreign policy advisers is a 2009 college grad who lists Model UN as a credential." *washingtonpost.com*. The Washington Post, 22 Mar. 2016, https://www.washingtonpost.com/news/

checkpoint/wp/2016/03/21/meet-the-men-shaping-donald-trumps-foreign-poli-cy-views/?utm_term=.e7f0a2457055.

168   Mufson, Steven and Hamburger, Tom. "Trump adviser's public comments, ties to Moscow stir unease in both parties," supra, ftnt. 149.

169   Nechepurenko, Ivan. "Carter Page, Ex-Trump Adviser With Russian Ties, Visits Moscow." *nytimes.com*. The New York Times, 8 Dec. 2016, www.nytimes.com/2016/12/08/world/europe/carter-page-donald-trump-moscow-russia.html; see also Mazzetti, Mark and Goldman, Adam. "Trump Campaign Adviser Met With Russian Officials in 2016." *nytimes.com*. The New York Times, 3 Nov. 2017, www.nytimes.com/2017/11/03/us/politics/trump-campaign-page-russian.html.

170   Prokop, Andrew. "Carter Page's bizarre testimony to the House Intelligence Committee, explained." *vox.com*. Vox, 7 Nov. 2017, www.vox.com/poli-cy-and-politics/2017/11/7/16616912/carter-page-testimony-trump-russia.

171   In hiring Epshteyn as "the Russia guy," the Trump Campaign appears to have been attracted by his abrasive "attack dog" style, which had created legal problems for Epshteyn in the past. Two years earlier, Epshteyn had been charged with misdemeanor assault in Scottsdale, Ariz., after a bar fight. The charge was dropped, however, after he agreed to undergo anger management counseling and perform community service. See Meier, Barry and Craig, Susanne. "The Obscure Lawyer Who Became Donald Trump's TV Attack Dog." *nytimes.com*. The New York Times, 13 Oct. 2016, www.nytimes.com/2016/10/14/us/politics/boris-epshteyn-trump.html.

172   Haberman, Maggie. "Boris Epshteyn, Trump TV Surrogate, Is Leaving White House Job." *nytimes.com*. The New York Times, 25 Mar. 2017, www.nytimes.com/2017/03/25/us/politics/boris-epshteyn-white-house-press-official-is-let-go-from-his-job.html.

173   Marans, Daniel. "When It Comes To Donald Trump's Russia Ties, It's All About The Aides." *huffingtonpost.com*. Huffington Post, 12 Aug. 2016, www.huffingtonpost.com/entry/donald-trump-advisers-russia-ties_us_57acd474e4b-007c36e4db94c.

174   Marans, Daniel. "When It Comes To Donald Trump's Russia Ties, It's All About The Aides," supra, ftnt. 166.

175   Meier, Barry and Craig, Susanne. "The Obscure Lawyer Who Became Donald Trump's TV Attack Dog," supra, ftnt. 164.

176   "War Hero's Father Speaks Out Against Trump Attacks . . ." *cnn.com*. CNN, 31 July 2016, www.cnn.com/TRANSCRIPTS/1607/31/cnr.05.html.

177   Bo Williams, Katie. "Former Trump official Epshteyn testifies in House Russia Probe." *thehill.com*. The Hill, 28 Sep. 2017, thehill.com/policy/national-security/352918-former-trump-official-epshteyn-testifies-in-house-russia-probe

178   Toobin, Jeffrey. "Roger Stone and the Trump-Nixon Connection." *newyorker.com*. The New Yorker, 25 Apr. 2017, www.newyorker.com/news/daily-comment/roger-stone-and-the-trump-nixon-connection.

179   Duray, Dan. "Donald Trump's 'Hit Man' Hones His Dark Arts." *vanityfair.com*. Vanity Fair, 20 July 2016, www.vanityfair.com/news/2016/07/roger-stone-donald-trumps-hit-man.

180   Hellmann, Jessie. "Roger Stone: If Clinton wins, I'm moving to Costa Rica." *thehill.com*. The Hill, 27 Aug. 2016, https://thehill.com/blogs/ballot-box/presidential-races/293554-roger-stone-if-clinton-wins-im-moving-to-costa-rica.

181   "Stone defends meeting, says FBI sought to entrap him." *thehill.com*. The Hill, 21 June 2018, thehill.com/hilltv/rising/393430-stone-defends-meeting-says-fbi-sought-to-entrap-him.

182   Thomsen, Jacqueline. "Roger Stone email about Assange dinner leaks." *thehill.com*. The Hill, 4 Apr. 2018, https://thehill.com/homenews/administration/381554-roger-stones-email-saying-he-met-with-assange-leaks.

183   FitzGerald, Drew and Holliday, Shelby. "Mueller Investigators Probe Roger Stone Conference Calls." *wsj.com*. The Wall Street Journal, 30 Oct. 2018, https://www.wsj.com/articles/mueller-investigators-probe-roger-stone-conference-calls-1540899120.

184   @GUCCIFER_2. "@RodgerJStoneJr thanks that u believe in the real #Guccifer2". *Twitter,* 12 Aug. 2016, 7:23 p.m., http://archive.ph/tTbWX.

185   Bump, Philip. "A timeline of the Roger Stone-WikiLeaks questions." *washingtonpost.com*. The Washington Post, 30 Oct. 2018, https://www.washingtonpost.com/politics/2018/10/30/timeline-roger-stone-wikileaks-question/.

186   Graves, Lucia and Morris, Sam. "The Trump allegations." *theguardian.com*. The Guardian, 29 Nov. 2017, https://www.theguardian.com/us-news/ng-interactive/2017/nov/30/donald-trump-sexual-misconduct-allegations-full-list.

187   Breuninger, Kevin. "Right-wing conspiracy monger Jerome Corsi says he would 'rather sit in prison' than say he lied . . ." *cnbc.com*. CNBC, 26 Nov. 2018, https://www.cnbc.com/2018/11/26/jerome-corsi-says-robert-mueller-offered-plea-deal-on-perjury-charge.html.

188   Tau, Byron and Holliday, Shelby. "Conservative Activist Jerome Corsi Says He Expects to Be Indicted in Mueller Probe." *wsj.com*. The Wall Street Journal, 12 Nov. 2018, https://www.wsj.com/articles/conservative-activist-jerome-corsi-says-he-expects-to-be-indicted-in-mueller-probe-1542063143.

189   Mazzetti, Mark, Sullivan, Eileen and Haberman, Maggie, *"Roger Stone's Dirty Tricks Put Him Where He's Always Wanted to Be: Center Stage,"* New York Times, Jan. 25, 2019, https://www.nytimes.com/2019/01/25/us/politics/who-is-roger-stone.html

190   Ibid.

191   Ibid.

192   Ibid.

193   Ibid.

194   Ibid.

195   Ibid.

196   Ibid.

197   Ibid.

198   Ibid.

199   Ibid.

CHAPTER 10 - TRUMP AND THE PRO-RUSSIAN REPUBLICAN PLATFORM

1   Wilkinson, Tracy. "In a shift, Republican platform doesn't call for arming Ukraine against Russia, spurring outrage." *latimes.com*. Los Angeles Times, 21 July 2016, https://www.latimes.com/world/la-na-pol-ukraine-gop-20160720-snap-story.html.

2   "Trump campaign guts GOP's anti-Russia stance on Ukraine." *washingtonpost.com*. The Washington Post, 18 July 2016, https://www.washingtonpost.com/opinions/global-opinions/trump-campaign-guts-gops-anti-russia-stance-on-ukraine/2016/07/18/98adb3b0-4cf3-11e6-a7d8-13d06b37f256_story.html.

3   Bronston, Sally. "Trump Chairman Denies Any Role in Platform Change on Ukraine." *nbcnews.com*. NBC News, 21 July 2016, https://www.nbcnews.com/meet-the-press/trump-chairman-denies-any-role-platform-change-ukraine-n620511.

4   Mak, Tim and Corse, Alexa. "Trump Campaign Changed Ukraine Platform, Lied About it." *thedailybeast.com*. The Daily Beast, 3 Aug. 2016, https://www.thedailybeast.com/trump-campaign-changed-ukraine-platform-lied-about-it.

1   Wilkinson, Tracy. "In a shift, Republican platform doesn't call for arming Ukraine against Russia, spurring outrage." *latimes.com*. Los Angeles Times, 21 July 2016, https://www.latimes.com/world/la-na-pol-ukraine-gop-20160720-snap-story.html.

2   "Trump campaign guts GOP's anti-Russia stance on Ukraine." *washingtonpost.com*. The Washington Post, 18 July 2016, https://www.washingtonpost.com/opinions/global-opinions/trump-campaign-guts-gops-anti-russia-stance-on-ukraine/2016/07/18/98adb3b0-4cf3-11e6-a7d8-13d06b37f256_story.html.

3   Bronston, Sally. "Trump Chairman Denies Any Role in Platform Change on Ukraine." *nbcnews.com*. NBC News, 21 July 2016, https://www.nbcnews.com/meet-the-press/trump-chairman-denies-any-role-platform-change-ukraine-n620511.

4   Mak, Tim and Corse, Alexa. "Trump Campaign Changed Ukraine Platform, Lied About it." *thedailybeast.com*. The Daily Beast, 3 Aug. 2016, https://www.thedailybeast.com/trump-campaign-changed-ukraine-platform-lied-about-it.

5   Ibid.

6   Ibid.

7   Ibid.

8   Ibid.

9   Ibid.

10   "Why the Crimean Referendum Is Illegitimate." *cfr.org*. The Council on Foreign Relations, 16 Mar. 2014, https://www.cfr.org/interview/why-crimean-referendum-illegitimate.

11   "Is floating a $50 million Trump Tower penthouse for Vladimir Putin Illegal?" *washingtonpost.com*. The Washington Post, 30 Nov. 2018, https://www.washingtonpost.com/politics/2018/11/30/is-floating-million-trump-tower-penthouse-vladimir-putin-illegal/.

12   Trump Doesn't Rule Out Recognizing Russia's Annexation of Crimea." *rferl.org*. Radio Free Europe Radio Liberty, 30 June 2018, https://www.rferl.org/a/trump-doesnt-rule-out-recognizing-russian-annexation-ukraine-crimean-peninsula/29328403.html.

CHAPTER 11 - TREASON AT TRUMP TOWER

1   Wolff, Michael. *Fire and Fury*. Henry Holt and Co., 2018.

2   Ibid.

3   Goldstone's emails explained to Don Jr. that the documents "would incriminate Hillary and her dealings with Russia and would be very useful to your father." Goldstone, who was acting as an intermediary between the Russians and the Trump Campaign, added: "This is obviously very high level and sensitive information but is part of Russia and its government's support for Mr. Trump." See "Read the Emails on Donald Trump Jr.'s Russia Meeting." *nytimes.com*. The New York Times, 11 July 2017, https://www.nytimes.com/interactive/2017/07/11/us/politics/donald-trump-jr-email-text.html.

4   Ibid.

5   Becker, Jo et al. "Trump Team Met With Lawyer Linked to Kremlin During Campaign." *nytimes.com*. The New York Times, 8 July 2017, https://www.nytimes.com/2017/07/08/us/politics/trump-russia-kushner-manafort.html.

6   Ibid.

7   Cohen, Marshall. "Trump lawyers say he 'dictated' statement on Trump Tower meeting, contradicting past denials." *cnn.com*. CNN, 2 June 2018, https://www.cnn.com/2018/06/02/politics/trump-lawyers-statement-trump-tower-russians/index.html.

8   Becker, Jo et al. "Mueller Zeros In on Story Put Together About Trump Tower Meeting." *nytimes.com*. The New York Times, 31 Jan. 2018, https://www.nytimes.com/2018/01/31/us/politics/trump-russia-hope-hicks-mueller.html.

9   If Trump, Hicks, and others who participated in these discussions intended to conceal and cover up the disclosure of the relevant emails for the purposes of obstructing the ongoing criminal investigation by Special Counsel Mueller's office, this would be a violation of Title 18, United States Code, Section 1519, which states: Whoever knowingly alters, destroys, mutilates, conceals, covers up, falsifies, or makes a false entry in any record, document, or tangible object with the intent to impede, obstruct, or influence the investigation or proper administration of any matter within the jurisdiction of any department or agency of the United States or any case filed under title 11, or in relation to or contemplation of any such matter or case, shall be fined under this title, imprisoned not more than 20 years, or both.

10   Becker, Jo et al. "Mueller Zeros In on Story Put Together About Trump Tower Meeting," supra, ftnt. 8.

11   "Read the Emails on Donald Trump Jr.'s Russia Meeting."

12   Kramer, Andrew E. and LaFraniere, Sharon. "Lawyer Who Was Said to Have Dirt on Clinton Had Closer Ties to Kremlin Than She Let On." *nytimes.com*. The New York Times, 27 Apr. 2018, https://www.nytimes.com/2018/04/27/us/natalya-veselnitskaya-trump-tower-russian-prosecutor-general.html.

13   Weisner, Benjamin and LaFraniere, Sharon, "Veselnitskaya, Russian in Trump Tower Meeting is Charged in Case That Shows Kremlin Ties," New York Times, Jan. 8, 2019, www.nytimes.com/2019/01/08/nyregion/trump-tower-natalya-veselnitskaya-indictment.html.

14   Becker, Jo et al. "Trump Team Met With Lawyer Linked to Kremlin During Campaign," supra, ftnt. 8.

15   Conspiracy to commit an offense or to defraud United States is punishable under 18 U.S. Code § 371 by up to five years imprisonment.

16   Kruzel, John. "Lewandowski wrongly says Trump in Florida day of Trump Tower meeting with Russian lawyer." *politifact.com*. Pundit Fact, 14 July 2017, https://www.politifact.com/punditfact/statements/2017/jul/14/corey-lewandowski/lewandowski-wrongly-says-trump-florida-day-trump-t/.

17   Merica, Dan. "Recreating June 9: A very consequential day in the 2016 campaign." *cnn.com*. CNN, 21 July 2017, https://www.cnn.com/2017/07/11/politics/trump-campaign-june-9/index.html.

18   Parker, Ashley et al. "Trump dictated son's misleading statement on meeting with Russian lawyer." *washingtonpost.com*. The Washington Post, 31 July 2017, https://www.washingtonpost.com/politics/trump-dictated-sons-misleading-statement-on-meeting-with-russian-lawyer/2017/07/31/04c94f96-73ae-11e7-8f39-eeb7d3a2d304_story.html.

19   Ibid.

20   Ibid.

21   Shane, Scott and Mazzetti, Mark. "The Plot to Subvert an Election." *nytimes.com*. The New York Times, 20 Sep. 2018, https://www.nytimes.com/interactive/2018/09/20/us/politics/russia-interference-election-trump-clinton.html.

22   Grieve, Pete. "Warner: 'Clear evidence' that Trump officials met Russians to get info." *cnn.com*. CNN, 11 July 2017, https://www.cnn.com/2017/07/10/pol-

itics/mark-warner-clear-evidence/index.html.

23   Apuzzo, Matt. "Mueller Issuing Subpoenas Through Washington Grand Jury." *washingtonpost.com*. The Washington Post, 3 Aug. 2017, https://www.nytimes.com/2017/08/03/us/politics/robert-mueller-russia-investigation-grand-jury.html.

24   There is also substantial evidence that George Papadopoulos and Carter Page, both Trump Campaign foreign policy advisors, also had substantial contacts with Russian operatives and officials during the 2016 presidential campaign, and that one of the consistent themes of these meetings was that the Russians confirmed that they had embarrassing "dirt" on Hillary Clinton that would be useful to the Trump Campaign. 17   Merica, Dan. "Recreating June 9: A very consequential day in the 2016 campaign." *cnn.com*. CNN, 21 July 2017, https://www.cnn.com/2017/07/11/politics/trump-campaign-june-9/index.html.

18   Parker, Ashley et al. "Trump dictated son's misleading statement on meeting with Russian lawyer." *washingtonpost.com*. The Washington Post, 31 July 2017, https://www.washingtonpost.com/politics/trump-dictated-sons-misleading-statement-on-meeting-with-russian-lawyer/2017/07/31/04c94f96-73ae-11e7-8f39-eeb7d3a2d304_story.html.

19   Ibid.

20   Ibid.

21   Shane, Scott and Mazzetti, Mark. "The Plot to Subvert an Election." *nytimes.com*. The New York Times, 20 Sep. 2018, https://www.nytimes.com/interactive/2018/09/20/us/politics/russia-interference-election-trump-clinton.html.

22   Grieve, Pete. "Warner: 'Clear evidence' that Trump officials met Russians to get info." *cnn.com*. CNN, 11 July 2017, https://www.cnn.com/2017/07/10/politics/mark-warner-clear-evidence/index.html.

23   Apuzzo, Matt. "Mueller Issuing Subpoenas Through Washington Grand Jury." *washingtonpost.com*. The Washington Post, 3 Aug. 2017, https://www.nytimes.com/2017/08/03/us/politics/robert-mueller-russia-investigation-grand-jury.html.

24   There is also substantial evidence that George Papadopoulos and Carter Page, both Trump Campaign foreign policy advisors, also had substantial contacts with Russian operatives and officials during the 2016 presidential campaign, and that one of the consistent themes of these meetings was that the Russians confirmed that they had embarrassing "dirt" on Hillary Clinton that would be useful to the Trump Campaign.

CHAPTER 12 - THE GATHERING STORM: DEMOCRACY IN CRISIS

1   *United States v. Nixon*, 418 U.S. 683 (1974).

2   President George Washington's Farewell Address (1796), https://www.ourdocuments.gov/doc.php?flash=false&doc=15

3   "The richest 1 percent now owns more of the coutnry's wealth than . . ." *washingtonpost.com*. The Washington Post, 6 Dec. 2017, https://www.washington-post.com/news/wonk/wp/2017/12/06/the-richest-1-percent-now-owns-more-of-the-countrys-wealth-than-at-any-time-in-the-past-50-years/.

4   Goodman, Peter S. "Too Big to Fail?" *nytimes.com*. The New York Times, 20 July 2008, https://www.nytimes.com/2008/07/20/weekinreview/20goodman.html.

5   Silver, Mark and Whitehead, Nadia. "The U.N. Looks at Extreme Poverty In The U.S., From Alabama to California." *npr.com*. NPR, 12 Dec. 2017, https://www.npr.org/sections/goatsandsoda/2017/12/12/570217635/the-u-n-looks-at-ex-treme-poverty-in-the-u-s-from-alabama-to-california.

6   Goodman, Nicole. "Mitch McConnell Calls for Social Security, Medicare, Medicaid Cuts After Passing Tax Cuts, Massive Defense Spending." *newsweek.com*. Newsweek, 10 Oct. 2018, https://www.newsweek.com/deficit-budget-tax-plan-social-securi-ty-medicaid-medicare-entitlement-1172941.

7   Marcos, Christina. "GOP lawmaker: Donors are pushing me to get tax reform done." *thehill.com*. The Hill, 7 Nov. 2017, https://thehill.com/homenews/house/359110-gop-lawmaker-donors-are-pushing-me-to-get-tax-reform-done.

CHAPTER 13 - DRIFTING TOWARDS "ILLIBERAL DEMOCRACY"

1   Scheiring, Gabor. "Hungary's 'illiberal democracy'." *theweek.com*. The Week, 27 Apr. 2018, https://theweek.com/articles/768453/hungarys-illiberal-democracy.

2   Ibid.

3   Ibid.

4   Ibid.

5   Ibid.

6   Milbank, David. "Of course it's Soros' fault. It always is." The Washington Post, 23 Dec. 2018, reprinted Montgomery Advertiser, www.montgomeryadvertiser.com/story/opinion/2018/12/23/course-its-soros-fault-always/2401245002/_.

7   Ibid.

8   Ibid.

9   Brooks, David. "The Chaos After Trump." *thenewyorktimes.com.* The New York Times, 5 Mar. 2018, https://www.nytimes.com/2018/03/05/opinion/the-chaos-after-trump.html.

10   Levitsky, Steven and Ziblatt, Daniel. *How Democracies Die* (Crown Publishing 2018)

11   Ibid; see also Kristof, Nicholas. "Trump's Threat to Democracy." *nytimes.com.* The New York Times, 10 Jan. 2018 https://www.nytimes.com/2018/01/10/opinion/trumps-how-democracies-die.html.

12   "Trump Defends Putin Killing Journalists: U.S. Kills People, Too," www.thedailybeast.com/trump-defends-putin-killing-journalists-us-kills-people-too.

13   Ibid.

14   Kristof, Nicholas. "Dictators Love Trump, and He Loves Them." *nytimes.com.* The New York Times, 14 Mar. 2018, https://www.nytimes.com/2018/03/14/opinion/trump-dictators-human-rights.html.

15   Ibid.

16   Ibid.

17   Ibid.

18   Ibid.

19   Ibid.

20   Perlez, Jane. "President for Life'? Trump's Remarks About Xi Find Fans in China." *nytimes.com.* The New York Times, 4 Mar. 2018, https://www.nytimes.com/2018/03/04/world/asia/donald-trump-xi-jinping-term-limits.html.

21   Ibid.

22   Borger, Julian and McKernan, Bethan. "Khashoggi death: Saudi prince may have been involved, Trump says." *theguardian.com.* The Guardian, 24 Oct.

2018, https://www.theguardian.com/world/2018/oct/23/jamal-khashoggi-trump-cover-up-sanctions-visas.

23   Ibid.

24   O'Connor, Tom, Newsweek, Dec. 24, 2018, ww.newsweek.com/trump-never-wanted-syria-war-election-2020-1268719

25   "Trump decided to withdraw troops from Syria without consulting advisers, allies."*cbc.ca*. CBC, 21 Dec. 2018, www.cbc.ca/news/world/trump-withdraws-troops-syria-without-consultation-1.4955697.

26   Ibid.

27   Capaccio, Anthony. "Mattis Resigns as Defense Chief, Citing Differences With Trump." *bloomberg.com*. Bloomberg, 20 Dec. 2018, www.bloomberg.com/news/articles/2018-12-20/mattis-to-step-down-as-defense-secretary-in-february-trump-says.

28   Ibid.

29   *"Mitch McConnell 'Distressed' Over Mattis' Shock Resignation,"* The Daily Beast, www.thedailybeast.com/mitch-mcconnell-distressed-over-mattis-shock-resignation

30   Ibid.

31   Goldberg, Jeffrey. "A Senior White House Official Defines the Trump Doctrine: 'We're America, Bitch'." *theatlantic.com*. The Atlantic, 11 June 2018, www.theatlantic.com/politics/archive/2018/06/a-senior-white-house-official-defines-the-trump-doctrine-were-america-bitch/562511.

32   Ibid; see also Schake, Kori. "The Trump Doctrine Is Winning and The World Is Losing." *nytimes.com*. The New York Times, 15 June 2018, https://www.nytimes.com/2018/06/15/opinion/sunday/trump-china-america-first.html.

33   Ibid.

34   Edevane, Gillian. "Donald Trump at G7 Summit: Past Presidents Allowed Countries to Rob U.S. like 'Piggy Bank'." *newsweek.com*. Newsweek, 9 June 2018, https://www.newsweek.com/donald-trump-g7-summit-speech-justin-trudeau-canada-967978.

35   Ibid.

36   Ibid.

37   Ibid.

38   Ibid.

39   "Trump at UN: I didn't expect that reaction." *cnn.com*. CNN, 25 Sep. 2018,   https://www.cnn.com/videos/politics/2018/09/25/trump-un-general-assembly-reaction-speech-nr-vpx.cnn/video/playlists/.

40   Tamkin, Emily. "Diplomats Say They Were Definitely Laughing At Trump At The UN." *buzzfeed.com*. Buzzfeed, 26 Sep. 2018, www.buzzfeednews.com/article/emilytamkin/diplomats-un-laughed-donald-trump.

41   Ibid.

CHAPTER 14 - CAN A SITTING PRESIDENT BE INDICTED FOR TREASON AND OTHER CRIMES

1   18 U.S. Code § 2381 provides: "Whoever, owing allegiance to the United States, levies war against them or adheres to their enemies, giving them aid and comfort within the United States or elsewhere, is guilty of treason and shall suffer death, or shall be imprisoned not less than five years."

2   Article 2, Section 4 provides: "The President, Vice President and all civil Officers of the United States, shall be removed from Office on Impeachment for, and Conviction of, Treason, Bribery, or other high Crimes and Misdemeanors."

3   "A Sitting President's Amenability to Indictment and Criminal Prosecution," U.S. Dept. of Justice, Office of Legal Counsel, Oct. 16, 2000, https://www.justice.gov/olc/opinion/sitting-president's-amenability-indictment-and-criminal-prosecution; *see also*, e.g., *"Can a president be indicted?,"* The Hill, May 29, 2018; *"A Constitutional Puzzle: Can the President Be Indicted?",* The New York Times, May 29, 2017; Epps, Garrett, *"The only Way to Find Out If the President Can Be Indicted,"* The Atlantic, June 5, 2018; *"Can the President Be indicted? A Long-Hidden Legal Memo Says Yes,"* The New York Times, July 22, 2017.

4   Article 1, Section 3 states: "Judgment in cases of impeachment shall not extend further than to removal from office, and disqualification to hold and enjoy any office of honor, trust or profit under the United States; but the party convicted shall nevertheless be liable and subject to indictment, trial, judgment and punishment, according to law."

5   Can the president be indicted or subpoenaed?" *washingtonpost.com*. The Washington Post, 22 May 2018, https://www.washingtonpost.com/news/fact-checker/wp/2018/05/22/can-the-president-be-indicted-or-subpoenaed/.

6   While the Supreme Court, in *United States v. Nixon*, did not specifically address the issue of presidential immunity from prosecution while in office, it did forcefully rule that the President Nixon did not have immunity or an unqualified privilege from judicial process; Chief Justice Burger perhaps summarized it best by writing in the majority opinion that " . . . neither the doctrine of separation of powers, nor the need for confidentiality of high-level communications, without more, can sustain an absolute, unqualified Presidential privilege of immunity from judicial process under all circumstances." See United States v. Nixon, 418 U.S. 683, 94 S. Ct. 3090 (1974).

7   Memorandum from Carl B. Feldbaum et al to Leon Jaworski, dated February 12, 1974, reprinted in Hofstra Law Review, Vol. 27, Iss. 4 (1999) Art. 3, at 1; https://www.documentcloud.org/documents/3896903-Legal-Memos-About-Whether-a-Sitting-President.html#document/p65

8   Ibid.

9   Ibid., quoting *United States v. Lee*, 106 U.S. 196, 220 (1882).

10   Ibid at 4.

11   Ibid at 5.

12   Ibid.

13   Ibid at 6.

14   Ibid at 7.

15   Ibid at 7-8.

16   Ibid. at 10.

17   Ibid at 14.

18   Ibid at 15.

19   Ibid at 17.

20   Ibid at 18.

21   Reply Brief for the United States of America, by Special Prosecutor Leon Jaworski and Philip A. Lacovara, June 21, 1974, https://drive.google.com/file/d/0B6mkR0LD6dl3aWJHd3pOUkxWeWc/view

22   Although Agnew's tenure as Nixon's Vice President was relatively uneventful prior to being charged with tax evasion and resigning his office, Agnew

developed a reputation as Nixon's chief defender hit-man when it came to the relentless pursuit of the Watergate story by the Washington Post and other reporters. In fact, Agnew can be considered as an early precursor of President Trump's full-throated attack on the press and attempt to discredit the Fourth Estate and all others who question his conduct and even his legitimacy. Agnew referred to Nixon's critics as "Nattering Nabobs of Negativism," showing a reasonably strong command of alliteration, if not truthfulness or honesty.

23   James M. Naughton, "Judge Orders Fine, 3 Years Probation," Oct. 11, 1973, The New York Times, https://www.nytimes.com/1973/10/11/archives/judge-orders-fine-3-years-probation-tells-court-income-was-taxable.html

24   "Ford Is Approved By Senate, 92-3; House Set To Act," The New York Times, Nov. 27, 1973, movies2.nytimes.com/learning/general/onthisday/big/1127.html

25   Walter Dellinger, "Indicting a President Is Not Foreclosed: The Complex History," Lawfare, June 18, 2018.

26   See Hofstra Law Review, Vol. 27, Iss. 4 at 677 (1999), citing 3 Farrad, Records of the Federal Convention of 1787, 625 (Rev. Ed. 1966). See also, Federalist 69. In Federalist 65, Hamilton wrote that a President, "after having been sentenced to a perpetual ostracism from the esteem and confidence, and honors and emoluments of this country, he will still be liable to prosecution and punishment in the ordinary course of law."

27   See Charles Savage, *"Can the President Be Indicted? A Long-Hidden Legal Memo Says Yes;"* July 22, 2017, The New York Times, *https://www.nytimes.com/2017/07/22/us/politics/can-president-be-indicted-kenneth-starr-memo.html*

28   Ibid, see Memo by Professor Ronald D. Rotunda, dated May 13, 1998 at 8-9; https://assets.documentcloud.org/documents/3899216/Savage-NYT-FOIA-Starr-memo-presidential.pdf

29   Ibid; see also, U.S. Supreme Court decisions holding that no one is "above the law." See, e.g., United States v. Lee, 106 U.S. 196, 220 (1882); United States v. United Mine Workers of America, 330 U.S. 258, 343 (1947); Malone v. Bowdoin, 369 U.S. 643, 651 (1962) (Douglas, J., dissenting); Johnson v. Powell, 393 U.S. 920 (1968) (Memorandum Opinion of Douglas, J); Brandzburg v. Hayes, 408 U.S. 665, 699 (1972); Gravel v. United States, 408 U.S. 606, 615 (1972); United States v. Nixon, 418 U.S. 683 (1974); Butz v. Economou, 438 U.S. 478, 506 (1978); Davis v. Passman, 442 U.S. 228, 246 (1979); Nixon v. Fitzgerald, 457 U.S. 731, 758 & n. 41 (1982); Briscoe v. LaHue, 460 U.S. 325, 358 (1983); United States v. Stanley, 383 U.S. 669, 706 (1987); Seminole Tribe of Florida v. Florida, 517 U.S.

44, 103 n. 2 (1996); Clinton v. Jones, 117 S.Ct. 1636, 1645 (1997).

30   487 F. 2d 700, 711 (D.C. Cir. 1973) (per curiam) (en banc).

31   See Open Jurist, *Nixon v. Sirica*, 487 F. 2d 700 (D. C. C. 1973).

32   Nixon v. Sirica, 487 F. 2d 700 at 711.

33   Ibid.

34   Ibid.

35   Memo of Professor Rotunda, dated May 13, 1998, at pp. 6-7.

36. Oona Hathaway, "Three Options for Prosecuting a President's Offences – Plus a Wildcard," August 23, 2018, Just Security, https://www.justsecurity.org/60423/options-prosecuting-presidents-offences-plus-wildcard/;

See also, Emily Birnbaum, "Adam Schiff: Justice Should Re-examine Whether It Can Indict Sitting President," The Hill, Dec. 13, 2018,

36   doj-must-re-examine-olc-opinion-that-you-cannot-indict-a-sitting president.

37   See 18 U.S. Code § 3161 (Time limits and exclusions).

38   Congress could also pass a statute suspending the running of criminal statutes of limitations as applied to a sitting president. Congressman Jerrold Nadler, Chairman of the House Judiciary Committee, has already suggested proposing such legislation. Naomi Lin, *Top Democrat: Constitution allows Trump to be indicted in Office,"* The Washington Examiner, Dec. 9, 2018, https://www.washingtonexaminer.com/news/top-democrat-constitution-allows-trump-to-be-indicted-in-office. On December 9, 2018, in an interview with CNN, Nadler has also taken issue with the Dept. of Justice and its Office of Legal Counsel's position that a sitting president cannot be indicted. Ibid.

39   Walter Dellinger, *"Yes, You Can Indict the President,"* The New York Times, March 26, 2018, https://www.nytimes.com/2018/03/26/opinion/indict-president-trial.html

EPILOGUE - AMERICA STRONG

1   See Eleveld, Kerry. "Comey on Russia: 'They're coming for America' . . ." *dailykos.com.* Daily Kos, 8 June 2017, https://www.dailykos.com/stories/2017/6/8/1670017/-Comey-on-Russia-They-re-coming-for-America-but-

Trump-didn-t-give-a-damn-about-it; see also "Full Transcript and Video: James Comey's Testimony on Capitol Hill." *nytimes.com*.The New York Times, 8 June 2017, https://www.nytimes.com/2017/06/08/us/politics/senate-hearing-transcript.html.

2   See Montanaro, Domenico. "Why the Russia Investigation Matters and Why You Should Care." *npr.org*. NPR, 24 May 2017, https://www.npr.org/2017/05/24/529781094/why-the-russia-investigation-matters-and-why-you-should-care; see also "Former CIA Director John Brennan offers a stirring explanation of why Russia's election interference matters." *theweek.com*. The Week, 23 May 2017, https://theweek.com/speedreads/700872/former-cia-director-john-brennan-offers-stirring-explanation-why-russias-election-interference-matters.

3   "We have met the enemy and they are ours," is part of a message from American naval officer Oliver Hazard Perry in 1813 after defeating and capturing British Royal Navy ships in the Battle of Lake Erie. "We have met the enemy and he is us," is a cartoon poster parody of Perry's quote by *Pogo* creator Walt Kelly; see also, Susan Rice, January 25, 2018, www.nytimes.com/2018/01/25/opinion/national-security-polarization.html

4   Zimmer, Ben (12 May 2013). ""Boston Strong," the phrase that rallied a city." The Boston Globe. Retrieved 3 March 2014; see also Dubois, Lou (April 21, 2013). "'Boston Strong' emerges as rallying cry, from stadiums to tweets". NBC News.

TRUMP - RUSSIA TIMELINE

1   Ward, Alex. "Trump Tower Moscow and Michael Cohen's lies about it, explained." *vox.com*. Vox, 18 Jan. 2019, https://www.vox.com/world/2018/11/29/18117910/cohen-trump-tower-moscow-mueller-buzzfeed.

2   Ibid.

3   Ibid.

4   Ibid.

5   Ibid.

6   Barrionuevo, Alexei. "Divorce, Oligarch Style." *nytimes.com*. The New York Times, 5 Apr. 2012, https://www.nytimes.com/2012/04/08/realestate/big-deal-dmitry-rybolovlevs-divorce-oligarch-style.html.

7   *www.huffingtonpost.com/entry/donald-trump-advisers-russia-ties_us_57ac-d474e4b007c36e4db94c*

8   Ibid.

9   Ibid.

10   Ibid.

11   Ibid.

12   Weiss, Lois. "Real estate startup Cadre raises whopping $50M." *nypost. com*. New York Post, 26 Jan. 2016, https://nypost.com/2016/01/26/real-estate-startup-cadre-raises-whopping-50m/.

13   Hayoun, Massoud. "Trump and his Advisors Are Connected To A Self-Professed Friend of Putin." *psmag.com*. Pacific Standard Magazine, 12 Jan. 2017, https://psmag.com/news/trump-and-his-advisors-are-connected-to-a-self-professed-friend-of-putin; see also Madsen, Wayne. "Jared Kushner: A Suspected Gangster Within the Trump White House. *strategic-culture.org*. Strategic Culture, 17 Apr. 2017, https://www.strategic-culture.org/news/2017/04/17/jared-kushner-suspected-gangster-within-trump-white-house.html.

14   Schreckinger, Ben. "The Happy-Go-Lucky Jewish Group That Connects Trump and Putin." *politico.com*. Politico, 9 Apr. 2017, https://www.politico.com/magazine/story/2017/04/the-happy-go-lucky-jewish-group-that-connects-trump-and-putin-215007; see also "Trump and his Advisors Are Connected To A Self-Professed Friend of Putin."

15   *jewishnews.timesofisrael.com/putin-on-our-side-says-russias-chief/*

16   Ibid.

17   "Trump Tower Moscow and Michael Cohen's lies about it, explained."

18   Apuzzo, Matt and Haberman, Maggie. "Trump Associate Boasted That Moscow Business Deal 'Will Get Donald Elected'." *nytimes.com*. The New York Times, 28 Aug. 2017, https://www.nytimes.com/2017/08/28/us/politics/trump-tower-putin-felix-sater.html.

19   Ibid.

20   Ibid.

21   "Manafort held secret talks with Assange in Ecuadorian embassy, sources say." *theguardian.com*. The Guardian, 27 Nov. 2018, https://www.theguardian.com/

us-news/2018/nov/27/manafort-held-secret-talks-with-assange-in-ecuadorian-embassy.

22   Helderman, Rosalind S. and Hamburger, Tom, "How Manafort's 2016 meeting with a Russian employee at New York cigar club goes to "the heart" of Mueller's probe," Washington Post, February 12, 2019.

23   Ibid.

24   Ibid.

25   Ibid.

26   Ibid.

27   "4 meetings with Russians disclosed by Jared Kushner." *chicagotribune.com*. Chicago Tribune, 24 July 2017, https://www.chicagotribune.com/news/nationworld/ct-jared-kushner-russian-meetings-20170724-story.html.

28   "Ivanka Invites Russian Billionaire's Wife to Inauguration Weekend."

29   "Ivanka Invites Russian Billionaire's Wife to Inauguration Weekend."

30   "Trump clears way for controversial oil pipelines."

31 *www.whitehouse.gov/briefings-statements/press-gaggle-principal-deputy-press-secretary-sarah-sanders-en-route-orlando-florida/*

32   Goldman, Adam et al. "F.B.I. Opened Inquiry Into Whether Trump Was Secretly Working on Behalf of Russia." *nytimes.com*. The New York Times, 11 Jan. 2019, https://www.nytimes.com/2019/01/11/us/politics/fbi-trump-russia-inquiry.html.

33   Email from CNN reporter Erica Orden @eorden, Nov. 29, 2018.

34   Ibid.

35   Vogel, Kenneth. "Trump Administration to Lift Sanctions on Russian Oligarch's Companies." *nytimes.com*. The New York Times, 19 Dec. 2018, https://www.nytimes.com/2018/12/19/us/politics/sanctions-oleg-deripaska-russia-trump.html.

36   Ibid.

37   Ibid.

38   Ibid.

39   Ibid.

40   Adam Goldman, Michael S. Schmidt and Nicholas Fandos, *"F.B.I. Opened Inquiry Into Whether Trump Was Secretly Working on Behalf of Russia,"* The New York Times, January 11, 2019, https://www.nytimes.com/2019/01/11/us/politics/fbi-trump-russia-inquiry.html.

41   Leopold, Jason and Cormier, Anthony, *"President Trump Directed His Attorney Michael Cohen To Lie To Congress About The Moscow Tower Project,"* BuzzFeed News, January 17, 2019, https://www.buzzfeednews.com/article/jasonleopold/trump-russia-cohen-moscow-tower-mueller-investigation

42   Vogel, Kenneth P., *"Deripaska and Allies Could Benefit From Sanctions Deal, Document Shows,"* New York Times, Jan. 21, 2019, https://www.nytimes.com/2019/01/21/us/politics/oleg-deripaska-russian-sanctions.html

43   Ibid.

44   Grise, Katherine, "Kushner's top secret security clearance," CNN, January 25, 2019 https://www.cnn.com/2019/01/25/politics/jared-kushner-security-clearance-overruled/index.html

45   Ibid.

46   Ibid.

47   Ibid.

48   Mazzetti, Mark, Sullivan, Eileen and Haberman, Maggie, *"Roger Stone's Dirty Tricks Put Him Where He's Always Wanted to Be: Center Stage,"* New York Times, Jan. 25, 2019, https://www.nytimes.com/2019/01/25/us/politics/who-is-roger-stone.html

49   Ibid.

50   Layne, Nathan, "Mueller Eyes Manafort Meeting With Russian Partner in 2016-Court Filing," Reuters, February 7, 2019.

51   Johnson, Carrie and Taylor, Jessica, "Manafort Intentionally Lied to Special Counsel, Judge Says," NPR, February 13, 2019 https://www.npr.org/2019/02/13/694565971/manafort-intentionally-lied-to-special-counsel-judge-says

52   Goldman, Adam and Haag, Matthew, "McCabe Says Justice Dept. Officials Had Discussions About Pushing Trump Out," New York Times, Feb. 14, 2019 www.nytimes.com/2019/02/14/us/politics/mccabe-trump.html.

53   Lynch, Sarah N. and Layne, Nathan, "Mueller Seeks Tough Sentence for Ex-Trump Campaign Chairman Manafort," Reuters, February 15, 2019

54   Chalfant, Morgan and Thomsen, Jacqueline, "New filing suggests Mueller has evidence Stone communicated with WikiLeaks," The Hill, February 15, 2019 https://thehill.com/policy/national-security/430299-new-filing-suggests-mueller-has-evidence-stone-communicated-with.

55   Thebault, Reis and Flynn, Meagan, "Trump suggests Rosenstein, McCabe are 'treasonous,' citing Fox News," The Washington Post, Feb. 19, 2019 www.washingtonpost.com/politics/2019/02/18/illegal-treasonous-trump-says-rosenstein-was-part-coup-attempt/?utm_term=.900b65a78438.

56   Mazzetti, Mark, Haberman, Maggie, Fandos, Nicholas and Schmidt, Michael S. , "Intimidation, Pressure and Humiliation: Inside Trump's Two-Year War on the Investigation Encircling Him," New York Times, Feb. 19, 2019, www.nytimes.com/2019/02/19/us/politics/trump-investigations.html?action=click&module=RelatedLinks&pgtype=Article

57   Dos Santos, Nina, "Senate investigators pursue Moscow-based former Trump associate," CNN, Feb. 21, 2019 www.cnn.com/2019/02/21/politics/senate-trump-russia-david-geovanis-intl/index.html.

58   Tackett, Michael , "Five Takeaways From Cohen's Testimony to Congress," New York Times, Feb. 27, 2019 www.nytimes.com/2019/02/27/us/politics/cohen-testimony.html.

59   McCallion, Kenneth, "Cohen has just made Trump's crimes vividly clear," New York Daily News, Feb. 27, 2019 www.nydailynews.com/opinion/ny-oped-cohen-has-just-made-trumps-crimes-vividly-clear-20190227-story.html.

INDEX

H